TASTING
PLEASURE

Also by Jancis Robinson

Jancis Robinson's Guide to Wine Grapes
Jancis Robinson's Wine Course
The Oxford Companion to Wine (editor)
Vintage Timecharts
Jancis Robinson on the Demon Drink
Jancis Robinson's Food and Wine Adventures
Vines, Grapes and Wines
Masterglass
The Great Wine Book
Which? Wine Guide (editor)
The Wine Book

TASTING
PLEASURE

Confessions of a
Wine Lover

––––––

Jancis Robinson

VIKING

VIKING
Published by the Penguin Group
Penguin Putnam Inc., 375 Hudson Street,
New York, New York 10014, U.S.A.
Penguin Books Ltd, 27 Wrights Lane,
London W8 5TZ, England
Penguin Books Australia Ltd, Ringwood,
Victoria, Australia
Penguin Books Canada Ltd, 10 Alcorn Avenue,
Toronto, Ontario, Canada M4V 3B2
Penguin Books (N.Z.) Ltd, 182–190 Wairau Road,
Auckland 10, New Zealand

Penguin Books Ltd, Registered Offices:
Harmondsworth, Middlesex, England

First published in 1997 by Viking Penguin,
a member of Penguin Putnam Inc.

10 9 8 7 6 5 4 3 2 1

LIBRARY OF CONGRESS
CATALOGING IN PUBLICATION DATA
Robinson, Jancis.
    Tasting pleasure : confessions of a wine lover /
by Jancis Robinson.
        p.   cm.
    Includes index.
    ISBN 0-670-85423-9
    1. Robinson, Jancis.   2. Wine writers—
England—Biography.   I. Title.
TP547.R63A3   1997
641.2'2'092—dc21   97-17451
[B]

This book is printed on acid-free paper.
∞

Printed in the United States of America
Set in Garamond No. 3
Designed by Virginia Norey

In memory of
W.v.S, K.v.S and E.H.L.

Acknowledgments

I take full responsibility for this book's execution, but all credit or blame for its existence must go to Al Silverman of Penguin Putnam Inc., who dreamt it up in 1993, before we had even met, and waited with extreme courtesy and unprecedented patience until I was ready to write it. He has been a delight to work for and with.

On the other side of the Atlantic, Clare Alexander oversaw its birth, while Helen Fraser responded magnificently to the challenge of publishing such a personal book by an old friend at a time when she had many other more important matters to see to.

Professional *éminence grise,* as always, has been my splendidly colorful, claret-loving literary agent Caradoc King.

Writing this book has shown me powerfully just how much I owe to those in and around the world of wine—not just the generous friends described in these pages, but a host of others who have been deemed to distract from such narrative line as there is, and many who may only have been passing acquaintances. In this gracelessly inclusive way, I would like to thank the hundreds, possibly thousands, of people in and out of the wine business who have opened a bottle or door for me, shared a taste or their knowledge with me, or devoted even a few minutes to me and my questing palate.

And finally, my family. All authors, and particularly those with young children, inevitably owe an enormous debt of time and support to their nearest and dearest. But I am acutely aware that they play an even more important role in a book as autobiographical as this one. I could not possibly have written it if I had not been lucky enough to enjoy a happy and indulged home life both during childhood and with my own family. For the last seventeen years I have owed most of all to my husband, Nick, but my children, Julia, Will and Rose, have also been endlessly forbearing, just like their grandparents.

Contents

TASTING
PLEASURE

A Tale of
Two Wine Producers

―――――

François Mitjavile was born in 1948 into a family synonymous in France with road transport. Mitjavile trucks pound France's auto-routes; Mitjavile calendars hang in offices all over the country. When he was old enough he was given the chance to run one of the family's subsidiaries in Leeds in the north of England, but at the age of twenty-six he discovered something that made his heart beat much, much faster. Because of that, and his extreme dedication, there is now another world in which Mitjavile is an important name, the world of wine.

François is interesting because he was one of the first examples of a phenomenon that is revolutionizing the way that world works, and is dramatically improving the quality of what it produces. Until quite recently, vine growing and winemaking were thought of as activities fit only for the uneducated. The aristocracy and haute bourgeoisie might well earn considerable sums from the wine produced on their land, but they would not dream of physically involving themselves in the production process. Wine's image in France was that of peasant lubricant. Wine was typically a crude drink made and drunk in quantity by shuffling old countrymen in berets. Young people were encouraged to aspire to the professions or an executive desk in some office block, with perhaps something as chic as *un malt* to enliven their social lives. But in France, as throughout much of the Western world, this has changed considerably in the last twenty years. Just as disaffection with urban life (particularly life in the cities of northern France) has become widespread, so the life of a vigneron has taken on a new nobility. Wine is more readily associated with craftsmanship, its appreciation come to be regarded as an art.

All over France, and the rest of the world, individuals who in another era might have earned their living in a role more traditionally associated with the highly educated are turning to wine production with a passion. Some of them are motivated by a bucolic vision that almost certainly incorporates the word "lifestyle." They tend to produce serviceable rather than exciting wine. A few of them are motivated by money. Their wine is usually worse. But there are some who are driven by the sheer magic of being so in tune with their plot of land that they can coax the best wine possible out of it.

Like all of these self-propelled enthusiasts, François Mitjavile is very much a loner. Even as recently as June 1994 when I last visited him, when the name of his property was well known by bordeaux lovers throughout the world, there was still no sign giving a hint which turnoff from the smallest of back roads out of Saint-Émilion might lead to Château Le Tertre Roteboeuf. And there was nothing about the modest farmhouse, apparently plonked down in the middle of an orchard full of long grass, nettles and fig trees, that suggested it had any link with wine, much less one of the world's most sought after. The Mitjavile residence in fact is one of the very, very few of the thousands of modest farmhouses around the tourist mecca that is Saint-Émilion that does *not* advertise its claim to be a wine château. But then with only about 2,000 cases of wine to sell each year (1,999 after I've bought mine), this is perhaps not surprising. In any case, as he has explained to me, he wants to be free to work his vines and his wines, and have just enough free time to entertain properly a small handful of true *amateurs de vin*.

But this is strange in a way because talking is so obviously what he likes. An intense and thoughtful man, he speaks rather breathlessly with unmistakable enthusiasm and lots of smiles. But then again what he says is not really talk, it is rather what the French would call *ré-*

flexions, not artful or polished disquisitions, but ideas with a spin on them. It is typical that he says with pride that "Tertre" enthusiasts are nonconformists. This is one of the four reasons he gives for the extraordinary fact that he has never applied, and probably never will apply, for membership in Saint-Émilion's official elite, the Grands Crus Classés. The others are that there are anyway enough people who love Tertre, for it is probably the only Saint-Émilion other than the top-ranking Ausone and Cheval Blanc—and nowadays he would have to add Valandraud—to sell out as soon as it's released. He also argues that not having the magic word "Classé" on his label imposes the discipline of having to make a wine every year that is good enough to sell on its quality alone.

I'd rung while filming in the area and he had obviously been delighted I could visit only in the evening. *"Je suis bête,"* he admitted happily, a fool in his devotion to work. I arrived as the warm sun was lengthening the shadows cast by his extremely beat up old Volvo to find that he'd added some gray hairs since I'd seen him last but that, like his apple-cheeked wife, Miloute (a persistent corruption of Emilie), he still had a marvelously unlined, outdoor face. Framed by curly hair, his face reminded me again, with its long upper lip and lazy lids, of Chico, the Marx brother with the hat, although François's humor is wry rather than slapstick. He showed me with pride how they had faced the simple eighteenth-century farmhouse with clay and chalk from the vineyard since my last visit, and how much finer this looked than the sand and chalk facing on an adjoining outhouse.

The house stands on the edge of the ridge on which Saint-Émilion was built so many centuries ago, and any visitor is naturally drawn to wade through the orchard and look out, over François's amphitheater of vines, to the plain of the Dordogne, then bathed in the golden light of a long summer's evening. He told me proudly how this small but favored property, which had been in his wife's family for years before they took it over, now included a prime parcel at the heart of his vineyard that until very recently had belonged to a cousin. It is the most wonderful view. I remembered that on my first visit François had described it, with no hint of cliché, as "a true corner of paradise only one kilometer from the city of Saint-Émilion." This time he explained with a smile how when his young son Henri had nightmares he would bring him out here to be calmed by the landscape. I can imagine them easily, standing in the moonlight, just waiting to be drawn by Edward Ardizzone.

Since I hadn't been to Tertre Roteboeuf for ten years, François gave me a rhapsodic progress report—not about the prizes and praise, but how much better he thinks he's got things organized now. "The vineyard's like a racing car," he said enthusiastically, "a finely oiled machine with a team of trustworthy, well-trained, devoted mechanics—mainly Moroccans who were originally taught to nurse vines from the point of view of quantity not quality." Now, François says, he is more of a teacher than a doer.

The Mitjaviles have been here since 1975, more or less the same amount of time that I have been involved in wine. I visited in the mid-1980s, when the property was still relatively unknown, and I remember him pursuing me as I drove away, yelling, "But tell me, which did you *prefer,* the 1983 or the 1985?" The powerful American wine critic Robert Parker began to write him up soon afterwards, and Tertre became a commercial *succès fou,* making wonderfully concentrated wines dominated by Merlot, always from almost uneconomically low yields of dangerously late picked vines and, as the Mitjaviles' income grew, with increasing proportions of new oak barrels. The wine has been described as a Pomerol from Saint-Émilion but I can't imagine François approving of that cliché. What he is trying to do is put the essence of that particular south-facing amphitheater of vines in a bottle, slopes that were planted with vines in Roman times.

By 1988, just as Tertre looked financially secure at long last, François went and risked it all on another possible failure. He fell in love with the potential of another vineyard, Château Roc de Cambes in the viticultural wilderness of the Côtes de Bourg, on slopes that run right down to the Gironde estuary, very Atlantic influenced. Restoring and setting up this second property had clearly been a Very Big Commercial Adventure for the Mitjaviles, involving banks, more employees and so on. The production costs at "Roc" were actually higher than Tertre's, he explained, but he couldn't get anything like the same price for the wine. Although he could now afford 100 percent new barrels for Tertre, he could not yet justify more than 50 percent for Roc, which, he admitted, with so much still to be done there, was still far from a finely tuned racing car.

Now that he has demonstrated that great Saint-Émilion doesn't have to come from an officially classified vineyard, he has taken it upon himself to convince people that "Roc" has just as good a *terroir* as Tertre, even though it is technically in a much lesser appellation. He told me he already had customers who are completely wedded to Roc, even though the first vintage was only in 1988.

As we walked around the yard to the small barn that acts as his winery, he started talking about the many friends of his who had become doctors. "They finish work at six," he told me (unlike him; I got the impression that he spends most of his time in the office in the middle of the house), "and so they have time to read far more widely than I do, but I honestly think I have a much better grasp of the world as it really is because I've had to immerse myself so fully in it while running my business. I now know how to manage money, how to farm, how to process, how to package, how to sell, how to manage people. All sorts of things!" He is delighted, in the manner of one discovering a new school of art or literature, with the notion that his wine depends not just on Nature and himself, but on a complex network of commerce, finance and other individuals. I remembered John Dunkley, who gave up a high-profile career in advertising in London to buy the Riecine Chianti Classico estate in the 1970s, pointing out to me that being a wine producer offered one of the very rare chances for one person to be involved in every single aspect of both production and sales, from soil to consumer.

As we prepared to taste François's 1993s, from many more barrels than I remembered from my first visit, he asked urgently, "What would you prefer, Jancis, to taste in the *chai* or out of doors? Yes, I too like very much to taste out of doors. The 1985, for example, can really be improved by the extra bit of aeration that involves." To be honest, I felt there was hardly room for both of us, a couple of glasses and a pipette in the tiny cellar.

The 1993 Roc reeked of spice and super-ripe fruit but had very obvious, rather coarse tannins on the palate. I marveled at how sleek and suave the 1993 Tertre seemed by comparison. "The *cave* at Roc is built into the riverbank, so it's much cooler and slows down the maturation, whereas here the warmer *cave* virtually works the wine itself. In many a year Roc will outlast Tertre. But the tannins are rougher and I need to understand why. I need to tame Roc," he said, almost to himself.

I suggested, half joking, that if he were Robert Mondavi in California, he would find the answer by doing a series of experimental microvinifications, varying different factors each time. François looked at me quizzically. "Oof! There are researchers for that sort of thing. I'm a practitioner. I'm too small." I had a sense that, whereas most wine producers, and certainly practically all with anything like his reputation, are extremely conscious of their place and rank in the world of wine, François Mitjavile really does work almost entirely to satisfy himself and his own goals, rather than to earn points and high prices.

As the darkness fell we talked about his plans for Roc and the goals he had set himself for Tertre. It was ten o'clock by the time he took a bottle of Tertre 1985 from a small stack in one corner of the cellar ("the one that I remember you liked so much on your last visit—and indeed I think it is the most charming of the decade") before going inside to eat a late supper. "We keep very late hours here." Miloute smiled apologetically.

The Mitjaviles ate in a perfectly square room with bright Monet blue paneling up to the bottom of the large windows on either side of the house. A tall armoire was stuffed full of lovingly collected china. Henri, who was about seven years old, and Nina, in her late teens, joined us round a beautifully darned white linen tablecloth, Henri fretting because he'd rather be with his new discovery, television. I had been warned at least four times about the simplicity of this snack. Four courses of snack there were: cold tomato soup; antipasti including piquant caper leaves and aubergine purée; thick slices of smoked salmon with sweet new potatoes boiled in their skins; and a chèvre and brebis, summer cheeses at the peak of perfection, with good crusty sourdough bread.

I was not surprised to hear that their oldest child, Louis, in his early twenties, was also involved with wine. He had been working all over the world for the Bordeaux-based "flying winemaker" Jacques Lurton. He has since come back home to work Mitjavile magic at Château Bellefont-Belcier next door. At Tertre Roteboeuf it would be difficult to escape the benign infection of wine fanaticism.

François is utterly unselfconscious about his winemaking gifts. "My first solo vintage was 1978, and I began to make exciting wines in 1981. I was a good learner but at first I didn't have any talent. I learnt a lot by working two years at Figeac and after that it was like following a recipe. But once you know well your job, and you've integrated the technique as a reflex, then you start to work from feeling."

He paused, trying to refine his thoughts. Frowning, he said, "Someone who makes wine is not creative like a painter. You can't make whatever you want. You can only make what the fruit produced by your soil can give you. The most important thing is to understand what you've got."

Nina was ready for bed. She kissed her parents on both cheeks and went off after Henri. I thought of my early start and rose too. But François was still looking thoughtful and I could see he had one more *réflexion*. "You know," he said, smiling, "many people were surprised that with no real background in wine I started to make exciting wine so soon. But I think it was because I was so afraid of my ignorance that I was extremely anxious and curious compared with those people who had grown up on wine property."

Few of this new breed of fanatically quality driven wine producers I continue to come across throughout the rest of the wine world have followed a father's footsteps into the cellar. François Mitjavile's Tuscan counterpart, for instance, ruddy-faced Paolo De Marchi, was born into a family of lawyers in northern Italy. He fell in love with agriculture in general and wine in particular while spending summers on his grandmother's farm in the alpine foothills above Turin. When he arrived at the Tuscan property that has been his life for more than twenty years, Isola e Olena were adjacent huddles of buildings hovering somewhere between a dilapidated farm and an abandoned hamlet. Like François, he had to build up the vineyards from scratch. It was only in the mid 1980s that he began to feel any sense of financial security, and it will probably be the mid 2010s before he feels confident enough to renovate his house.

These passion-propelled wine producers rarely operate in luxurious wineries with expensive equipment. Dany Gantenbein makes his wine in an old Swiss cowshed straight out of *Heidi*. Hätsch Kalberer has been known to use a scythe on the (also Swiss-owned) Fromm Vineyards of Marlborough in New Zealand. Dr. Bailey Carrodus, an Australian national treasure (even if he still sounds like an Oxford don) ferments his dense Yarra Yering reds in steel-lined tea chests. In the

Minervois in southern France, Daniel Domergue and Patricia Boyer's family live in one room so that they can afford the luxury of a destalking machine—and a fax machine to keep abreast of the labeling quirks required by their American importers. And in the glamorous context of California, Paul Draper of Ridge Vineyards is as exceptional for the hillbilly aspect of his winery high above Palo Alto as for the faithfulness of his geographical renditions of Cabernet and Zinfandel, wines he has been bottling for even longer than François Mitjavile.

The achievements of Draper and a handful of wine craftsmen in America's wine state are all the more remarkable because California is such a funny place to make wine. Not because of any natural disadvantage—the place is blessed—but because it is *so* dominated by one company, of Italian origin like so many California wine enterprises, Gallo.

The name haunted my encounters with wine in the state that was to become my home away from home from my very first visit there in the summer of 1969. I remember even then, years before I had any professional connection with wine, being struck by the inherent absurdity, and marketing acuity, of the names of the company's two big sellers, cheap blends labeled Gallo Hearty Burgundy and Gallo Mountain White Chablis.

As I learned more and more about wine, I became more and more aware of how little I knew about the Gallos. For all their power, they were intensely secretive. Secrecy is common in family businesses but this one was and still is the biggest wine company anywhere in the world, making about twenty times as much wine as, for instance, the whole world-famous, would-be-world-conquering Robert Mondavi operation. Over the years the Gallos had to my knowledge admitted only a handful of high fliers from the press to their vast production site in Modesto at the northern end of the Central Valley, the hot plains that are home to well over 80 percent of all California vineyards, and about 2 percent of its public image. Marvin Shanken had been granted an audience for an indulgent interview in his *Wine Spectator*. I knew that Hugh Johnson had also visited there, and that the Gallos had stayed at his home several times. But such was their obsession with secrecy that they refused Hugh's request to use their particularly extensive library when he was researching his monumental history of wine.

By the early 1990s, however, there were signs that even the Gallos realized that concealment is not exactly in tune with the ethos of the late-twentieth-century wine market. The Gallo brothers were getting seriously into exporting, targeting Britain, one of the most obviously expanding wine markets, with the most glamorous and lavish advertising campaign it had ever seen for wine, priced at around $6 million. (The Gallos didn't actually spend anything like this, cunningly persuading the U.S. Department of Agriculture to subsidize the campaign.)

I'm sure it was because they were so keen to increase sales in Britain that early in 1995 I suddenly received an invitation to visit Gallo the next time I was in California. As it happened, my husband, Nick, and I were due in San Francisco to pick up an award earned by my editing of *The Oxford Companion to Wine*. We were intrigued by the thought of this little day trip. Which is why one morning in late April 1995 we found ourselves speeding north over the Golden Gate Bridge in an enormous stretch limo with two typical Gallo executives. They had between them precisely fifteen months' experience with the company. "I confess I'm not a very wine knowledgeable person," warned one of them, slumped tieless against the burgundy velveteen.

By this time of course the Gallos weren't really plural. The company had been built up in the immediate aftermath of Prohibition by Ernest Gallo, a marketing genius, with his younger brother Julio in charge of production. Julio had recently died in an accident on a family farm and so it was even more obvious than ever that this vast company was basically run by one man (hence the high executive turnover), Ernest Gallo, vintage 1909.

The main point of our visit so far as he was concerned was to show off the new Gallo wine estate in Sonoma, already famously producing a $50 Cabernet, a major departure for a company that had built its fortunes on basic jug wine, even if the output of this model farm represented hardly a drop in the ocean of wine Gallo produced each year. The old Frei Ranch, clearly being geared up to be Gallo's public face, was in a beautifully peaceful corner of northern Sonoma—or Not Napa, as the Gallo line has been. For the moment, however, there were no outward signs of a Gallo link, just a small wooden gateside sign saying 3387 DRY CREEK ROAD and some tanks and concrete blocks that had obviously only recently been shoehorned into this bucolic scene.

We were introduced to Matt and Gina Gallo, children of Julio's son Bob, and clearly the two "G3s" (as the twenty grandchildren are known) who are most in tune with true wine quality. Big, broad Matt, a political science major, drove us round the estate. "You're probably familiar with the Gallo development style," he said confidently, "where we move mountains, literally, recontouring, changing the topsoil. See, we want to have hillside vineyards because they're best, but we like to get slopes down to less than fifteen percent. So we take the topsoil, stockpile it at the side of the vineyard, fill up the gullies with it, rip it all. Then put the topsoil back. Put in the drainage systems. This year erosion was a problem. Recontouring allows machine picking—not that we've used machines much so far, but we want to keep 'em as an option. We're mapping soil types to match rootstocks and varieties."

We wound up the hillside on an increasingly muddy track, past live oaks, manzanitas and red-barked madronas, orange California poppies, purple wild lupins and strawberry clover, all bursting forth in the bright spring sunshine, evidence of the much-trumpeted commitment to (a fairly expedient version of) organic farming. We came to a mouthwateringly beautiful glade which, on further inspection, turned out to provide shelter to what looked like *dozens* of earth movers. I am bad at grasping numbers over 100, particularly in relation to money, but I couldn't help feeling more digits were involved in this little ranch than probably any other wine estate I had ever visited.

This was confirmed when we got back down to the concrete shells that were set to become the winery and barrel hall, the domain of a long-serving winemaker as delightful as his name, Marcello Monticelli. It probably helps tenure at Gallo if you're Italian. On one side were stacks and stacks of brand-new barrels, still swathed in plastic for their long journey from the crème de la crème of French cooperages. But this was clearly just the start. "I'm sure you'll find a way to get sixty thousand barrels in here, won't you, Marcello?" said Matt, with the assurance that limitless funds generate. I thought of how that extraordinary investment could be divided up between, say, two thousand of France's most talented winemakers—and still they'd probably have more new casks than they needed. I knew that my friend Mel Knox, the San Francisco barrel broker, was already salivating at the avenues of commercial possibility opened up by Gallo's new commitment to quality—and this was supposed to be small scale compared to what we would see at Modesto!

To our surprise, our request to visit the company's headquarters had been acceded to and, furthermore, we had been invited to have lunch with the great man himself. An extremely comfortable Gallo helicopter was duly pressed into service to ferry Nick, me, Gina and the two increasingly superfluous execs over the Napa Valley and Sacramento delta to Modesto, transforming two and a half hours by road into forty-five revealing minutes in the air. This was just after one of Napa Valley's periodic floods and I'd never seen the northern California countryside looking so beautifully green. It was easy to see how anyone with an aerial view of California's vineyard preparation, new plantings, replantings and phylloxera damage would have a huge advantage over his rivals.

Gina, a thoughtful, deep-voiced young woman, was obviously quite smitten by wine. She'd been through the mill of the enology department at Davis, and seemed to have inherited her grandfather Julio's sensitivity. In between her pointing out notable vineyards and wineries, we settled down to the sort of gossip that wine nuts indulge in between themselves, but which does not bear repetition. She even quizzed me about the possibility of her taking the grueling London-administered Master of Wine exams, which I took as a sign of real devotion to the subject (at this stage she was neither engaged nor married). I was also amazed by her candor—an entirely different approach to that of the surviving G1. "There is definitely a stigma associated with the name Gallo in relation to quality wines," she admitted with admirable realism. An executive woke up at this point, realizing what a potentially treasonable statement had just been made, and added bullishly, "Ernest said that it just wouldn't be any fun doing it *without* the Gallo name." Ernest has certainly done his damnedest to acquire exclusive right to the Gallo name, contesting the Chianti Classico consortium's long-standing right to the Gallo Nero (black cockerel) name, and even going to court with his youngest brother, who was using it for his cheese business.

We fell silent as we approached Modesto, wheeling over a few of the extended Gallo family's sprawling modern homes set in parklike gardens before we were lowered right into the heart of the 250-acre site, unsettling the peacocks as we landed on the well-sprinkled lawn just in front of the main office block, a monument to sixties corporatism. We all climbed up a Washingtonian bank of steps—useful for photographs and statesmanlike farewells—to a large, open-plan entrance hall, complete with all the requisite murals and fountains. As Gina led us toward some impenetrable-looking wooden paneling in the far left-hand corner, a very strange thing happened. The paneling seemed to give way at Gina's approach, and our executive minders disappeared, hung back and backed away, somehow just melting into the offices of the lower orders as we entered the inner sanctum, a suite of heavy offices plus dining room where the Gallos themselves are based.

Ernest was waiting for us, dapper, diminutive, bespectacled and well briefed on my work. We went straight in to lunch, with two of the G2s, Gina's father, Bob, and Ernest's son David, and our inquisition began.

I had intended to interview the founder of this great dynasty, but it didn't turn out like that. Despite his quite severely impaired hearing, Ernest was determined to find out as much as possible from us, and to give as little as possible away. As we munched our marinated red peppers I asked him why he was beginning to get serious about exporting. So as to give the rest of the world the chance to taste his wonderful wines, of course. So when did he expect his British business to be profitable? "Profitable?" he said, and paused for a long chew, considering this inflammatory word. "We've never operated at a profit in our life, anywhere. We're in business for fun." Bob and David chuckled dutifully. "You know, because we've never charged what our wine is really worth, we don't have the image that some people think we deserve," Ernest added in his deadpan staccato.

We'd barely started Maureen-the-office-cook's ravioli, the second of four courses, before he turned the tables and we were quizzed at length about how California wines were regarded in Britain relative to those of Chile, Australia, France and South Africa. Communication was hampered by his hearing and there was much repetition and explanation from his son and nephew, but he still managed to extract far more from us than vice versa. Questions ranged from our opinion of the food at Claridge's where he always stays in London ("a very satisfactory hotel, extremely high standard of service"), to the evolution of pubs, the Master of Wine exam, the British cider market and the performance of California wine's new generic representative in London.

At one point George the butler was instructed to get hold of a bottle of one of their new ciders (the Gallos own almost as many apple orchards as vineyards) and soon I had a bottle of Hornsby's Draft Cider in my hand (made "in the best tradition of the finest European pubs" according to the label). Ernest was planning to launch it in England and was using me for market research. I tried out a straightforward factual question on him, asking how sweet it was. "Some people think it's sweet. Some don't," was his typically enigmatic reply.

From here on, we were encouraged to give Ernest a couple of hours' intensive consultancy on how Gallo wines could do better in Britain. I learnt virtually nothing, except that he is an extraordinary individual, with tunnel vision. He obviously knows the American market inside out, but isn't remotely interested in anything that will not benefit Gallo directly. Try as Robert Mondavi, Gallo's extrovert antithesis might, he could never get Ernest to cooperate on an industry-wide basis, which was disastrous when antialcohol sentiment in the United States was at its height.

Not that Gallo Senior was a stay-at-home. He'd just got back from North Vietnam. Vacation? Mmm, half and half. And all three Gallo men seemed suspiciously well informed about Chile for a company that continues to deny that it would ever be interested in investing abroad. Ernest assured me that although Chilean wines looked okay when tasted in situ, once you got them back to Modesto and tasted them side by side with Gallo's California wines, they didn't look too good.

The G2s were allowed to take over for a while, with some tricky questions about Britain. "How are we perceived over there?" Bob Gallo asked (his daughter Gina hardly spoke during the meal except to translate some of our anglicisms). I prevaricated, mumbling about the visibility of their ads and so on, but he'd have none of it. "No, no. People-wise, I mean." Ah, well. Good old Nick jumped in here. "I think you're seen as the great unknown," he said tactfully.

David Gallo wanted to know where I stood on whether it was the grape grower or winemaker who was more responsible for wine quality, a sensitive question for the world's most important purchaser of grapes. "Is the vine the true winemaker or should the winemaker's influence predominate, whereby he chooses more or less oak, more or less *sur lie* and really fashions the wine himself?" I got the distinct impression he favored the second view.

The only time Ernest became at all animated was when we described the chaotic nature of Italian generic promotion in Britain, where the money finally comes through in the last month of the financial year and is routinely spent on one absurdly lavish, ineffectual banquet. "I don't know why I'm laughing," he chuckled. "My father was born in Italy."

He was particularly interested in Hazel Murphy, the woman who had done so much to boost Australian wine sales and visibility in Britain. I learnt that he had already heard about Murphy the Human Dynamo and once had her summoned to meet him between planes at Heathrow airport. His minion couldn't believe Hazel when she said that, since she worked for the Australian government, there was no point. "You're missing out on the opportunity to meet the Mr. Ford of the wine industry," she was told.

This vinously omnipotent Mr. Ford turned out to have, like so many magnates, the most extraordinarily bossy secretary. From about the time the 1991 Estate Cabernet was served, she kept opening the door of the small, increasingly airless dining room to remind Ernest of his next appointment. We finally tore ourselves away from each other, me feeling frustrated because I was no nearer to understanding what Ernest Gallo really thought, he doubtless frustrated that he hadn't managed to prize more out of me.

Bob Gallo, a production man like his father, Julio, had been, was detailed to give us a tour of the site, and picked up one or two of their many winemakers on the way. We'd already seen from the air the number of railway lines that were needed to ship out what Gallo produced, but with each new fact our jaws fell further. They have their own trucking company, make their own cartons and labels, their furnaces produce *more than two million bottles a day,* some of the tanks hold 600,000 gallons—but it all looked very old-fashioned. This was basically a wine factory. They had long since outgrown the site, hemmed in by the town and two rivers, and did all their grape crushing elsewhere, but the underground cellars were stuffed full of old wooden vats of their own strange design.

I had long wondered why so many of their red wines were so acid and asked one of the winemakers whether they routinely did the second, softening malolactic fermentation. "Routine malolactic is an oxymoron for us, Jancis," was one of the more intriguing things I was told, along with how they keep a dozen examples of every bottling in their wine library, six stoppered with traditional cork and six by crown cap. For test purposes, they always choose a bottle with a crown cap, "because it's such a great preserver."

We were also told that ten of the twenty G3s were already working in the family firm, but Gina was "the most enology-minded." Imagine those family dinners. And what happens when Ernest makes a joke.

Gina flew back with us, dropping us at the little Angwin airstrip where we were met by an old friend, a curious and long-standing exception to the rule that everyone who lives in the Napa Valley is in the wine business. I thought about Gina and her fellow G3s afterwards. In a way they're the nearest California has to our Royal Family, bowed down with both responsibilities and opportunities, yet for the moment bound by the wishes and management style of the reigning head of the family. Gina struck me as the Gallos' Princess Anne, workmanlike, unaffected, and with real potential for dedication—and the crucial awareness of how the results of it might fit into the rest of the world.

So, this is a tale of two wine producers, driven by completely different forces and histories but at long last going in the same direction. It is easy to see which of these two men has come the farther, made the greatest transition in objectives. Yet he is the one who still has farther to go.

Liquid Magic—
Birth of a Wine Lover

What was it that started it all?

Perhaps some alcohol-impermeable genes inherited from my paternal grandmother. At the age of eighty-eight, she heard on the wireless that too much gin was bad for you. So for her last ten years she drank whisky instead.

Or was it a more romantic, cultural inheritance from my mother's maternal grandfather, James Forfar Dott, who owned a bit of French forest, a cooperage beside it and a warehouse on the quayside in Bordeaux? James Dott, a Scot of Huguenot descent, may have felt the same sort of subconscious resonance that I did when I first lived in France on acquiring this bold stake in what was once the mother country. The main business of the cooperage, which his children described vaguely as "sheds and barrels," was to supply casks for Britain's east coast herring trade. The family would decamp from Brighton and spend their summer holidays in a bleak-looking house known as Le Château Dott, overlooking the railway station nearest the cooperage at Bussière-Galant, the visit of *les Anglais* being regarded as quite an event in this small village south of Limoges. While James ran his business interests from a green and brown painted office in The City of London, his French investments were entrusted to Mr. Reynolds, a grumpy expatriate. His French wife, according to my distant cousin David Chaundy, put up with his moods, pointing out, "at least he is faithful."

Cousin David visited the old warehouses in Bordeaux in 1954, driving his parents (including the oldest of James's four daughters) down to Spain for one of their much-loved holidays in Torremolinos, then a small fishing village. French bureaucracy had slowed the sale of these sagging-roofed sheds to a standstill, even though James had died more than twenty years earlier and this was a final attempt to cut the cross-Channel thread. Some of the many lawyers and agents they consulted remembered James Dott well and all described him as *"un homme honnête,"* which made his survivors wonder about the rest.

In three or four decades, cooperages in general, and French oak barrel-making in particular, would become the most glamorous and financially interesting cog in the wheel of the world's wine trade. And, had this family connection been maintained, I would not perhaps have devoted quite so many column inches to mocking emergent wine producers' apparently limitless veneration of expensive new oak barrels— and drawing attention to their suppliers' profits.

But I managed to spend my own first four decades ignorant of this nugget of family history, eighteen years of them almost entirely ignorant of wine in any form. My father hates it when I say this because he thinks it reflects badly on him. But the truth is that in the Britain of the fifties and sixties wine was still a rarity. Our wine imports were negligible in the postwar years and it was not until the early seventies that we began to lose our suspicion of this inherently foreign drink. In the fifties and sixties the lives of even solidly middle class families such as ours impinged on wine only on very special occasions. Beer was the drink of choice not just in the local pub, The Drover's Rest, but in the cellar of the local lord. Once the concept of eating out began slowly to establish itself, the more adventurous local farmers could report on "five courses for three bob—smashing value." We knew just enough to be snooty about others drinking (Spanish) "Sauternes," sweet oily lubricant, with steak. But the rest of the limited selection of wines available in mid-twentieth-century Britain was not much less filthy. Typically they reeked of the chemicals that bottlers, many links along the distribution chain from any vineyards involved, rammed into the wine to stop it going fizzy, cloudy or some strange color.

No wonder so few of my fellow countrymen regarded wine with any enthusiasm, and no wonder I was barely aware of wine while growing up in the far northwest of England. Eden House, center of my life and still home to my parents, had been built by my father's great-grandfather nearly a century before in his native Kirkandrews-on-Eden, a village of forty-five people, one post office and no mains drainage in Cumbria's Eden Valley (no less pretty but very much colder than the South Australian version, one of the state's famously "cool" wine regions).

The headache potions once sold as wine in Britain undoubtedly belong to another era, but the era ended barely twenty years ago. Their period feel owes less to my great age than to the remarkably swift evolution of the wine world since the seventies. Unwittingly I have witnessed at close range one of the most extraordinary social changes of the late twentieth century, the popularization, and in some quarters near-deification, of wine—and food.

Food, and my relationship to it, is the real basis of my love of wine. Picture this. Fashion-conscious, country-based but innately urban grammar school teenager lives an infrequent bus service away from the nearest shop and coffee bar (how sad, I can hear my elder daughter groan). Twiggy, an emaciated blond model, is the national role model. Our particularly numerate seventeen-year-old discovers calories. She decides she's overweight—there's too much puppy fat to squeeze into a size 10 Dollyrocker from Richards Shops—and begins to keep a tally of her calorie intake. This is fun. Math plus willpower equals minus pounds. Minus even more pounds, about twenty-five in five weeks as it turned out (for this seventeen-year-old is nothing if not determined), and the body is so weak that the mind is also enfeebled. It wonders whether the brambles eaten on a walk contain more calories than those expended on that walk. It knows that food taken from other people's plates, and leftovers, contain no calories at all. It sees no contradiction in the concept of skeletal beauty. I can quite see how anorexics shrink to their childish body weights, although luckily I stopped "banting," as my godmother called it, well before this. Frustratingly, I can't remember why or how, but my poor parents must have been terrified. Between April and June 1967 I went from being a robust, reasonably good athlete to a state of weak, sunken-eyed deflation. Pale, specter-thin, but—so much luckier than some—very much alive.

All this physical turmoil had one fateful, pivotal side effect. It is obvious that whatever one deprives oneself of, one becomes absolutely fascinated by. I became an obsessive cook. I devoured recipes instead of calories. I made the most extraordinary things, always determined by what happened to be in the larder, cupboards and a throbbing fridge called a Coldrator, since in our rustication we were able to indulge only in *in*convenience shopping, heaving bulging baskets on to the bus. I forced these strange dishes down my parents and brother James and, during the banting period at least, wallowed in the virtue of not eating them myself.

The long-term effect was that I acquired an enduring interest in and passion for food. For flavors, for textures, for the interplay between them, for the mental stimulation and physical comfort that they bring. So it was hardly surprising that, once exposed to it, I would have the same feelings for food's quintessential companion, liquid food, wine.

The first wine I was exposed to as an independent being, rather than as one of my parents' dependents, was fairly horrible, but it taught me an invaluable lesson. On the day in July 1968 when I finally left school I caught an overnight bus to London and then, quivering with nervous excitement, set off on a long sea and rail journey to Grosseto on the Tuscan coast. I was off to work the summer as a chambermaid in what was then Italy's most expensive hotel, Il Pellicano near Porto Ercole on Monte Argentario.

I'd found out about this exotic vacancy from some friends of my father who had a villa just along the hair-raising coast road from the hotel and knew its Scottish-American owners. Because the local Italian girls preferred to work at the tomato canning plant, the Grahams had taken to recruiting chambermaids via the classified columns of the *Times* in London. They didn't dare use the paper's new section called "Crème de la Crème" (aimed at nice girls prepared to work hard for awfully well paid men) but every spring inserted a brutally honest few lines in the "Situations Vacant" section: "Hard Work, Long Hours, Rotten Pay," was how they began. They said they'd had two hundred replies that year, but that someone had dropped out at the last minute. So here was I, a pale, northern Englander sitting in an unbelievably hot, slow train mysteriously called an *espresso,* about to start my working life at about $6.50 a week (although I was to find that tips averaged twice that).

Thanks to my post-anorexic state, I was immediately christened La Grissina by the mainly Italian team working in this luxurious twenty-room establishment. The work *was* hard. The hours were long. The conditions were not exactly *simpatico*. The three (out of the five) British chamberslaves who were not (yet) shacked up with local Italian boys and their families had to share a tiny, dark room whose only virtue was a small terrace overlooking one corner of the terrace where guests were served a buffet on Saturday nights. If we were suitably pert with one of the waiters (without being brazen, which would have terrified these boys exposed only to the ways of the heavily protected, tomato-canning local girls), they would covertly throw the throwable items from this buffet up to us. I remember squares of chocolate cake and squidgy round rolls like pincushions that seemed so much more re-fined than the coarse unsalted bread served by the naked slice with staff meals. "Sergio, Sergio. *Burro, per favore,*" we'd whisper urgently from our second-class darkness, desperate for something as novel and northern as a small packet of creamy white butter.

While guests left mounds of uneaten food on their plates, and picked and chose between carefully assembled salads of various crus-taceans, pulses and vegetables (*vitello tonnato* or *calamari fritti*), staff meals consisted chiefly of pasta and the produce of the canning plant, although I do remember how richly exotic the smell of stewing pep-pers seemed then. But it was the drink provided that was to teach me such a lot. We could drink as much of the rough red wine on offer as we liked with our meals, but if I wanted to drink reliable, bottled water guaranteed not to shock my metabolic flora, as carefully pro-tected from hot-blooded mediterranean violation as the girls of Porto Ercole, I had to pay for it.

This was a dramatic reversal of the value system in which I'd been raised. To this day my mother carefully restoppers and treasures the remains in every bottle of wine, even if less than half an inch is left in the bottom. Wine, after all, is the expensive imported stuff on which a heavy duty has been levied; water simply falls from the sky, with depressing frequency if you live in northern England.

It dawned on me that for millions of people, those living in coun-tries like Italy, France, Spain, Portugal and Argentina where wine is made in huge quantities and sold at very low prices, wine was not something obfuscated by mystique and fraught with social symbolism

but just an everyday, commonplace drink. A drink that was ubiquitous, dirt cheap, and one in which harmful bacteria tend to be usefully
killed off by the combination of acid and alcohol.

This seemed wonderful to me. I began to get a glimmer of a world
in which it was possible to relax with wine. Perhaps it was even possible to erase the audible quotation marks habitually used to enclose
the word in 1960s Britain, a self-conscious practice designed to signal
recognition of the fact that wine was an exotic substance, associated
with solecism, holiday madness and gastric turmoil.

Wine for the Pellicano hotel staff came in large straw-covered *fiaschi*
which I realize in retrospect must have been used over and over again to
transport the local red from the local co-op's tank to our table under an
awning in the kitchen yard. The stale, slightly vinegary whiff that
hung over it is a telltale sign, I now know, of overexposure to air and
heat. The previous autumn's produce was probably at its best fresh from
the fermentation vat early in the year when temperatures were much
lower and there was less risk of boiling off vital elements in its flavor.
By the time I got to taste it, in the torrid dog days of July and August,
it had lost much of its youthful appeal but was still perceptibly
different from the overworked liquids sold as wine in Britain.

Along with being introduced to *potentially* vivid wine, a once-
vibrant liquid which had not passed through dozens of grimy middlemen's fingers, I was introduced as well to an entirely new spectrum of
colors in Italy. My pastel Liberty print frocks looked wan in the
brilliant mediterranean light. I understood why the Pellicano's
customers (who included Charlie Chaplin and family, a Getty who
pressed 25,000 lire, untold riches, into my hand on my second day,
and, I think, the queen of the Netherlands although I should have
been more impressed in retrospect) wore the shocking pinks, purples
and oranges of Emilio Pucci and the like. I did not understand why so
many of them discarded their possessions—either dropping silk shifts
into wastepaper bins, airily handing them over to us, or simply leaving
them behind. When I left in September, it was with a suitcaseful of
exotic clothing, which looked as outlandish in Cumbria as my black
PVC raincoat had in Tuscany.

Not long after this exchange of brilliant sunshine for soft gray
drizzle, I proudly used what remained of my Pellicano tips to take my
parents to dinner at Sharrow Bay in the Lake District, a member of a

strange new breed called country house hotels, before being driven down (or was it up?) to Oxford with a large trunkful of clothes.

It was from a tiny student bedroom at St. Anne's, then the most modern of Oxford's five colleges for women, that I was to properly make the acquaintance of wine, or rather wine connoisseurship, which is such a very different thing from drinking. (One of the three questions I had chosen from a possible thirteen on the general Oxford entrance paper was a discussion of the statement "Drunkenness in ordinary cases is not a fit subject for legislative interference.")

The word "connoisseur" is not an attractive one. It smacks of exclusivity, preciousness and elitism. But there is a very distinct quality to wine connoisseurs, as distinct from wine enthusiasts and wine bores. I thought for many years that it was a French word but of course the French equivalent is *connaisseur,* and the French are wise enough to know that not many of them truly know, or *connaissent,* wine. The French use the much more attractive and positive term *amateur de vin,* lover of wine. All wine connoisseurs are wine lovers but not all wine lovers are connoisseurs.

Connoisseurship is not a necessary state for wine appreciation. It is perfectly possible to enjoy wine enormously without really understanding it. But a connoisseur sees each individual wine in its historical, geographical and sociological context and is truly sensitive to its possibilities. Connoisseurship is a rather old-fashioned concept. Many wine enthusiasts today view each wine as something to be judged rather than enjoyed. They feel the onus is on the bottle to knock their socks off rather than on the person who pulled the cork to appreciate and flatter the wine. Connoisseurs, on the other hand, make a conscious effort to open each bottle at a stage in its evolution when it is likely to shine. They serve wine at a temperature likely to make the most of its attributes and the least of its shortcomings (a fine young red bordeaux or Cabernet Sauvignon tastes perfectly horrid drunk cool without food, for instance). Rather than just reaching for the most expensive bottle they feel they can afford, they take a strange sort of pleasure in trying to match particular wines to particular occasions, people, weather and food.

I am very aware that these strange connoisseur creatures, who clearly allow their conduct to be swayed by previous experience, may sound a bit precious, perhaps suspiciously snobbish. But the difference between them and, say, a stickler for protocol or etiquette, is that they do what they do for the entirely sensible, selfish and laudable reason of maximizing pleasure. There is nothing whatever wrong with wine lovers who simply pour wine with careless gusto down their throats. There are times when that and only that will do. But those who will not meet a wine halfway, and who consistently ignore the story each wine has to tell, deprive themselves of a large part of the potential pleasure associated with each bottle. As I was to learn, a wine is more than just a liquid.

I, by the way, consider myself a wine connoisseur some nights (and most days) and a wine lover every night, sometimes an excessively ardent lover. Like "wine expert," "wine connoisseur" is an appellation I would never insist on for myself. It sounds horribly off-putting. In fact, I would find it hard to like someone who described himself or herself as a connoisseur. Like "intellectual" or "prodigy," it is a term which invalidates itself if used self-referentially.

The person who introduced me to the notion of wine as an intellectual entity was a true connoisseur, however, with all the slightly paradoxical asceticism that that implies. Alison Forbes was in the year above me. She was studying classics and I was engaged in a strange, brand-new hybrid course designed to bridge the gap between the arts and the sciences, maths and philosophy. I came to hate the maths but enjoyed the philosophy and the logic that bound them together. I'm not sure how Alison and I met, although we may have shared a Moral Tutor (who, two years earlier, would have been Iris Murdoch). Alison was a most unusual person in many respects, being much taller and more spiritual than the average Oxford undergraduate, but what I found most fascinating was that she, most unusually for someone born (just) in the 1940s, had been brought up to be a wine connoisseur. Her father, a Devon doctor, was one of the few dozen men who joined The (International Exhibition Co-operative) Wine Society each year during and immediately after the war. (There are nearly ten thousand new members each year in the 1990s.) Like any well-informed medical man, he ensured that his children were brought up to admire and savor wine in moderation. They would be given small sips from a very young age, and were taught, if Alison was anything to go by, to take serious note of its character and origins.

One of my first memories of learning about wine is that of standing on the High Street outside the shop window of Oxford's then leading wine merchant G. T. Jones listening to Alison's German wine mantra: "Green glass for moselle, brown for hock."

She would tell me in advance when she was planning to open a half bottle of this or that—and what she was planning to celebrate and/or eat with it—before giving me a taste, plus instruction. She found a very absorbent pupil. Alison Forbes subsequently worked for Penguin Books and then went to live in Italy, so presumably the wine never dried up. I owe her a great deal.

She knew someone who knew someone else who was part of a wine-tasting society at Oxford. I have been asked why I didn't join. It didn't occur to me for a second. Like most aspects of Oxford, indeed like most aspects of sophisticated southern life, such a society sounded far too glamorous and exclusive to accommodate me. Coming from a village school where it was considered an achievement to pass the 11-plus, and a girls' grammar school which sent an average of one pupil a year to Oxbridge (the 1956 vintage had yielded the biographer and novelist Margaret Forster, who has written similarly about how she felt at Oxford), I always felt an outsider, as though I was there only by virtue of some extremely fortuitous mistake. I learnt many years later that had I summoned up my courage and joined the Oxford University Wine Society, I would have met my fellow wine writers Oz Clarke and Charles Metcalfe a decade earlier than I did—although I would have had so much less confidence than they had that I would probably have abandoned wine forever.

As it was, my wine epiphany took place more privately, in the circumstances for which wine is designed, with a good dinner. Like so many other wine lovers before and since, I found my love affair ignited by a single, outstanding and still memorable bottle. Even though you might have spent years swigging ordinary commercial wine of varying degrees of deliciousness, it takes just one sniff and sip of something in a completely different class to make you realize that wine is capable of reaching not just your throat and nose but your brain, your heart, and occasionally your soul too. You just know that there is *more* in every way in an incontrovertibly fine wine. This could be proved empirically by boiling all the water off it, leaving so much more in the petri dish (the wine's dry extract) than in similar remains of a vapid commercial blend. But such a demonstration is unnecessary because you can tell by the way your senses are vibrating and your heart is racing that this is a completely different experience from drinking normal wine. Perhaps the two most significant attributes in a great wine are the range of nuances in its smell (so variegated it is known by insiders as a "bouquet," as opposed to the simple "aroma" of a basic young wine) and the length of time the flavor lingers in the mouth after it has been swallowed, the wine's "length."

For years I have bleated that expensive wine is not necessarily an extravagance because a mouthful of it can last so much longer than a mouthful of cheap wine. I find that my instinct after downing a mouthful of very ordinary wine is to gulp another to check whether it really did taste of so little. Over the last two decades, the quality gap between basic and special wines has narrowed, but when I tasted my seminal bottle, it was vast.

In the early 1970s wine drinkers were infinitely less knowledgeable and demanding. There were some skilled winemakers (even if they were much less formally trained than their counterparts today), but most commercial wines were transported in bulk, blended beyond recognition and bottled extremely carelessly—partly because no one complained about the results. I remember that for much of the 1970s all I demanded of a wine was that it didn't actually smell disgusting. (If it did, and it was white or pink, the solution was—and still is—to chill it so viciously that it was impossible to smell anything from it.) Winemaking faults were commonplace. White wines were routinely deadened by exposure to oxygen which would brown them to a dull gold and leave them with off-putting, flat, sherry-like smells, particularly in warmer wine regions where the grapes would often start fermenting even before they reached the cellar. Hot country reds often came with lovely deep colors but also the vinegary smells associated with volatility. White wines then were generally much sweeter than now, and lashings of sulphur were added to stop that sugar from fermenting explosively in the bottle—so that whites were commonly tainted with the acrid reek of excess sulphur dioxide.

In those days almost every bottle was masquerading as something else. More than 10 million bottles of coarse, raisiny Cypriot wine labeled Emva Cream were sold each year dressed up as sherry. Tall brown bottles with gold labels promising Lutomer Riesling (always pronounced "Rize-ling" in those days) were pretending to be hock from Germany, which still had some cachet then, with fine German wine easily commanding the same prices as fine red bordeaux. In fact the best-selling Lutomer brand was a blend of the light, fresh, *cheap* produce of Slovenia in northern Yugoslavia, brutalized by bulk shipment to London's still-maritime Dockland, by heavy additions of coarse grape concentrate to sweeten it up, and by even heavier doses of sulphur. (It took many years for the Germans to lobby the authorities in Brussels so relentlessly that they managed to reserve the exclusive right to the term "Riesling" for their own grape, which has nothing to do with that now properly called Lasskirizling in Slovenia. So efficiently did they do this that it took me almost as many years to realize that there was nothing inherently wrong with "the other Rizling"; it just doesn't happen to be German. Austria makes some stunning Welschriesling—yes, the other one.)

In the days before Britain joined Europe's Common Market, bottles of even the most basic red wine were habitually dressed up with psuedo medieval labels to look like some rather smart burgundy. They typically contained a great deal of North African red. But then so did the real thing at that stage. (Many years later in the early 1980s, when *The Sunday Times* news editor had the misguided idea of sending me to Sète, France's principal wine port on the Mediterranean, to sniff out a wine war, or least some wine scandal, I remember how shocked I was by such brazenly incriminating dockside street names as Quai d'Alger.)

After 1973, when Edward Heath finally got our entry papers signed— helped by some 1955 claret served to the dubious French at the British embassy in Paris—we all imagined the chief benefit would be that wine would become as cheap in Britain as it is in France, but it was no longer so easy for British wine merchants to stick names as famous as Pommard and Nuits-Saint-Georges on different bottles (often taken from exactly the same tank). These were the names of places. Which meant that the French appellation contrôlée system, outlined by the Institut National des Appellations d'Origine and therefore European law, was specifically designed to protect them. Britain's wine bottlers (very much more numerous then than now) had to exercise their imagination a little. The curlicues remained but the names had to become more inventive—even if the small type revealed these wines were mere Vins de Table, French wine's dregs. My favorite was the quite splendidly deceptive Côte de Villages, widely available in the late seventies throughout Britain's largest hotel group.

It was no wonder then that my seminal bottle of red burgundy made such an impression. I had a boyfriend at the time who was as keen on eating and drinking as I was (and in those puritanical days, I remember, was roundly dismissed as "a bit of a bon viveur"). His delightful German professor father was extremely generous, which meant that we ate out far more often than was the norm—and I became the restaurant correspondent for the university magazine *Isis* (not quite my first journalistic assignment, which had been writing and illustrating a riveting article about fashion for *The Cumberland News* when I was sixteen). The revelatory bottle of red burgundy was consumed at a restaurant called the Rose Revived just outside Oxford.

In those days the Rose Revived was famed within Oxford not just for its pretty name but for quite respectable cooking for the period, a period defined gastronomically by kipper paté and duck à l'orange. An expedition as far out of Oxford as Newbridge in 1970 gave undergraduates like us a feeling of real exploration. What we were about to experience on this sunny summer's evening in the English countryside represented sophisticated liberation from hurried early evening dinners in hall.

I suppose David, my boyfriend of the time, ordered the Chambolle-Musigny, Les Amoureuses 1959. I don't remember. It almost certainly came propped at an angle in one of those strange little wicker cradles designed to leave the sediment unshaken in the bottom of the bottle. I would probably scorn the heavily cut glasses today. And nowadays I would know that the most important information on a burgundy label is the name of the producer (so shockingly diverse are their winemaking skills to this day), but then I thought the name of the wine was all that mattered. It may well have been a wine imported and bottled by Averys of Bristol, a firm with a particularly strong reputation for the robust style of burgundy then in vogue. At this point Averys was still very much a family enterprise, ruled by the idiosyncratic Ronald Avery, whose hold on the cellars around Oxford must surely have been strengthened by his son John's recent stint at Lincoln College, supposedly studying agriculture. The Avery style of burgundy was deep-colored, full-bodied, headily scented and voluptuous. No wonder it made such an impression. Here was a wine that positively demanded attention.

I may have remembered Alison's instructions to smell, or "nose" the wine first—and was overwhelmed by a clean, sweet perfume so ineffably more real, more vivid, more of the earth than of the factory, than any wine I had ever come across before. This wasn't a difficult wine to enjoy—not like the dry austerity of the odd red bordeaux that had come my way at one of the grand dinners occasionally organized to give undergraduates a taste of college cellars' riches. This was brazen and fleshy and each mouthful entranced me, even if I found it impossible to describe. I doubt whether we even tried to discuss the wine other than to grunt and drool. It is, after all, only professionals who are forced to try to transform those essentially visceral sensations into words.

Of course I did not get up from that table determined to be a wine writer, but that wine did make me realize that wine can enhance life for far more and nobler reasons than its alcohol content alone. The best wines express a place, a person, and a point in the historical continuum as well as being capable of providing sensual thrills which, because of all this and also perhaps because there is no need for the messy business of chewing, can seem more spiritual than those associated with most food. Or is this absurdly far-fetched? Wine certainly needs food even more than food needs wine, although I was to learn that there are occasions when it can cope without solid ballast.

Going to stay with the German professor at his house on the plain near Interlaken, chosen for its heart-stopping view of the Eiger, the Jungfrau and the monk, or Mönch, shielding the virgin from the ogre in snowy perpetuity in the Bernese Oberland, opened my eyes to new possibilities for wine, as well as for music appreciation. This eminent international lawyer followed the German custom of drinking beer or water with his evening meal and then sitting, in his case listening to Schubert or Mozart on a record player of, to me, quite astounding clarity, with a bottle of wine. He kept his favored bottles in a wooden

chest, to distinguish them from the liters of Fendant and Dôle bought
to sluice his four sons and their entourages. The great majority of them
were examples of the delicate, fruity essences produced in the Mosel
Valley, a taste which I have shared ever since. These razor-sharp wines,
often with only about 8 percent alcohol, are perfect for sipping without food—ideally when listening to music or reading (although for
some reason it seems all wrong to *eat* while listening properly to
music, perhaps again because of that chewing business and the way it
interferes with the rhythm). Many years later it gave me enormous
pleasure to take bottles from the great Mosel wine dynasties such as
Prüm and von Schubert whenever we went to visit him in his London
flat. He told us the same joke reassuringly often, about the visitor who
is served a vineyard's produce in situ, to which the punchline is "I'm
afraid it doesn't travel," giggling more helplessly each time.

I cannot be the only Oxford graduate to regret not having taken
more advantage of the contents of the best college cellars. In those days
the less-rarified bottles from some of the very few cellars in the world
that had been maintained more or less continuously since the Middle
Ages were available to undergraduates at virtually the prices they had
been bought for, which was very little. But then this was an era when
inflation was still something that happened to the tires of our bicycles
rather than the economy. None of us could believe that a classed
growth claret, which was probably on sale for 25 shillings ($2) or so in
1970, would ever seem ridiculously cheap at that price.

Poor old St. Anne's, founded as recently as 1952, could offer little
more interesting than a bike shed full of sherry, the drink dons served
in tutorials to dull the senses while listening to students read their
essays. But beneath some of the older colleges were medieval treasure
troves I should have plundered, via friends at those colleges. (It should
not have been too difficult to persuade someone to cooperate; women
enjoyed an absurd social advantage then, outnumbered ten to one by
students at the men's colleges.)

One of the first assignments I set myself when finally writing about
wine was to go and investigate the legendary cellar of All Souls, a college of immense interest to undergraduates because it was open only to
particularly high powered professional academics. I was duly shown

round by the man in charge of the cellar, Head Butler Walter Quelch
(surely a transplant from an Iris Murdoch novel). I had, in fact still
have, never seen such quantities of mature and maturing top-quality
wine, case after case of first growth 1961s stretching into the vaulted
darkness.

But I left Oxford without even thinking about finding a career in
wine. My years there, 1968 to 1971, coincided neatly with students at
their most revolting, or at least revoltingly sanctimonious. Oxford's contribution to the great student demonstrations of 1968 was to occupy the
ancient Sheldonian Theatre for a few hours—I forget why—and to have
one young man dress up as a woman for matriculation, a strange ceremony requiring all new undergraduates to dress up in black and white
subfusc. This was before it was possible to be both a socialist and a
champagne drinker. Eating was a bourgeois habit. And every time
Bernard Levin mentioned a particularly delicious meal or wine in one of
his columns in the *Times*, he was berated on the "Letters" page for days
afterwards.

It was not just that the British public were still imbued with the
puritanical idea that eating and drinking were merely refueling
processes, as mildly embarrassing and as worthy of attention as dis-
posing of the waste matter from them. They had not yet, apart from
the likes of my great-aunt and -uncle, been exposed to mainland
Europe's more hedonistic approach. I noticed that more and more of
my contemporaries, especially women who had been lured by the
Twiggy trap like me, were becoming fascinated by food, but they felt
guilty about it. The word "foodie" had not yet been coined. Elizabeth
David, who had been writing beautiful prose and biting culinary criticism for two decades, was still regarded as a mere writer on women's
topics. Food and drink were not considered respectable interests—perhaps partly because famine was a much more, perhaps I should say *even*
more, serious issue than it is today. The word "Biafra," then suffering
the terrible aftereffects of trying to secede from Nigeria, was one which
frequently appeared in those letters to the *Times*.

So rather than follow my instincts and try to find a job in what I
really enjoyed, I cravenly followed the herd and thought I should go
into something called Marketing (a few years previously it would
probably have been Advertising). But I was determined to market a
product I was interested in so I took the risk of applying for only two

jobs, one with Thomson Holidays because I liked travel and one with United Biscuits because I liked biscuits. I struck lucky and missed out on a life entwined with custard creams, perhaps because at the shortlist session at some dire motel on the Great West Road in Osterley, when we were asked to rank the candidates we thought should get the job, I automatically omitted myself—although at least I didn't put myself third, which one of the others did. She was also female of course.

Becoming
a Wine Writer

And so I became a graduate trainee in Britain's burgeoning package tour business, unwittingly playing a small part in introducing the nation to the habit of wine drinking by means of cheap foreign travel. In September 1971 I started off on a year-long tour of the different departments in the old cigarette factory that is Greater London House at an annual salary of £1,400 ($2,200), and thought myself lucky to have an income at all. Most of my friends were prolonging the agony of exams, either academically or on the lowest rung of a profession.

Nearly twenty-five years later I was invited to a dinner for wine stewards of various Oxford colleges, those with the power to fill their cellars. It involved staying one winter's night in the slightly damp visitor's room of one of the older men's colleges, which meant that I had the novel thrill of wandering around misty quadrangles without being late for a tutorial, feeling touristy enough to want to go to Choral Evensong, and seeing through the illuminated windows of the Bodleian Library the warm glow of scholarship rather than guilt-inducing swots. I was surrounded by students in the throes of interviews and job offers. I heard someone boasting of being offered exactly ten times what I had been offered by Thomson Holidays, when it need only have been seven times to keep pace with inflation. Perhaps my new job was not the best rewarded in terms of sheer cash, but we did reap other benefits.

We could fill free airline seats, provided we could travel at short notice. One of the secretaries used to fly out from Luton to Majorca and back of an evening simply, she said, for the in-flight meals and the duty-free (profits from which were the financial raison d'être of Thomson and its airline at that stage). We were also allowed a 60 percent discount on Thomhols for ourselves and our partners. The razor-sharp marketing director Roger Davies and his wife, Adele Biss, my immediate boss and later to become head of the British Tourist Authority, therefore argued that they were actually *owed* 20 percent of the cost of any Thomson holiday they took together. Thanks to Thomson I discovered that parts of Majorca are extremely beautiful, although not the dreary strip of sixties concrete that was Arenal when I was sent to do my one-week stint as a rep, the cliché tour guide one rainy November. The female Thomson rep's uniform at that stage was a lovely little Crimplene number in Jif lemon yellow and royal blue. Since I was quite clearly the most temporary of staff, putting in this week simply because it was, quite rightly, demanded of all graduate trainees that they should experience package tourism at its rawest, I was not given the luxury of a uniform that fit.

Then there was the problem of my name. It certainly wasn't worth getting that right just for one week, and anyway which of the guests at the Arenal Park, who had paid $29 all-in for their week of coach trips and cheap booze, could care less that my name was that of the heroine of Mary Webb's *Precious Bane*—even if it had made such a lasting impression on my mother and her sister when they read it in their teens? So for a week of damp concrete, sangria parties and "I Belong to Glasgow" on the bus, I was Jan. I went the whole hog and had my hair backcombed by the hotel's hairdresser.

Having gone to a state school but living in one of the more socially stratified corners of Britain, I grew up with an almost priggish horror of snobbery and prejudice in any form. My egalitarianism has never been more severely tested than during that week in Arenal, however. The general rule in tourism is that the more people pay and the more the sun shines, the less they complain. I found myself at the other end of both spectra, and the general gloom was compounded by the temperamental nature of the lifts in this multistory tourist park. I have

forever associated the smell of damp concrete and Ducados cigarettes
with Spain.

Although student travel had taken me to Beirut, the Soviet Union
and all over the United States, including more Greyhound bus stations than I now like to recall, this was my very first taste of package
tourism. It fascinated me to see how important a part alcohol in general and wine in particular played. Lightly taxed alcohol seemed to
rival sunshine as the single greatest attraction of southern Europe for
northern Europeans who had to pay vast amounts to their governments
for the right to drink at home. The "welcome party," the tour operators' chance to secure an even higher proportion of their customers'
discretionary income by selling them expensive excursions, would be
nothing without its promise of free punch, sangria or Glühwein. And
throughout my three years with Thomson I was to see how the Brits
were introduced to the strange new notion of drinking wine with
meals, in between all those cheap Cuba libres and Gintonicos.

In the era of price controls, the fiercely competitive tour operators
would rival each other for the number and value of "free" tidbits included in the price. Wine was a common weapon in this battle, for
custom, and wine was frequently part of the package. The ration on
offer was often far more of this exotic liquid than the Brits could
handle, however. Hotel dining rooms had medallions marked with
each room number which could be hung round the neck of each bottle,
saving its contents for the next meal. Bottles were thus eked out over
several meals, even over a week, without any dispute as to their ownership—even if the condition of their contents must have deteriorated in
those hot summer dining rooms. It is a wonder the British wine revolution ever got off the ground, now I come to examine it more closely.

I don't remember being exposed to any superior wine during my
stint in tourism, but one great advantage of joining a nascent industry
was that we graduates tended to be given far more responsibility than
we deserved. Within a year I was hard at work putting together a "program" called Lakes, Mountains and Fjords. The Norwegian component
was smartly dropped once Brits discovered how expensive everything,
especially drink, is in Norway, but not before I had the challenge of
taking a posse of telephone salesgirls more used to trawling the bars of

mediterranean sunspots, on an "educational" to a tiny farming village near Bergen. Their disappointment as they struck out from our homely lodgings in their glad rags in search of a good time was palpable. Perhaps it is not surprising that so few people ever managed to book one of those holidays.

I graduated from summer to winter and put together a set of hotel beds, flight seats and bus journeys in between that constituted the Thomson Winter Sports offering. Andorra and Formigal in the Spanish Pyrenees had been a great success (cheap alcohol again), so we added a small village there called Panticosa whither I had once to accompany a group of journalists. This taught me a great deal and I thought of it often when, subsequently, I belonged to the press rather than the trip of a press trip.

On Friday night when we reached Luton airport, hub of the packaged world, we were told at check-in that the flight was overbooked and we'd been off-loaded (how much more jargon can a desperate tour guide take?). One of our hired cars broke down en route from Barcelona to the village. I left the non-skiing editor of *Travel Trade Gazette* at the top of the mountain after the lifts had closed. A large part of the inside of our (Thomson-owned) aircraft fell across the laps of myself and the ski experts of *The Sunday Times* and the *Financial Times*. I followed conventional advice and whenever anything went wrong, administered alcohol.

But even the constant traveling offered by this job was not enough to compensate my impatient nature for all the meetings it involved. Besides, this was the era of flower power and my immediate predecessor had set a dangerous precedent by giving it all up in favor of an ashram in Nepal (although not before posing for a photo opportunity for *Travel News*). I also had itchy feet and therefore had to leave the travel business. But there was something about the Indian subcontinent that did not appeal. It had the wrong sort of recreational drugs.

My beloved German professor came to the rescue. He agreed it would be a jolly good idea for his youngest son to perfect his French. Yes, a course at the university of Aix-en-Provence sounds perfectly reasonable. Oh dear, your semi-ruined farmhouse is too far away from the town to complete your studies? Ah well, enjoy yourselves, my darlings.

And we did, sporadically, for the academic year 1974–75. We rented a beautiful heap of stones in a valleyful of cherry trees in the Lubéron. Peter Mayle was yet to make it world-famous but it was already a playground for foreigners. Our best friends were an elderly American couple (I would probably call them middle-aged nowadays) who professed themselves Marxist but said they didn't believe in sharing their own wealth, and a Norwegian poet who was allowed to drink only on specified nights by his strict Lutheran wife. The consequence of this was that at about five o'clock on designated drinking evenings he would rattle up our stone track, clanking an unimaginable number of bottles. He would carry them into the house, beaming "I'm going to feel really, *really* bad tomorrow morning." I have since come to think that that approach may be more honest than that of most British and Americans which is to pretend that drinking doesn't make them drunk, and that hangovers don't exist.

But what this year of dropping out taught me was that if you are a certain sort of person, not having a job is no more relaxing than having one. I simply filled the gap left by no longer worrying about whether anyone would sue about the number of meters I'd said the hotel was from the ski lift (there were one or two known litigants who spent their evenings comparing different companies' brochures to this end) for worrying about whether we had enough oil for the lamps and logs for the hearth. The farmhouse had no electricity, its own very limited well and a leaky water tank. It could happily have absorbed all our attention, and frequently did, but for Werner's sake we did occasionally try to do some reading and writing in French, in between a steady stream of (generally English-speaking) visitors.

My overriding memories of this corner of Provence are smells— thyme and wild garlic particularly, rather than the lavender of tourist shops, or the pines of Aix and even further south. Then the man-made aromatic overlays of scented basil (then virtually unknown in Britain), meat charred on an open fire, the piercing but sweet anise of pastis, the almost rancid reek of olives.

This was not an important wine area. The most common local wine was a light red and pink Côtes du Ventoux made on the flanks of windblown Mont Ventoux to the north. Such wine as was made on the lower Lubéron massif itself had just qualified as a VDQS, a Vin Délimité de Qualité Supérieure, as the French officialdom cautiously puts it, and would not be reckoned worthy of full Appellation Contrôlée status until 1988, just in time for Mayle-mania.

I felt completely at home in this combination of French culture and mediterranean landscape. My Buddhist sister-in-law is convinced that I have experienced southern France in a previous life. I did not feel French, I must say, but I felt utterly in tune with one, or rather two, very important aspects of French life: attitudes toward eating and drinking. The excitement of living here was not in experiencing great, classic wines and haute cuisine, but in exposure to a culture in which food and drink were not scorned as disgusting or dismissed as frivolous, but embraced as central to life itself.

Within a week of arriving I had thrown off my British prudery about refueling and by the time the end of our year in Provence was in sight and I had to start earning my living again, I was determined to find a job that involved one of my two major interests, food and drink—I didn't mind which. I never dreamt, however, that I would be lucky enough to combine one of them with another of my passions. I found it very easy to list my recreations in *Who's Who*: wine, food and words.

I have always felt the need to describe, whether orally or literally. Like many others, I suspect, I don't really feel as though something has happened unless I have described it to someone else, usually trying to amuse with the description and often putting some sort of spin on it by omission or exaggeration. It was natural therefore that I began to write an article about dropping out in Provence. I sweated away for weeks and eventually sent it to an editor at *The Sunday Times*. I no longer have Ian Jack's letter accompanying its return, although my memory treasures his phrase "but I think you write very nicely" to this day. I see from the yellowed pages I still have that I changed the last paragraph (specifying sun and cheap wine as the chief advantages of this exile) and sent it off to a girls' magazine instead. They wouldn't print it either—a sound decision.

There was a summer of reentry into British life. Diary entries such as "Gimme Shelter," "Abbey Road then bed 3 a.m." and "straights to lunch" bring back the southern English part with as much clarity as is possible. There is a sharp change of tone as I went north to spend some time in Cumbria: "marsh mushrooms w. Granny" and "croquet all family after supper."

Back in London in autumn 1975, I had first of all to readjust my
ears. It was not a case of swapping birdsong for heavy traffic—the
French had long since wiped out the local bird population, leaving the
Lubéron so quiet that my ears hurt for the first few days back in
Islington. I had also to reacclimatize myself to being a wine drinker in
a country whose government levied a tax on every bottle far in excess
of the average cost of the wine inside it, although I don't remember my
consumption declining as a result. I think the stint in France had
changed my taste, though not very much.

A wine I remember buying in Earls Court supermarkets pre-France
was Hirondelle rosé, the pink version of a brand owned by one of the
brewers who were taking on an increasingly demonic role in their
domination of the British drinks business. Hirondelle was energetically advertised and promoted (by the man who now represents the
wine interests of Baron Philippe de Rothschild in Britain), but its geographical origins remained deliberately vague so that the brewing
brand owners, Bass, could go and buy in bulk wherever prices were
lowest. A retail price of a dollar a liter (bigger bottles were a sign of a
bargain then) sticks in my mind from this era of my wine buying.

It is hardly surprising perhaps that a year in Provence failed to convert me from rosé; to the southern French in general and Provençals in
particular, pink wines are not silly, sickly and manqué but basically
the hot-weather version of dry red wines. So the wine I sought out on
my return to London was the dry(ish) pale pink Listel Gris de Gris
made in the Camargue, a reminder of southern French sunshine. So
easy to appreciate, pink wines.

Then began one of the happiest, or at least most carefree, periods of
my working life, an autumn spent doing temporary work in search of
something permanent and gastronomic. I toyed with the idea of starting
up a business cooking directors' lunches; the City was full of girls with
velvet hairbands converting a Cordon Bleu course into profitable meals
in boardrooms. As one of them put it to me, "So long as you give them
carrot soup once a week, you can be sure of making your margins."

My first port of call was the *Good Food Guide*—the restaurant-goer's,
indeed my own, bible. After some sort of written test, I was given a
sheaf of folders to turn into entries for the Guide. The 1976 Guide con-

tains several of my parodies of the then editor Christopher Driver's style, although the only one I still remember writing was an entry on the Lavender Hill Restaurant in south London, whose owner, Robin Jones, moved two years later to the Croque-en-Bouche in Malvern Wells where he created arguably the best restaurant wine list in the country. (In 1996 he dismembered it, in recognition of the fact that the sort of people prepared to pay the going rate for fine wine in a restaurant are not the sort of people who go out to eat in rural Herefordshire.) I remember getting terribly hungry as I sat reading diner's reports and menus.

I also worked in a wine bar in the City, actually the nearest wine bar to Vintners' Hall, one of the medieval livery halls and the spiritual home of London's wine trade, although I did not know it at the time. Wine bars were an important phenomenon in seventies urban Britain, a visible symbol of female emancipation. Women were regarded with suspicion in pubs but this new wave of wine bars offered them a meeting place where they could drink alcohol and eat slightly more adventurous food than was provided by their precursors, the cafés and teashops of suburban England that served as nests of female gossip.

Whittingtons, named after Dick, was a big wine bar more specifically tailored to meet the needs of the City businessman, i.e., a very stiff pink gin on the dot of 11 A.M., when the day's legal drinking window was allowed to open, and drafts of vintage port until long after it closed. I occasionally helped out in the wine bar's restaurant and kitchen but basically I was employed as a glorified barmaid. I can still remember how liberating it felt to walk out of those converted coal-holes in the afternoon knowing that—in stark contrast to Thomhols days—I was taking home not a single care or responsibility.

And then, toward the end of October, I spent one fateful week in the press office of the British Waterways Board. My job, filling in while an assistant was on holiday, was to cut out those stories in the press which had been marked up as of relevance to those in charge of Britain's canals by my temporary boss. I did not impress this lady. I just couldn't cut straight enough and probably, I realize in retrospect, made far too many personal telephone calls in the hours that dragged between the excitement of wielding my scissors. When I wasn't snipping or gossiping, I was reading the piles of print delivered to that office each week, and without that I might never have become a wine writer. I was introduced to two trade journals, *Campaign* for the mercurial advertising industry and the more prosaic *UK Press Gazette* for people who write far more words for much less money. In both of them was an intriguing classified ad: "TECHNICAL MAGAZINE covering the Wine Trade requires a young assistant editor. Knowledge of trade (other than that gained through the bottom of a glass) is essential and proven writing or journalistic experience is a definite advantage."

I wonder now how I had the nerve to apply, but I was so glad I had when I had my interview with Simon Taylor, now the BBC's motor racing commentator. One of his jobs then was publisher of Haymarket's *Wine & Spirit*, a glossy but dangerously slim monthly that was then just one of hundreds of trade publications published by Michael Heseltine, the man who would be tipped to oust Margaret Thatcher. "We've had a lot of applications for this job," Taylor said, "and we're having a great deal of difficulty choosing the right person. Either they're wine experts and we have to teach them how to write, or they're trained journalists and we have to teach them all about wine." He paused and looked down at my carefully embellished application form. "You, of course, are neither of these things. Nevertheless, you are the favorite for the job."

I carefully tried to anchor my eyebrows and look noncommittal. The pay was no great shakes (the "young" in the ad should have told me that) but, hey, who's counting when a lifetime in wine beckons (as thousands of wine trade employees have reasoned before and since). And so, on December 1, 1975, with absolutely no relevant experience, I started work in a tiny, paper-strewn office just off Carnaby Street.

A year later, when I reckoned that even if there had been a gross misunderstanding I wouldn't be sacked, I took this exceptionally lateral-thinking publisher to one side at the staff Christmas party and asked him why on earth he'd decided to take me on. "Was it the writing for *Isis* or the *Good Food Guide?*" I asked. "Or the year in France, or working for the wine company?" (Luckily for me and my application form, Whittingtons wine bar was owned by a wine company, Ebury. It survived the increasing coagulation of the British wine trade for another twenty years.) "No, no, no, none of those things," he said impatiently. "It was because you'd shown you could run the skiing side of Thomson Holidays. We reckoned that what we needed was a good organizer, and that even though you didn't know very much, you'd soon organize yourself to learn."

But he must have assumed I could type. Thank goodness he didn't ask. The magazine, aimed every bit as much at the deep advertising budgets of the Scotch whisky industry as the more rarefied concerns of the British wine trade, was at that stage edited by Colin Parnell. A career journalist in his forties who had proved himself on a wide range of Haymarket magazines (which tended to be called things like *What Car, What Camera* and *SLR*), he had improved *Wine & Spirit* enormously during his tenure and willingly allowed wine in general and red bordeaux in particular to sink its gorgeously savory claws into him. Frustrated by Haymarket's unwillingness to invest in a consumer wine magazine, he and my predecessor, Tony Lord, were then in the throes of launching their own, called *Decanter*. This meant that Colin was a slightly semi-detached editor as far as *Wine & Spirit* was concerned, and my chief mentor in the early days was a highly intelligent, chain-smoking secretary in thrall to a biker who made frequent visits to our office, creaking his leathers around such space as was left between the three desks, bookcases and filing cabinets, stacks of old magazines and layouts, and Colin's locked bottle safe. Liz and I would look dolefully at Colin as he slunk in from a long lunch to deposit a free bottle or two before churning out an editorial with enviable ease.

I cannot imagine what poor Colin thought when he first clapped eyes on me. At that stage I wore my hair in a sort of pre-Raphaelite frizz that was the result of tiny braids and a cache of small elastic bands (which I found, still rather whiskery, in one of my antique snuffboxes the other day). My clothes were distinctly more gypsy than executive—in fact I think I bought my first suit just before having a photograph taken for the cover of *Decanter*, which was *many* years later. I was recently taken on one side by one of the wine trade's longer-serving Champagne Charlies, men who sell bubbles by hanging around high-class bars, restaurants and racecourses in expensive suiting. "I remember you when you were in your hippie phase," he gloated.

I certainly can't have looked very promising as editorial material, writing things out in longhand and then painfully picking them out with two fingers on a manual typewriter. I went back to Cumbria for Christmas, my head full of deadlines, the stink of cowgum and a sense of achievement at having put together a whole-page report on the 1975–76 season's prices of raw young Scotch. There were pages to be filled on the movements of vodka brand managers, sherry marketing budgets and cunning new products such as pink vermouth and cream liqueurs. In fact so busy was I trying to fill these pages that I hardly noticed how little involvement I seemed to be having with the liquid I joined to love, wine.

Early Days—
Wine-Sodden Nights

___

Simon Taylor's hunch that I would quickly make up for my most obvious shortcomings was well founded and by mid-January I was enrolled in the most basic course of the British wine trade's official educational body, the Wine & Spirit Education Trust. It wasn't in truth the most challenging exam, even for someone as untutored as me. I told my friends self-deprecatingly there would probably be a question "Valpolicella is (a) red, (b) white, or (c) rosé" and there was actually one that went "Valpolicella is (a) French, (b) Spanish, or (c) Italian." I passed, and immediately enrolled for the next stage of theory. But the practical of course is by far the most important aspect of wine appreciation, and I was to experience two seminal tastings in my first few months.

I shall never forget my first formal wine tasting. Invitations to tastings rolled in to the *Wine & Spirit* offices but they tended to have Colin's name on them. In mid-February, however, I was at long last allowed out to a wine tasting. Ontario wines were not perhaps the most illustrious stars in the wine firmament then, but that did nothing to lessen my nervousness at having to swirl and spit with others far more experienced than I.

Wine tasting looks and sounds disgusting, there's no getting away

from it, which is strange when you think how much fun it can be—
well, perhaps not. My wine classes had prepared me for what to do—
swirl, sniff, scribble, slurp, scribble, spit—so I didn't feel too worried
about that aspect. What worried me was that this, unusually, was to be
a tasting with all participants seated round a table, so comments would
be expected—and the dozen or so participants in this case included not
just my mysterious predecessor at *Wine & Spirit*, Tony Lord, but also
the world-famous demigod of wine, Hugh Johnson.

Lord turned out to be an aggressive young Australian who was presumably compensating for his near-slavery squeezing a *Decanter* a
month out of a shed beneath the arches of Waterloo Station. Johnson
was his urbane antithesis, but then who needs aggression when they
have just written the classic of the modern wine world, its definitive,
beautifully produced *Atlas*? I listened carefully to what these much
more experienced tasters had to say about the wines. And the most
extraordinary thing was that they all used contradictory expressions,
and yet acted as though they were in complete accord. "It's a bit tart,
isn't it?," someone would say. "Absolutely. Nice roundness," another
would add, while yet another would volunteer, "I'd like a little more
acid." And the amazing thing to me was that no one argued. They
seemed oblivious to the inbuilt contradictions. Reassured, I subsequently worked out, by the irrefutable fact that wine appreciation is an
entirely subjective process, that professionals simply carried on express-
ing what they thought, impervious to any apparently opposing view.

This was an invaluable lesson, and most encouraging. Even at this,
my very first professional tasting, I ventured the odd, very quiet little
comment—and nobody contradicted me! In fact they tended to nod
agreement, before going on of course to express their own views. Two
decades of tasting and talking about wine myself and listening to
others do the same have convinced me that there will always be as
many opinions of a wine as there are tasters of it, and sometimes more
even than that. To this day I observe this phenomenon of unconscious
and benign contradiction in professional wine tasters, particularly
Britain's ultra-polite breed.

Early in 1976, when I'd been on *Wine & Spirit* only a few weeks, I
went to my first tasting of really young smart red bordeaux, the wine

that makes up the bulk of most collectors' cellars and the fine wine market. These wines, so commercially significant, are regularly offered *"en primeur,"* in the spring after they're made and more than a year before they are bottled. The 1970 vintage had been a marvel, the 1971 much less so, and the 1972, 1973 and 1974 positively disappointing (you could, eerily, substitute a nine for all but the last of these sevens). The wine trade desperately needed 1975 to be worthy of investment and one of the larger wholesalers accordingly organized a giant tasting of these infant clarets in London in late March. All these pinstriped men—and the wine trade was overwhelmingly male at that stage, hence the chip on my shoulder perhaps—were nodding approvingly over the spittoons, wooden wine cases filled with sawdust and black trails of expectorated wine, about what a wonderful vintage this was.

Now this, unlike our lack of concordance over Ontario's wines, was something I couldn't understand. These wines, with their modest, workmanlike labels showing they were mere *échantillons* drawn straight from a cask rather than the properly matured final blends that would eventually be bottled, tasted like ink to me. Superior red bordeaux is not meant to be much fun to drink at this stage, admittedly. Along with vintage port, it is one of the few wines which is specifically designed to be aged in bottle for many years before mellowing into subtly nuanced drinkability. Serious British claret lovers of the old school abide by what they call the ten-year rule, whereby bottles of serious claret are kept firmly stoppered until the wine is at least one decade old. The substance that preserves red wine as it ages is tannin, the cheek-drying element in stewed tea and walnut skins. It is considered normal for young bordeaux to be high in tannin, and deciding when a red wine is drinkable is largely a question of somehow working out the optimal balance between declining tannins, developing bouquet and fading fruit (which is next to impossible to do without opening the bottle). But the wine will only be worth aging if there is considerable fruit there to begin with and, as it turned out, many 1975s have shown themselves over the years to have been too full of tannin and too light on fruit. This vintage's rating in the charts has fallen since its debut.

I didn't know this at the time, and I suspect I would have found *en primeur* samples of any Bordeaux vintage too chewy for me, just as most wine neophytes do. Ambitious, young red bordeaux is one of the most difficult wines to appreciate, and yet it can often be the most expensive, glamorous-looking bottle in a wine store. I often wonder how many people spend a fortune on such a wine as a gift and then feel cheated by how little pleasure it gives.

So, shakily, over Canadian wines and one of the toughest Bordeaux vintages ever, I gingerly pushed off from the edge of complete ignorance into the shallows of a little wine knowledge. My diary for early 1976 shows an increasing frequency of lunches with public relations men, typically representing one of the better-funded companies that *Wine & Spirit* might write about. There were many pages of magazine to fill, and no excess of advertisers to do the job, so these middlemen probably found me a hopelessly easy target—although some of the approaches were so desperately unsubtle that they imbued me with a skepticism I have never managed to shake off. I remember one of the less sophisticated managers detailed to liaise with the press (as the media were then) being crass enough to say that if I were good he'd give me a bottle of Southern Comfort, and if I were bad he'd give me two.

By April I was on my first press trip, as a guest. Now this was more to my taste than playing distressed hostess at Luton airport. The purpose of this particular jaunt was to make us feel more warmly about a certain whisky but it was organized by one of those people who know exactly how to spend other people's money to best personal gastronomic effect. After a leisurely tour of Speyside, Scotch whisky's Médoc, in the spring sunshine, we stayed in a Georgian mansion-turned-hotel overlooking Culloden Moor near Inverness and began our evening sipping glass after glass of Krug. The only-top quality champagne I had previously been exposed to was the odd, very late night sip of Dom Pérignon when I used to hang around with one of the Pink Floyd (who, of course, had it written into their contract). But now, sunk deep into a well-worn leather chair with my tastebuds in the peak of condition, I could really appreciate what makes expensive champagne so expensive: the sheer depth of flavor that takes years to develop, the way each mouthful lingers in your throat like a comforting, slow-release capsule of explosive warmth, the fact that it wafts rather than gets up your nose. I suppose that later that evening we were given some whisky to drink, after a bravura performance by some of Scotland's finest raw ingredients in the paneled dining room, but I certainly can't remember it.

This was the first of my short visits to Scotland, for Scotch was the most important wine or spirit advertised in *Wine & Spirit*. In the summer of 1976 I also flew north of the border to look around a most important aspect of the drinks industry, a giant glass furnace near Edinburgh, which in fact offered some relief from the torrid temperatures then unexpectedly scorching southern England. On this trip one real journalist, a man from the *Financial Times*, supplemented the usual group of us compliant trade writers. I was terribly impressed by him. He seemed to be noticeably alert, even after dinner. He didn't necessarily laugh at his hosts' jokes, but asked tricky questions and took an awful lot of notes. The man from United Glass gave me to believe that he was a bit of a troublemaker. That sounded fun, I thought.

Slowly but surely I was acquiring knowledge of both wine and journalism—in the privacy of my own office with, apparently, no one but the long-suffering Liz to notice my mistakes. By July specific wines were beginning to make an appearance in my diary, even though it was meant to be merely a record of engagements rather than innermost thoughts. "M. Frayn's Donkey's Yrs then Lynch Bages at Le Chef" says July 23.

The following week I was taken on my very first foreign wine trip, so the diary boasts, all within forty-eight hours: "John Arlott, then Southampton–Le Havre. Chantovent. Lunch overlooking the Seine. Gewurz on board. Krug and kippers with John Arlott. Frantic. Glyndebourne." (The next day, Friday, mentions a more prosaic visit, to some freight forwarders in South London, and dinner at the Italian restaurant Meridiana. The entry for Saturday morning says simply but tellingly "Headache.")

John Arlott, the late, great cricket commentator, was to play a very important part in my wine writing career. He thought that in my female wine writing state I might make a good subject for the women's page of the newspaper for which he wrote about cricket and wine, *The Guardian* (or *Grauniad* as it was known because of its inventive misprints). This indirectly resulted in my being asked to write my first book. But I was initially introduced to him by a coauthor of his own, the Burgundy specialist and peripatetic wine importer Christopher Fielden. At the time Fielden was responsible for selling the wines of the giant French bottler

Chantovent in Britain. He invited me and wine merchant Richard Taylor to visit Chantovent's headquarters near Paris via John Arlott's home in the Hampshire village of Alresford. It was an old coaching inn, still virtually intact round a courtyard just off the wide main street, with its original cellars reached via a perilous ladder. Presumably for this reason John Arlott, then a less than sprightly hulk in his sixties, would try to bring up from the cellar beforehand everything he planned to drink of an evening. This was reasonably frightening, for he was a man of gargantuan appetites, his expression veering unexpectedly from its customary lugubriousness to uncontrollably wheezy laughter.

When we dropped in en route for the cross-Channel ferry, on a beautiful golden evening, we clambered down to the cellar (whose extensive contents were auctioned off by Christie's so that he could decamp to the island of Alderney and start collecting all over again) and brought up six bottles of his favorite wine, Beaujolais. John identified with the earthy peasants and uncomplicated wines of this region, which were much more fashionable then than now. All I remember is a heady cocktail of his erudition (although he wore his lovingly acquired knowledge of sport, poetry and literature lightly), the beautiful and carefully chosen contents of this house and the flagrantly fruity nature of the wine.

I recall the lunch by the Seine perfectly, however. In those days, as it had been for centuries, wine from the south of France was shipped in bulk to the population centers in the north of the country to save money, so Bonnières-sur-Seine was a logical place for Chantovent's vast bottling plant. I spent the morning there inspecting the first of the many hundreds of foreign bottling lines I have by now been invited to admire (presumably because they cost so much, although they are infinitely less exciting for a wine writer than the liquid itself). This might not have been the most romantic wine producer to begin with, but lunch on the sunny terrace of a restaurant high above the broad, sleepy river Seine made up for it. I had that French classic, salmon with creamy sorrel sauce, a dish I had never come across before, with a full-bodied, golden Meursault, a dry white wine with so much more ambition than the listless British-bottled blends labeled Chablis that were the closest to white burgundy I had so far come across. The export director of Chantovent, Richard and Christopher seemed equally courteous and amusing, and I reflected on how lucky I was to have found a way of being paid to do this.

The overnight crossing back to England was not exactly luxurious (although I see that I carefully noted what we drank on board) but the breakfast John Arlott had waiting for us was: Krug and kippers, the most extraordinary combination of de luxe drink and subsistence food (the smoked version of those herring my great-grandfather had packaged). It provided the perfect opening chapter of a book I later wrote on how well unlikely combinations of wine and food can work, provided the circumstances are right.

At that stage the proud, conservative family house of Krug was in a state of radical upheaval. It had not yet got into bed with the huge Remy-Cointreau distribution group but they had exchanged more than chaste kisses. Krug had been admired for decades as producers of an incredibly good, incredibly expensive, seriously full bodied, franglais-named blend called Private Cuvée. It came in a standard champagne bottle and carried no vintage date, but still managed to command the same price as a vintage-dated prestige cuvée such as Dom Pérignon and its host of imitators. Chez Arlott, we washed away the grime of the ferry with a bottle of Private Cuvée. If it could stand up to kippers at eight o'clock in the morning it could stand up to anything. Unbeknownst to us, however, Krug was about to launch a rosé (over several dead bodies), a single vineyard all-Chardonnay champagne and, most controversially of all, had maturing in its cellars as we sipped our kippered Krug a replacement for Private Cuvée, a distinctly lighter blend called Grande Cuvée, to be launched with much razzmatazz in a completely new, swan-necked bottle in 1978, just months after my first in-depth look at their cellars. Champagne cellars, more than any others, consist of piles and piles of maturing bottles. This taught me to look more closely at their shape in the future.

Krug is run by two archetypal brothers. Henri is the sober winemaker and Rémi, the younger one, is a monomaniac who wants to "Krugize" the whole world. Important new recruits to Remy-Cointreau's champagne group, which includes Charles Heidsieck and Piper Heidsieck, are required to visit its most glamorous component. After two days of proselytizing Krug to a new managing director for Charles Heidsieck, Rémi turned to him over lunch and said, "Now tell me about you. What do *you* think of Krug?"

I think of myself as being quite a frequent traveler nowadays, but I'm amazed looking back to see how many trips I managed to cram in to my first full year on *Wine & Spirit*. Between October 29 and November 15 in 1976, for example, I toured De Kuyper's multi-colored liqueur factory in Rotterdam, spent what was almost a lost weekend in the company of Messrs. Fielden and Arlott at Dijon's Gastronomic Fair, and dashed to and from Mâcon in the back of a Ford Granada to play a part in the ridiculously dangerous Beaujolais Nou-veau Race, then in its prime. The Mâcon trip was the least fun for me, for it was commandeered by motoring correspondents and organized by Piat, hardly the most *echt* Beaujolais producer and soon to become famous for producing Piat d'Or, a heavily advertised branded wine they claimed the French "adored" until being forced to admit that most of them had never heard of it.

After hours on the motorway in the rain, we were put up in one of those concrete boxes that French hotel chains are so keen on and served the sort of plastic food they specialize in. This contrasted so miserably with the Burgundian bounty we'd been treated to in Dijon the weekend before that I'm afraid I consoled myself with a quarter bottle of champagne from the minibar in my hotel room and have felt guilty about it ever since.

The weekend at Dijon's Gastronomic Fair was vividly debauched, as only Burgundy—and Bordeaux never—can be. On Saturday morning John Arlott and I were memorably "intronised" into the Grand Order of the Escargot de Bourgogne, swearing eternal allegiance to the Bur-gundian snail and forswearing all others (although I am told that any escargot sold in France today is statistically most likely to have come from Turkey). The Order's plastic snail hangs from its yellow riband in my bathroom to this day. On Sunday we had an incredibly long lunch in the country, followed by an incredibly long dinner in the town. John Arlott told us dolefully when he came down on Monday morning, "I knew as soon as I woke up it had been a heavy night by how carefully I'd folded up all my clothes." We did not undertake our first job that morning, judging a Grand Marnier cake contest, with gusto.

I look at photographs of myself during the late seventies and can hardly wonder at the size of my cheeks. I seemed to spend most of my life eating and drinking—which was, after all, exactly what I'd planned from Provence. Although most of the British still regarded food and drink with suspicion, I seemed to have managed to surround myself with the exceptions to that rule.

At around this time I met up with a group of friends from St. Anne's. One of them, now famous for having walked out with a future president of the United States, was virtuously offering legal aid. She made me feel guilty. Another, Sarah Maitland, was already establishing herself as a novelist. She made me feel envious. But the brightest one of all, someone who was so young at Oxford that she then went to Cambridge to do another degree there, had become an accountant. She told us excitedly about her work and the perks involved. One week she might go and look round a lavatory paper factory, and we'd be surprised how fascinating that was. And once she'd even been sent to France to look round a cognac company. She told us how she'd been put up in a beautiful château with a marble bathroom and a little decanter of brandy and some sugar lumps on the dressing table. Ah yes, this sounded familiar to me from my trip to Martell earlier in the year. She made me feel very, very lucky indeed.

Nineteen seventy-six was America's bicentennial year, so the particularly hot summer was awash with special, celebratory bottlings of champagne. It was also the first year, of many, that I went on holiday and managed to combine it with the pleasures of work. For a wine writer, the line between work and play is inevitably a blurred one. Vines tend to be grown in some of the more beautiful parts of the world—a mediterranean climate suits both them and the tourist perfectly. Wine producers generally like to show off their wares, either in a tasting room or round a table. (The only wine producer I ever visited who didn't offer me a taste of his wine was the late Major General Sir Guy Salisbury-Jones, a pioneer of modern English vine growing. He and his wife very politely poured me a glass of sherry instead, explaining that their own wine was too rare and heavily taxed to open.) The wine business is also truly international and extremely sociable, with almost mafia-like connections. So as a wine writer, it is possible in most countries to find a congenial wine producer, merchant, commentator or plain old fanatic. (This used to be true only of specific parts of the world, but wine has spread its tentacles dramatically in the 1990s, especially in the Far East, so that today I think only the polar regions are relatively free of wine maniacs.)

People may be marginally more welcoming to someone who has

spent as long as I have in the wine world, but I don't remember any
lack of warmth even when I had only a few months' experience under
my belt. But I suppose my 1976 holiday could not have been to a more
hospitable place, northern California. Ever since my first trip to the
United States as a student in 1969—the summer of the moon landing,
Chappaquiddick and Woodstock—a part of me had been in love with
America and Americans. Most of my friends were concentrated in and
around San Francisco and for much of the late 1970s I half wanted to
live on the open-hearted, sun-crazed West Coast. As usual, I associate
it with particular smells—the warm, sweet, resinous, slightly stuffy
smell of sun on redwood, and the ubiquitous cinnamon.

   This was meant to be vacation, but my holiday notebook had a list of
wineries to visit: Hans Kornell, Mondavi ("very advanced"), Freemark
Abbey, Beaulieu and an outfit I called Moët-Hennessy because it had not
yet been named Domaine Chandon. The topics I noted in advance that I
wanted to cover included the relationship between the boffins at the
University of California at Davis and the growers and winemakers under
their influence (a question that was to take on particular significance a
decade later as the consequences of Davis's advice on rootstocks—a
full-scale phylloxera invasion—became all too apparent), the trend
from red to white wine (now reversed) and varietal versus generic wines,
those labeled by grape variety as opposed to a supposed, usually cor-
rupted, wine archetype such as burgundy and chablis.

   While in San Francisco, between engagements at the Renaissance
Fayre, hot tubs and juggling lessons in Golden Gate Park, I contacted
two wine writers who had written for *Wine & Spirit*, Julius Jacobs and
Gerald Asher, now wine king of *Gourmet* magazine. Jay Jacobs was kind
enough to take me to a wine writers' gathering on Treasure Island where
I ungraciously noted "some horrid American-vine wines from British
Columbia, Ontario, Ohio, Missouri and, *vino mirabile*, Arkansas."

   The really memorable engagement, though, was a dinner party Gerald
was kind enough to invite me to (billing me as "my editor"), having
vetted me over a glass of Souverain Riesling-Gewürztraminer first. This
was an almost physically exciting time for California wine. The wine
improvement graph was virtually vertical and the dozens of hopeful new
winery owners had just received confirmation of their unstated belief
that California was about to wrest the wine crown from France. Steven
Spurrier's seminal California versus France tasting in Paris in May had

suggested that even French tasters preferred California's best to France's best provided they didn't know what they were tasting. (The result was that the French have refused to taste blind ever again.)

Also invited to dinner in Gerald's elegantly furnished apartment at some very high altitude over Green Street, overlooking the sunset and Golden Gate Bridge, was James Beard, the culinary master who would spawn an institute and a host of annual awards, and a bullish young wine producer called Robert Mondavi. I say young, he must have been in his fifties, but he was so energetically visionary that youth clung to him, and still does. The first wine served in that candlelit dining room was a curiosity called Fumé Blanc, Mondavi's richly smoky, vanilla-scented spin on the then-reviled Sauvignon Blanc grapes of California. This was followed, after much discussion, by a deeply blackcurrant-scented Cabernet Sauvignon 1973 from Clos du Val—a brand-new winery started up by Bernard and Helia Portet, a young French couple with Château Lafite connections who had also been invited to dinner—before the classic 1966 red Graves Château La Mission-Haut-Brion and a golden Sauternes from a tiptop vintage, Château Sigalas-Rabaud 1967.

The Portets demonstrated that foreigners were beginning to be interested in California wine, but it was the huge Moët investment in making champagne-like California sparkling wine that seemed a real, grown-up story to me in my new journalist mode. Moët & Chandon was and is the giant of the champagne industry, and to see them earthmoving, buying and planting hundreds of acres with champagne grapes, importing yeast cultures and special presses from France and even shipping over a sixty-three-year-old bottle-riddling expert to teach the Americans how to do it was extraordinary. Yet none of this, to my knowledge, had reached the international press. Could it be that I had stumbled across *un petit scoop*?

So, on my return to England, I cobbled what I'd learnt into a story and, via my friend Alex Finer who worked on the paper, lobbed it into the newsroom of *The Sunday Times*. I must have chewed my pencil for quite a while because it didn't appear until two weeks after I flew back, but it did appear, with a Michael Heath cartoon captioned, with a nod to the current Coca-Cola campaign, "Things Go Better With Moët et Chandon," on the front page. Admittedly in the graveyard along the bottom, but so what? I was edging toward being a proper grown-up journalist and I obviously enjoyed it so much I see I had three more articles printed by the paper that autumn—all of them the sort of easy-read pseudo news that Sunday papers have to specialize in.

By this time I was starting to be a bit more fastidious about the wine I drank. I liked the crisp directness of Sauvignon grapes grown in and around the Loire Valley. I had a little flirtation with Sauvignon de Saint-Bris, famous for being grown not far from Chablis and therefore classified as a burgundy but in fact from the greater Loire basin, and then decided it was time I bought myself some wine at auction. I'm not sure I have ever bought at auction, with the exception of the odd bid in a charity sale, ever again. Not that my case of Marcel Gitton's Sancerre 1973 Les Belles Dames was in the least disappointing (specially not at $34), but since then I have heard collectors and merchants over and over again grimly deciding that the only thing to do with their disappointments is to send them to the sale room. Undoubtedly most bottles that come up for auction are in good condition, but there are just too many middlemen, risks and commissions along the way to suit my cautious nature. I also tired of Sauvignon, except on a very hot day, but that's another story.

The real thrill of this period was wine bargain hunting, with my wine knowledge increased, or rather extant, thanks to the Wine & Spirit Education Trust. It would take me ages to get home at night, because I liked nothing more than to idle in every wine shop I passed, scanning the shelves looking for something unusual or particularly well priced. Augustus Barnett, owned by a bluff, charismatic, barrow boy character called Brian Barnett, was the most exciting group of off-licenses at that time, challenging the increasingly moribund Grand Met-owned Peter Dominic chain, but there were far more independently-owned wine shops than, sadly, there are today. I would linger in an Augustus Barnett in Soho, and snoop in Milroy's too. The sort of thing that made my heart beat faster—believe it or not—was a pink rioja, full-bodied but dry—or a Gigondas, all the fun of Châteauneuf-du-Pape but half the price—or, also from the southern Rhône, an extraordinarily sweet, powerful, grapey thing called Muscat de Beaumes-de-Venise, then all the rage by the glass in the restaurants I spent far too much time in.

The Old Wine Trade

When I wasn't eating and drinking in a restaurant (the Tate Gallery restaurant with its Olde English cooking and benevolent fine wine pricing policy was the wine trade haunt of those days while Langan's Brasserie was my evening haunt), I seemed to be doing the same thing over lunch in the offices of some wine or spirit peddler. My diary entry for September 30, 1976, reads "Lunch: John Davy. Evening: Recovering." (This was when the free vintner, the quiet man behind so many discreet London wine bars with names such as the Boot & Flogger and the Tappit Hen, introduced me to Château Grillet, the overpriced and all too heady white from the northern Rhône.) I suppose I must have spent the odd moment back at the office because I had uncomfortably many pages to fill each month, with help from only a small network of underpaid contributors, but it's not that particular aspect of this long-gone era that sticks in my mind.

In the late seventies the bulk of the wine trade was still coasting along on a virtually Edwardian timetable. The typical wine merchant was a gentleman who reached his offices at about ten, did a bit of paperwork and made a few calls and then settled down for a three- or four-hour lunch, which constituted work because it was with other members of the trade, and occasionally even customers, before swaying back to the office in a porty haze to check on the messages before going home. I know this because this is what I used to do, except that I think I tended to stay in the office until six or seven when I would then meet a friend for a drink before going out for dinner.

Things must have reached some sort of nadir for my liver one day in January 1977 when I was researching an article about the state of the gin business (and London was surely the place to do it). At ten o'clock in the morning I had a meeting at Gordon's monolithic headquarters near my Islington home, where bureaucracy and inebriation so bizarrely collided. I followed my early morning nip with a trawl of a wine tasting organized by Stowells of Chelsea, which at the stage had never even heard of the wine boxes which are now its specialty, slotting in a brief meeting with unknown Spanish wine producer Miguel Torres before lunch at Christie's. In the afternoon I had to continue my gin studies chez Beefeater, and then in the evening went to a hardly abstemious dinner with Richard Taylor (fellow Krug-and-kipperist) and his wine writer wife.

One or two newcomers to the trade were reputed to be operating to a different rhythm to the old ways. Brian Barnett of Augustus Barnett, for example, started work famously early—so early that he was able to play defiantly and ostentatiously all afternoon. There were beginning to be rumors that some people were thinking about cutting down on drinking at lunchtime, but certainly not those "in the trade." The spirits companies were most staggering to me. It was absolutely normal to begin drinking at or even before noon—and this with a carefully standardized product, often a single household name, which hardly needed to be consciously tasted by visitors, let alone employees. I remember that in *Wine & Spirit* days I sometimes met trade writers who specialized in either beer or spirits, and the gossip between them always seemed to be about whether old So-and-so had been trundled off to a drying-out clinic yet, or about the midnight antics of a colleague who had not quite reached that stage.

Curiously, in my two decades in and around wine, I have come across remarkably few incidents of harmful or even embarrassing excess. Admittedly I'm an inside and doubtless partial observer. Wine people seem to me on the whole sympathetic and jolly, and get more sympathetic and jollier as the evening wears on. If antialcohol campaigners were to turn up at my dinner table late at night I couldn't guarantee that they wouldn't be shocked, but if they were shocked it would only be because they disapprove of high spirits, loud voices and laughter. Journalists interviewing me, usually at the insistence of some book publicist, seem obsessed by a question which basically boils down to "How drunk do you get?" It would be stupid to claim that I have somehow escaped with body tissue completely impermeable to alcohol, but it's a difficult question to answer. I have certainly been known to repeat myself; I forget a lot; and my great claim to fame is that I once poured wine over a fellow writer's head. But I don't think my name is synonymous with inebriation, and nor are many of us wine writers. We are in general self-employed and have to be rather too industrious to overindulge very often. On the other hand, we have the perfect excuse to keep on consuming, and some wine passes my lips practically every single day, or at least every single evening.

The greatest mistake I ever made in print was to repeat the health education wisdom prevailing in Britain in the late 1980s that it was sensible to abstain from drinking alcohol at all for a couple of days every week. By the time my friend and literary agent Caradoc King murmured to me that a liver specialist friend of his said this was simply temperance propaganda and that such a short period of abstinence would make no medical difference, my consumer's guide to alcohol was already being printed and it was not until the Department of Health unexpectedly issued new, more liberal drinking guidelines at the end of 1995 that officialdom admitted its mistake. I feel very guilty about something most of the time, but particularly about depriving some faithful, health-conscious readers of the pleasures of wine consumption in vain. My life, like that of so many others, feels like one long agony of culpability, from which I have occasionally to escape via the wine glass.

Nowadays I go to perhaps two or three wine trade lunches a year, when we all sit around a well-polished table and drink perhaps five different wines and mutter about how like the old days it is. For many of the older members of the London wine trade, lunch didn't really start until the Benevolent box was on the table, however. The trade's charitable organization, the Wine & Spirit Trades' Benevolent Society, looks after those who have fallen on hard times. Every time I hear the name, an image of aged gents in wheelchairs comparing cirrhotic notes in some south coast resort rises uncontrollably before me, even though I know that it is genuinely a Very Worthy Cause. Since the fifties the Benevolent has had the bright idea of distributing collecting boxes throughout the trade, and the most common practice was to bet on the identity of the vintage port, or occasionally ports, served after a typically extended wine trade lunch. Most offices would have some cellar slave whose job it was to decant the port and put the telltale cork in an envelope so that even the home team could play—although the slaves, deprived of the long lunch and fine port, must sometimes have been tempted to play a trick or two. The stake was usually one pound ($1.60) and the rule was that if you correctly guessed either year or shipper you could keep the money. If you managed to guess both shipper and vintage, a rare occurrence, you were given a bottle to take away—although if you were classified as "trade" rather than "customer," you would merely share the kitty.

There were and are certain people with special expertise in port, either buyers or sellers in real quantity such as Bill Warre, a descendant of the eponymous port shipper, who surely has a port stream instead of a blood stream, and John Davy with his many City wine bars (for which, being a member of the Vintners' Company of the City of London, he needs no license). Even they are easily flummoxed. Whatever happened, the Benevolent has been the beneficiary of this practice, which continues today, with decreasing frequency and increasingly dilapidated collecting boxes. Typically today, however, guests at wine trade lunch tables are carefully cossetted high-spending private customers whose knowledge of vintages and shippers has to be supplemented by a prompt card listing all the possible combinations. (So embarrassing to declare that it just has to be Cockburn 1966 when such a port never existed . . .)

There were at that time many delightful gentlemen in the wine trade. A few of them are still there, clinging on by the skin of increasingly wine-stained teeth in the face of the combined and invincible forces of the supermarkets. In the late seventies the pinstripes still ruled the roost. Supermarkets were beginning to sell wine but at this stage they bought most of it straight off the lists of the established trade with its complicated and ever changing network of agencies and importers. The supermarket chappies were seen as useful but basically ignorant upstarts in the world of wine who probably didn't even know which way to pass the port. My exact contemporary Allan Cheesman, who began work at Sainsbury's in 1972 and was to become Britain's most influential wine merchant, still remembers being told by a young man behind the counter of ultra-traditional Fleet Street wine merchant El Vino (owned by a Conservative Member of Parliament) that he wouldn't like Gewürztraminer, it was rather a complicated wine. The British wine trade, which gave up almost a week each year to congregate at the Bristol Wine Fair, had no idea it was on the brink of total transformation.

So for the moment it was a round of genteel tastings, lunches and receptions, with wine trade and press alike quite willing and able to give up several hours (more if you counted the aftereffects) to celebrate the launch of a new label or taste the wares of one small producer. It was at an occasion like this that I met Jack Rutherford, whose family firm of fine wine importers, fast disappearing into the vermouth-scented maw of Martini, gave Serena Sutcliffe, now Sotheby's mistress of wine, a toehold in the wine trade. They had imported Louis Roederer for years and old man Rutherford told me how at home he had a substantial stock of champagne in a superseded bottle size, imperial pints. "Just the right size for an aperitif for two," he confided, "but a lot of them have lost their fizz. You'd be amazed what a pinch of bicarbonate of soda can do."

The traditional British wine merchant had no qualms about improving on the work of the vignerons he bought from (the word "winemaker" did not exist then, and most of those he dealt with were French). Why should he? The British, after all, had a long tradition of dominating the world's wine trade. They were masters of it. Only the Dutch had, in their time, imported anything near as much wine, but the British could also claim to have virtually invented sherry, port, madeira and marsala as well as ruling Bordeaux for three centuries and playing a crucial role in the development of claret and champagne. This imbued the British wine trade, or The Trade, as they called it, with a feeling of enormous superiority. The wine merchant Charles Walter Berry was thought to be quite extraordinarily adventurous when, in the 1930s, he actually toured the wine regions of France. Then in the 1950s Harry Waugh and Ronald Avery, representing the rival Bristol merchants Harveys and Averys respectively, broke new ground by actually selecting wine in situ, tasting young wine straight from the barrel rather than placing orders from offices in Britain.

Along with André Simon the champagne salesman who founded the International Wine and Food Society, Ronald Avery is one of the grand old men I would love to have met. He died just after I began at *Wine & Spirit* but lives on in many a story and was clearly one of the great wine trade meddlers. Those invited to his famously disorganized household were routinely served old wines "refreshed" with a shot of a younger one, even champagne; or hard young clarets softened with a dash of vintage port. Bristol was twinned with Bordeaux and when charged with entertaining a grand delegation of visiting Bordeaux wine merchants Ronald Avery decided to serve them a Château Rausan-Ségla from the notoriously tough vintage of 1896, subjected of course to his famous softening treatment. Christian Cruse smelled it and sipped it and then smelled it and sipped it again with rapt attention before turning to his host and observing, "Do you know, I think the 1896s are beginning to come round at last."

Once Britain entered the Common Market and had to subscribe to the principle of authenticity, however, Ronald Avery's magisterial methods became more difficult to apply in the cellars of his family firm (now owned by the Pieroth group of door-stepping wine salesmen). Britain's EEC entry in 1973 marked a turning point in the fortunes of the British wine trade, even if its effects were just beginning to make themselves felt as my wine trade lunching reached its peak in the late 1970s. Before we tagged ourselves on to a culture steeped in the importance of Roquefort that comes exclusively from Roquefort and Chablis made only in Chablis, British wine merchants got away with murder, or at least forgery on a massive scale. Wine would be imported in bulk and bottled in dark, damp, cramped cellars under the London or Bristol pavements where it was extremely difficult to tell which pipe led where. Red burgundy was the most frequently traduced wine type. The British public were familiar with names such as Pommard and Nuits-Saint-Georges (Burgundian villages many miles apart producing distinctly different wines) but few of them had any clue how they really should taste. And no wonder since for years they had been sold blends of earthy reds from the southern Rhône or, even cheaper and even earthier, Algeria under these names, often from the same vat. Such wine cost a fraction of real burgundy.

But soon after EEC entry, British wine bottlers had to start obeying European wine laws. Which presented a dilemma since Burgundy was undergoing its own trauma, also the result of how easy it was to sell wines labeled with Burgundy's famous names, whatever they tasted like. Over the years, as Burgundy's farmers learnt to depend on agrochemicals and began to plant new, higher-yielding clones of the Pinot Noir vine that is solely responsible for red burgundy, the red wines of Burgundy had become less and less red, and often much less concentrated. Only the greatest, most expensive Grand Cru reds of the region were at all like the rich velvety archetype that the British (and Swiss and Scandinavian) merchants had kept alive. The fake burgundies of the Rhône and Algeria tasted nothing like the contemporary real thing, and Britain's wine consumers (and merchants) had to be reeducated. There was much discussion in the late 1970s and early 1980s about these vapid new burgundies, and many a palate preferred the old style. Burgundy itself had its share of scandals, for some of the region's own merchants had been using the same sort of recipe as their British counterparts; it made sound commercial sense. It was to be many years before Britain's wine policemen, just nine inspectors working under the auspices of the newly formed Wine Standards Board (based just next to Vintners' Hall at $68^{1}/_{2}$ Upper Thames Street), swept out the murkiest cobwebs from wine bottlers in Britain—chiefly by waiting for the decline of British bottling. Such has been the continuing drive for authenticity, and the narrowing cost differential between shipping in bulk and bottle, that today there are only about a dozen commercial bottlers of any size left in Britain (there were 46 in 1991).

If I found the traditional wine merchants lovable but quaintly out of touch, what did they make of me, I wonder? I recently asked Michael Broadbent, who resurrected wine sales so successfully at Christie's in 1966 and without whose palate and immaculate tailoring no serious wine tasting anywhere on the globe is complete. Nowadays we are good enough friends for him to smile and say, "Well, all I remember is that we thought you had a bit of a chip on your shoulder about being a woman."

This came as a complete surprise to me. There's no note of this chip in my diaries, but it was obviously there all along. Now that I've established myself as some sort of a figure in wine I don't feel remotely exceptional because of my sex. When I started, Jilly Goolden and Jane

MacQuitty were already reasonably well established wine writers, and Pamela Vandyke Price had been at it for years. We were soon joined by Kathyrn McWhirter, Joanna Simon and a host of other Englishwomen writing about wine, including Masters of Wine Rosemary George and Serena Sutcliffe. But perhaps it's true that in the late 1970s I was singing an overtly feminist tune. Every other woman in the media was, after all. I know that we all felt rather sad when the matriarchal line of editors at *Wine & Spirit* ended with Joanna Simon handing over to Tim Atkin. Today they are the wine correspondents respectively of the big rival Sunday newspapers *The Sunday Times* and the *Observer*.

I remember thinking at one stage that if I were a man of my age writing about wine I'd complain of discrimination, so frequent seemed to be the articles and features about women in wine. And the other great advantage in those courteous days was that as a woman you tended to be seated next to the host or important visitor, making it so much easier to get the scoop. (The fair, doe-eyed Kathryn McWhirter had much better stamina and wiles than me. She would stay up long into the night listening to the increasingly revealing confessions of various men in the wine and spirit trades, before going to the Ladies to write it all down.)

The traditional British wine merchant also seems, for some unaccountable reason, to find women easier to distinguish than men. Our male colleagues Stephen Brook (*Vogue*), Robert Joseph (*Sunday Telegraph*) and Anthony Rose (the *Independent*) are continually mistaken for each other by such pinstripes as remain.

Of all the wine writers in Britain (and by 1996 the Circle of Wine Writers had more than a hundred members) about a third are women. The proportion in most other countries, including the supposedly egalitarian United States, seems to be much lower and in Latin countries is virtually negligible.

Whether we bring anything specifically feminine to the art of wine writing I do not know. Those of us with young children have felt less able to travel than many of our male counterparts, I know, but we do have one theoretical advantage at least, and this is not my chip speaking. Every time that tasting ability is monitored objectively, not necessarily with any wine connection, women seem to perform better. A typical such experiment would take untutored palates, expose them to certain aromas or flavors and test their ability to recognize them.

Medical specialists acknowledge that the tasting faculties are generally better in women and, as in men, tend to be keenest between the ages of thirty and sixty. Children have very sensitive palates but presumably lack the experience and vocabulary needed to identify and describe the sensations, whereas tasting is just another of our faculties supposed to decline quite sharply once we reach the seventh decade.

For the moment, then, I fall in to Most Privileged Taster bracket (even if I was slightly too young when I started writing about wine), but you must understand that I am making no personal claim here. I do not consider myself an exceptionally gifted taster; I think I just followed instructions and that, provided I concentrate, I can be as perceptive as the next person, of either sex. Anyone, with the sole exception of that small proportion of people who for entirely medical reasons— accident or illness, for example—have a damaged sense of smell (*the* important sense for wine tasting), can do the same. All it takes is sufficient interest to want to learn, to concentrate on what the nose and palate communicates and to try to log those sensations so that they can be recognized again. For filing purposes it can help to attach a description to each sensation but it is only absolutely necessary for those who want a career as a wine commentator.

There are all sorts of different reasons for tasting wine, which entail different techniques and abilities. The most common sort of conscious wine tasting (as opposed to just drinking, which anyone can do) is the most admirable one, tasting for the purposes of pure pleasure. This involves just a moment's concentration for each nose—and mouthful— in recognition of the effort most winemakers nowadays put into every bit of their output. It also makes perfect sense because just throwing something as heavily taxed as wine down the gullet—as a surprising number of people do—is a waste of someone's money.

The technique here is the much-derided swirl and sniff, to encourage and then appreciate the wine's volatile flavor messages, followed by a thoughtful mouthful, also swirled around the palate before being swallowed.

The essential questions are "Do I like this?" (so you can pursue, or avoid, other wines like it). "What does the smell remind me of?" (trying to track relationships with other wines). "Are all the essential elements—acidity, sweetness, tannin, alcohol—in balance?" And "Does the flavor linger after swallowing?" An affirmative answer to the last two questions suggests the wine is good quality and ready to drink. Top-quality wines that are still very young, especially reds, tend to tan the inside of the cheeks just like leather, thanks to their heavy charge of tannins, which are precipitated as sediment while it matures inside the bottle. Everyday wines tend to leave very little trace after they've been swallowed, whereas a mouthful of seriously fine, multi-faceted wine can still titillate the palate even a minute after it is swallowed. I have heard of some French tasters who keep numerical records of this *période de persistance* for individual wines.

The most common reason we professionals taste a wine is not to maximize the pleasure it gives us, but rather the reverse: to assess it in terms of quality and, often, value. Usually we know exactly what the wine is—we're tasting it in some merchant's or producer's lineup—so we're using it to add to our total knowledge of a given winemaker, vineyard, region, grape or vintage. The most noticeable difference in technique (apart from the fact that we generally taste in silence and take notes) is the crucial one for our health: we spit rather than swallow. I suppose I must have felt inhibited about spitting in public once but I certainly can't remember it. Nowadays it seems the most natural thing in the world is to cluster with my colleagues round a spittoon writing notes, gargling, and occasionally communicating with eyes, eyebrows and grunts above cheeks bloated with wine samples.

There are other practical differences between tasting for pleasure and for work. When assessing a wine, I want to be able to taste every nuance, good and bad, so I tend to taste white wines very slightly warmer than I would choose to drink them. The one thing that most fascinated me about wine when I first started out was the science behind tasting, so I realized pretty soon that the warmer a liquid is served, the more of the volatile aroma is given off. And since flavor is best sensed using the nose (texture by the mouth), it makes sense to err on the side of warmth when assessing a wine. (The obverse is that aggressive chilling will rid a nasty white wine of its unappealing flavor.) Warmth also tends to make tannic young reds taste slightly less tannic and tart young whites slightly less acid—and since, sadly, we wine scribes tend to spend very much more time tasting wines that are too young than too old, this warmth can help.

In practice, I tend to taste most wines at comfortable room temperature when I can. The classic wine tasting scene, in a chilly, dank cellar full of barrels, is also the most uncomfortable. Your toes and your nose feel like ice. The wine tastes like chilled ink and it's too dark to see the color properly. Such tasting as I do at home I do mainly round our dining table which is at one end of our kitchen. This would horrify many of the wine writers I first came across in the late seventies when wine lore was a matter of unchallenged dogma.

The conventional beliefs were, and still are for many people, that there should be as few distracting smells as possible in a room where wine tasting takes place. I remember Pamela Vandyke Price used to enter a wine tasting, usually held in some rentable public space in a hotel or livery hall, like a bloodhound. The nostrils of her already upturned nose would flare with distaste and she would start muttering not so sotto voce if she caught sight of a lily in no matter how splendid a flower arrangement, or if she scented perfume, aftershave or a whiff of dry-cleaning fluid on any fellow taster. But she reserved complete disdain for anyone, usually some hapless southern European wine producer who couldn't understand what all the fuss was about, unwise enough to light up a cigarette within smelling radius.

I am just as distracted as Pamela by someone suddenly lighting up while I'm trying to taste a wine, but I think it is the sudden, intense smells that cause the problems rather than, for example, the poor lily. Just as people who live in a town producing something particularly smelly don't notice it, I think we all get used to the smell of any room we're in pretty quickly. In recognition of other tasters' sensibilities, I try never to wear perfume on a day when I know I am going to be tasting wine with others, except that this constitutes such a high proportion of my days, that I usually forget to dab on my Eau d'Issey even when I may. As a consequence, like most wine professionals I hardly bother to buy scent or eau de toilette. It seems a shame that so many people whose finely developed sense of smell would enable them to enjoy the parfumiers' work to the full are so rarely able to.

There is no doubt, however, that even if we're forced to forgo added perfume, our own natural auras are quite powerful enough to be distracting. Someone at a wine tasting will quite often hand me a glass of wine they find remarkable in some way, encouraging me to "taste [or smell] that." On the basis of repeated experience I always try to take the glass from them before raising it to my nose so that I'm not distracted by the smell of their hands. Not that my hands and body are any less smelly than anyone else's, I'm sure, but my smell is the one I'm used to, the smell I taste through all the time and therefore don't notice. It is for similar reasons, I'm sure, that heavy smoking does not destroy the palate, it just adds another layer of blithely unnoticed odor.

Pamela never smoked, despite her mother's going to the trouble of teaching her to inhale as elegantly as she herself did, and still pays a supplement to have her clothes dry cleaned without smellable trace. When I joined the fringes of her world more than twenty years ago when she was the *Times* wine correspondent, she was already known as the doyenne of wine writers (however much she hated the title), a commanding presence with blond curls, kittenish smile and stubborn chin above a colorful robe. Nevertheless she was very kind to me. One evening very early in my wine writing career she invited me to the flat in South Kensington where she has lived forever. I don't think I'd ever seen so many wine bottles in a place of residence; I'd certainly never seen so many wine books. As we downed a bottle of Mosel, she cheerfully told me that I would eventually discover that there was "a very special hole in hell" for publishers.

Pamela wielded considerable power in the world of British wine retailing. A recommendation in the Saturday *Times* was not to be sniffed at. Pamela belonged to the school of wine writing which believed in maintaining very close links with the trade itself, and she was violently opposed to any written criticism (although wedded to the spoken sort). There were other members of the Circle of Wine Writers whose opinions of individual wines did not really have any commercial power, but the wine trade was expected to kowtow to all of them and they did rather capitalize on this. Lunches had to be of a certain standard, and woe betide the publicist whose press trip was drier than the norm.

I had a particularly useful experience very early on during an expedition to watch horse racing sponsored by a trade organization known then as the Rhine and Moselle Shippers (i.e., importers of German wine). We all traveled together by train from Victoria station and I, at that stage unknown, settled myself into the corner of one compartment which soon filled up with the shippers and their wives. Just as the train pulled out of the station, one of them stood up, looked round and said with ill-disguised relief, "There aren't any wine writers in this carriage, are there?" So *that's* what they really think of us, is it, I thought to myself, as a cross to be borne.

And ever since that time I have determinedly downplayed the importance of wine writers to such an extent that by the early 1990s I was probably underestimating their clout. Most of those writing about wine in Britain in the late 1970s, with the exception of Edmund Penning-Rowsell of the *Financial Times* and the already best-selling Hugh Johnson, had a fraction of the wine knowledge that today's wine writers do. The archetypal wine correspondent then was a semi-retired specialist writer, perhaps literary editor, who had been pensioned off with a wine column and an entrée to lots of good lunches and trips. Lunch was seen as the most important part of a tasting (whereas now remarkably few wine writers allow solid matter to interrupt the 100-sample flow). John Arlott was such a gifted cricket commentator that he could afford to be modest about his wine accomplishments. Cyril Ray wrote so beautifully that he had no qualms about confessing, "I never claim to be any sort of an expert." And Derek Cooper, then the *Observer*'s wine columnist, had such a good nose for a story that it didn't matter that his olfactory senses were more attuned to whisky than wine. When *The Sunday Times* invited a number of us wine writers to taste a selection of mystery wines (which turned out to be our own recommendations) for the purposes of an article in their consumer "Lifespan" section, Derek refused, saying, "I'm not making a fool of myself in public—and you can quote me." Which brings me to that most discussed sort of tasting of all.

Blind Tasting

There is no doubt that guessing a wine's identity on the basis of taste alone is one of the most impressive tricks a human can perform. It is seen as the defining act of wine expertise. Wine outsiders seem endlessly fascinated by it, presumably because it demonstrates skills they have never developed themselves. Wine insiders call it blind tasting, and it always surprises me how many outsiders think this involves putting masks on the tasters (which would be a very dangerous undertaking) rather than masking the identity of what is to be tasted, typically encasing the bottle in an opaque bag or cardboard sleeve.

I am more impressed by the possibly more common ability to identify music and performers from a short phrase, because I find it more difficult than blind tasting, but I suspect it involves a similar combination of one-third natural gift and two-thirds application guided by varying degrees of luck. Blind tasting for the purposes of identification is a very specialized sort of tasting of little practical use but great entertainment value. One would naturally assume that tasting experience and a good memory were the most important elements in blind tasting but experience can be a real bind, I have found. I have never been as good at identifying wines as I was in the late 1970s when my palate memory (and actual memory) were uncluttered by accumulation. Every new wine made a crystal-clear impression and, since I had experienced so few of these impressions, it was dead easy to relate practically everything I tasted to just one of them. Then, as we accumulate more experience, more impressions and increasingly discover exceptions to the rules that seemed so simple at first, our poor old palates and memories become increasingly befuddled.

This, we wine professionals argue, is why we make so many mistakes round the dinner table and why our spouses or partners tend to be so much better at guessing the wine than we are. It's their uncluttered palate memories, you see. Michael Broadbent, veteran of many a fine wine dinner, rather wearily makes a similar point in his classic on the subject, *Wine Tasting*: "It is not uncommon for the highest scorers to be amateurs, for their greatest performances are usually set in an even more limited (however excellent) context, that of their own and their friends' cellars."

If blind tasting itself is difficult for insiders, the nuances of it are even more difficult for outsiders to understand. On the face of it, for example, it seems as though to guess a 1988 red bordeaux as a 1987 would be a better guess than to guess it as a 1986, but insiders know that both the 1986 and 1988 vintages in Bordeaux produced deep-colored, tannic reds at about the same stage of evolution, whereas the 1987s are the lightest, puniest clarets of the decade, i.e., nothing like the 1988s. I have frequently identified top-quality Chardonnays as white burgundy when they have actually been, say, a Kistler creation from California or Antinori's Cervaro from Italy. On the face of it, these guesses are thousands of miles out, but insiders know how very similar the wines can taste, sometimes because exactly the same grapes and techniques, even the same clones and barrels, are used. To outsiders, we professional tasters can seem the most dreadful bunch of fraudsters.

It can be difficult for outsiders to ask the right questions too. I remember very early on in my wine career being invited to Sunday lunch by someone who was such an old and fiendish friend that he reckoned I should be tested on my newfound expertise. (We had previously shared many a Harvey Wallbanger and Margarita.) With the roast beef he poured us all a glass of purple wine and challenged me to identify it. One look at the color suggested it was a young (bluish) wine made from fairly thick-skinned grapes (deepish color) such as, well probably all I could think of at that stage were the Bordeaux grapes Cabernet and Merlot. I took a sniff and sure enough, there were the telltale terribly well-mannered smells I'd been taught to describe as "blackcurrant" of young claret. "Bordeaux?" I ventured. Steve took a furtive look at the label. "That's right. What year?" I tipped the glass away from me against my white plate to see whether the wine had taken on any brick tinge with age, just as I'd been taught to in my wine classes. Still crimson but quite watery at the rim, it must be young and probably not that wonderful quality (the best red wines tend to be very intensely colored in their youth) so I guessed it was probably some commercial bordeaux two or three years old. "Yes, yes," said Steve impatiently, "but what *château* is it?"

Now this was a really tricky one. If it did carry the name of a Château on the label, it was almost certainly a pretty inconsequential one and could have been one of literally thousands of small wine farms allowed to call themselves "Château" Such and Such. Eventually, after a thoroughly unsatisfactory dialogue for both of us, the wine was revealed as the mass-market blend Mouton Cadet. How to turn a drink meant to spread goodwill into an embarrassing argument.

Happily, although outsiders remember when you get it wrong, insiders do seem to remember when you get it right—mainly because they know how difficult it is. Notable feats are discussed widely; the odd bravura performance can cling flatteringly to one's reputation for years and years. I will always remember Lindsay Hamilton of fine wine traders Farr Vintners telling me that he had seen Oz Clarke, fellow wine writer and extremely gifted blind taster, given a wine that was actually a blend of Jaboulet's 1982 and 1983 Hermitage La Chapelle, hesitate between identifying it as a 1982 or a 1983. Now that's impressive.

On those rare occasions when I have managed to be more right than wrong, it has usually been remembered and repeated back to me. As the French wine writer (and once owner of Château Margaux) Bernard Ginestet puts it, "I know of tasters who live by a reputation forged on the basis of two or three inspired guesses." I sometimes feel like that.

The only time I have ever felt that I was being *tested* by a fellow professional was when I first visited Château Cheval Blanc, the great Saint-Émilion property whose wines have over the years become some of my absolute favorites for their grace and balance. I was researching my second book, *The Great Wine Book*, and wanted, fairly predictably, to include Cheval Blanc as one of thirty-seven properties profiled therein. The man who had been in charge of this first growth since 1970, after managing rubber and cocoa plantations in Africa and the Far East ("the same as vines really"), was the lofty Jacques Hébrard. His wife was one of the Heritiers Fourcaud-Laussac still prominently and proprietorially featured on the label of Cheval Blanc. When I turned up early one evening in 1981 as agreed, he was not particularly forthcoming. He answered my questions but volunteered not a word more. He made sure I realized that one of his jobs was to judge books written about Bordeaux. As I got up to go, he rather doubtfully invited me to stay for dinner. It must be a very small class of people who would refuse an invitation to dine at a first growth château and one which certainly does not include me, however reluctant the host.

The hostess, Madame Hébrard, turned out to be charming, as was their snow-white cat (Chaton Blanc?), and the table in the salon had already been laid for three. Before dinner we watched the landing of the first space shuttle on a television distractingly acting as plinth for a model of the plane which his father had piloted across the Atlantic half a century before. He was still distinctly gruff until he'd served the contents of the two decanters sitting on the sideboard. It is hardly a great feat to guess that at Cheval Blanc the wine they are most likely to serve is Cheval Blanc. My job was clearly to guess the vintages. The first wine was still very lively with a great thwack of Saint-Émilion warmth and sweetness. It was relatively concentrated in color still but had developed quite a brickish tinge at the rim. The smell, or "nose," was both fascinating and seductive and there was still lots of firm fruit. This must be a robust middle-aged vintage, but that rim looked too mature for it to be a 1970, yet it tasted too young to be any older than that. It was too good a wine to have been made in 1974, 1973 or 1972, so was it by any chance 1971? M. Hébrard smiled for the first time that evening and his wife looked approving. "Some more lamb perhaps?"

Now to the second decanter. Professional protocol dictated that it would be older than the first wine, and that was certainly confirmed by its lighter, browner color. Here was a fully mature wine I thought (although I thought the same when drinking it fifteen years later) which smelled so sweet, luscious and thoroughly charming that it could have been a 1966, but it was terribly impressive, very powerful and underneath all that charm something with enormous guts. Something, some divine intervention, made me plump for 1964, a great year for Cheval Blanc, rather than 1966, and then my host visibly melted. We all had a lovely time after that (and who wouldn't with these two decanters to help them?) and Jacques Hébrard was charm itself whenever I came across him subsequently.

My most embarrassing trial by tasting took place not long after this Cheval Blanc visit but in much more public circumstances. The broadcaster Terry Wogan was at the height of his fame, hosting a live, early evening chat show during which all he had to do was look coyly at the camera and raise an eyebrow to have the entire audience of the Shepherd's Bush Theatre and his millions of television viewers across Britain either swooning or chortling, depending on their sex. For some reason—the performing dogs principle, I suppose—Hugh Johnson and I were invited to appear together to taste some wine. Ever-generous Hugh, for neither the first nor last time, saw it as his duty to make sure we had some champagne to drink—bought from a dubious local off-license and drunk in a cramped dressing room. That bit was fine. But then eventually we were led, increasingly zombie-like in my case, to the set on stage and, under cover of some musical act, installed on the regulation sofa beside a coffee table on which were two wine glasses from hell. They were tall, narrow cones, heavy and ornately cut, just the sort of thing you would find in a boardroom but never in a wine lover's house because there was no bowl for the telltale aroma to collect in and no nice thin lip to put you in really close contact with the wine. And, as if that wasn't enough, the wine must have been sitting out since rehearsal time that afternoon under strong studio lights so that such smell as there had been had long since dissipated. Well, that's my excuse anyway, for failing, in front of probably five million people, to identify Château Lafite 1976, hailed as "the wine of the vintage."

Needless to say, I had been much more successful on a much less important show when asked to identify six wines for local TV in Newcastle several years previously very early in my career. The more of a nonentity you are, the more relaxed you can afford to be when blind tasting in public. It was the same sort of early evening show in Newcastle but a much more cramped studio. The stage manager tiptoed in with the wines on a tray as I sat watching the previous guest, a weatherman. I signaled to him that because he'd filled the glasses right up to the top rather than the usual tasting level of about a quarter full, he'd have to pour most of the six wines away. He signaled to me that he had nowhere to pour them, shrugged, and downed the equivalent of half a bottle in the thirty seconds before we were due to go on the air.

Blind tasting as performance art appeals to me less and less as I get older, for obvious reasons (although I see that I first made the analogy between it and crossword puzzle solving, both of them impressive but fairly useless, in 1980 when *The Sunday Times* tested our ability to identify our own recommendations and my palate was inexperienced enough to perform well).

There is another reason for blind tasting, however, which is invaluable for any wine professional: assessing the quality of a wine (as opposed to identifying it) without knowing what it is. Most of us consumer writers on wine acknowledge that the best way of testing a wine's real quality is to taste it blind with its peers, and we try to base our recommendations on that process as often as possible. Similarly, the best way of assessing a completely unfamiliar wine—some new offering from the hills of Attica, for example—is to taste it blind and try to work out what price you'd be prepared to pay for it. This was the basis on which the enlightened London wine merchant James Rogers made all his wine-buying decisions. If only more retailers followed his example.

Blind tasting is a truly humbling experience and teaches us all just how heavily influenced we are by labels and reputations rather than inherent quality. If I had just half the cost of all the wines with a "Montrachet" in their name which have turned out to be expensive disappointments, I would be a very rich woman. The French are fiercely opposed to blind comparisons between their wines and those from other countries. They claim it is as senseless as comparing apples with pears. I'm not so sure. If you want to come to grips with, say, the essential Pauillac-ness of Pauillac, then of course it's a waste of time to taste five of them mixed up with five top California Cabernet Sauvignons. But if you want to test the hypothesis that Pauillacs are a better buy than California Cabernet Sauvignons, then such a blind tasting is one way to do it—especially since even quite experienced tasters can have difficulty telling some of them apart.

Just as the world of wine has been transformed in the last twenty years, so have the mores of blind tasting. When I started, blind tasting round a wine trade lunch table was a relatively simple matter. It was chiefly a question of deciding whether the red wine was bordeaux or burgundy. If it were burgundy, you progressed gently via Côte de Nuits or Beaune to whether it was a village wine, premier cru or grand cru and took in the vintage somewhere en route. If it were bordeaux you worked out which of the "Big Four" (Médoc, Graves, Saint-Émilion or Pomerol) and, if Médoc as it so often was, which of the "Little Four" (Saint-Estèphe, Pauillac, Saint-Julien or Margaux). Just occasionally someone served something really outré such as a Rhône or Château La Lagune or Cantemerle, a bordeaux from outside the little four communes of the Médoc.

Today all but the most conservative hosts serve wines from all over the world, many of them aping each other so successfully that they hardly carry a recognizable geographical origin at all, making blind tasting even more perilous. And a uniformity of aspiration has swept even the old stalwarts of the Médoc so that traditional communal differences are often subordinated to winemaking technique. In fact, Professor Emile Peynaud of Bordeaux University, the grand seigneur of wine tasting and a winemaking consultant at numerous topflight châteaux, claims that such differences between villages are "really just the commercial styles which were followed when blending in merchants' cellars years ago; the reality is quite different. For my own part, I would not claim to be able to identify the communes of a series of Médocs tasted blind. The problem is just as difficult in Burgundy where the distinction between wines from the Côte de Beaune and the Côte de Nuits is a matter for endless debate."

It is probably worth repeating the wine trade's most often told story here. The personnel change but the sentiment doesn't. A wine professional is asked when he, or she, last mistook bordeaux for burgundy. "Oh, not since lunch" is the answer—although nowadays it is getting harder and harder to find people who drink at lunchtime at all.

First Steps
Abroad

———

As editor of *Wine & Spirit* I had the perfect excuse, nay obligation, to travel to inspect the places where wines and spirits were produced.

Because of the orientation of the magazine's editorial and, particularly, advertising, I seemed to spend a lot of the late 1970s touring the distilleries of Scotland, from foot stamping in the crisp Highland air outside, to the vegetal smell of barley on the malting floor inside, to the warm maltiness of the mash tun, the sweet, beery perfume of the wash-backs, Scotch's wooden fermentation vats, then the cranium-piercing reek of the clear spirit that flowed from the shiny copper stills, and finally to the damp, peaty scent that hangs over any warehouse filled with maturing Scotch.

Each distillery has undoubtedly as much individuality and character as a top wine château. The Highlands are beautiful. Scotch whisky is a fine spirit. But it is not my preferred drink or subject. I can enjoy the pungent aroma of a well-aged malt after a particularly good meal, and I can even savor a mouthful or two if I find myself out of doors north of the border.

Similarly, on weekend breaks in Moscow and Leningrad organized by my old employers at more or less this time, I discovered that a fiery slug of vodka gulped in the snow seems just the thing to ward off the savage cold of a Russian winter. But for every day, spirits seemed, and still seem, just too strong for me, even when thoroughly watered down as all malt whisky connoisseurs insist their distinguished spirit should be. The drink that made my heart beat faster, and my food taste more flavorful, was wine.

Happily, I was to discover that wine is made in some of the most attractive parts of the world. Too cold a climate and the vines won't rippen. Too uncomfortably hot and they get no rest. A mediterranean climate suits the vine every bit as well as it suits me. Vineyards also tend to be, for obvious reasons, in the heart of the countryside (although Paris still harbors a few small patches of vines, Vienna is overlooked by several, and in Britain some Midlands council has encouraged vine growing as youth employment opportunity on the edges of industrial Dudley).

There's also something very special about the shapes, textures and colors of vines and vineyards themselves. I don't think I'm being perverse in finding aesthetic delight in the sight of parallel but widely spaced rows of vines snaking across the countryside, often etching out the contour lines, sometimes forming a patchwork with a neighboring plot. Many fruit trees (which is, after all, what vines are) are planted in straight lines, but few have such satisfying foliage as the vine. The pointed, witchlike symmetry of the leaves mirrors that of the Virginia creeper to which the grapevine is related. The vine, however, has the added decoration of delicate tendrils and, of course, succulent fruit, in so many different colors and packaged in bunches of such attractive, and varied, shapes. Grapes, even fully ripe grapes, can vary from little blue-black pea-sized Cabernet Sauvignon through brownish mauve Pinot Gris and amber-gold, discreetly sized Chardonnay to balls the color and shape of a greengage, as in some of the grapes grown for the table rather than for the fermentation vat. The smaller the grape and the thicker its skin, the greater the ratio of solids to liquid and, usually, the more concentrated the flavor in the resulting wine.

During my year in Provence in 1974 and 1975 I had witnessed what still seems to me one of the greatest natural miracles, the annual transformation of a vineyard from the sullen little black stumps of winter to the luxuriant green canopy of summer, followed by the dramatic and definitively autumnal golds and reds of vine leaves as the sap falls and the plants gather their carbohydrate resources for a long winter sleep. (Wines from tropical Brazil where grapes are harvested up to five times every two years suggest that dormancy is essential if good wine is to be made.) It has now been more than twenty years since I have been able to monitor a single vineyard for a whole year but I hope to again one day.

One of my first official sorties abroad as a wine writer was, naturally enough, to Bordeaux, France's biggest fine wine region and one about which we British still feel proprietorial. Good heavens, it was barely more than five hundred years ago that we relinquished Aquitaine to the French. Out of the blue, just eighteen months into my wine writing career, I'd been contacted by a wine producer then of relative youth and minor importance, Jean-Michel Cazes of the fifth growth Pauillac property Château Lynch Bages (where stainless steel had just replaced wood as favored material for the fermentation vats for the tough old 1975 vintage). He still hasn't explained to me satisfactorily how he even knew of my existence, let alone picked me out for the honor of being sworn in as a member of the Commanderie du Bontemps du Médoc et des Graves, one of the smarter gastronomic brotherhoods of which the French are so proud.

The week before I took my first trip to the world's most famous wine region I'd been discussing it with Nick Clarke, a young Master of Wine. His job then was to buy fine wine for Bass Charrington, the giant British brewer which had decided a few years before to diversify into wine, thereby upsetting the global market in it. In a misguided attempt to beat inflation, people like Nick Clarke were given absurd sums of money, something like $30 million a year even then, and told to buy as much fine wine as they could lay their hands on. Clarke, who was nearly fired for not buying any of the mean, nasty and thoroughly overpriced 1972 bordeaux, remembers buying Mouton, the first growth, ten tonneaus at a time in his buying heyday of 1960 to 1971. It was quite normal then to buy fine wine in this, the traditional Bordeaux measure of wine volume, the equivalent of 100 cases of a dozen bottles each.

Today there are hundreds of possible buyers of each individual case all over the world, but in the early 1970s there were really only a very few dozen principal purchasers of claret *en primeur,* in youthful bulk before it is bottled: the big British brewers, Seagram's Château and Estate fine wine division in the United States, the Scandinavian monopolies and a few long-standing importers in Switzerland, Germany and the Benelux countries. In such a position, the handful of buyers entrusted with spending the British brewers' wine budgets could visit even the finest Burgundy cellars and buy up virtually its entire contents.

Allied Breweries insured the nose of its chief buyer, Colin Anderson, at Lloyds, so crucial was it seen to be to their fortunes. Nick Clarke remembers being able to order 500 cases of domaine-bottled Chassagne-Montrachet from Gagnard-Delagrange, so open the field and so deep the brewers' pockets.

But Nick lost his edge when Bass's adventures in wineland were brought to an abrupt and very visible halt by some corporate volte-face in June 1974. Virtually all of its fine wine stocks were disposed of in a Christie's sale which still holds the record for the largest number of bottles to be offered at once: half a million, or more than 40,000 cases. Even first growths were being offered in 100-case lots, at prices that delighted both the syndicates of individual buyers and the likes of Brian Barnett, who was subsequently able to offer surely the greatest wine bargains ever at his Augustus Barnett shops. Foolishly, at this stage, on less than $5,000 a year from Mr. Heseltine's publishing company, I thought £3.99 (about $6.50) far too much to pay for a bottle of wine for myself, even if it was Château Pétrus 1970. The handsome cellar of bordeaux chronicler Edmund Penning-Rowsell on the other hand was considerably enriched by Mr. Barnett's bargains. He has always been a much wiser wine buyer than me.

Three years later, just before my Bordeaux trip and just before Barnett sold out to the highly dubious Rumasa sherry-and-banks group, Nick Clarke was still working for Bass, but in a more conservative mode simply filling the cellars of its restaurants and hotels as and when needed. I went to his office just across Regent Street from mine to be briefed on a day-long conference I'd been invited to at Château Lascombes, the Margaux second growth Bass had bought from Alexis Lichine in its wine expansionist days in the early 1970s. When I told him I was staying with Jean-Michel Cazes at Château Lynch Bages the weekend before, he told me to "ask them what they put in it." This half-joke was inspired by this particular claret's exceptional exuberance and richness of flavor, probably my first conscious introduction to the extent to which a particular location (not additive, Cazes was to assure me) can affect flavor.

I had the most idyllic introduction to Bordeaux. Never one to settle for a simple journey, I was to arrive via a night in Cognac which, wearing my *Spirit* rather than *Wine &* hat, I had already visited once. Whereas Scotch whisky country is brisk and prickly with tweed, heather and gorse, the atmosphere in Cognac country just north of Bordeaux in southwest France is langorously soft, limpid and almost soporific, like Bath. In the case of Bath it is perhaps the result of the sulphurous vapors which still rise from the Roman baths. In the case of the cognac towns Jarnac and Cognac itself, it may be that the air is heavy with alcohol evaporating from the sheer concentration of black-roofed warehouses full of brandy. There is much rueful talk in cognac country of "the angel's share," the significant, and extremely expensive, proportion of precious cognac which escapes into the heady Charentais atmosphere each year.

I drove down to Bordeaux with a young man from Courvoisier on the most beautiful golden June evening. That night the city looked beguilingly mellow, the handsome old stone arches and intricate statuary alight with a rosy glow. We rolled over the cobbles of the famous Quai des Chartrons, the quayside from which wine has been shipped since the Middle Ages. We dawdled past the Grand Théatre and whizzed up and down the broad, open Allées de Tourny which looked as though they should be full of little boys and girls rolling hoops under the watchful eye of Nanny. This was the thoroughly acceptable face of commercial prosperity and my favorable impressions were sealed by a dinner next to the limpid river Dordogne (or was it Garonne?), still bathed in that heady golden, slightly mayfly-blown light.

It was the world-famous Médoc the next morning that disappointed. Here was the greatest concentration of famous wine properties in the world, hallowed châteaux and village names streaming past the car, yet there was so little air of romance, so few beguiling aspects, so little evidence of humanity. The Médoc is basically an almost flat plateau stretching northwest from Bordeaux, overlooking a wide stretch of gray water (the Gironde into which the pretty Dordogne and Garonne

are transformed) on the other side of which is a very low hill. There is
the occasional copse, and the architecture of the grander châteaux has a
certain ambitious grandeur to it, of a distinctly nineteenth century
sort, but if the vineyards themselves seem neat, low and conservative,
the châteaux are equally closed and inexpressive.

This is not to reproach the wines. The Médoc makes no claims to be
a tourist center, even if nowadays one or two châteaux actively welcome visitors (notably those run by the now hugely successful Jean-
Michel Cazes). In the late 1970s Alexis Lichine was reviled for erecting
signs actively soliciting personal callers to his third growth Château
Prieuré-Lichine, virtually the only evidence then that the Médoc housed
anyone with an interest in selling wine.

The other, a few miles north on the same narrow road which twists
through the Médoc, was (and is) a giant replica of a wine bottle in the
grounds of Château Gloria. Described by Edmund Penning-Rowsell as
"huge, hideous," it advertises in very large letters the fact that the best
wines in the world are produced in Saint-Julien. I was told a story
about this bottle recently in Connecticut which illustrates what might
be called the Médocain mentality. Ken Onish, now trying to persuade
Americans to buy South African wine, was in the 1960s working several villages away as a *stagiaire,* or apprentice, at Château Lascombes,
the Margaux second growth that Alexis Lichine was about to sell to
Bass Charrington ("we used to see him sitting on the lawn with men in
suits"). Being only twenty-three, and passionately enthusiastic about
his newfound French base, Onish reckoned the legend on Saint-
Julien's giant bottle needed some amendment. One night, therefore,
he and an English girl also based in Margaux set off in his car with a
pot of green paint. Standing on his shoulders, she painted out "Saint-
Julien" and replaced it with "Margaux." They returned, giggling, to
Lascombes, well pleased with their work.

They should have known that secrecy and French village life are
incompatible. Someone had taken note of Onish's car's numberplate and it was not long before a carful of gendarmes drew up at Lascombes. The two suspects were immediately separated—these guys
had read the right books—and pretty soon one of them sang. There
could be no resistance to the policemen's pièce de résistance, a sample
of the fateful green paint. "Have you ever seen this before, sir?" they
asked the increasingly somber young American.

Onish was told to go and apologize to the owner of Château Gloria, and highly successful propagandist for Saint-Julien, Henri Martin (later recruited by Château Latour). Monsieur Martin, however, still bristling with indignation, refused to accept his apology, let alone admit this might just be a youthful prank. The upshot was that Onish's *carte de séjour* was rescinded and he had to leave the country. An escapade that became a reluctant escape. (The coda to this story is that Martin did eventually come to see the joke and his progeny have been to stay with the Onishes in the United States.) Knowing that Saint-Julien has no first growths but many a second, I can't help wondering whether the reaction would have been identical if the pranksters had substituted the name Pauillac, incontrovertible hotbed of Médoc wine quality, with three of Bordeaux's five first growths rather than sleepy, then underperforming Margaux.

By coincidence the Commanderie that I had been invited to Bordeaux to join had been founded by Henri Martin, to mirror the hugely successful Chevaliers de Tastevin in Burgundy. The French love these *confréries,* brotherhoods long on ceremony and red velvet usually designed to promote a particular gastronomic product and, along the way, the girth of the confreres. There are hundreds of these associations, devoted to a certain sort of biscuit, or way of cooking tripe or, in the case of my previous distinction, the Burgundian snail. Most of them are thoroughly modern inventions, despite the mock medieval robes, insignia and pomp. Certainly none of them can boast a history as long as the Jurade de Saint-Émilion, which can trace its origins back to the twelfth century and is today a particularly active life force behind the wines of Saint-Émilion, the prettiest town on the Bordeaux wine route. The Commanderie du Bontemps du Médoc et des Graves was designed to be its "left bank" (of the wide Gironde estuary) counterpart but is in fact only one year older than me, having been founded in 1949. Never mind, it seemed a very great honor to the inexperienced editor of *Wine & Spirit.* There I was sticking down page proofs in a dingy little office in Soho one minute and in the next I was lining up in a red velvet robe with the Japanese ambassador to France to be sworn in to this most impressive-looking order.

Twice a year, at the notional time of the vine flowering (the Fête de la Fleur) and the start of the grape harvest (the Ban de Vendange), the Commanderie assembles at a volunteer château and "enthrones," or

intronises, a tranche of new members before, of course, getting down
to the real business, a meal even more copious and bibulous than the
French rural norm. This summer of 1977, a particularly dismal vintage it must be said, the owners of Château Phélan-Ségur in Saint-
Estèphe had nobly agreed to entertain us all, and the swearing-in
ceremony was to be in their *parc,* as the French call any garden with
trees. We stood in line, uneasy in our robes, and waited our turn for
what looked like a quite terrifying test. Commandeur Martin himself
would approach us, his back to the audience, with a mystery glass of
wine and ask us, in front of everyone else gathered there, to identify
it. What the crowd couldn't see, but most of them must have guessed,
was that we were all discreetly prompted with the name of the wine.
(Whoever imagined in the first place that suitable candidates would be
able to blind taste in such circumstances, I wonder?)

   In my diary for this Bordeaux weekend I have casually scribbled
"Pétrus 45" over the Friday night. What should have been a memorable introduction to what was then the world's most expensive Bordeaux château and this century's most famous vintage is in retrospect a
lesson in how wine is, all too frequently, misused. The heir to an
American fortune whom Cazes did not know particularly well had
bought a bottle of this famous Pomerol. He and his wife were visiting Bordeaux and invited him to join them for the great denouement
of this purchase. (That's the thing about wine; the inevitable auto-
destruct pull of the corkscrew.) Their hearts may have sunk slightly
when he told them he had a young British wine writer staying, but
perhaps Jean-Michel's wife, who must have experienced many of these
dinners, was not too sad that I would be taking her place. We dined at
La Réserve in what was then the northerly limit of the Graves region
on the outskirts of Bordeaux. (Today this smartest bit of the Graves
has its own appellation, Pessac-Léognan.)

   I would love to say that this was an evening made magical by wine,
but I'm afraid the overload of expectation hung heavily over our table.
The wife of the Pétrus purchaser was a teetotaler (this is far from
unusual) and the other couple traveling with him felt somewhat
oppressed by all this wine talk. Who can blame them? Shocking to
recount, I have no recollection of the wine itself except for the uncomfortable feeling that I was unworthy of it, and yet it, a dark, slightly
soupy monster, could not possibly be wonderful enough to melt the

social unease bred by a group of virtual strangers united by a single bottle. I don't mean that we drank only the Pétrus. We had the most famous local white, Domaine de Chevalier, first. But our host, instead of sharing his wine with friends and feeling relaxed enough to admit it if it didn't bring ecstasy, was using his superior buying power to entice us to his table. No wonder we all felt awkward. I remember my casual supper by the Dordogne (or was it the Garonne?) with much more affection.

Today Jean-Michel Cazes, whose great-grandfather came to the Médoc as an itinerant farmworker, is one of the most important figures in Bordeaux. Under his aegis the family wine property, Château Lynch-Bages, has gone from strength to strength, beating first growth Château Mouton-Rothschild to the dubious merit (but marketing triumph) of launching an overpriced dry white sister to the main red wine. (The longer I have been writing about wine the more wary I am of making generalizations, but I cannot think of a white wine produced in the Médoc that is anything like good value. They tend to be expressions of vanity or commercial acumen.)

Cazes, like so many successful proprietors today, runs his own wine merchant's business and has his own branded red and white bordeaux blended from wines bought in bulk on the Bordeaux market, again like Mouton Cadet. But his chief distinction is his role running AXA Millésimes, the wine division of the huge French insurance group AXA which owns a dazzling array of smart properties in Bordeaux, Burgundy, Hungary and, the birthplace of Madame Jean-Michel Cazes, Portugal. These wine interests, however, manifold as they seem in the wine world, apparently represent a tiny fraction of the turnover of AXA, which has been built up by an old schoolmate of Cazes.

We winos are always being put in our place. For something that gives as much pleasure as wine, it occupies remarkably low economic ranking. South Africans, for example, point out somewhat ruefully that their most lavish winery, Vergelegen, recently constructed on top of a mountain and equipped without thought for expense, must have cost its Anglo-American owners what they earn in a few minutes from one of their diamond mines.

Perhaps of more relevance to consumers of this delicious drink are comparisons between the cost of acquiring a wine collection and that of investing in fine art. I know of many male wine enthusiasts who deliberately arrange for the telltale wooden boxes branded with expensive château names to be delivered at times when they know their wives will be out of the house, so they can secrete them in a dark corner, covering the tracks of their obsession. My suggestion is that they justify themselves aggressively rather than defensively by pointing out just how relatively inexpensive fine wine is. The wine departments of Sotheby's and Christie's make hardly a dent in the auctioneers' annual accounts, even though they sell the lion's share of the world's resources of seriously captivating wine.

In between my increasing number of forays abroad, I was exposed to a remarkable number of great wines—far more than are opened nowadays for pipsqueaks such as wine trade journalists. London boasted a hectic timetable of wine tastings put on by one of the trade's many importers to try to flush out orders from the hundreds of independent wine merchants there were then. Returning from my Bordeaux intronisation, for instance, I immediately went to one tasting of marvelous German relics from the exceptional 1959 vintage—all copper color and fruity vivacity—and another, an established highlight in the wine trade calendar, in the candlelit Lebègue cellars under London Bridge station, of the near-mythical, richly perfumed burgundies of the Domaine de la Romanée-Conti. We tasted the 1966, 1971 and 1973 vintages of Grands Échezeaux, Richebourg, La Tâche and, the rarest grand cru burgundy of all, Romanée-Conti itself. I didn't realize at the time that such venerable treats would become rarer and rarer.

I didn't realize that the oldest and therefore rarest wines that wine lovers come across are likely to have been tasted at the beginning of their love affair with wine, possibly even before they have built much confidence as a taster. I began a collection of memorable (empty) bottles in the late 1970s, thinking this would be just the start, but of course as time wears on the vintages become less venerable, and most of the bottles I open today seem less significant. Dust now gathers on the forest of great bottles that I planted on top of a cocktail cabinet in the early 1980s, and in the 1990s I seldom add more than two bottles a year to this increasingly historic collection.

The Thirsty
Tour Operator

Our family holidays had always been spent in a fisherman's cottage in Southwold on the Suffolk coast, so I went abroad only once before leaving school. Perhaps it is this, together with having been brought up in such a small, relatively isolated community, that made me a particularly enthusiastic traveler, and accepter of invitations. I was always trying to cram too much into my life—and this has not changed much. In the late 1970s, when I was bound to London by nothing and no one, I made literally hundreds of visits to distilleries, bottling plants, vineyards and cellars.

My three years with Thomhols the tour operator, which ended in 1974, left me a sort of thwarted travel agent. To this day, I love trying to work out the most efficient way of getting from A to B and feel real distress if I get to an airport and realize there was a better connection than the one I'm committed to. I love poring over maps and time-tables. My mother says I must have inherited this from her father, who ran Northern Ireland's railway system, and her brother, who insisted on running one in miniature in the house where they grew up, not letting his sisters up or down the stairs until the signals changed.

Perhaps the most luxurious trip I ever went on, virtually untroubled by anything like work and certainly completely devoid of bottling line inspection, was organized by David Russell, an aristocratic bon viveur who represented the likes of Baron Philippe de Rothschild and Krug champagne by insisting that they treat us hacks like the most exigent monarchs. He has recently retired finding, slightly to his dismay, that the house in Kent on which he'd set his heart came complete with a vineyard. Young male wine writers were much less interesting to him than young female ones (and possibly vice versa), but I found him a delightful traveling and dining companion. He was the sort of public relations man who would tell you the whole story, warts and all, but made you like him so much that you respected his confidence. Other, more brutal practitioners were fair game for forcing into damaging admissions and leaks. (I continue to be surprised, however, by how few people with valuable knowledge seem to realize that journalists are taught to twitch and respond whenever they receive classified information, however informal the circumstances. I'm very good at keeping a secret, but it has to be clearly labeled.)

This particular trip was one of David Russell's most ambitious, a sort of Grand Tour of northern Italy, taking in Bass Charrington's major Italian wine suppliers. They—Bolla of Verona and Ruffino of Tuscany—were pretty incidental to the whole thing. Venice and Florence were the stars of the show: David had his priorities right. He also somehow managed to persuade those paying for these outings that wine writers, even lowly trade writers such as myself, would be mortally offended if asked to fly anything other than first class. But being Mademoiselle Agent de Voyages, I did not fly out first class Alitalia because en route I managed to squeeze a magical trip to watch the grape harvest in Alsace.

This is the time of year when the prettiest villages of this Franco-German region are filled with raiders from across the German border. Milky, stomach-churning half-fermented grape juice is served by the jugful, with bowls of damp, new season's walnuts, on the flower-bedecked terraces above cobbled streets. Being able to to enjoy this treat as well as the Italian one meant an overnight train from Colmar to Chiasso, a bus to Milan, and then a taxi to Venice if you please. David Russell, who took over responsibility at Milan, didn't believe in trains.

I had last encountered Venice as a student armed with a guide to the city's cheapest *pensione.* This time I stayed at the Gritti Palace, dining on a terrace which seems almost to be floating on the Grand Canal. Also in the party was Charles Mozley, the leonine artist and illustrator whom David had persuaded to do some work for Bass Charrington's wine company Hedges & Butler in exchange, I suspect, for vast amounts of wine. His impressionistic pastels of the Bordeaux châteaux are now collectors' items and join all sorts of bargain bottles as purchases I wish I had made. Charles was mercurial, however, and although this trip was virtually fault-free, he needed cosseting and humoring. Indeed, David Russell made a specialty of humoring difficult characters such as Mozley, the Rothschilds of Mouton and Cyril Ray, an elegant and urbane writer whom he also cajoled into ornamenting Hedges & Butler's public face. Ray, a military historian and distinguished journalist for *The Sunday Times,* was an excitingly senior figure to an untrained newcomer like me. He wrote monographs on all sorts of wine producers and undertook commissions from wine retailers and wholesalers without a second thought. The mores of wine writing were subtly different then.

Another memorable Italian trip of the late 1970s was a Tuscan tour of Chianti Classico *castelli* and *fattorie* led by the region's British representative David Peppercorn and his new bride, Serena Sutcliffe, the first matrimonial union of Masters of Wine. The governing body of the Chianti Classico properties was a Consorzio that was tying itself in terrible linguistic knots trying to decide how its emblem should be described in English: black cock? cockerel? rooster? Gallo Nero? America's most powerful wine producer, Ernest Gallo, would prefer not. The Consorzio was housed in an elegant mansion on the outskirts of Florence with jumps in the garden for its director and his mounts.

This messing about with the highly qualified rubbed off. I learnt all sorts of useful things, such as that Steradent solution is one of the few things capable of cleaning the inside of a decanter; that in the previous growing season, miserable 1977, the Bordeaux growers had to spray their vineyards against rot up to seventeen times; that the Chianti Classico producers weren't terribly keen on the restriction and bureaucracy involved in the supposed glory of the DOCG wine denomination looming on the horizon; that the grand Florentine wine merchants Antinori were experimenting with an exotic import from Bordeaux, small French oak barriques (just as Cordier of Bordeaux were trying out larger barrels, according to Serena). It was all fascinating stuff for someone trying to soak up wine knowledge as fast as possible.

I took advice on which wines had shown best in Peppercorn and Sutcliffe's tastings of the infant 1976 vintage (much more generous, if faster maturing, than the 1975s) and ended up buying a case of fleshy La Lagune and rather dull Branaire-Ducru on my return to London, the first of many wine purchases *en primeur.*

On our last morning we were free to roam in Florence. I certainly ducked into the Duomo and marveled at its deep entrenchment in the heart of the city (so much more atmospheric now that it has been cleared of traffic), but rather than immerse myself in the Uffizi, I sought out an *enoteca,* one of the specialist wine shops that have since sprouted throughout Italy. I spent a happy hour in the Enoteca Internazionale de Rham (founded seven years previously by an early German enthusiast for Italian wine) examining bottles and wines I had previously encountered only in print: an exceptionally aromatic Gewürztraminer from the far northeast of Italy; the famous Biondi-Santi Brunello di Montalcino (the 1970 Riserva already 27,000 lire); Vin Ruspo, a pink Tuscan oddity from Carmignano. I carefully spent 7,000 lire on a bottle each of Bricco del Drago 1974, Carema 1971 and Vino Nobile di Montepulciano 1971 to take back to my embryonic wine cellar.

The places I inspected in *Wine & Spirit* days (including Hereford for cider, Normandy for calvados, Clerkenwell for gin and Warrington, a.k.a. Varrington, for Vladivar vodka) faithfully reflect the wines and spirits on the international marketplace of the time. Europe was the focus, although eastern Europe was virtually terra incognita. Germany was still important enough to swallow up a week at a time, notably the wine academy in the Cistercian monastery Kloster Eberbach in the woods above the Rhine where I was indoctrinated into the German way of wine alongside the American wine educator Harriet Lembeck. She brought along her husband, Bill, who made artificial limbs ("Bill never believed in God until he tried to create a knee"). Much time was spent in Oporto and up the Douro valley in port country and in Jerez (or more particularly in the pool of the Hotel de Jerez), center of what was then an extremely lucrative sherry business.

The sherry business was very much more confident then than the much smaller port business, even though much of the talk was about this crazy upstart José Maria Ruiz-Mateos whose wild borrowings and sherry/hotel/banking Rumasa group was completely upsetting the stately old order, building stocks and bodegas that would eventually prove the downfall of the local economy. Harveys Bristol Cream had been one of the great successes of the mid-twentieth-century wine trade, profits from exporting this sweet British blend having subsidized the wine education of a whole generation of gentlemen wine merchants such as Michael Broadbent. One of his fellow ex-Harveys Masters of Wine, Robin Don, accompanied me and others on a visit to inspect the wine industry of Catalonia in northeast Spain. Things were still relatively primitive here in the late 1970s. As we descended through dark and dust into a particularly rustic cellar my nostrils flared at a stingingly familiar smell. Robin Don saw my brow furrow as I tried to identify it. "Vin-e-gar," he whispered helpfully into my ear. Masters of Wine continue to educate, if not always to learn.

My most constant companions on the commercially inspired tours d'horizon which occupied so much of my time while at *Wine & Spirit* were two fellow hacks. My predecessor Tony Lord was one of them, enjoying his increasingly important role as editor (and part-time advertising salesman) of *Decanter*. As a guest Tony can only be described as Australian, or rather stereotypically Australian: boorish, demanding, rude and thoroughly badly behaved. His usual ploy was to criticize his hosts and their products nonstop while demanding vast quantities of what he really liked drinking: beer. In print, he was a lamb. A fine journalist, he would somehow pick up the story between glasses and could sit down at a moment's notice and regurgitate accurate, readable prose whose only fault was that it was too laudatory.

As *Decanter*'s reputation grew, so did Tony's demands. It must have become increasingly difficult for his hosts to weigh up the long-term publicity gains against the short-term assault on their tempers and drinks supply. Eventually Tony went back to his native Western Australia (where he now has his own vineyard) but in the late 1970s, however unlikely this seems to many of the younger wine writers who emerged during his last years in Britain, he still made an agreeable member of our trio of wine travelers. (Steven Spurrier tells the story of running on Clapham Common in the misty wastes of south London at seven o'clock one morning in the 1980s, when Tony had also, most uncharacteristically, taken up running. Out of the fog emerged Monsieur Lord running toward him on the same wide path. "Out of my fucking way, Spurrier," he grunted as he drew near. "Don't you know to stick to the left?" And with this typically brusque greeting, he disappeared into the early morning mist.)

My own approach, incidentally, has always been the opposite of Tony's, possibly less honest, and certainly more cowardly. As a visitor I try to be scrupulously polite, but in print I find myself being dispassionately objective, even sometimes to the point of brutality. I don't know where this comes from. It would be easy to blame the particularly acerbic, cynical national newspaper I was to work for later, but I have a horrible feeling that I have always written this way. I know that I try never to think about the effect of what I write on its subject until after I have written it. Perhaps this is all a reaction against the relatively indulgent school of wine writing that prevailed when I started out.

The third member of our trio was Pat Straker, a name less well known to wine consumers but one synonymous with the workings of the British wine trade through his editorship of the tame trade weekly, the other *Harper's*. For many of the old guard in the trade, something had happened only if it had been recorded in Pat's organ (usually word for word according to the press release). Pat's distinction is a nose that looks as though it has been glanced by a cricket ball, irrepressible good humor, much deeper knowledge of wine and the wine world than he ever suggests in print, and an impressive number of sons and stepsons. Pat, Tony and I were to spend hours and hours together, sitting in airports, somewhat gingerly inspecting vineyards, blinking our way through dank cellars and, the bane of any visiting drinks writer, inspecting bottling lines.

To a wine enthusiast one bottling line looks very much like another but in the late 1970s and early 1980s they often represented a producer's most substantial recent investment, so we were habitually required to worship at the altar of their speed and efficiency. To this day the whisper "bottling line" is enough to evoke a sort of freemasonry of shared suffering between drinks writers who on the whole just aren't interested by something as aridly mechanical. I was, much later, to discover another group of professionals who view bottling lines as the most interesting aspect by far of any winery, however: cameramen. The bottling line, after all, is one of its very few reliably moving parts.

We three spent so much time waiting in airports together in fact that my notebooks for the period are littered with pages of digits, the debris of a number-guessing game we used to play called Bulls and Cows (Bull was right digit, right place, Cow right digit, wrong place). Ah, life was simple then. Not that we didn't gossip—we did a lot of that—but we all had noncompeting roles. Tony was the consumer writer, representing what was then the only wine magazine in Britain. Pat was Mr. Trade Weekly and I was Ms. Trade Monthly. Today there are two consumer magazines and a host of scribes writing columns for competing national newspapers. For years the *WINE* versus *Decanter* rivalry soured relations among the writers, most of whom wrote for one or the other. (I have done neither, now I come to think of it, and was for long viewed with suspicion as a rival by *Decanter* on the basis of my monthly column for the American *Wine Spectator*.) We all breathed a huge sigh of relief when *Decanter* recruited someone from the *WINE* camp—and pretty soon vice versa—so that nowadays relations have become much more normalized.

Pat and Tony were my companions on my first long-haul wine trip, to South Africa in 1977 in the dark days of apartheid. In retrospect I was extremely naive. I simply wanted to see this extraordinary place for myself and it is a sign of how exceptionally apolitical my milieu was at that time, and perhaps how insignificant I felt, that I could not imagine that my visit might be construed as support. The excuse for the trip was the Nederburg auction, an annual garden party which continues to this day as a social distraction and a way of bolstering prices for the Cape's finest wines.

South Africa was fascinating—such a vivid clash of natural beauty and human brutality. I remember the casualness of a leather sjambok hanging on the back of a door in a handsome homestead with its shadowy black servants where we were entertained to a braai, an Afrikaaner barbecue. I remember the stunning scenery of the Cape, the elephant's-hide texture of the rocky mountains, the luminous purity of the white shacks against the tall eucalyptus trees, the picturesqueness of the barefoot black children and their mommas with their giant cans of water . . . Hang on, this wasn't picturesque, this was despicable. No running water! No shoes!

But these impressions followed our first night in South Africa (no direct flights allowed then; we reached Cape Town via Las Palmas, "Salisbury" and Johannesburg). We stayed next to the extraordinary flat-topped Table Mountain at the Mount Nelson Hotel which, even to someone used to the archaic British wine trade, seemed like a relic from the 1920s. I wandered around a carefully manicured rose garden, and saw a diminutive but incontrovertibly grand old lady go into a private room signaled "Lady X's Cocktail Party" wearing a long black dress, a short cape beaded with jet, and carrying an elegant cane.

The hotel management obviously mixed up our genders, taking Pat for female and me for a man, because Pat was greeted with a large bouquet of flowers in his room, while in mine was a bottle of the local sparkling *vonkelwyn* on ice with a couple of glasses. I must have been crazy but when a maid appeared, I invited her to have a glass with me. I've no idea what was going through my mind, but I know that she agreed immediately and within a minute we were sitting side by side on my bed, her telling me how she had to get up at four-thirty every morning to get in to work on time, and how she saw her children twice a year if she was lucky. I hope she didn't get into trouble. Especially since the management thought I was a white man.

South African whites in those days were as defensive as one would expect, virtually greeting you off the plane with statistics about how much more repressive certain other regimes were. Eastern Europe figured, I seem to remember. But then in their cups late at night they'd mutter, "Any chance of a job in London, do you think?"

The red wines were well and truly old-fashioned and, thanks to South Africa's enforced isolation, remained that way until very recently. Because South Africans themselves were hardly exposed to any non–South African wine, both winemakers and wine drinkers were happy with the status quo—which suited both parties perfectly well until South African wine producers needed to export. They were particularly proud of their crisp, fresh white wines at that stage. They'd had an influx of expertise from Germany (crazy when you consider how dissimilar their climates are) and reckoned they had now mastered how to make stable, appetizing whites.

This was a real breakthrough, made at various points during the

1970s and 1980s in all of the world's warmer wine regions, which rid the market of the sort of deep brownish, heavy-tasting, almost sherry-like white (and pink) wines that were the norm until an investment was made in enough refrigeration to keep grapes, juice and wine cool. Without the benefit of a man-made cooling plant or some particularly deep, cool cellar, grape juice tends to brown and start fermenting straightaway—especially when grapes, always picked in daylight in this premechanical era—often arrived at the cellar baked by the midday sun. Since fermentation generates its own heat, it was all too common for freshly picked grapes to become a hot, seething, uncontrolled mass of skins, juice and half-wine before the winemaker knew it. Lots of the more interesting flavors were literally boiled off and, provided the mixture didn't get so hot that the yeasts were stunned into torpor and the fermentation process came to an inconveniently sticky halt halfway through, the result was a dull, varnishy liquid without finesse or interest but often with some distinctly off-putting smell. All sorts of bacteria thrived in the world's warmer wine production centers.

Refrigeration plants such as those the South Africans were so proud of meant their winemakers could slow everything down. Giving them control over the temperature inside a tank (the next step on from simply trying to keep temperatures as low as possible, as some Bordeaux winemakers had done by simply throwing ice into the fermentation vat) put them in control of the process. Winemakers could now afford to drain juice off the grapes slowly, extracting a bit of character from the skins while running off the first, gentler "free-run" juice and keeping it separate from the more astringent juice that was physically squeezed, or pressed, out of the grapes. The cooler the fermentation, the slower it took place, and therefore the greater the chance of making a refreshing wine with enough acidity and fresh, fruity aromas, went the theory.

The recent history of wine style evolution is one of action and reaction. Because we were so delighted to find white wines we could actually describe as "crisp" (winespeak for an agreeable but not tart degree of acidity), it took us some years to realize that they didn't actually have much flavor or character. Certainly South Africa's most common grape, Chenin Blanc, the most usual candidate for this modern cool fermentation trick, was produced at such high yields that there was all too little flavor to preserve from the grapes and into the wine. Never mind. The South Africans regarded themselves as ahead of the pack back in the late 1970s, helped of course by the fact that the KWV, a sort of government wine division, kept such a tight grip on what went on in the industry. The Californians and Australians were technically ahead of them, but at that stage they were only just turning their attention to trying to export their new generation of crisp whites. To the winery visitor of the late 1970s, stainless steel with its assurance of temperature control was the sign of a modern establishment.

Old-fashioned white wines, or rather pale tawny wines, were still much more common then in Spain, Italy and much of France. Marqués de Cáceres, a modern white wine made in Rioja by Henri Forner (whose family also owned the largest château in the Médoc, Larose Trin-taudon) was so unusual in Spain in the late 1970s and well into the 1980s that it remained a rather anodyne model for the whole Spanish wine industry for years. (Chivite of Navarra grabbed the country's considerable favor for fresh, temperature-controlled pink, or rosado.) In the same way, dry whites made in the cool northeast of Italy, in Friuli on the border with Slovenia, were so refreshingly different from the tired old ferments that came from the south, that they have remained the Italian archetype, no matter how little fruit or flavor many of the modern reproductions have had.

The wonders of temperature control were hardly known in what was called Yugoslavia when I visited it as wine writer at large in the late 1970s. A group of us, writers and wine importers (a combustible mixture but one that could yield a wide range of totally unconnected background information to a trade reporter such as myself) were invited to spend eight days touring this already obviously fragmented country in the hope that our visit would eventually yield some nice hard currency. With six republics, two autonomous regions, three mainstream religions, three languages and two alphabets (Roman and the Cyrillic script I had picked up the bare bones of during an extended driving holiday through eastern Europe to the Soviet Union in 1970), it was clear that Tito must have represented some human form of Superglue. As if our destination weren't fractured enough, we had been invited by four different export organizations, all of whom were using our tour as a useful excuse to do some spying on the opposition within their own country.

The Yugoslavia of the late 1970s seemed strangely liberal and well provisioned compared to what I'd seen in Czechoslovakia, Hungary, Romania, Bulgaria and, especially, Russia and the Ukraine a few years earlier. When we landed in the south, the first of many indispensable interpreters wore Gucci shoes and a scarf very ostentatiously labeled Pierre Cardin. Our guide in the northeast of the country told us airily he was just off to Venice that weekend to do some shopping. Admittedly, they still used tractors to ferry luggage around Skopje airport, and vehicles could only be used on alternate weekends (according to whether their red-starred license plates ended with an odd or even digit), but there were none of the stark food shortages endemic in the rest of eastern Europe. In fact one of our fist meals, in Macedonia in the far south, was an embarrassingly copious feast. There spread out in the heat of an eastern Mediterranean midday among the roses were not only stacks of kebabs, piles of little meatballs, platters of feta with salad and mounds of strawberries and a giant trout from Lake Ohrid but the entire components of the two whole sheep which had been roasted on a spit outside. This included two sheep's heads, which of course yielded four supreme delicacies—sheep's eyeballs. Being the only woman of this particular party was not an unmitigated pleasure.

Outside, women in long gypsy skirts worked in the fields of what we were told were purple opium poppies. Our tour of the giant central Macedonian wine-processing plant (winery is too modern a word) had been followed by the all-important *degustatzi* in an immaculately decked out hospitality chamber. Typically for eastern Europe, there were ashtrays but no spittoons in this tasting room. Spitting is for wimps. I probably asked for a bucket. "Whites all unpleasant," I noted sternly. "Hot brownish color and hot, sweet smell. One Rizling was ok." They recommended we drink the local brandy with our first course of tzatziki, a soothing blend of yogurt and cucumber. With the feast that followed, the winery manager drank beer and his staff chose the local extremely sweet cream soda. We should have taken this as a sign— although later on we were to lunch to a guitarist singing a refrain which was translated to us as "He who doesn't drink wine should commit suicide."

The Yugoslavs ("very handsome" is another comment from my notebook; I still marvel at how much better looking are most men of these ethnic groups than the women) were basically trying to impress on us all that they had masses of delicious wine that the Germans and Japanese were importing in great quantity (sweetish red for the Amselfelder brand and Sauvignon Blanc respectively), and couldn't Britain try a bit harder in this respect? At this stage the dreaded Lutomer Riesling was just about all we imported from Yugoslavia, although the wine arm of the Courage brewers, represented on this trip by a charmingly indiscreet senior Master of Wine, were developing a rival called Cloberg Riesling, which has since died a well-deserved death.

The Yugoslav way of making white wine was to keep it for many months in large old wooden vats. We saw not a sign of the shiny stainless steel that was fast being installed in western wineries. They were still at the stage of being proud of their filtration machines rather than trying to downplay them (the machine in one winery was stamped "Gasquet Bordeaux—Pairs, London, Madrid, Alger, Oran"). One winery manager explained without shame how his wines were kept in outdoor tanks in the heat without any temperature control for months on end. In the coolest part of the country, however, near Maribor in inland Slovenia, it was already clear, tasting the wine fresh from a cask deep in a cool cellar, that there was the potential to make really fresh, sappy, exhilarating Sauvignon Blanc—just like the wines that sell for a fortune in Friuli and Styria over the borders with Italy and Austria respectively.

This being eastern Europe we had to be heavily organized in our "free" time too. One night we were whisked from our hotel, whose nightclub promised "Berlin Strip, Can Can, Arabian nights," to a "folklore supper" in a local wine cellar. Had this not been behind an admittedly flimsy Iron Curtain, I think most of us would have had enough experience to skip *this* experience but this was clearly not an ordinary outing. We had wine poured down us, snacks pressed down our gullets, all to the twang of local music, punctuated by children doing local folk dances and, as the evening wore on, we were moved on to the obligatory slivovitz and some noise and deliberate glass smashing. We felt very ethnic, very carried away. Then a rather bossy woman in black started to organize congas around the old wine vats, pressing the table napkins, which happened to be red, into our hands. Look, like this! she went, waving her red napkin in the air. As we dutifully copied her, a photographer whom none of us had noticed before went flash, flash, flash—and there we were, recorded forever, the party of western wine buyers so enthralled by socialism we were all waving the red flag.

I felt particularly awful the next day. Not just because of the industrial wine and industrial-strength slivovitz, but because none of us was in exactly top tasting form. The one region omitted from our tour was poor little Montenegro which produces a sturdy, concentrated red called Vranac which I have since recommended enthusiastically many times. Two men had come five hundred miles north to Slovenia from the "Enterprise 13 July" in Titograd just to watch us taste their wine. (One can only guess at the political background to this.) Unfortunately the Vranac was grafted on to the end of a big tasting of Slovenian wines and I fear the men from Titograd must have felt their journey was completely worthless (unless of course they managed to incorporate a night at the Berlin Strip into their visit).

The silliest wine trip I ever made was to Paris, a jaunt organized by IDV, the wine subsidiary of Grand Met, to mark the launch of a new range of very ordinary French wine called Les Grands Vignobles. This trip owed its existence to the old-fashioned belief that journalists will report something only if bribed to to do so by a notable meal. We were to fly to Paris for lunch, the connection being that these were French wines, right? The problem, however, was that this was French wine the inimitable International Distillers and Vintners way, i.e., bottled in a factory in Harlow, in the south of England. It was therefore necessary for us to fly to Paris accompanied by several dozen bottles of Les Not Very Grands Vignobles at all. Their weight and frangibility was inconvenient, but nothing compared with the difficulty of getting the wine through customs. The French find it quite impossible to imagine why anyone would want to import wine into their country. Close examination of French wine lists and wine shops confirms that most people who ever tried gave up eventually (although, mysteriously, trade figures show that France is the single biggest importer of Italian wine in the world). Certainly, the men at Charles de Gaulle were not impressed by IDV's publicity stunt which, I seem to remember, was to provide a photo opportunity involving these cases of wine being driven through Paris in some sort of open carriage. I may be wrong, but I think the bottles were eventually jettisoned in bonded limbo, empty boxes were photographed, and we all breathed a sigh of relief that we had an excuse to order something much more exciting to drink with our lunch in the brasserie at the Gare du Nord.

The silliest travel plan was an 8:35 A.M. flight to Turin (Barolo, Barbaresco) the morning after my thirtieth-birthday party in April 1980. I was living then in a beautiful Georgian house in Islington, house-sitting supposedly for my dear friend the German professor who was based in Freiburg and had introduced me to Mosel-sipping to music. New Zealander Johnnie Gordon (to whom my 1989 book *Vintage Timecharts* is dedicated) and the energetic friend yet to flower into the dauntingly successful novelist Rosie Thomas helped me get ready during the day. No hired caterers in those days, the eighties had hardly begun.

That evening the tall, narrow house strained at its fine-boned joints with people. My choice of wines for the evening was a telling barometer of the times: Jean Descombes's exceptionally meaty, concentrated 1976 Morgon (who drinks top cru Beaujolais nowadays?) already bottled by the canny Georges Duboeuf, and an Alsace Riesling from Trimbach (who, apart from me and Hugh Johnson drinks Riesling in any form at all?). So, with a high concentration of these two liquids still in my bloodstream, I found myself in Turin airport with chef David Chambers and many wicker baskets full of pudding basins and smoked salmon being sniffed appreciatively by the airport's tracker dogs. Chambers and colleagues were for some reason to cook a thoroughly British meal to accompany the fine wines of Piedmont—another, even more regrettable than the Grands Vignobles, case of coals to Newcastle.

I was busy, but not too busy to enjoy the odd moment of reflection. Had I really stumbled across a way of earning my living which involved spending a significant proportion of my time in some of the world's most beautiful countryside, in a position in which hospitable and often interesting people seemed keen to make me even happier by forcing delicious food and drink down me? There was perhaps nothing particularly novel about what I was fed in France; this was the sort of cooking that many British chefs aspired to then. Often the difference was merely that in France ingredients were much more carefully chosen and techniques applied with more confidence. It was on wine-foraging trips that I was introduced to cèpes. I also met black lampreys of Bordeaux and the irresistibly creamy richness of foie gras which my own liver seems finally to be rejecting at more or less the same time as public opinion.

Less refined but more fun was eating further south. Throughout Italy I continued to learn how very different from the real thing was the food served in Britain's Italian restaurants. And how the Italians have a real, and how thoroughly contemporary, respect for vegetables. In Rioja there were silvery slivers, the tiniest of baby eels, served hot and garlicky in individual terra-cotta dishes with a wooden fork because of their charge of electricity. Sherry country turned out to be full of my favorite foods. The only trouble was that they were all served before rather than during meals, themselves entirely superfluous. Coming from the quiet, cool north, where "dinner" and "tea" can be served so early that a fourth meal, a super-sweet carbohydrate infusion called "supper," is often routinely slotted in after the nine o'clock news, I have always found it supremely luxurious to eat meals late, which is part of the appeal of southern Spain.

In pre–European Community entry Andalucia, breakfast was never served before nine. The locals would rarely sit down to the lunch and dinner table before three and eleven respectively, but the tapas served beforehand made it unnecessary anyway. Visitors to the whitewashed cathedrals that were traditional sherry bodegas were told that if they didn't have one (copita of sherry) at eleven (A.M.), they'd have to have eleven at one. The midmorning sherry was usually an historic, dry tawny Amontillado or more usually even nuttier Oloroso with about as much resemblance to the cream sherry beloved by the Brits as to lemonade. Then sometime between one and three (and then again between seven or eight and eleven) the pale, dry appetite-revivers called Fino and Manzanilla would lubricate dish after dish of salty almonds warm from the pan, slivers of juicy crimson *jamón serrano* (surely no relation to the pink, rubbery, sodden slices called ham in England), fruity green olives, cubes of tortilla, and sweet, briny shellfish.

In Oporto, or Porto as the Portuguese call both their most famous
wine and the city it is matured and bottled in (a port), I had one of the
most educational experiences of my wine writing life. I was joining a
party of fifty-four people from the world's seventeen most enthusiastic
port-drinking countries to celebrate the three hundredth birthday of
port shippers Croft—or at least the three hundredth birthday of the
arrival in Portugal of its forebears. (Britain's trade wars with France in
the late seventeenth century meant that keen young merchants went to
seek their fortunes in northern Portugal then, resulting in the birth of
port as we know it and, in the late twentieth century, a flurry of
these Anglo-Portuguese tercentenary celebrations.) By this stage
the company belonged to my old friends Grand Met, then trying to fit
this ancient and in many respects primitive wine into its thoroughly
modern international marketing strategy ("the active brand will be the
winning brand," we were told by Ben Howkins, who has since sensibly
left the world of market shares and promotional budgets to look after
Lord Rothschild's more intuitively managed wine interests).

This was 1978, just four years after revolution in Portugal had
brought Croft's expansion plans to an abrupt if temporary halt. Wandering around the backstreets of Oporto I saw all sorts of reasons for
revolutionary fervor. As in South Africa I caught myself on the beginning of the thought loop that begins "bare-footed, bare-bottomed
urchins—how quaint." There were even adults who had to negotiate
Oporto's steep cobbles without shoes. Children begged, carrying plaster
statuettes of saints as a totem in streets only a puzzlingly unthrown
stone's throw from the Factory House, the eighteenth-century fortress
in which the port shippers still congregate, and which is still considered a part of British not Portuguese jurisdiction.

This was chastening stuff, and has perhaps informed all my subsequent visits to the port producers, even though European Community
entry has now transformed the standard of living of the average Portuguese (however uneasy the relationship between the foreign port
shippers and the native grape growers continues to be).

I was chastened professionally too. I arrived early one evening when
the rest of the party was on some expedition elsewhere and therefore
went in to the gloomy dining room of the Hotel Infanta de Sagres to
dine alone. I had been writing about wine for two and a half years now.
I had come top in my wine exams, the Diploma course run by the

Wine & Spirit Education Trust, so naturally I thought I knew it all. I spoke no Portuguese but navigated my way round the menu because there were some English translations (Oporto is, after all, so influenced by the English as to have its own cricket club). I was looking forward to studying the wine list, to learning more about Portuguese table wines. The wine list was quite long, but the more I studied it, the more I realized I understood only two words on it: "Branco" (white) and "Tinto" (red). There was clearly a great, unbroached divide between the sort of wines the Portuguese exported (Mateus rosé, Lancers and the odd Dão) and those they actually drank. Virtually all I could do was choose a color and a price and then leave it to chance. It dawned on me that this was presumably what most consumers have to resort to most of the time when confronted with a wine list. I happened to have spent many an hour in a wine classroom and poring over wine books. But that was my job. I realized how extraordinarily unfriendly most wine lists are and it was probably this experience which inspired me to try to come up with something a bit more useful when I became personally involved in restaurant management several years later.

I traveled frenetically in those days, as I had no one to read goodnight stories to back home, and I learnt an enormous amount, reveling in trying to dig out the trade story, the economic background, the commercial reality, rather than the rose-tinted version dished out to the consumer press. And one thing had the delightful habit of leading to another. It was only because of a weekend at Château Loudenne in the Médoc that I went to Australia in 1981, much earlier than most of my peers.

I was invited to Loudenne for a late summer's weekend in 1980 by the super-urbane Martin Bamford, the vinously acceptable face of Grand Met who cleverly persuaded the conglomerate to install him at Loudenne and establish what was virtually an English country house there, an outpost of a much more gracious life than most people in the British wine trade by then were experiencing back home. A man with a natural talent for hospitality in its nonplastic sense who died early and suddenly, he had assembled a most agreeable party, which included the Johnson-Hills, premature émigrés from Hong Kong who had just bought Château Méaume in the northern boondocks of the region. They were hard at work on the relatively common, but all too impossible, dream of turning it into a serious competitor to the classed growths of the cosseted Médoc. We were sitting on the terrace of the low, pink *chartreuse* overlooking the Gironde (which, funnily enough, looks less gray with a glass of champagne in one's hand), Union Jack flapping. The subject of Australia came up and I repeated my usual line about how I would love to go there but ideally without paying for the airfare. Oh, that's no problem, said the Johnson-Hills. The head of Cathay Pacific's a very good friend of ours. I'm sure he'd be delighted to fly you out there in exchange for writing an article or two for his in-flight magazine . . .

Similarly, I'm sure Willie Landels invited me to write for his glamorous *Harpers & Queen* magazine only because during our initial meeting he happened to ask me where I was going that weekend and the answer was Cap Ferrat. (He didn't know it was to sleep in a corner of the kitchen of an ancient, rambling summer house which had been in the family of some sensible but ungrand Luxembourg friends since you could buy a hectare of this bejeweled Riviera promontory for a few thousand francs.)

The *H&Q* connection, like the Australian trip, was to lead indirectly to pastures very new, but they belong to another era, the eighties.

My Very Own
Imprint

I have never had a career plan, and often wonder what would have happened if I had. Instead my working life has been entirely reactive rather than proactive. This is what happens if you embrace the grammar school ethic. People put hurdles in front of you and you obligingly try to lumber over them. Ambition may play a reflexive part but free will does not.

When I was working at *Wine & Spirit* in the late 1970s we had two American correspondents. One was a mustachioed young man with a newsletter about the corporate machinations of the drinks industry. He worked out that one good way of increasing his sales in Britain would be to feed us with a column written from a U.S. perspective, full of appetizing tidbits, with the subscription details of his newsletter at the bottom. It says something about my commercial naïveté that as editor of *W&S* I was prepared to offer this free ad for what was effectively a competitive publication. It said something about the commercial instincts of the young American that he had the nerve to propose this scheme. His name was Marvin Shanken and he has since gone on to transform the *Wine Spectator* from a two-color broadsheet into the world's glossiest and biggest circulation wine magazine. More of him later.

The other American columnist predated my arrival in Foubert's Place. John McCarthy was already established as a regular commentator on the American spirits scene and I was accustomed to panicking monthly that his column would not arrive in time. (We seemed to have so much space to fill on a very limited editorial budget, I don't think it ever occurred to me to reject a contribution.) McCarthy was an old hand, recently retired from the New York advertising business, confident enough to spot a trend but too autumnal to establish or act on one. Sometime early in 1977 he made a state visit to London and we finally had the chance to meet after many months' courteous correspondence. We had lunch together in one of the many slightly down at heel "Italian" restaurants which then populated Soho. He drank Scotch and soda; I had a half bottle of overproduced Valpolicella.

"You know what," he said, "we got these new things in the United States. Newsletters about wine. You ought to start one up here." At about this time a young Californian, Robert Finigan (who was to be married briefly to Marimar, the daughter of the winemaking Torres family of Catalonia), was causing a certain amount of stir with a monthly or bimonthly pamphlet recommending what and what not to buy on the American market. Finigan had started in the early 1970s, had been followed only a couple of years later by the *Connoisseurs' Guide to California Wine* and a host of flimsier but no less opinionated homespun publications. Normally I would have thought McCarthy's suggestion far too ambitious. After all, I had a full-time job, wine courses to take and an awful lot of travel and socializing to fit in. (I wasn't married then, so my social life and all the mate-hunting it involved was far more time-consuming.) But it so happened that it had just been proved to me that it *was* possible to slot another responsibility into my life, so I toyed with the idea of slotting in a second.

After only a year or so at *Wine & Spirit*, I'd been headhunted to take over editorship of *Wine Times*, a small wine quarterly, from Cyril Ray by one of the most underrecognized forces in the modern world of wine. Tony Laithwaite had been bitten by the wine bug in 1965 when he spent some time with a winemaking family in the outlying vineyards of Greater Saint-Émilion as part of his university course—geography at Durham. He came back home determined to try to make a living introducing the British to French wine with greater authenticity, made by real peasant farmers rather than industrial blenders.

He was not the first with this idea. As early as the 1950s Frank Schoonmaker had pioneered this in his selections of domaine bottled burgundy in particular for the American market. At about the same time Harry Waugh and Ronald Avery had also made strenuous efforts to circumvent conventional supply chains when importing French wine to their respective bases in Bristol. And Gerald Asher, now America's most elegant wine writer, was tussling with how to make money out of Asher, Storey, his ground-breaking importer of lesser-known country wines of France. (It has always amused me that the ragbag of not-bordeaux and not-burgundy, etc., is known as French Country Wine, or Regional France, as though the classic wines of France came instead from industrial estates or were interregional blends.)

Tony Laithwaite's connections were more modest to begin with. He literally drove a truckload of decent wine back home and virtually sold it door to door. He did pull off a masterstroke though. He contacted *The Sunday Times*'s most swashbuckling editor ever, Harry Evans, with the idea of a wine offer through the pages of that influential paper. Had Tony been a conventional pinstriper, he would almost certainly have been ignored, but the romance of his story appealed to Evans and Tony was soon introduced to the paper's wine correspondent, Hugh Johnson. Thus was born the Sunday Times Wine Club, which flourishes to this day alongside many parallel mail-order wine companies that form part of the extremely profitable Laithwaite empire. By steadfastly remaining a cherub-cheeked, slightly bemused ingenu on the fringes of the conventional wine trade, Laithwaite steadily became one of its few substantial beneficiaries.

Part of this process was establishing a series of bonhomous services and activities associated with the "club," helped enormously by the image, imagination and actions of its celebrated president, Hugh Johnson. To this day Hugh continues to dream up exciting schemes, typically involving potentially hazardous sea voyages. What Tony wanted to talk to me about, however, was the club's quarterly newsletter, a little black-and-white publication called *Wine Times*. Cyril Ray wanted to retire. Would I take it on? What was good enough for the grand old man of Albany (whom Edmund Penning-Rowsell met one day in St. James's Street carrying his shoes to Lobb's to be cleaned) was certainly good enough for me.

Arthur Lancaster, a delightful and experienced designer and printer of such things, was already in place. He would come to Duncan Terrace. I would hand Arthur a pile of contributions in various forms and some possible illustrations and, after a certain amount of proofreading, he would miraculously turn it into a publication.

The Sunday Times and Cyril Ray connections gave me the excuse to approach possible contributors of giddyingly high stature, for even then I had grasped that wine is often viewed as an infinitely more valuable currency than cash. The playwright Michael Frayn was a long shot, admittedly. He refused to play ball, as did Bernard Levin, but Levin replied so politely that his letter has remained a model for my own correspondence ever since.

As I got used to this second editorial role, it seemed to fit quite easily into my life alongside my day job on *Wine & Spirit*. Perhaps therefore I could also squeeze in writing and publishing a newsletter every month? I discussed it with David, the German professor's son, the one with whom I'd shared the seminal red burgundy, who was now a merchant banker between nine and five. He was ready for some weekend divertissement, something a little more interesting to talk about at parties than shuffling money round the world. He would help launch this modest new publication. So we agreed to invest a few hundred pounds each in designing a layout and printing the first few trial issues. If we got enough subscriptions we would carry on. An illustrator friend, Conny Jude (subsequently hired by *Decanter*), drew us a languorous champagne drinker to lie across the bottom right-hand corner of our front page, framed with stars. We also needed a title, and the one we chose was a sign of those liberated times: *Drinker's Digest*. We couldn't afford to advertise, so we decided we'd launch the *Digest* by simply sticking it through letterboxes ourselves in suitably well-heeled districts of London.

So it was that we spent several weekends in the fall of 1977 pounding pavements in Chelsea, Kensington and Islington. I suppose in view of the facetious title we'd chosen, I shouldn't have been so surprised when a lady in Highbury Fields, through whose door one of us had just pushed the first, complimentary issue, marched down the street to press it firmly back into my hand saying, "There's quite enough trouble in the world without *this* sort of thing, thank you very much."

It makes me feel exhausted now just to think of all this work on top of *Wine & Spirit* and *Wine Times*, not to mention the travel, but I must have had more energy then, and certainly fewer domestic calls on my time. The prose of *Drinker's Digest* and *Wine Times* is certainly breathlessly energetic. Just as I relished the lack of responsibility involved in my temporary jobs back in London after Provence, I made full and exuberant use of my junior status during my first years as a consumer wine writer. No one would take me very seriously, I felt, so I just wrote exactly what I thought, however flippant or iconoclastic.

The focus of *DD*, as we soon called it, was peculiarly British. The British continue to feel guilty about spending money on things to eat and drink. Unlike Americans who want a fast track to the best, at any price, what the British want most of all is a bargain. We therefore decided we'd trawl British wine retailers and draw readers' attention to the best buys. "Inside—150 bargain bottles," we promised on the cover of the first October 1977 issue, which includes a rave review of a new pocket book from Hugh Johnson ("£2.95—£2 to *Drinker's Digest* subscribers"), a gloomy report on the recent 1977 grape harvest in Europe, the start of an alphabetical guide to Weirder Wines (Argentina, Australia and Austria). "Do you ever buy at Oddbins?," we asked in our accompanying flyer. "We hope so because they have many good bargains. And some not so good . . . like Château Fourcas-Hosten 1966 at £4.19. We tell you where to buy it at £2.56," etc., etc. In the champagne section we showed where you could find Moët & Chandon NV for around $6 and, an even greater bargain, Dom Pérignon 1969 at less than $14 (this last at Steven Spurrier's Caves de la Madeleine in Fulham whose specialty, he later admitted, was losing rather than making money). Under the Table Wine heading we alluded only to the price, about $1.50 a bottle, and sensibly steered clear of making any qualitative claims about a Spanish wine on sale at Barretts Liquormart by the name of El Bullox.

Amazingly, this extremely amateur publication managed to find a market. Subscribers seemed to be literate and to enjoy joining in the bargain hunting. One of our first letters came from the novelist Sybille Bedford of Chelsea, who seemed to understand exactly what we were up to. Neville Abraham, a London Business School graduate who is now one of London's most influential restaurateurs but at that stage had not yet realized how difficult it was to make financial sense of the wine business, wrote remonstrating that we seemed to care too much about price and not enough about quality. Clearly he had a point. There was a limit to the entertainment value of a monthly list of wine names with stockists and prices. We needed a monthly theme and even, a revolutionary concept at the time, a comparative tasting.

It is now taken for granted that much of the content of wine magazines and newsletters is based on blind assessments of individual wines that are related in some way, but this is a distinctly late-twentieth-century concept. *Decanter*, the only other regular publication for British wine drinkers in the late 1970s and early 1980s, was made up of sedate articles, profiles and vintage assessments rather than anything as vulgar as a comparison of variations on a theme. (It was still widely held that it was impolite at best and improper at worst to criticize any particular wine, producer or, closer to home, importer. The British wine trade was still a fairly cozy little clique.)

By the fourth issue, the upstart and extremely skeletal editorial team at *DD* was starting to get into its stride, with a timorous but detailed look at burgundies available, incredible as it now seems, under $6.50 a bottle. Christopher Fielden was recruited in his capacity as author of a book on Burgundy to keep my tastebuds on the straight and narrow, and we ended up carefully distinguishing between wines that managed to be both attractive and authentic, pleasant but apparently fake wines (some London bottlings from the most reputable merchants provoked considerable incredulity), and wines that could not be recommended. "Very much a British-style burgundy" was the ominous tasting note on Berry Brothers' Chambolle-Musigny 1972. The difference essentially was between relatively pale, sprightly, fruity wines that genuinely had been made from grapes grown as far north as Burgundy, and deep, soupy, more alcoholic blends that almost certainly incorporated some Rhône if not Algerian red. (The great Auguste Clape of Cornas regularly shipped some of his wonderfully beefy and thoroughly unBurgundian wine north to one of Beaune's négociants, according to Remington Norman's book *Rhône Renaissance*.)

The next issue of *Drinker's Digest*, dated February 1978, marked a turning point. The ten wines treated to a full description were drawn from a tasting of fifty bottles from Spain, then considered a thoroughly exotic provenance for any wine weaker than sherry. First under the inelegant heading "Names to Look Out For," was a strange new wine region called Rioja, complete with pronunciation guide ("a bit like a Scot would say Ree-ocher"). Rosi and Anthony Hanson, billed as "one of the 99 distinguished members of the Institute of Masters of Wine," helped us taste these wines and the tasting marked a coup for this tiny scrap of a publication. Subscriptions were still at such a low level that every time I went to pick up the mail from the local post office in Islington, my heart would beat faster if I saw it needed an elastic band to keep the envelopes together. The marketing of *DD* needed a shot in the arm.

Michael Bateman, editor of the then famous "Lifespan" section of the *Sunday Times* magazine (in the late 1970s still distinguished as a *color* magazine), provided it. Our taste test was just the thing this rampant organ of consumerism was looking for. The results of *DD*'s Spanish wine tasting appeared in full color on page 26 of the *Sunday Times* magazine, giving the nascent newsletter some much-needed publicity. Subscriptions edged up steadily, which made the monthly midnight drops of untidy text to a small printer near Pentonville prison feel more worthwhile. We must have done some hard work sending out free copies to the press because by the time the annual subscription was $8.80 a year, we could quote praise from writers in the *Observer*, the *Times*, the *Guardian*, *Time Out* and *Good Housekeeping*, most of whom obligingly said that you could save the subscription on one or two shopping trips.

The next entry in my first cuttings book after the Spanish page in the *Sunday Times* magazine is a yellowing copy of an article in the *Guardian* headed "Bouquets and a nose for news." Alongside it is a photograph that looks like a heavily inflated rubber model of me (fewer wrinkles and hamster cheeks, the result of all those lunches and dinners). This was the short profile instigated by John Arlott, the *Guardian*'s wine and cricket master. He'd suggested to one of their feature writers that I'd make a suitable subject for the paper's famous Women's page—young(ish) woman doing a man's job and all that. The article made me sound much more important than I really was, infuriated my father by repeating my allegation that he hadn't brought me up to drink wine, but did paint an accurate portrait of my general philosophy of wine: that it should provide as much pleasure for as many people at as low a cost as possible.

As a direct result of this I received a letter from a book packager who said he wanted to produce an introduction to wine and that I sounded like just the sort of person to write it. I worked on a synopsis, sent it to him, only to have it returned with the comment that he now realized his publishers had a moral objection to books about alcohol. I have a pathological hatred of wasting effort, reinforced by the years of trying to fill *Wine & Spirit* on a shoestring. If I hadn't spent some time on that synopsis, I would never have dreamt of inching toward hard covers (as Pamela Vandyke Price had so incredibly said I would). But my maths teacher's smug refrain "Mathematicians are economical of effort" keeps coming back to haunt me. I asked a publisher friend, Helen Fraser, then nonfiction editor of the Fontana imprint for Collins, what I should do with my synopsis. She told me I needed an agent and introduced me to a charming, claret-loving contemporary, Caradoc King, who had recently jumped ship at Penguin to join A. P. Watt, the world's oldest literary agency.

Caradoc and I met in one of the wine bars then proliferating in London and began what has been a very happy friendship and, I suppose I have reluctantly to call it, business association. I have always felt that he slightly disapproves of my libertarian approach to wine provenance. He has been nagging me to write a definitive book on bordeaux for two decades now and I serve him non-French wine only gingerly. But he has always been enthusiastic about any wine book project and this meager outline for a wine primer was no exception. He took my synopsis and ended up selling it—to Helen, for an advance of £1,000 (about $1,600), I seem to recall, thereby clearing £100 for introducing me to the person who had introduced him to me in the first place.

The Wine Book was launched in October 1979. I wrote most of it over the 1978 Christmas holidays in Cumberland and adopted two authorial bad habits that have stayed with me ever since: cutting deadlines dangerously fine and carelessness over, or rather an inability to feel responsible for, maps. I love poring over good, proper, cartographically precise maps, but absolutely hate designing or proofreading maps in my own books. Debbie Jarvis, who has since extremely confusingly adopted her food-writer pseudonym Elizabeth Kent, was the book's energetic publicist. We organized a blind tasting for women's magazine journalists, comparing a well-known wine with one that I suggested was a less expensive, better alternative. She somehow managed to persuade papers as diverse as the *Telegraph* and the *Daily Mirror* to write about the book.

I'm surprised this slim introduction to wine received as much attention as it did. What strikes me now when I read it, and old copies of *DD*, is the amazing confidence with which I wrote then. The less you know, of course, the smaller the boundary with your ignorance. Over the succeeding years as I have learnt more and more about my chosen subject, I have become increasingly aware of exceptions to every rule, and of how much I don't know. I have also met more and more people who know more than I do about a particular area of wine knowledge. It fair knocks the wind out of your sails, and the youthful arrogance— one might almost say quintessential Sunday *Times*ness—out of your prose.

The launch proper of my impudent *Wine Book* was at the Chelsea Arts Club. It was notable for an unexpected cameo appearance by Reginald Bosanquet, famously bibulous newsreader (whose entirely fictional romance with fellow newsreader Anna Ford was then being chronicled in *Private Eye*), and for John Arlott's appearance, which at one fell swoop disillusioned my friend Johnnie Gordon who had spent so much of his New Zealand youth listening to his cricket commentaries. I think he rather unfairly expected him to look ready for the crease himself. The sensation of seeing and cradling a book one has written is supposed to be deeply moving. I can't remember being very moved, probably because I was too busy worrying about what I would put in the next *Wine & Spirit*, *Wine Times* and *Drinker's Digest*. I was almost certainly spreading myself, or rather my meagre grasp of wine news and opinion, far too thinly even then. And worse was to come in the 1980s, a decade of driving in too high a gear.

Casting
Adrift

———

Two meetings in late May and early July of 1980 were to change my working life. But during the month of June between them I managed to cram in a fair amount of play. There were activities that spanned both work and play, such as a committee meeting for a quaint-sounding quasi-social outfit called the Under 40 Wine Trade Club (which has since dropped the first two words of its name with the inevitable aging of its members) and meeting for the first time Oz Clarke, an actor beginning to dabble in wine. (I asked him to guest-edit an issue of *Drinker's Digest*. His jokes about Bulgaria drew a swift but unamused response from ex-communist Edmund Penning-Rowsell who was by then the newsletter's "consultant.")

It was at this time too that I met someone who could have played an even greater role in transforming and normalizing the average Briton's relationship with wine—James Rogers. James was slightly older than me and had been born into a family, archetypal members of the Surrey haute bourgeoisie, which owned a chain of licensed grocers called Cullens. He'd been exposed to accountancy, but it ill suited his lateral creativity. He joined the family firm in 1971 and soon afterwards discovered a wine, a Viña Ardanza 1964 rioja which convinced him of something that his contemporaries then found heretical: that good wine could be found outside Bordeaux and Burgundy. James, typically, got to it first, but eventually we all made the rioja discovery (as *DD* subscribers were encouraged to seven years later).

If there was one wine that broke France's hegemony as far as British wine drinkers were concerned it was—nothing to do with the New World—red rioja. The wines on sale in the mid to late 1970s, those made in Rioja in the 1960s and early 1970s, offered an enormous amount of mature, sweet, oaky pleasure—at prices that compared extremely favorably with the rather mean petits châteaux clarets that had been the British red wine drinker's basic fare. It may have been Rioja's history, as a sort of refuge for Bordeaux wine producers fleeing French viticulture's phylloxera crisis in the late nineteenth century, that soothed some of the traditionalists and made the region seem less foreign. Whatever the reasons, we all wallowed in rioja until the early 1980s when the producers dramatically raised prices and cut corners so that too much of the stuff suddenly tasted thin and horrid.

This was to pose no difficulty for James Rogers, who had gone on discovering further proof that the wine world extended beyond France, Oporto and Jerez—always tasting wines blind and trying to put a price on them so that he could never be swayed by label and reputation. By the time I met him, Cullens was one of the most interesting places to buy wine in the country. He operated out of a dusty corner of the firm's warehouses in the London suburbs and that day showed me a range of wines, blind of course, from places as truly exotic then as California, Austria, Chile, Portugal and, his big new find, a wine labeled Cabernet Sauvignon from Bulgaria. (This last, served in an anonymous claret decanter as recommended, was the current hit with Cullens' solid, middle-class wine-drinking customers. Tony Laithwaite discovered Bulgaria's bargains at more or less the same time.) James's distinction in his relations with the wine press was that rather than pushing wines at you, in the way of most wine merchants, he gave you the feeling that you were discovering them together. When the family firm was sold five years later, he became a trail-blazing wine educator.

Also in June 1980 was a memorable weekend, a weekend that transformed my associations with Southwold on the Suffolk coast from teenage romance and stale ale (our cottage was next to a pub) to full-blown wine passion. When I discussed this shared experience recently with Liz Morcom, a contemporary in the wine trade with whom I spent many a tasting and drinking hour in the late 1970s, she reminded me how very different the pace of our lives was then. We both had to take off work all of Friday for the Southwold jaunt.

She also reminded me of a lunch designed around her birth year, 1953, which I'd given at Duncan Terrace earlier in 1980 for her birthday to which at least eight of us devoted most of a weekday without a second thought, or any obvious disapproval from our employers. We each brought bottled contributions, including a golden honey-and-lemon Laville-Haut-Brion from my birth year, 1950, a restrained Pape-Clément 1961, Domaine de Chevalier 1953 (very correct) and a Cheval Blanc 1953, which was unfortunately waning, bottled by Liz's then employers British Transport Hotels, a sweetly meaty 1953 Aloxe-Corton, and a 1952 Grands Échezeaux from Domaine de la Romanée-Conti that was in even better shape, with the most amazing power. But the best wine of the lot was a tawny sweet Forster Jesuitengarten 1953, proving that, yes, Riesling is the greatest white wine grape in the world, a proposition I continue to disseminate to this day.

This sunny Friday three months later Liz and I were driven out to Suffolk in an unbelievably grand chauffeur-driven car with Sheldon Graner, the man who started Majestic Wine Warehouses and now drives a minicab, Clive Coates (then Liz's boss), and a member of one of London's most successful brewing families. (This, by the way, was much the same tasting group as had devoted a day in February of that year to a vertical tasting of Château Pétrus at the Curzon House Club that took us back through every single vintage from 1973 to 1952, and then included the four greatest vintages of the 1940s and an over-the-top 1926! This bounty fully deserves an exclamation mark.)

It seemed to take forever in those premotorway days but we had wine gossip and some extremely good champagne to keep us amused en route. A comparative tasting of 1976 red bordeaux had been organized by Simon Loftus, wine buyer for Adnams, Southwold's brewer, wine merchant and main employer. We tasted in the whitewashed parlor of his house by the Blythburgh marshes, atmospheric enough to be used subsequently as setting for a Peter Greenaway film. Clive was teased, not for the first time, for his refusal to taste blind. Simon, with his precocious gold earring, gypsy eyes, keen brain and devastating lack of tact, is still one of the British wine trade's greatest assets, and most generous hosts. He, Sheldon and others had been plotting this event for some time. The "work," and *much* discussion, was over by about two. (There was some argument about the relative merits of Lafite and Latour, so we retasted the same bottles, recorked, the next day and Latour, as usual, coped most manfully with this brutal treatment.) I thought I detected "a touch of H_2S" on the Lagune 1976— how could this be when I had not yet visited Australia where every wine taster seems to have this stinky sulphide compound up his nose?

We then went on to a restaurant nearby for one of the most extraordinary lunches of my life, to the gentle play of a fountain in a walled garden, an enclave of hedonism in the pretty market town of Halesworth. The staff must have cursed our late arrival, I realize with hindsight, but it was magical. Soup is the perfect antidote to wine tasting whatever the weather because it dilutes the alcohol stream a bit. Bassett's thoughtfully served us chilled mint and cucumber soup and warm bread with our golden Château Sénéjac 1934, a slightly dried out old white bordeaux but one whose perfume had something of the richness of my beloved Laville-Haut-Brion. An almost treacly sweet, intensely fruity Haut-Brion Blanc 1968 washed down a daring galantine of duck, including pistachios, tarragon and even kiwi fruit. Stuffed pike with sauce verte stood up sturdily to Vidal Fleury's still-lively 1976 Condrieu as we stuffed ourselves, and at this point we hadn't even got to the serious wines. And they were very serious indeed, the most famous being the Cheval Blanc 1947, a legend of a red bordeaux, to which everyone had been looking forward all morning.

But do you know what? The wine at this lunch could have been Beaujolais. In fact it probably should have been Beaujolais. A lighter, simpler, more directly fragrant, more refreshing wine would have been much more the thing for drinking out of doors on a hot sunny day than this revered, complicated, intensely rich relic (which I have been lucky enough to be able to swoon over, indoors, three or four times). This mismatch between great wine and the great outdoors is a most regrettable fact of life to someone like me, brought up to cherish every ray of sunlight, and to believe that there is hardly any pleasure greater than eating out of doors. The answer I am working toward, with much pleasurable trial and frequent error, is never to eat and drink in direct sunlight, and to be hawklike over a red wine's temperature, carefully keeping the bottle in something that keeps it from heating up. And, of course, you have to pour sparingly and drink quite quickly. The Cheval Blanc '47 was served alongside Pétrus '47, another trophy wine that, in château-bottled form, is at least as rich but not quite so fine; if anything it showed rather better in these less-than-ideal tasting conditions.

But what the heck, we had the lunch of a lifetime. A monstrously magnificent Château Latour 1949, a red with enough stuffing to stay in the glass even out of doors, following the lamb with the cheese before a vivaciously sweet little thing from the Loire came to wake us all up. About this Quarts de Chaume 1961 I wrote "honeyed acidity—makes you feel sprightly not sickly." The Tokay Essencia 1934, the most amazing toffee-like syrup from pre-communist Hungary, managed an extraordinary whiff of gunpowder before something I described as a "swift farewell." Just as well too, I should think.

I stayed that weekend with Simon and his wife, Irène (this must have been before their dauntingly talented daughter Hana was born). I spent Saturday reveling in nostalgia and rooting about in Southwold's unparalleled universe of small specialist shops beneath the lighthouse, and Sunday testing out the theory that Bollinger went with new English strawberries. Weekends like this I might callously classify as having something to do with work, but I see that in the month-long interval between my two seminal meetings I also managed to squeeze in considerable play: Glyndebourne's *Falstaff*, something called the Rose Ball, two sessions at the Notre Dame rock and roll dance hall by Leicester Square, a concert in Blackheath, dinner at the Garrick with dentist–cum–wine merchant Robin Yapp, a radio appearance on the *Food Programme*, a wedding, a party, a (week) day at Wimbledon not watching tennis in the rain, a Joan Armatrading concert, a performance of *The Tempest*, a particularly long lunch at a restaurant in deepest Kent with the chief inspector of the *Good Food Guide* and thirteen dinner engagements. No wonder I used to try to rewind the day's events and play them back before falling asleep each night.

The important meeting that took place just before this particularly hectic June was with the publisher of the *Good Food Guide*, the man charged with the printed output of the powerful Consumers' Association whose most famous publication *Which?* would submit everything from washing machines to socks to the most rigorous testing and comparative analysis. He wanted to launch a liquid version of the annual *Good Food Guide*, provisionally and somewhat cumbersomely called the *Which? Wine Guide*. Would I be interested in editing it? I think that was the impetus for the meeting, but the upshot within the next few weeks was that I agreed to edit the *Guide* and Consumers' Association, the august voice of intelligent, middle-class Britain, agreed to buy *Drinker's Digest*. This gave me far more satisfaction than seeing my name on the cover of a book. What thrilled me was that we had created something entirely without parallel from nothing, which a body as authoritative and value-conscious as Consumers' Association thought was worth paying for. I think the agreed-upon sum was £2,000 ($3,200)—hardly a fortune—but meaty enough then to provide consolation to someone who could see a long chain of responsibility and possible debts stretching into the future. One thing CA would have none of was the title, however. It was promptly changed to *Which? Wine Monthly*, a wine newsletter they continued to publish, ad-free as at its inception, for more than fifteen years.

I had, unknowingly, been tested out for suitability as a Consumers' Association employee a few months previously when the editor and chief inspector of the *Good Food Guide*, Christopher Driver and Aileen Hall respectively, invited me out to lunch at San Frediano on the Fulham Road. Nowadays, for reasons that will become clear, I take eating out with a restaurant critic for granted, but in those days I was fascinated to see what effect the particularly recognizable features of someone as gastronomically powerful as Christopher Driver would have on a waiter. The answer in this case was the most revolting display of fawning and flattery—including bringing out the bottle of olive oil from the kitchen to demonstrate that, yes, it really was virginal—all aimed exclusively at Christopher, even down to slopping coffee into all our saucers but wiping up only his. In the early days my newsletter copy was read by this distinguished upholder of good English. One penciled comment in the margin read: "the most inventive spelling of 'idiosyncrasy' I have ever come across."

My next fateful meeting, in July 1980, was to provide me with the time to prepare this new annual 400-page wine guide from scratch. I'd had wind of the fact that *The Sunday Times* was looking for a wine correspondent. So when Harry Evans's henchman Brian MacArthur invited me out to lunch, I had a good idea why. Besides, over the years since my very first little story in the paper about Domaine Chandon in 1976, I had regularly written for the paper as a freelance.

We met at a geographically convenient French restaurant by Gray's Inn. I remember thinking that my choice of wine was critical: it had to taste good but show some individual flair. I'd been partying the night before and would have been quite happy with water, but I chose a red Loire, a Chinon, which is still a favorite for its silky texture, reviving smell of pencil shavings and refreshing raspberry fruit. It did the trick (helped apparently by a behind-the-scenes recommendation from Hugh Johnson, the previous incumbent). By August I was able to hand in my notice to Mr. Heseltine, hand over editorship of *Wine & Spirit* to Kathryn McWhirter, and begin the supposedly blissfully liberated life of the self-employed.

My brief was a strange one. The paper had no regular wine column; I was paid a retainer and my job was to persuade the paper's notoriously powerful space barons to print my articles wherever they seemed most appropriate. Most of them liked to drink, but they also liked to bully. The best story in their view was the one that involved maximum suffering and inconvenience for the journalist. There was no point in being a baron unless there were some obvious serfs.

Michael Bateman, now food editor of the *Independent on Sunday*, was an exception. He was an extremely good editor, unerringly spotted my most careless contributions, and had inordinate enthusiasm for wine and food coverage. Bateman's problem was my congenital lack of confidence. Bolstered by *The Sunday Times*'s giant circulation and unlimited funds (this was the pre-Murdoch era) he would paint a grand picture of, say, an international wine competition in which we'd pit the first growths against the best of Italy. I couldn't possibly do something as daring as that, I'd say, giving him instead a myopic little diatribe about the evils of British sherry.

And then soon there was to be the problem of my time. The whirligig of the 1980s may have been exciting for me but must have been extremely frustrating for my increasingly numerous employers.

A New World
of Wine

There is no reason why life should divide itself neatly into decades, but the first year of the 1980s did herald a quite distinctly new phase, not only in my own life but also in wine.

In the wake of the well-publicized California versus France taste-off in Paris in 1976, California wine producers were on a roll. No cap-in-hand hopeful exporters they, but a well-funded, energetic, cohesive, thoroughly modern wine industry producing elegantly labeled bottles which, if we were lucky, we might just get our hands on. I had spent some time in California in 1979 researching a long article for the *Sunday Times* magazine about the state's emergence as a fine wine producer. While there I had stumbled across the news that Robert Mondavi and Baron Philippe de Rothschild of Mouton were to undertake a joint venture, to make a California wine of matchless price and, they hoped, repute. This was the next significant achievement for California, after the Paris tasting, the first time such a transatlantic alliance had been forged—and a dazzling feather in Mondavi's cap.

There had been a flurry of California tastings in London in 1978 and 1979, but inflation and the relatively weak dollar of the very early eighties helped, too. Suddenly California wine looked not just appetizing but affordable. The golden allure of the West Coast began to attract interest from a new breed of potential wine importers, most notably a handsome, well-connected young man named Geoffrey Roberts.

What was significant about Geoffrey's interest in these New World wines was his background. An impeccably mannered Old Etonian quartered in Chelsea, he'd trained as a lawyer but found the law too arid. He already had an appreciation, indeed cellarful, of the classic wines of France but was genuinely impressed by the quality of wine being made in California. He made sure he was well established in the grandest wine trade circles, helped considerably by the sums his friend Christopher Selmes was spending on wine in the auction rooms and, presumably, investing in Geoffrey's nascent California wine importing business.

By 1979 Roberts had managed to have himself appointed U.K. agent for that most dynamic of Napa Valley wine producers, Robert Mondavi, who came to London to lecture a few of us wine writers (for the first but by no means the last time) on his determination "to fill the gap left by the price increases of classic wines." He told us, "It takes time to get people to accept that we can be up to that top level." But over the next decade this robustly ambitious Californian, the strongest and most positive force I have ever encountered in the world of wine, regularly turned up in London to trumpet his latest vintage, thereby running down the three previous ones which Geoffrey still had to sell.

On March 20, 1980, Mr. Geoffrey Roberts requested the pleasure of our company at the Tallow Chandlers Hall for his first comprehensive trade tasting of wines from the likes of Joseph Phelps, Heitz, Chateau Montelena, Chalone, Chateau St. Jean, Mayacamas and, yes, Mondavi. Hugh Johnson, both auctioneers (Michael Broadbent and at that time Pat Grubb of Christie's and Sotheby's respectively) and all the great and the good of the wine trade and press were there, as well as a bevy of beautiful young men in very well cut suits to do the pouring. What did we all make of these wines?

We found the Chardonnays a bit facile and sweet (a few of them were veering toward excessive oakiness even at this early stage) but this nation of claret lovers could hardly fail to see the exciting potential in the reds, however tannic some of them seemed. I was particularly impressed by Mondavi's Cabernet Sauvignon Reserve 1974 ("absolute essence of Cabernet," I wrote enthusiastically), Chalone 1978 Chardonnay ("much richer, fatter and more characterful than the Chards so far") and another 1974 Cabernet, from Mount Eden "individual but v g").

Serena Sutcliffe, David Peppercorn and I had been entertained the night before chez Selmes in his eighteenth-century house on Cheyne Walk. Anders Ousback, the Australian who has since gone on to glittering careers in both restaurateuring and ceramics, was in charge of the distinctly superior things we ate and drank.

Geoffrey may have been the most successful passenger on the California wine wagon but he was by no means the only one. Wine merchants were signing up agencies all over the West Coast. Willie Lebus and John Walter opened a smart little Wine Studio in Belgravia and welcomed producers of the caliber of Dick Graff of Chalone. We Brits were flattered that these California producers seemed to think it was important to export to us (presumably they realized there was not a chance of persuading the French to take California wine seriously, so a thirsty nation with no wine industry of its own and a shared language was the obvious bridgehead in Europe, the home of wine). At the industrial end of things Grand Met was importing vast quantities of cheap blends under the Almaden label. Seagram was in the process of signing up Orson Welles to do a series of TV ads for the Paul Masson carafes it had aimed in profusion at Britain. And many of us were already drooling over an ultraclean, grapey sweet wine in a convenient screwtop bottle, Christian Brothers Chateau La Salle.

All this enthusiasm needed a focus. An American, Paul Henderson, had retired from McKinseys, the management consultants, and decided with his wife, Kay, to open a luxurious country house hotel in Devon, Gidleigh Park, in 1978. He was very keen on California wine, and frustrated by how difficult it was to find good examples in Britain. So thrilled was he by the prospect of specialist importer Geoffrey Roberts that he bought practically half of his first shipment (and still has about a dozen Cabernets from the early 1970s on the list at Gidleigh to prove it).

Later that year the Hendersons, the Averys, Hugh and Judy Johnson and Johnny Apple of the *New York Times* and his effervescent wife,

Betsey, met at the house of Harry Waugh, the grand old man of the British wine trade who had directed Harveys of Bristol in its heyday and was California wine's earliest supporter in Britain. They decided to form a club to focus attention on this exciting extension of the fine wine world and named it after California's very own grape. Paul Henderson was the first secretary of the Zinfandel Club, and in February 1979 organized a dinner at the Garrick at which BV Georges de Latour 1970 and Heitz 1968 Cabernet Sauvignon were the stars. Later that year he ran a Chardonnay fest attended by Robert Mondavi at Joseph Berkmann's restaurant in King Street. I went along to both of these dinners with great pleasure, partly in my Californian manqué persona. California still felt like my second home.

I did not need much persuasion therefore to take over from Paul as secretary to the Zinfandel Club. One of my first jobs (after another Garrick dinner at which a mystery Zinfandel was served—a 1978 from Cape Mentelle in Western Australia, an early offering from the man who was to dream up Cloudy Bay Sauvignon Blanc, New Zealand's flagship wine) was to organize a giant California wine tasting on November 24, 1980, in the bowels of the American embassy in Grosvenor Square. We had thirty-six wines, which I see I put in a very strange tasting order, with reds first and the dryish Gewürztraminers between the sweet Rieslings and a Late Harvest Zinfandel (then all the rage), a California "port" and, finally, some sparkling Domaine Chandon imported specially.

These wines were drawn from thirteen active California wine importers, including one that was new to me, K & L Associates. I met the L that night, a young man called Nick Lander who told me he was refurbishing a large old restaurant in Soho called L'Escargot and was about to open it as a specialist in American wines. He was also about to become, as he has complained many a time since, Mr. Jancis Robinson.

The gearing up that was the eighties began here: the ridiculous concentration of events, emotions, duties and devotions. By December 19 when Nick flew off to spend Christmas in Hong Kong and I sped north over Shap Fell to the usual family Christmas in Cumbria, we'd agreed that I would fly to California early in the New Year to join him on a wine-buying trip for the restaurant.

There is something magical to the British about the sun shining somewhere in January, even if the vineyards of the Napa Valley would be wreathed in early morning mists. We even managed to swim out of doors in a pastiche Hotel California setting, the San Jose Hyatt, site of our romantic transoceanic tryst. It nearly went disastrously wrong when they kept us in two separate rooms for the first five hours, not telling either of us that the other had arrived. We overcame this early setback, however, and bought not only such California wines as were left after so many other British importers had gone a'trawling, but also some fine Pinot Noir from Oregon, Riesling from Washington, and even Sainte Chapelle's full-blown Chardonnay from Idaho. Nick also found himself forced into recruiting staff on this trip. Robert and Claudia Hardy, a young couple who had been working at the Wine Country Inn where we'd stayed in the Napa Valley, pursued us right to our departure gate at San Francisco airport protesting their keenness to work in a "wine bar" in London. Nick, who became known as a famously generous employer, promised to try to get permits for them to work as sommelier and greeter.

Suddenly taking this two-week absence from my desk constituted extreme impetuosity on my part, although I had to pay for all that pleasure with some particularly hectic days on my return. On the second night after our return we somehow found the energy to have the Zinfandel Club cabinet (Johnsons, Waughs and Averys) to dinner at Duncan Terrace to show them some special single bottles we'd brought back. They included a Kistler 1979 Chardonnay I was very taken with, and a Washington Merlot bottled in Oregon by Sokol Blosser, which struck me as a particularly successful combination of grape and place.

Part of the reason Nick and I accelerated our courtship was that I was due to disappear on my very first trip to Australia, all thanks to the nice man from Cathay Pacific, for a month in February. I flew from Gatwick after a romantic night in the snowy Tudor eaves of Gravetye Manor, keeping our bottle of Dom Pérignon cool on the window ledge. In retrospect I realize it was rather a waste of a month of sunshine during an English winter to have been so lovesick. I told everyone who would listen about Nick, and the Australians seemed particularly taken by the fact that he'd been to Cambridge and I'd been to Oxford. "S'pose you met at the Boat Race, then?" one of them asked.

The Australian wines we saw in Britain in the 1970s and early
1980s belonged to an entirely different era from the bright, breezy
ultramodern blends we see today. In sharp contrast to the novelty of
importing California wine, Britain had a long history of importing
wine from down under. Indeed, Australia had been known in some
quarters as John Bull's Vineyard for the quantities of "tonic wine,"
strong, sweet stuff bought on the basis of hit per penny, shipped to
Britain in the early twentieth century. The Australians had been
learning how to make table wines with scarcely more alcohol than
their French counterparts and as much refreshment value, thanks
to the introduction of refrigeration, and were slowly starting to drink
them. The man responsible for convincing Australians that wine was a
man's drink was the ebullient Len Evans, or Lyn Ivens as he is known
to most Australians. A swaggering, Napoleonic, congenital competitor
and raconteur who had progressed from glass washer to hotel manager
to restaurateur was now owner of The Rothbury Estate, arguably the
Hunter Valley's most famous winery. Len put his mark on it by
making it a very social, clubby affair with all sorts of associated high
jinks involving big dinners and blind tastings. When I first visited
Australia, Rothbury was suffering financially from having planted too
many red and not enough white grapes, Len always having been a bit
ahead of his time.

I'd first met Len to write a profile of him during my early days on
Wine & Spirit, interviewing him in the dingy Soho offices that served as
Australian wine's showcase in Britain. (The Australian Wine & Brandy
Corporation closed them down in 1981 when Soho was regarded as
sleazy beyond compare; at that time people thought Nick was mad to
be opening a smart restaurant there.) At that stage I didn't know Len
well enough to realize that he is even more talented than his own publicity suggests. It was already clear, however, that this was someone
who believed in the future of Australian wine down to his fingernails
but who, crucially, also had a thorough appreciation of the great wines
of the world. In fact, he had plans to take over the world. In the late
1970s, he'd persuaded his highly successful friend and business associate Peter Fox to buy not just some vineyard land in the Napa Valley,
but two châteaux in Bordeaux, if you please. Château Padouën was in
Barsac, sweet wine country, while Château Rahoul, the Australians'
Bordeaux base, produced red and white Graves.

Thanks to Christopher Selmes's Sydney connections, Rothbury, Rahoul and Padouën all featured in Geoffrey Roberts's first trade tasting. Also featured was a new winery run by one of Len Evans's protégés, Brian Croser, a young wine academic who'd been flown to Bordeaux from his own Petaluma wine operation to make the 1979 vintage for him. "From the 1979 vintage," boasted Geoffrey's tasting catalogue, "Padouën is the ONLY chateau in the Sauternes region to practice individual grape selection (even Château d'Yquem is a quarter bunch selection)." No prizes for guessing who wrote that.

How exciting life must have been for Len then. I'd bumped into him, with "Foxy," at the Stanford Court in San Francisco on Halloween 1979 when they must have been prospecting for a suitable California investment. I always associate Krug with Len. Wherever he is, it is too, in quantity. We drank lashings of Krug at the hotel and then went for a meal in Chinatown. Len likes a party.

In those days the vineyards and cellars of Australia were very much terra incognita to foreigners. Hugh had been prospecting—and given the Aussies a typically inspired and much-used quote about Penfolds Grange Hermitage being Australia's one undisputed first growth. And not long before my visit Edmund Penning-Rowsell had been met by Len in a Rolls-Royce and spirited off for a boozy sail round Sydney Harbor, an image I have difficulty with to this day. But there was hardly any mention of Australia in the wine articles of that era, other than a distress parcel of syrupy Hunter red under the Arrowood label and two much-derided basic blends memorably named Kanga Rouge and, after some competition from Bondi Bleach, Wallaby White. Hardly the stuff to bolster Australia's dubious wine reputation.

I arrived in Sydney to an old-fashioned Australian Saturday afternoon. The Menzies Hotel, a transplant from early 1950s English provinces except for the shorts, was in the heart of the shopping district, but all the shops were closed—in fact the city itself seemed closed. The carpets in the hotel seemed to smell of burnt Vegemite, Australia's self-defining yeast extract spread. The little welcome card from the Australian Wine & Brandy Corporation looked ominously bureaucratic. I missed Nick and I was too jet-lagged to be excited. But Sunday made up for it. Bob and Gwen Mayne, officially welcoming me under Wine & Brandy Corp auspices, drove me up in a car, numberplate VIN 111, to Berowra Waters, Gay Bilson's famous palace of delights on the Hawkesbury River, reachable only by ferry or, for ex-hibitionists, seaplane. This was better French bourgeois cooking than I had come across on most of my travels through the wine regions of France. Bob brought along a box of some of Australia's greatest wine treasures designed to soothe away jet lag, unguents like glori-ously full-throttle, feral Hunter Valley "Hermitage" (Shiraz) from the early 1960s, and coppery sweet Porphyry.

The next day I discovered the quite exceptional quality of fully mature Hunter Valley dry whites, in the form of some of the older releases of the then benevolent Lindemans, still an arch competitor rather than sub-sidiary of Penfolds (Australians regard apostrophes as an affectation). These racy long-distance runners, made entirely without help from the oak tree, were given names such as Riesling, Chablis and White Bur-gundy, but were actually all made from Semillon, a vine that is trans-formed into a prima ballerina, with a whiff of burnt toast, when planted in the Hunter and well aged in bottle. This wine style, unique not just to Australia but to the Hunter Valley, is all too often ignored in the current Chardonnay- and oak-besotted era.

I met up with Len Evans that evening and had a tour of the great sights of Sydney, including Doyles on the Beach for fish and, of course, his own vinous hideaway Bulletin Place, scene of many an extravagant wine guessing game. There was, perhaps inevitably, a tasting going on here and James Halliday, then a lawyer by day and partner in Broken-wood winery by weekend, slipped me a taste of the famous Grange 1955, a wine (then selling for an unbelievable $85 a bottle) of such unctuous concentration it knocked me sideways.

One of my objectives during this trip, other than finding out about an entirely new wine source and what it had to offer, was to research a book I'd been commissioned to write over the next year or so called—what else after *The Wine Book?*—*The Great Wine Book*, a collection of essays about some of the finest wines in the world. Grange, Petaluma and Tyrrell's were to represent Australia—which was quite a bold step then, for which I was roundly castigated by Auberon Waugh when he reviewed the book. ("To speak of Australian wine in the same breath as Lafite while ignoring whole areas of Burgundy is absurd.")

I spent a wonderful morning with Max Schubert, the creator of Grange. He told me how he had been so impressed by the wines he saw on a study trip to Bordeaux in 1949, that he had come back inspired to make wines as concentrated and long-living in South Australia. "I would have loved to have used the same grape varieties as the French, but we didn't have them. The only Cabernet Sauvignon I knew of at that time was a few acres in our own vineyards." A few years before my visit Penfolds had put the 1955 Grange into a class called Open Claret at the all-important Canberra Agricultural Show. It had still won a gold medal, despite being well into its third decade, "but we've decided to pension it off now."

The Grange story is now so well known, it should be inspiring many more ambitious winemakers to fly in the face of fashion. (Grange was initially rejected by Penfolds and dismissed as "dry port" or "tastes of crushed ants.") Max Schubert died in 1994 while I was filming in South Australia. I watched the stream of cars disappearing into Adelaide's crematorium, a roll call of the great and the good in Australian wine.

The most memorable day of my 1981 Australian trip was also its longest. It started with a dawn flight from Italian-speaking Griffith, part of the extraordinary, heavily irrigated interior that produces so much of Australia's basic wine, to Wangaratta, or "Wang" as they call it in those parts, abbreviation being a national sport. This was so I could spend the morning with Brown Brothers of Milawa in northeast Victoria. Head of a fourth-generation business with four sons, ultra-steady John Brown senior met me at the airport in his shorts and Mercedes. "That's Roger's house over there, and you can just see the roof of Ross's through the trees . . ." Ross and Roger, indeed all her sons, towered over their mother, in whose carefully tended rose garden we breakfasted on melon, new season's Muscat grapes, Mrs. Brown's kumquat marmalade, and Vegemite rendered genteel by being smeared onto a cut-glass dish.

Like everyone else in Australia in the early 1980s, indeed like most wine producers everywhere outside France, the Brown clan felt Australian winemakers had a lot to learn from California, and was interested in this new grape Chardonnay. Tyrrells of the Hunter Valley had had remarkable success with it, and the Browns were trying to plant some of their own. The trouble with the combination of early-budding Chardonnay and their carefully purchased high-altitude vineyards was the frost danger (Milawa is well on the way to Australia's snowfields). They quickly installed some overhead sprays to protect the nascent

crop with ice and were looking forward to harvesting their first proper
crop next month. "It's beautiful fruit. I can't wait to see the wine," the
vineyard manager Brown son told me excitedly. Even two Chardonnay-
booming years later in 1983, Australia had barely 2,000 acres of
Chardonnay vines old enough to produce a commercial crop of wine.
(Two decades later that figure was more than 14,000 acres, with a further 5,000 coming onstream by 1996.)

It is easy to forget just how recent a phenomenon Chardonnay-
mania is. In the early 1980s the variety was virtually unknown in, for
example, New Zealand, Chile, South Africa (they'd planted something
else by mistake) and southern France. Crucial to Chardonnay's success
has been a complete revolution in how wines are labeled. In Australia
John Brown was an early devotee of varietal labeling, calling a wine
after the grape variety from which it is made rather than, à la française,
after the place it comes from. Although his region was historically
famous for its heady fortified wines, his imagination had been captured
by the work of De Castella, an early Swiss-born Victorian viticulturist
who experimented with new grape varieties for table wine. He remembered going to tastings of these experiments before he left school. "No
one else was interested, but I thought it put a bit of interest into the
game."

Over lunch we tasted a blossom-sweet Orange Muscat, a Flora and
Ruby Cabernet, two fairly recent crossings imported and dragged
through the quarantine system from California, a Merlot 1978 (nowadays Australians are on their knees seeking out this Bordeaux grape), as
well as a minty single vineyard Cabernet and a Shiraz/Cabernet blend
from the early 1970s before three late-picked Rieslings back to 1962.
(They apologized for having run out of their 1953 sweet Riesling which
had still been in cracking shape two years earlier. It had been bottled in
an old whisky bottle and stoppered with a homemade cork because there
was such a shortage of materials after the war.) On top of that there were
six of their white varietals that took so long to ferment (up to a year for
one Semillon) because they chilled the fermentation vats so fiercely, and
cleaned up the must so vigorously beforehand, centrifuging out all the
solid matter in the grape juice.

Neither my palate nor my brain were at their freshest, therefore,
when John Brown dropped me off at the next stop on my Wine &
Brandy Corporation itinerary, at Morris of Rutherglen up the road.

Mick Morris was the most unlikely representative of the international conglomerate Reckitt & Colman (which then owned his family winery) I could have hoped to encounter. Australia's most lauded fortified wine maker greeted me in filthy shorts and an even filthier shirt. His first words were typical of the laconic understatement that characterizes the Australian male: "We'll have yer full before yer leave."

This hot northeast corner of Victoria is Australia's Douro Valley, famous for the quality of some unique, and uniquely strong and sweet, fortified wines. They're made from ultra-ripe, nearly raisined grapes which are allowed to just start fermenting before a great whack of fiery young brandy is added to the sweet, grapey mixture and the blend then added to be matured for years in a sort of solera system of ancient casks in furnacelike sheds. I can't think of any other winery anywhere in the world whose buildings qualify only as sheds. Nor a winemaker so difficult to imagine in the grandeur of the port trade's Factory House in Oporto where he told me he'd once dined.

Morris laid on a tasting for me not just of his own "ports," Liqueur Muscats and Liqueur Tokays, but of all his competitors' too, And, what made it triply taxing, the setting for the tasting was not some air-conditioned chamber, but out of doors with only a flimsy corrugated iron roof to keep the bottles in the shade, if not exactly the cool. He'd gathered together thirty examples (average alcohol content 18 per cent). I pleaded with him, reminded him of my early start, and so he mercifully cut the selection down to "just" twenty-three.

They were *wonderful* wines. The Liqueur Muscats in particular are quite unlike anything else, truly a sort of warm Christmas cocktail of sherry, port, madeira and Muscat de Beaumes de Venise, and I have remained a fan of this style ever since. I can taste them now, so strongly etched are they on the palate. But this was a particularly good example of the difference between tasting and drinking. Many a writer's evening I would delight in sitting down with a thimbleful of Liqueur Muscat after dinner, but having to write intelligible notes on and assessments of a score of these things in the baking Australian bush was quite a different experience.

I kept at it right up to the Morris Very Very Old Liqueur Muscat, a deep, dark treacle that had spent more than seventy years in one of those sheds, admittedly being refreshed with a little 1954 made from pre-phylloxera vines. "It's a curio," Morris told me dismissively. "If you drank a bottle, you'd be as sick as a dog." We discussed Australia's all-powerful wine shows, where medals that are answers to a salesman's prayer are awarded and withheld by judges who regularly tackle two hundred wines a day, the strongest wines always coming last of course. Morris harbored no illusions. "I've seen judges come up to look at the fortifieds and they're as full as ticks before they're started." Fullness was a state I could sympathize with.

But this was not my last appointment of the day. I had a dinner date with the eight most prominent wine producers of the area, Mick Morris and his cronies. The evening taught me more about rural Australia than any wine tasting. We went to the wine producers' regular haunt, the Corowa Bowling Club, crucially just across the Murray River in New South Wales, which meant that gambling was allowed on the premises. Decorous ballroom dancing was the draw for most of the other visitors. There was not just one electric organ here, but two. The couple who provided the music had been playing together for two decades. Her buttock work on the stool was wonderfully muscular. Just as the hefty blokes in white woolly kneesocks, paunches tucked into straining shorts, were surprisingly nimble, waltzing and wheeling away oh, so correctly, consistently leaving the width of a Fosters can between them and their partners, beaming in sprigged nylon frocks, tight little perms and sandals.

The wives of my eight hosts were not allowed to join us. They were each issued a polystyrene cup of tokens for the jukeboxes and effectively told to go and amuse themselves while the men got on with what they did best. The women probably thought I was as strange for wanting to spend an evening gossiping about wine as I thought they were for not protesting at their exclusion. We withdrew to a side room to taste, eat and pontificate.

There were some weird and not so wonderful table wines made from grapes baked by the heat of the Australian interior that by and large showed how far Australia still had to go at that stage. There was Campbells Chablis, actually made from Pedro Ximenez, the grape used to make sweetening syrup for sherry and jolly flabby too. "People love it or hate it," Colin Campbell observed placidly. Another "Chablis," this one made from a Portuguese grape they called Dourado, was followed by a powerhouse-in-a-bottle, Baileys Hermitage (which Tony Laithwaite had already got his hands on for the Sunday Times Wine Club) and a

1975 Shiraz from Stanton & Killeen ("a classic example of beautiful soft Rutherglen Shiraz made in the days before we started to throw in the acid," according to Mr. Killeen).

That night we heard that the ever-vigilant New South Wales police (stricter than their Victorian counterparts on permissible blood alcohol levels) were out to get as many positive breath tests as possible in the short stretch between the club and the border. "The boys are on the bridge," we were told, with a meaningful nod, by the management. Those abstinent wives were shown to have their uses.

Four days later, in one of the fanciest of Melbourne's fifteen hundred restaurants, my day in the country was to catch up with me. I'd been invited to a dinner Len Evans had organized for Melbourne's wine press to make them realize they ought to be writing nicer things about Rothbury's reds. His winemaker addressed the room first, pointing out gently, "We're sorry that our whites have been praised so much more." Then Evans got to his feet and looked threateningly around the room. "What he means is we're pretty cheesed off that you've been ignoring our reds." He had the power of course because he was about to con-duct, after our fourteen wines and five courses, several rounds of his famous Options game. The concept behind this cleverly democratic invention of Len's is dead simple. Everyone in the room tastes a wine blind and then stands up. Evans then progressively makes all but the winner sit down by asking a succession of questions based on increas-ingly narrow alternatives (e.g., "Is this wine French or not?" or "Was it made pre 1975 or post 1974?"). He can and frequently does use this opportunity to draw the room's attention to the poor performance of particularly cocky or high-profile participants. But the real joy of the game is that the complete novice seems to have at least as high a chance of winning as the most determined professional.

Somewhere between the Bass Straits muttonbird with ginger and the sweetbreads wrapped in sorrel a red-faced man who'd been staring at me earlier suddenly leaned diagonally across the table toward me. "I know who you are," he leered. "You must be the English tart who tasted twenty-three Liqueur Muscats with Mick Morris."

I didn't realize it at the time, but this rite of passage was to smooth my way into some form of acceptance by the fiercely male Australian wine establishment (which still seems to me to operate a form of tokenism toward women). Australia may have become a wine-drinking nation, but sharing a beer is still the true bonding experience as far as any Australian man is concerned. Not being a beer drinker, I was thrilled over the years to come to find myself invited regularly to judge those all-important wine shows in Australia, give keynote speeches and even, occasionally, share a platform with Len himself. If Hugh and Edmund were my early patrons in Britain, Len played that role in Australia, which was to make its presence increasingly felt on the world stage.

But for the moment, in the early 1980s, the New World of wine meant California, so much more sophisticated than roughneck Australia both in terms of wines and, especially, people. I was looking forward to getting back home to see how my personal stake in California wine was getting on in his Soho building site.

Lurching Toward
Respectability

On my groggy return from Australia (two stops en route then) to Nick's house full of wine samples and architect's drawings in north London, I was all too aware that I should be getting down to the second, 1982 *Which? Wine Guide* I was contracted to edit. I felt a certain reluctance. The previous year it had been a luxury to inaugurate the annual *Guide* with a blank canvas, but tackling the same giant problem a second time lacked much of the original excitement. Second time around I felt I'd made all the jokes and was simply correcting my mistakes. I rather halfheartedly tried to convince the *Guide*'s publisher at Consumers' Association that there was a potential conflict of interest, Nick being a wine importer and about to be a wine-minded restaurateur and all that, but he would have none of it.

The whole thing was made much, much easier, however, by the pen and efficiency of an assistant editor and friend who was in the process of transforming herself into Rosie Thomas. While helping me with the first two *Which? Wine Guides* she wrote her first novel, skilfully sold by her husband and our literary agent, Caradoc King. *Celebration* turned out to be about a young female wine writer torn in love between the owner of Dry Stone winery in the Napa Valley and Baron Charles de Gillemont of Bordeaux. I loved it.

Together, Rosie and I tried to assemble a complete guide to Britain from the wine lover's point of view. We had reports on wine regions from a lineup of contributors that looks very august today. Liz Berry, Bill Bolter, Clive Coates, Ian Jamieson, Tony Laithwaite, Simon Loftus, Edmund Penning-Rowsell (the *Guide*'s consultant), David Peppercorn, Jan Read and Serena Sutcliffe had all written or have gone on to write books about wine themselves. I'm amazed how ambitious we were, and how little the format has changed over the years— even though I handed over the third, 1983 edition with relief to Jane MacQuitty.

For Nick the spring and early summer of 1981 were a whirl of builders' broken promises, hopeful calculations on the back of envelopes, samples of the snail trail carpet that would be mentioned in so many reviews of the restaurant and long drives out to a warehouse in Rainham to try to resurrect something from the hardware that had been left in the old Escargot Bienvenu when it closed, condemned by the health inspector of the Westminster City Council on forty-four counts. This five-floor 1741 Soho townhouse, a listed building, had been home to London's first "French" restaurant in the 1920s and had enjoyed great success until a slow decline in the sixties. The Escargot Bienvenu had become the sort of place godparents took teenagers in the mistaken belief that it was still fashionable. Nick, realizing very early in his brief wine importing career that vertical integration was the only possible way of making it pay, had been looking for a small wine bar to sell his California wines in. His designer friend Tom Brent showed him the derelict townhouse instead and from then on both of them were hooked. Initially, it was only the fact that he was refused a wine-only license that propelled Nick into becoming a restaurateur.

Luckily for me, I had no idea of quite how great a risk was being run by a complete novice opening a 200-seat restaurant in the depths of the early eighties recession in an unfashionable, nay positively louche, area of London. Had I had anything to do with it, the new Escargot would have been furnished with coconut matting and furniture from Habitat. Instead I assumed Nick knew exactly what he was doing and Tom's vision was indulged, including the blue snail trail carpet woven by a mill on the brink of ruin, specially designed leather chairs that took up an awful lot of room (and were $130 each!) and daring rag-rolled eau-de-nil walls.

At this entirely speculative stage, Nick was alert to every augury. He was hugely cheered by the inexplicable good luck of having both of the Hardys' applications for work permits accepted in record time. By the beginning of May they were installed in the flat at the top of the building, with the furniture I had assembled for the property I had been about to buy for myself just before I met Nick.

The real coup, however, was persuading Elena Salvoni, London's most loved maîtresse d' to come round the corner from the old Bianchi's (now Bahn Thai). Elena, with her enthusiastic twinkle and confidential charm, had over the decades presided over hundreds if not thousands of alliances—licit and illicit, personal and commercial. Like so many before him, Nick used to eat at Bianchi's purely because he felt Elena was a friend. On a whim he explained to her what he was up to at L'Escargot. It was either Nick's charm, or his offer of a financial stake in the new business, or the fact that she felt sorry for him that lured her and her hundreds of devoted customers away. Nick used to tell me he wanted to have London's best restaurant and be its worst cook and that he'd already achieved one of those ambitions. His bachelor kitchen in Chalk Farm certainly proved it. Sue Miles, whom he'd admired when she'd run her own restaurant, was recruited to find suitable kitchen staff, most importantly of course the chef. There was no question as far as Sue was concerned that it should be an inspired young self-taught cook, Alistair Little, another Cambridge graduate. Many menu conferences followed.

But there had to be an important wine list conference too, for the cellars of L'Escargot had been stripped bare, except for the odd bottle of ZigZag vermouth from Chambéry, the restaurant's specialty. The new restaurant's chief wine advisor was *Sunday Times* wine correspondent and editor of the *Which? Wine Guide*. Perhaps using my experience in the Oporto hotel as inspiration, I was determined to make the wine list much more user-friendly than the terse, rigidly geographically segregated, padded inventories that were then the London norm. Desktop publishing was still unheard of so we printed a list only two or three times a year, but it was designed to be read. We decided to have relatively few wines, and to divide them by style, a revolutionary concept at the time. So our whites were carefully divided into "light and fruity," "dry and flinty" and "fuller Chardonnays," while our reds were either "light and fruity," "rich and fuller" or "aristocratic

Cabernet Sauvignons." Another innovation, much fueled by the owner's wife-to-be, was that every wine was described with a sentence or two. With increasing wine knowledge on the part of the restaurant-goer, and occasional whimsy on the part of the wine list-compiler, this has become a dubious practice, but at the time we had many comments from customers delighted to have something to read while they waited for their lunch or dinner companions.

In the frantic run up to the opening day, June 2, 1981, we'd already had a series of trial dinners, first for family, then for friends, including one, daringly, for the Zinfandel Club. This tall, thin restaurant had the terrible disadvantage of a basement kitchen up to three floors away from its customers. Two dumbwaiters and two electric hoists were absolutely vital to satisfying the desires of all in that building. When one of them broke down, as often happened, it was hell. Early waiting staff included several actors who have gone on to much more starry roles but in these early days contented themselves with playing the part of a human dumbwaiter.

The first proper trading day was no less frenetic and tense than any restaurant's opening. Nick's complexion matched the pale green of the walls exactly. Alistair was going crazy in his cramped, furnacelike quarters down below. The builders were still fitting the bar. I invited my colleague and columnist from *The Sunday Times*, Godfrey Smith, for lunch in a brazen attempt to attract some good publicity. Nick's sister Katie, nervously acting as cashier that first day, watched theater producer Michael Codron walk out because the service was so slow. She still feels sick when she thinks of L'Escargot's opening day. I just assumed that my hero had it all under control.

Nick particularly wanted to thank Winston, the foreman of the builders who had been far more energetic and helpful than he need, so we were due to have dinner with him and his wife that first evening, once Nick could be persuaded to sit down for longer than a minute. But because almost all the wines in the first list were American, the result of our wine-buying trip at the beginning of the year, we had an unexpected guest for dinner that night.

By the time I got there, dashing down Charlotte Street past Channel 4 for the first of several thousand times, who should be declaiming at the newborn bar but Bob himself, the great Mondavi. He'd just flown in by Concorde and had heard that there was this new restaurant specializing in California wines. He just had to come and have a look, so of course we invited him to join our small party. True to inimitable form, he managed to make us feel great for having this American idea, and guilty for not having any of his wines on the list. The *Times* diarist, dining three tables away, recognized him, came over to interview him for the next day's paper, and this was just the start of the media circus that Elena's windowless room on the first floor was to become.

As the days became marginally less frenetic and the bookings book increasingly overcrowded, Elena amassed a troupe of regulars which included Albert Finney, John Hurt, Michael Palin, Ed Victor, Melvyn Bragg and, when she was in town, Ella Fitzgerald. It was perhaps not so surprising that the restaurant took off with a bang. London's most celebrated restaurant critic, Fay Maschler, came straight off the plane from her Greek holiday and wrote a rave review. Nick was so ecstatic that he sent her flowers which took up the entire backseat of a taxi. I felt very jealous, when I should simply have been extremely relieved.

Some fine-tuning was needed, however—not least with the wine list. We started getting complaints that the California whites weren't dry enough. And one night during the first few weeks a party of eight Frenchmen walked in, ordered their food, took one look at the wine list and walked out. We thought we'd better add to the initial selection. A new house white was supplied by a diminutive, elderly stamp-collecting Czech called Ernst Gorge who made every female heart in the British wine trade beat a little faster. Anthony Hanson, then just starting work on his definitive *Burgundy*, provided a bordeaux-like red. For our second wine list we also grafted on some wine styles impossible to emulate on America's West Coast: Muscadet (very popular then), Sancerre (even more so; the archetypal smart restaurant wine), a Chablis, a Chassagne-Montrachet from the irreproachable (for quality) importer O. W. Loeb and three mature vintages of Château Léoville-Las-Cases for those claret-loving customers looking for a vertical tasting. At the same time, in homage to our first guest from the greater world of wine, we added a Robert Mondavi Reserve Cabernet 1975 and a sweet wine from Mondavi via Geoffrey Roberts.

A year or so later Mondavi came back for lunch, this time with his wife, Margrit. We had a lovely meal in the pretty first-floor drawing room of the old townhouse, so incongruously looking out onto the sex shops and the old Establishment Club. With the dessert we poured him some of his Moscato d'Oro, a sort of California Moscato d'Asti. "What's this, Margrit?" he barked. "Do we make this? We do? Well, how about that? I haven't tasted it in years." Both my sister-in-law and I had already fallen in love with him.

Thanks to many a foreign visitor like this and to the beau monde attracted by Elena's solicitousness and distinctive food cooked first by Alistair and then Martin Lam, L'Escargot was well and truly launched. It was helped by the proximity of Saatchi & Saatchi, the new Channel 4 up the road in Charlotte Street, the British Film Institute, all the attendant cutting rooms, casting agents and people in the music business, and Mitchell Beazley entering their prime as the world's foremost wine book publishers just across the street. I bought Nick an extremely grand Florentine cuttings book to house all the printed praise, and the paparazzi work on guests such as Mick Jagger and Princess Di.

At the same time as Nick was battling to convert a derelict townhouse and a gigantic overdraft into other people's pleasure and his profit, I was hard at work on *The Great Wine Book*. It is no wonder we found it impossible to find the time to get married. I had unwittingly stumbled across the most wonderful wheeze. To write about all these great wine producers, I would of course have to go and spend time with them, inevitably having to sample some of their most precious wines. It says much about the unquestioningly hospitable nature of the wine world that all these eminent people were prepared to welcome a young woman from England who had been writing about wine for such a short time. I'm sure none of them had ever heard of *The Wine Book* or the *Which? Wine Guide*—although perhaps the name of *The Sunday Times* cut a little ice.

April 1981 was dedicated to Bordeaux, an exhausting round of first growths. Nick took some palliative rest from the drills and hammers in Greek Street and joined me for the first half of this taxing research trip.

We flew off one Friday night and enjoyed that most luxurious of meals, an extended and refined Saturday lunch, in the sunny first-floor salon which then housed the St. James restaurant in the center of Bordeaux. The Bolters treated us to their exceptional blend of welcome and intellectual stimulation that evening. And on Sunday we were swept up in Les Noailles brasserie by Bordeaux's two resident Masters of Wine, Johns Salvi and Davies, who invited us to join them in their regular Sunday matinee box at the opera at a performance of *La Fanciulla del West*, during which, much fortified, they fell happily asleep.

Work didn't start until Monday evening when we went to research, and stay at, La Mission-Haut-Brion, home of the glorious long-lived golden Laville. Such a good dinner did we have that we woke up late for our appointment with arch-rival Haut-Brion across the road. Because of the rivalry between the neighboring properties, the stars of what was then the Graves appelation, we felt embarrassed to confess where we'd spent the night. This was my first meeting with Haut-Brion's immaculately groomed administrator Jean-Bernard Delmas and I was much impressed. Of all those with current experience of running a first growth château, his is the longest, and probably the most autonomous tenure.

At a black marble table, served hot little cheesy morsels (most unusual) by a uniformed waitress, we tasted Haut-Brion back from 1979 to 1975, which Delmas admitted was *"pour demain,"* confessing that he thought the 1970s would never be ready and that anyway it was the 1961, the first year of his beloved stainless steel fermentation vats, of which he is most proud. Monsieur Delmas has never allowed me to forget my description of him in *The Great Wine Book* as looking like a nightclub owner, but we share a passionate interest in ampelography, the science of identifying vine varieties.

It was to be a tough week: Tuesday evening at Château Lafite, where the beautifully knit 1962 and the elegantly silky 1953 provided some consolation for staying at the then antediluvian Hotel France et Angleterre on the noisy seafront of Pauillac; Wednesday afternoon at Château d'Yquem; Château Palmer after Nick's departure on Thursday; and then on Friday, just the way things worked out, Mouton, Latour *and* Margaux, a triple first growth day.

Mouton, a cluster of buildings rather than a single grand château building, inevitably involved a tour of the world-famous, Michelin-starred wine museum. Before examining anything to do with wine, I reached it by wading over the uncomfortably pebbly white gravel, so carefully raked every day according to the wishes of *le baron,* under the white doves who wheeled so obligingly for him. I marveled at the

Bugatti in which Baron Philippe de Rothschild (possibly at that moment skulking upstairs in his bedroom-cum-office) had completed the twenty-four-hour race at Le Mans in 1929. There was a picture of him grinning. Even in goggles and cap he was utterly recognizable. I was yet to meet him but when I did, I quite saw what a remarkable visionary he was.

I was shown round by Raoul Blondin, the front-of-house wine expert at Mouton. Just as cruise liners are supposed to have tanned, handsome "Captains" who can dance and do all the social stuff as well as the chap who actually sails the ship, so Mouton had the chisel-featured Blondin in his beret and *bleus de travail,* always ready with an opinion on the wines and intimate knowledge of Mouton's famously well-furnished cellar. His job was to deal with people like me and, importantly, to look after all the wine requirements of the Baron himself and his daughter Philippine when she came to stay in her own quarters, the eighteenth-century house, Petit Mouton.

I left this magical barony reluctantly to be taken afterwards to lunch by some of the sales and marketing men then busy ferrying millions of bottles of the brilliantly named Mouton Cadet around the world at the one businessmen's restaurant within striking distance. There we were served a vast terrine full of pâté de foie gras which had been cooked especially for us. Five days later I was to return to the same table with Michel Delon of Château Léoville-Las-Cases. The patronne served me the same dish, freshly filled with this assault on my own liver, without a blink.

Compared to the magic and drama of Mouton, Latour seemed rather dull and stodgy (occasionally the wines of each property display these respective characteristics). At this point in Latour's quite checkered recent past the first growth was still British-owned, partly by Allied through Harvey's of Bristol and partly by Pearson, owners of the *Financial Times.* A young member of the extended family Clive Gibson had been put in charge. I was shown round by the elderly Jean-Paul Gardère, a protégé of Henri Martin of Saint-Julien bloated bottle fame, and young Jean-Louis Mandreau, both of them sharing a small, smoke-filled office overlooking the vineyard and church spire of Saint-Julien. Both were soon to move on and a new regime would be installed to handle the richesse of the eighties.

On Monday I visited the minuscule Château Pétrus in the morning and had a memorable lunch in front of Christian Moueix's house in the trees on the banks of the Dordogne. The pretty house was being painted in pastels by a number of craftsmen suspended on scaffolding. It looked just like the backdrop for an operetta, but the wines were clearly more on the scale of a grand opera. This is what I wrote about the 1971: "I understand what they mean when they say you don't have to eat when you're drinking Pétrus." Not for the first time did I resort to textile similes in my tasting notes on the '52, ending with the phrase "red velvet with a pattern."

On Tuesday Madame Dubois Challon played hostess, Pascal Delbeck sommelier, with an ancient retainer waitress, at a lunch for me and the Fourniers of Château Canon, which culminated in a miraculously youthful and concentrated 1849 Château Ausone. On Wednesday I visited Château Léoville-Las Cases and gorged myself on foie gras one more time before flying back to Nick and the builders.

But the most memorable part of my stay was the weekend. Château Margaux is by a very long way the most stunning building in the Médoc, described thus in a late-nineteenth-century monograph on the most famous crus of Bordeaux: "the Versailles of the Médocain vineyards. It is a palace in the full sense of the word, a palace modeled on the Parthenon in Athens with gracious Doric columns, magnificent carvings and a truly royal avenue."

This handsome château and the estate surrounding it had recently been sold by the Ginestet family, who had long since run out of the money needed to maintain a first growth. The new owner was a newcomer, a Greek-born cereal and grocery magnate called André Mentzelopoulos. The sums he had immediately lavished on repairing the vineyards, updating the cellars and completely renovating the château was the talk of Bordeaux, but he died at the end of 1980, still a relatively young man, leaving his glamorous widow, Laura, in charge. "He always wanted the best," she was to tell me. Just after I had written asking whether I could visit the property for my *Great Wine Book*, she had been looking through her husband's papers and, for some reason I still don't understand, had found my name on a list of wine writers he thought should be invited to the property. Accordingly Laura, bless her, invited me for a weekend à deux in the newly refurbished national monument that is Château Margaux.

It was the most enormous fun for someone like me who enjoys easy conversation, good food and wine, and finds that the lap of luxury tends to fit like a glove. Those beautifully ironed, embroidered linen pillowcases . . . the posy and warm, buttery croissants on the breakfast tray . . . the profligacy of Roger et Gallet in the bathroom . . . and Laura promising so enthusiastically to come to L'Escargot and try "Nick's plates." (I was later to have the chance to compare the accommodation with that at fellow first growths Latour and Mouton and must report that, while things at Mouton were more dramatic—would Philippine or Joan Littlewood manage to delay their evening appearance longer?—Margaux wins Best Kept Château Award.) Paul Pontallier was yet to be recruited to run the property, so I was shown around by Laura and the old guard managers on Saturday morning—but not before a panic about the wines to be served at lunch when Peter Sichel, Alexis Lichine (both owners of Margaux classed growths) and Château Margaux's eminent consultant oenologist Professor Emile Peynaud were expected.

Margaux's cellar in the post-Ginestet era was not exactly the most lavishly provisioned, and there was an anxious search for a bottle of Peter Sichel's wine Château Palmer. Eventually one of the staff was dispatched to the Maison du Vin, the village wine shop, for "one—no, two bottles of a good vintage, 1976 or 1970, or 1971." It must have been tough for this warm Toulousaine ex-beauty queen to have been pitched into the arcane world of wine, and in such a prominent position, but she used her charm and what was evidently a firm grasp of commerce to great effect.

I already knew two men who were crazy about her and there must have been many more. One of them was clearly her neighbor Alexis Lichine, the American in Bordeaux who invited us for the most sumptuous lunch in his copper pan-bedecked kitchen at Prieuré-Lichine on Sunday. Well, at least he invited Laura and was probably rather disgruntled that I came along too to share his bottle of the ethereal 1953, then Château Margaux's most famous twentieth century vintage. (We don't know yet whether the 1983 will match it.) This langorous lunch followed a Sunday morning walk around the estate during which Laura got particularly excited about the new herd of cows ("so that our manure can be *fresh,* not bought-in stuff which loses its nutrients").

But before all this was dinner at a restaurant in Bordeaux where I saw Laura the businesswoman in action. We dined at Clavel with two of the *courtiers* that are still so important to the Bordeaux wine trade, the brokers who act as tactful middlemen between the château-owners and their customers, the merchants or *négociants*. They advised Laura to put on the market only half of the amount she sold the year before as an opening gambit. Her instinct was to sell the first tranche small and dear. But the main thing was that she felt that her special project, the recently revived oaky white wine Pavillon Blanc du Château Margaux, deserved a particularly good launch price. The *courtiers* looked a bit doubtful and suggested 35 to 40 francs a bottle. She held out for 60 francs until the end of the meal, when they dutifully gave in. "Consumers will have to wait at least five years before they can taste our red wines, so the whites can be the herald of the new regime at Margaux," she said contentedly.

One thing became very clear from my ludicrously rarefied tour of Bordeaux: the rivalry between the first growth châteaux is still intense, though perhaps not as bitter as it once was. When Baron Elie de Rothschild was in charge of Lafite, the stories of how he and Philippe would try to put their cousin's wine down (by serving it with curry, etc.) were legion, if sometimes apocryphal. Now that Elie's nephew Eric, a genuine friend of his cousin Philippine at Mouton, had taken over at Lafite, things had loosened up considerably. The Bordeaux elite—Lafite, Latour, Mouton, Margaux and Haut-Brion—now thought of themselves as a club, and had cozy little meetings in Paris (where they spend far more time than Bordeaux) to discuss policy—mainly opening prices—and strategy. But this did not prevent them from taking their exalted rank in the world of wine extremely seriously (I have heard one second growth proprietor complain that he has never been invited to several of the first growths) and—most importantly—from wanting to produce a wine recognized as incontrovertibly the best in as many vintages as possible.

One of the few public arenas in which the first growths were compared in those days was a small Cotswold dining room to which Nick and I were invited for the first time, appropriately enough, the Saturday after my return from Bordeaux, while my senses were still vibrating from all this high-class stimulation. Edmund Penning-Rowsell had for years housed himself, his wife, Meg, and his wine cellar in this handsome stone house a few miles from Blenheim Palace just outside Oxford. Best known by others as *Financial Times* wine correspondent, chairman of The Wine Society and the foremost Bordeaux chronicler in English, he had been a generous and supportive colleague of mine from the very start. He was already a consultant on *Wine & Spirit* when I joined, as I later persuaded him to be on *Drinker's Digest*. His seniority and impeccable reputation with traditionalists provided much-needed gravitas for publications edited by an inexperienced hippie like me.

His value to me was beyond question. What was surprising was how extraordinarily kind and open he was toward me right from the start. I have never been a direct rival, but I can hardly remember a time when he didn't discuss wine with me with genuine modesty. "Oh really? How very interesting." Or, "Of course you know far more about that sort of thing than me." With his pepper-and-salt tweeds, cane, homburg, devotion to the Traveller's Club and Enoch Powell whiskers, he might strike you as a supercilious hard-line right-winger. Instead he is famously, indeed extremely, left wing, and has consistently encouraged all young wine writers that have come his way in the time that I have known him (even though his failing sight prevents him from recognizing many of them nowadays).

Before this April Saturday in 1981 he had already invited me several times to stay with him and Meg and enjoy some of the extremely grand bottles in his cellar, the freshest of fruit and veg from the garden and Meg's infectious blend of intelligence and frivolity. This dinner, however, was not pleasure but work, as he kept trying to remind us. For several years Edmund had been comparing over dinner round his dining table (he is of the generation that believes restaurant-going to be an outrageously extravagant exercise) all the first growths of the vintage eleven years before, observing the convention that a first growth bordeaux is not seriously ready to even broach before its second decade. The results of these dinners were, and indeed still are, published on the pink pages of his paper, the *Financial Times* (another paradox; he personally subscribes to *Marxism Today*), and seem to be followed closely by the parties concerned. When, for example, in the early 1990s we rated Château Haut-Brion 1982 lower in the pecking order than Jean-Bernard Delmas believed was appropriate, he made this very clear to Edmund.

We tasters could be faulted for enjoying the exercise too much, but not for any variation of method. We have by now settled in to a rhythm that has hardly varied since that first dinner in 1981. There is a standard lineup of personnel—the Penning-Rowsells, Nick and I, and Michael and Daphne Broadbent—and a rigid procedure. Edmund asks us all to be there by teatime so that we can gossip before turning to the task in hand. We get there about five and Edmund spends the next two to two and a half hours wondering where the Broadbents are. We know that Michael is probably still clearing his desk at Christie's seventy extremely congested miles away. The Broadbents eventually screech to a halt on the Penning-Rowsells' gravel, Daphne having been terrorizing the fast lane on the M40, Michael as horizontal as BMWs allow, taking a nap. They dash upstairs to change—not that Michael Broadbent is known for the sloppiness of his dress, but Edmund insists on a suit and tie. Edmund will have brought the relevant bottles up from his chilly cellar and will have been anxiously cupping their shoulders to see how effectively his skeletal central heating system has warmed them. Some combination of menfolk pull the corks using Edmund's collection of antique corkscrews, and decant them against a shadeless table lamp with much suspicious sniffing and comment on any ullage—excessive space between the top of the wine and the bottom of the cork which can spoil the wine by exposing it to too much air. His assortment of elegant eighteenth- and chunkier nineteenth-century decanters is almost as enviable as his cellar.

We're then allowed to sit down around the stone fireplace (or just occasionally, when the weather plays ball, in their fairy-tale garden), surrounded by mementos of their travels and particularly fine celadon, and share a bottle of champagne. More antique glassware: delicate, trumpet-shaped *flûtes* in which the wine goes right down to the base of the glass. We nibble cheese biscuits, as one of the many rules of the Penning-Rowsell household is that it is bad for you to drink champagne on an empty stomach. We discuss the quality of the wine, often Alfred Gratien, Louis Roederer, Pol Roger or Laurent Perrier, all favorites. The bottle has usually been in that stone-cold cellar for a good many years, and the wine is beginning to turn deep gold and substantial, more often showing a certain meatiness than simple froth and refreshment.

And speaking of meat, we are beginning to smell it roasting, and Meg is keen that we move into the dining room. Like the rest of the house, this stone-flagged chamber is lined with William Morris wall-paper. Kelmscott is not far away and Edmund was a founder member of the William Morris Society.

The table is always covered with a beautifully thick white linen tablecloth whose demands on the laundress worry me but which pro-vides the regulation white background against which to judge the wines' all-important color. (Any sign of brown at the rim shows the wine has already evolved quite considerably; impenetrable purple sug-gests it has a long life ahead.) On the broad window sill is Edmund and Meg's giant glass goblet beautifully engraved *"Beva con noi* E P-R M P-R." There are two triangular corner cupboards stuffed with the glasses, minus those that Edmund will ritually wash by hand the next morning, drying carefully with Wine Society tea towels designed for the purpose. There are framed, signed menus from particular high-lights in a long life of wining and dining. Across the mantelpiece is strung a line of silver *taste-vins,* glinting in the candlelight. Beside each place is a small card on which Edmund has typed the château names in the approved tasting order. Beside Daphne's place is also a flashlight, annual recognition of her comments on how inconveniently dark this scene is.

When we began in 1981 tasting the 1970 vintage (what luck for us newcomers), we tasted Margaux first, because of its debilitated perfor-mance in the immediately pre-Mentzelopoulos era. Then came Haut-Brion, Lafite, Mouton, Latour, Cheval Blanc and finally Pétrus. Haut-Brion, being the only non-Médoc wine and also one that tends to mature deceptively fast, however long it stays on that delicious plateau, is usually tasted early on and is almost invariably more charming than most. We always group the three Pauillacs in ascending order of likely astringency so that the famously tannic, stately Latour does not eclipse the much more ethereal/evanescent (depending on your view) style of Lafite. The styles of these three neighboring kings of the red wine world can be summed up as electric, exotic and majestic respectively— although Michael has suggested that racehorse, thoroughbred and carthorse might be more appropriate. This, incidentally, did not go down well with the Pearson director in charge of Latour at the time. Michael's supposed partiality for Lafite, especially as opposed to Latour, has been a long-running theme of these dinners.

From the 1976 vintage, when the bearded young winemaker Pascal

Delbeck revived the fortunes of Château Ausone, the only wine other than Cheval Blanc to be considered a Saint-Emilion first growth, Edmund has added this wine to the lineup, so that we have been known to revise the order to: Haut-Brion, Ausone, Cheval Blanc, Margaux, Lafite, Mouton, Latour and Pétrus, or Haut-Brion, Margaux, Lafite, Mouton, Latour, Ausone, Cheval Blanc and Pétrus. Not without considerable discussion on this tricky subject. (The theory of wine order is that one should go from young to old—not a consideration in this case—from light to heavy, from soft to tough, upwards in alcohol level and, should this be relevant, upwards in quality.) Margaux was traditionally seen as the lightest, most "feminine" of the four Médoc first growths, supposedly without the tannic spine of the Pauillacs, but I must say that right from the 1978, the first proper Mentzelopoulos vintage, Margaux has always tasted extremely tough and chunky from our eleven-year vantage point. So there is an argument for moving it after the Lafite, but then that would split up the Pauillacs, and Margaux is not usually heftier than Latour. Such problems.

Juggling these decanters, identified only by an increasingly smudged felt tip numeral, becomes increasingly difficult as the evening wears on. We each have a separate glass for each wine in front of us, and the wines are poured two at a time, the first two with the first course, second two before the main, next two toward the end of the main course and the remaining wines with cheese. But what with constant top-ups, there is ample opportunity for confusion in the gloom, although, amazingly, we have yet to make a mistake.

Wine doth loosen the tongue and slacken the will, of that there is no doubt. So as the evening wears on, it becomes increasingly tempting to talk about subjects other than what is in our glasses (which of course is as it should be at most dinner tables, no matter how grand the wines). Edmund, our chairman and the man who has to deliver 800 words as a result of our deliberations, has repeatedly to call us to order. Meg in particular tends to have far more interesting things in mind than whether she prefers the Lafite to the Mouton. "Meg, Meg! Concentrate, *please.*" Michael tastes with his wristwatch alongside, taking timed notes in his famous little red tasting notebook, hundreds of which have served him and his readers so well over the years. His long experience has shown him how much wines change in the glass, the better ones improving, the more superficial ones deteriorating (this has been a recurring contrast between Old and New World wines). We all tend to take positions, and sometimes have to relinquish them during the evening when we see how the wines evolve.

The menu is very carefully circumscribed. Edmund has strict ideas about the sort of foods which do and do not go with fine wine (Meg is naturally more anarchic but does not often get her away). There must be nothing too strongly flavored, nor too acid, nor too sweet. All foreign cheeses are frowned upon, including the vast canon of France's *fromagiers* with the sole exception of Cantal. It tastes reassuringly like Cheddar. Over the years we have tended to supply, and Nick has tended to cook, an increasing proportion of the dinner. Nick and I have heated discussions beforehand about exactly which sort of charcuterie will be tolerated, or whether a light young English goat's cheese would or would not be welcomed.

The denouement arrives more or less with the dessert, generally the produce of the kitchen garden in some creamy incarnation. Gooseberry fool is a favorite.

The most important part of the evening in the long term is the totting up of our preferences. None of this scores-out-of-100 business, now so popular with wine commentators and consumers around the world, for Edmund, or even points out of 20. The Penning-Rowsell system (of which we have to be reminded every year) is that we each put the wines in order, the favorite getting one point, our second favorite two points and so on. These are entered on a grid by either Michael or myself and added up so that the wine that garners the least points is the overall favorite and the one with the highest total languishes at the bottom. Michael often drives us all mad by ranking two, three or occasionally four wines equally, but then he is only demonstrating how difficult it is to rank or score something as varied and sensual as wine.

The overall "winner," if that is the right term, after all these years is probably Cheval Blanc, regularly one of the least expensive of these wines. I am tempted to suppose this is because, with its predominance of Cabernet Franc grapes and ballast of approachable Merlot, it tends to mature sooner than the Cabernet Sauvignon–dominated Pauillacs (and yet is not as full-throttle, over-the-top as Pétrus so often is at this early stage). However, my dear friend Cheval Blanc is so often just as gorgeous at thirty, forty or even fifty years that it seems to have staying power too. Other wines certainly chime in to seize the crown in many years—Margaux in 1983, Mouton in 1986, for example—but few other properties have shown such consistency. As Jean-Bernard Delmas complained, rather plaintively, our results do not always reflect the common belief in current wine and vintage reputations, nor at all the relative values in the salesroom, but there would be no point to this exercise if we all came to the table convinced that the wine that is popularly held to be "wine of the vintage" is bound to be the best. If our little group has a distinction it is that it is genuinely free of prejudice—with the just possible exception of course of Michael's feelings about Latour. . . .

The addition of Ausone over the years has not been wholeheartedly welcomed by me because Edmund is usually very keen that we should finish up all the decanters. One bottle of champagne plus eight bottles of often extremely concentrated red between just six tasters is going it by any standards, and I can honestly say that I rarely feel worse than on the morning after one of these august gatherings. The glasses will have been stored in the hatch between dining room on one side and kitchen and the Penning-Rowsell cat on the other. A feline form called Pétrus, succeeded by a Cos, may well have been prowling around these wine-stained glasses, desperately trying to gain access to the rest of the house.

We are all so noisy and giggly when we go to bed, but in the morning we talk quietly and wash and dry up carefully, grimly describing interrupted sleep or lurid dreams. Since they bought a house outside Bath, the Broadbents have rarely spent the night in the Cotswolds, so it is just the four of us (or four plus our children) who eat a muted breakfast back in the dining room. The right size of brown china *cafetière* is carefully chosen and kept warm above a small candle, along with a jug of hot milk. And we have to make one highly political choice for so early in the morning, whether to favor the dark brown, chunky marmalade made by Edmund, or the golden, sweetly fluid one made by Meg. My favorite breakfast moment of all time was when our son William, then three or four years old, leaned over toward me and whispered very loudly, "Is Egmund the boy or the girl?"

We have been extremely privileged and spoiled to have sat round this hospitable table as many times as we have, and some of my happiest memories are of meals outside in the seriously classic English garden. It was typical of Edmund that for lunch the day after our tasting of the 1971s, the first first-growth dinner after our wedding, he served us a Château Léoville-Las Cases 1971, just to see how the lower ranks had fared, and the gloriously youthful, jewel-like Château Pétrus of Nick's birth year, 1952. (I guessed 1971 and 1961 as their respective vintages.) This last was bottled by Harveys of Bristol in their heyday, just before Michael arrived there. A comparison of it with my patterned velvet bottle served chez Christian Moueix after a visit to Pomerol showed eloquently that during this period English bottlings could be just as good as, and sometimes better than, the same wines bottled at the château. In those days few of them had their own bottling lines and they relied, as many smaller producers still do today, on mobile bottling lines, not all of the highest quality.

The great Californian wine lovers Belle and Barney Rhodes once served two bottlings of this 1952 vintage of Pétrus, one by Averys and one undertaken at the château, to dinner guests John Avery and Christian Moueix without telling them which was which. To everyone's delight, John Avery preferred the château bottling, while Christian Moueix preferred the wine bottled in Bristol.

Drinking wines of this quality with people who understand them, around a relaxed, sociable table, is the single greatest boon of my enviable métier. Already in 1981 I felt as though I had come a long way since failing to find any point of contact with that embarrassing bottle of Pétrus '45 before my Bordeaux intronisation in 1977.

Wine

on the Box

———

Much of the summer of 1981 was spent researching other wines and wine characters for *The Great Wine Book*, including an immersion in Burgundy which underlined for me just how different it is from at least the most famous wine region of Bordeaux, the Médoc. Buildings in Burgundy may be more modest but they are two or three centuries older, mellow, medieval, still functional, and inhabited, unlike the grand but ghostly châteaux of the Médoc. (I had to interview Clive Gibson about Château Latour in London rather than Pauillac, for example.) Many of the most famous Burgundy domaines are virtually one-man (occasionally woman) bands. The person who shows you around also makes the wine, drawing small samples out of each barrel himself and offering them initially with a farmer's reserve, warming to conviviality only if your judgments on them accord with his. (The convention is to ascend the quality ladder, so it is unwise to be overenthusiastic about the first wine.)

During our September trip to eastern France, because we were combining my researches with Nick's into the state of contemporary French *restauration,* there were two particularly pampered days during which we managed to consume the equivalent of six Michelin stars. And this was the era of beurre blanc, écrevisses, cheeses approaching

100 percent of greasy matter and foie gras *sans limite*. Our digestive systems must have been so much more elastic than they are now.

By October 1981 L'Escargot was reckoned to be in a fit state to hold our wedding reception (Bruno Paillard 1973) for roomsful of friends in the evening and the usual very disparate family members at a more formal wedding breakfast. I still have a photograph of my great-aunt, a fierce professional flower arranger of international repute, haranguing Kathryn McWhirter, my successor at *Wine & Spirit*, and another of Nick's uncle Manny from Liverpool manfully undertaking the job of papering over the cracks with a warm-hearted speech at the Jewish-Anglican family lunch.

We decided to combine our honeymoon—or what my mother was later to call rather pointedly the first of our three honeymoons—with the researches I needed to make into Alsace, the textbook-pretty region on the Franco-German border with the indulgent cuisine and the tall, tapered green bottles of aromatic, full-bodied wine. It was as fraught with disaster as convention requires. The airline left our suitcases behind. The chef of the hotel deep in the Vosges mountains chosen carefully because of its restaurant had left the week before. And Nick was sick during the supposed highlight of the trip, dinner at the famous Auberge de l'Ill at Illhaeusern. The Auberge, like all gastronomic enterprises in Alsace, is very much a family affair, and the Haeberlins routinely reserve their best tables for the likes of the Hugel family, run by Johnnie and their great rivals, the Trimbach clan, of whom Hubert is the best-traveled member.

We were thrilled, therefore, when at the end of our morning with Johnnie Hugel on our last day in Alsace, both of us feeling extremely hale and hungry, he suggested taking us for lunch at the Auberge. Now we could really enjoy that world-renowned cooking. We arrived at the restaurant and, such is Johnnie Hugel's standing, that the entire staff were lined up immediately to be presented to us. They all kept polite but completely impassive expressions until we got to the junior sommelier at the end of the line. "Ah, but you were here on Saturday night!" he exclaimed. Johnny Hugel's face turned to thunder, he wheeled round and interrogated us sharply. "Who brought you here? Hubert?" We had our work cut out to convince him that we'd been there in strictly neutral, self-propelled, and in fact rather unsatisfactory, circumstances. The lunch was memorable—not least because it showed us how, if the wine is substantial enough, like a Vendange Tardive Pinot Gris, for example, it is perfectly possible to enjoy a white wine with food as rich as heavily sauced venison.

My work life was every bit as busy in late 1981 as what is called personal life, a mark perhaps of how many people are unlucky enough to work at something they feel detached from. During the year three very different individuals had approached me with a view to exposing me to an entirely new medium for me, television. Until then my television experience was limited to a brief appearance on a late-night BBC chat show hosted by Tim Rice, Andrew Lloyd Webber's wordsmith, with a particularly urbane wine merchant and Kingsley Amis, who had dismissed the 1970 Cheval Blanc as "some cheap rioja."

The first would-be TV impresario was a mature, extremely well dressed (and therefore, I was to realize, suspiciously atypical) independent television producer who came to see me with an equally well groomed female assistant. They looked very much at home in the first-floor drawing room at Duncan Terrace, took a long list of contacts and telephone numbers of suitable wine producers to visit in France, and I never heard from them again.

My second potential colleague in this brand-new medium for wine was Fay Maschler, whom I had met on a gloriously sybaritic trip to the Michelin galaxy around Lyons with wine importer Joseph Berkmann just before I met Nick. (Good practice for our own subsequent eating trip.) She had an idea for a magazine-format, studio-based BBC television series that would be called *Food and Drink*. We went to see Will Wyatt, then controller of the BBC's more upmarket channel BBC2, about it and were commissioned to make a pilot version.

In a BBC studio we had food writers Paul Levy and Richard Olney and chef Michel Roux, who showed how to joint a chicken. Actor Leonard Rossiter talked about his love of wine. I lectured the little black hole in the camera on some iniquity of wine labeling, probably the blends of "EEC," European Economic Community, i.e., mainly Italian, wine that were sold masquerading as German, however unlikely a commercial proposition that seems in the late 1990s. I found it very easy to talk to this little black hole. For a start it couldn't heckle or answer back and therefore posed no threat, but more importantly, it was expected of me that I should address this hole. No imposition or interruption is involved—unlike the business of, for example, butting into the conversations of friends round a dinner table to make an announcement, or even say a hello or farewell, all of which I still find excruciatingly embarrassing.

Will was not thrilled by our pilot. Too elitist, he said it was, particularly my demonstration of how to open a champagne bottle. He may have been right. Certainly neither Paul Levy nor Richard Olney would be seen dead on the determinedly populist series that eventually surfaced under Fay's title. For these three words she was paid £500 ($800), and after several years it eventually became one of BBC2's most popular programs, partly, I suspect, because it is a quintessentially mainstream BBC1 format. It was screened on BBC2 because then the idea of a television series about food and drink was regarded as frivolous and indulgent. The phrase I particularly remember from its early years was, as a presenter tasted some dish, "Ughh—garlic!"

I was asked to do some filming for the first series of *Food and Drink*, but by then I had already been lured away to BBC2's new rival, an addition to what had previously been a choice of just three channels in Britain, the independent, mold-breaking Channel 4. The man who lured me was Barry Hanson, then on a roll having produced Bob Hoskins's first big hit *The Long Good Friday*, an unusually hip, realistic London thriller. Barry was being funded by Goldcrest, a grandiose 1980s film and television company then housed in a villa in Holland Park and splashing out on movies such as *Chariots of Fire* and *Gandhi* and, its eventual nemesis, the unthinkably expensive turkey *Revolution*.

For Goldcrest a six-part TV series on wine, *The Wine Programme*, was relatively small beer, so to speak, and no one seemed to be counting the pennies. Barry's real coup had nothing whatever to do with me: it was persuading a broadcaster to devote thirty minutes of prime-time television to a subject as potentially inflammatory as an alcoholic drink. The BBC, which is still dominated to a certain extent by the ascetic legacy of its founder, Lord Reith, had consistently rejected any proposals involving liquor. There had been the odd film about, for example, the famous Hospices de Beaune annual auction of burgundy, which could be dressed up as travelogue, but wine per se was seen as a subject that was not just dangerously alcoholic but dangerously elitist.

It was typical of the swashbuckling head of the embryonic fourth channel, Jeremy Isaacs, that he would choose to break this convention. There was also sound sense to his decision to commission Barry to produce a series called *The Wine Programme*. Wine was no longer the drink of a privileged few. Average per capita consumption of wine in Britain had almost tripled to more than a bottle a month between 1970 and 1982. This increase in per capita wine consumption was to slow during the later 1980s and early 1990s so that by the mid 1990s we Brits drank on average about a bottle and a half of wine a month— twice as much as Americans, even if less than a quarter as much as the French.

I could see with my own eyes what a democratic drink wine had become by the early 1980s. It was clear that the sort of people who, like me, spent their own money on evening wine tastings such as those organized by the wine shop La Vigneronne constituted a fair cross-section of society. Taxi drivers would regularly lecture me on their wine drinking habits ("we try not to open the third bottle of an evening, my girlfriend and me"), and wine was already most women's drink of choice. But public perceptions take time to catch up with reality. Wine was, and possible still is, popularly associated with mystique and snobbery.

Barry's thought was that wine information would be more palatable if delivered by someone as unlike the stereotype wine bore as possible, which was presumably what made me a candidate as presenter of this new series. What caught his and his producer wife Susanna's attention initially was an article I'd written for *Harpers & Queen* called "I Spit for a Living," but I suspect that he was also quite attracted by the connection with the bright new star in London's culinary firmament, Nick's Escargot.

After a screen test I had to write a script for a fully grown-up series. This was quite incomprehensible to me. I asked Barry and Susanna if they could lend me a book that would teach me how it was done. They seemed to think this was funny. So I sat down and wrote a script that was basically like *The Wine Book*, read to my friend the little black hole. This, as you may imagine, was less than scintillating. Eventually, after many a meeting in the pale green armchairs at the front of L'Escargot, we had something on paper that might just translate into interesting moving images on the screen.

The next stage was to make a pilot program, a sort of introduction

to wine, which included an interview with Napa Valley–based Frenchman Bernard Portet of Clos du Val, half of the young couple on the
exciting new Franco-California wine cusp I had met in Gerald Asher's
dining room five years earlier. We also had me stomping grapes in the
garage of an Italian family who lived in a London suburb and still
made their own wine from grapes flown in to Covent Garden market
for the purpose—much more convenient than flying us all out to
film the real thing. The pilot did the trick and our commission was
confirmed.

The only problem was that, in the way of recent brides in their thir-
ties, I was pregnant. Our baby was expected in July, about the same
time as sweet little Princess Di's first, in fact. I was determined to
spend the baby's first few weeks doing something people (although
definitely not my deeply skeptical northerner father) were starting to
call bonding. But I blithely agreed to start filming the main series in
September 1982, just in time for the grape harvest in Bordeaux.

It is common in Britain nowadays to blame the collective maternal
folly of the early and mid 1980s on Shirley Conran (American women
have other scapegoats). Terence Conran's second wife, Caroline, is a
warm, domesticated, thoroughly humane food writer with, as far as I
know, a full grasp of family obligations and limitations. His first wife,
Shirley, on the other hand, had in 1975 published a book called *Superwoman* whose thesis was that women could and should Have It All. (Her
recantation, *Down with Superwoman*, did not create half such a stir when
published in 1990.) I realize now that it was misguided at best and
potentially hugely damaging to suggest that having babies and children was just another achievement or leisure activity to be slotted in
between executive politics and baking one's own bread, but it would be
wrong to blame Shirley Conran. *Superwoman* was regarded as an influential work only because it carried the message we all wanted to believe at
the time, that it was completely unnecessary, indeed rather wet, to
make any concessions to motherhood in our careers.

This meant that my very first television contract, negotiated with
much pain on both sides by Caradoc and Barry, the worlds of publishing and television feeling equally suspicious of each other, had a
clause in it stipulating that there had to be provision for a nanny or
nanny substitute (Nick) wherever we went on location. It also meant
that poor Julia, our firstborn, spent much of months three to five on

planes, in hotels and being wheeled round vineyards and cellars in between feeds.

Julia was born on July 10, 1982, a day when Escargot customers were treated to exceptionally lavish hospitality and I tried to graft this new, entirely unfamiliar role on to all my old ones. (Significantly perhaps, the one thing both Nick and I have wanted to do immediately after the birth of all our children is write, whether personal accounts or just thank-you letters. Strange but by no means uncommon.)

Within a couple of days I was back home. But being a self-employed freelancer meant that there was no safety net of maternity leave or solicitous employer. And my determination that Julia's first friend would be me meant there was no nanny or nurse either. I had been back from the hospital for just a day or two, in a state of such tension at the unaccustomed responsibility of motherhood, that for the first and last time in my life I actually craved the mental massage of a gin and tonic, before *The Sunday Times* newsdesk put in its first call. With a baby at my breast, I must have sounded less than enthusiastic about the story they wanted me to follow up. "Don't worry. You've got till Friday," they told me cheerfully.

The Great Wine Book was also being printed over that summer but I was already succumbing to the blandishments of a new publisher, Kyle Cathie then at Pan, who wanted a paperback on wine tasting. I dreamt up the idea of a book which would have one page of wine theory facing another page of practical exercises to demonstrate that theory. I must claim personal responsibility for the grimace-worthy title of *Masterglass*. It was not due until the spring of 1983 when *The Wine Programme* would be edited, but illustrates well my regrettable habit of reacting with collusive overcommitment to an external stimulus.

This is how it came to pass, on the morning of September 27, 1982, that just as a driver rang the bell of our house in north London I was ramming poor little Julia's legs into an outfit specially saved from the dozens that kind family friends had given her. Nick, Julia and I were setting off on my first-ever trip filming on location, staying for the first few nights at Château Margaux, no less, my Médoc home from home. On the way to the airport, for the first, perhaps only, time in my life I had a serious crisis of confidence. I'd spent the last ten weeks in an admittedly cozy ménage à trois but doing something I turned out to be thoroughly incompetent at, looking after a baby. And here was further proof. I'd left that outfit too long on the hanger and couldn't get all of Julia into it; instead of a chic all-in-one in which to arrive at her first first-growth château, she had to wear the bottom half with the top half inelegantly tied round her waist (I'd cut things too fine—another shortcoming—to find her a backup). By now I was convinced that I'd be an inadequate television presenter too. What evidence did anyone have that I could do this, for heaven's sake? I could hardly bear to watch myself on that pilot film. I'd have to remember all those lines, and how on earth was I going to combine the work with doing right by Julia?

When I look with the benefit of hindsight at the filming schedule for what I believe was the world's first television series devoted to wine, it all seems terribly relaxed compared with the intense demands on today's much more streamlined film crews. The typical location film crew nowadays consists of one person in charge of pictures, one in charge of sound, a director and, probably, a fixer person, researcher or production assistant. Our team for *The Wine Programme* consisted of director Paul Fisher, a cameraman already dreaming of the movies, his assistant, *two* sound recordists, an electrician to take care of any extra lights that might be needed, a production assistant, a continuity girl and, the ultimate luxury for a television crew on location, a makeup artist. Oh, and Barry flew out for the night that that elegant Laura Mentzelopoulos invited the entire crew to dinner in Château Margaux's vine-painted dining room, surely the only time it had entertained anyone with as many tattoos as the electrician.

The first morning was a confused flurry of duties—which should I do first, feed Julia, feed myself or wash my hair?—mixed with more of the luxury I remembered from my weekend with Laura. The housekeeper brought in an even bigger breakfast tray this time with an approving coo at the gurgling *pigeonette*. I was terribly, terribly nervous but there was one good omen. The sun was shining on the vineyards round the château where we were due to click our first few clapperboards (what a literally resonant symbol they are, ever more so in this dully whirring age of videotape which takes its cues not from an audible clap but from digital timecodes).

The trouble with putting wine on television is that so little moves, and when it does, it tends not to move for very long. Thus, vineyards and wineries make marvelous fodder for photographers, but there is a limit to how long you can sustain television viewers with a beautiful view. For most of the summer the rustling of wind in the vines is about the most exciting event in the world's vineyards. And even less happens inside cellars and wineries. The odd barrel may be topped up, and in particularly commercial cellars there is always the cameraman's favorite, the bottling line, but it is really only during the grape harvest, vintage or crush that there is much action in cellars and vineyards. This is why we'd chosen to come to Bordeaux at the end of September. And why the vineyard just in front of Château Margaux this sparkling autumn morning was thronged with grape pickers (no machines for a first growth), obligingly bent double in their delightfully obvious exertions.

They had been up since six and had probably started work before eight. It was at least ten-thirty before we had captured any images at all. By eleven o'clock we had probably shot one or two minutes' worth. (The normal expectation is to end up with about five minutes' transmitted film per day, what with traveling, unloading and assembling the kit, waiting for the sun to come out from behind a cloud, for a plane to fly out of earshot, retouching the makeup, etc., etc.) The crew were exhausted. They were also well versed in what were then regarded as their dues. Bacon sandwiches were what they got in the middle of the morning on a decent production. This one was obviously not up to this standard, but surely the production assistant could rustle up some coffee? A delightful girl, she was too young to put her foot down, and too inexperienced to have anticipated the problem of location catering when the location is a vineyard, so off she dutifully trotted toward the world-famous eighteenth-century château. The French have never been able to understand the Anglo-Saxon desire for hot liquid and caffeine between meals anyway, but the grape pickers could not believe their eyes when she eventually returned from Madame Mentzelopoulos's kitchen with a gold-handled tray bearing the salon's set of delicate, gilded coffee cups and a silver jug of coffee.

We somehow settled down to the demands of working in the countryside. It had been raining the weekend before we arrived, so the vineyards were pretty muddy. The good old pickers, needless to say, were wearing all the right gear, but for some reason none of us had thought of bringing suitable footwear. (But then this was the first time a British film crew had roamed at large in wine country.) Nick, between wheeling the pram, was dispatched to the Margaux village shop to buy nine pairs of rubber boots.

By day three we knew we had some beautiful images—an old man in a beret obligingly biked slowly along Château Margaux's avenue at just the right moment. But our plans were subject to last-minute revision. Contrary to popular belief, the famous 1982 vintage in Bordeaux was not conducted in continual sunshine. Toward the end of the first week we had to drop our plan to film more picking and, thanks to the ever-accommodating David Russell, I arranged an interview at short notice with Baron Philippe de Rothschild in his bedroom just up the road at Mouton. In his work clothes of silk pajamas he was a marvelous old ham, and showed me the label designs for the new Mondavi joint venture wine, the same two-faced head that eventually graced the Opus One label, except that at this stage the plan was to call the wine Janus. Presumably this was before someone told them this was a common name for sex shops (and people whose real name is Jancis) in Britain.

The extremely technical, essentially artificial process of filming seemed so at odds with the simple, bucolic traditions of the grape harvest, an observation I make unclouded by personal experience of ever having done it myself. I'm sure it is backbreaking work (which is precisely why I have never done it), but grape pickers always look happy. There must be some special Prozac-like compound in the air above a vineyard full of ripe grapes finding their way from vine to bucket, so long as the weather is fine. (Picking in the rain is as demoralizing as picking in temperate sunshine is invigorating.) It could be alcohol, as grape pickers are habitually given so much (fairly basic) wine to drink in the evening that they may still be under its influence the morning after. But I fancy there is something else too. Perhaps the satisfaction of taking part in a ritual that has changed so little over the centuries, or a sensation that I can only guess at, that of engaging in hard physical teamwork in the great outdoors.

Inside a winery at harvest time the atmosphere is more obviously highly charged. Grape reception areas that spend fifty weeks a year in dusty solitude are suddenly the focus of attention. Normally sullen, empty fermentation vats bubble away, exuding warmth, alcohol, carbon dioxide and the smell of grape skins. Adrenaline levels in winemakers and cellar staff, who spend most of the year in their boots, have to surge to such heights they can almost dispense with sleep.

Adrenaline adjustment has always seemed to me to be a major problem for television presenters working mainly on location. That first trip I was probably kept suitably on edge worrying about Julia's feeds, nappies, temperature and whether she would cry within range of the microphone, so my adrenaline level remained high. Normal life on location, however, involves hours and hours of waiting—rarely free enough to go off exploring, or gathering material for a book or article—for that magic moment when it's your turn, all conditions are at last perfect, and you are expected to deliver a stunningly sparkling performance.

I think I err on the side of being too normal, too adrenaline deficient. I have since interviewed Philippe's daughter Baroness Philippine de Rothschild, who trained as an actress. I watched admiringly how, as soon as she hears the camera whirring, every muscle in her face, especially those at the corners of her mouth, seems suddenly to have been tweaked by thousands of invisible threads. Her eyes sparkle, her words tumble and fight with a ready giggle, and her body is invaded by a language all its own.

While at Margaux we filmed Edmund and Meg being entertained at lunch in the dining room, supposedly being transported by the quality of a bottle of 1953 except that it was a double fake. Firstly because Laura wanted the crew to film the beginning rather than the end of the meal so that it would be less intrusive. So in fact we were drinking a much less exciting vintage while pretending to enthuse about the '53 that Lichine had served a year previously. I asked Nick recently whether he could remember which vintage this lesser one was and he was distinctly unhelpful. "All I can remember from those lunches was starving because I was always served last, but Laura was usually smoking by the time I'd finished my first helping so I never felt I could accept a second." (One habit I have happily adopted from the French is to start eating as soon as I am served; it seems so much more sensible than letting the food get cold, but it's true that Château Margaux first helpings were feminine sized.) When the real '53 was finally served with the cheese (the poor film crew by now banished to find a decent lunch in the sleepy village of Margaux), the first bottle was corked, made unappetizing by a moldy cork, so a second had to be broached.

Two days previously the château's consultant oenologist, the great Professor Emile Peynaud, came to lunch and made no bones about making sure he had enough to eat with his 1971 and 1962 Margaux and the delicious Yquem 1975. I interviewed this world-famous wine authority in a corner of the winemaking quarters about his policy on decanting. His entirely scientifically based view that you risked more than you gained by decanting wines any earlier than just before they are served was to create quite a stir with traditionalists when it was eventually aired back home. My grandmother passed on the message from one of her set in deepest Somerset that he liked the program but couldn't agree with the bit on decanting.

For my part, I have always had the greater respect for science—even if my recurring nightmare is having to take A-level Physics again— and have also found Peynaud's views to be consistently sensible. I generally decant wines as close to serving them as is convenient. With tight-knit wines such as young red bordeaux or northern Italian, I usually decant them before guests arrive. But I am wary of decanting red burgundy at all, so fragile do its perfumes seem to be. A red burgundy can smell flat and oxidized after less than an hour, although white burgundies often benefit so obviously from oxygen's blowing through their most secret corners that we often decant them before serving. I know there is a school of thought that believes opening a bottle and letting it stand an hour or two before serving allows it to improve and "breathe," but I'm with scientists here too. How can the reaction between oxygen and so small a surface area as a bottleneck possibly affect the great bulk of wine in the bottle? In the old days this may have helped dissipate noxious fumes, "bottle stink," or perhaps more correctly "bottling stink," but this is not a modern problem.

While in Bordeaux we also filmed the deceptively humdrum farmhouse that is the world-famous Château Pétrus and I interviewed its young director, Christian Moueix, in a misguided attempt to get him to condemn the high-profile recent French investments in California wine, such as those of Moët and Baron Philippe. I wondered then why he was so difficult to draw out on this subject but realized in retrospect he was at just that time himself in the process of negotiating the Napa Valley joint venture, which would be called Dominus, with Robin Lail, whose father had left her and her sister some prime vineyard (and who would twelve years on help to publicize *The Oxford Companion to Wine* in and around San Francisco). In the early 1980s it seemed as though everyone in the wine world wanted to invest in northern California.

Other filming trips in late 1982 included Champagne, during which I discovered that the dank catacombs in which champagne is matured, enviable as they seem to winemakers in warmer climates, do not provide a perfect milieu for four-month-old babies. The Napa Valley in November on the other hand seemed just the job. The Mondavis in particular really took to Julia and vice versa. I have several photographs of her being passed delightedly from lap to lap round the famous lunch table at the Mondavi winery. This table, as mobile as "the Baron's" back in Pauillac, became a magnet for the world's wine commentators because of the Mondavi policy that it is only possible to appreciate how good their wines are by tasting them alongside the sort of irreproachable classics—first growth bordeaux and grand cru burgundies—that in fact come the way of the wine writer all too rarely.

One night after filming, Bob Mondavi took Nick and I, and therefore Julia in her carry cot, out to dinner at the old Miramonte in St. Helena. This filming business, for all its prolonged longueurs, was pretty tiring, particularly for someone still feeding a baby in the middle of every night. And now I come to think of it, Paul had ordered a dawn shot the next morning. We'd ordered our food and now heard Mondavi ordering the wine. "We'll have a bottle of our Chardonnay, and the Chateau St. Jean, the Freemark Abbey, the Chappellet and the Cuvaison, and then for reds . . ." Hang on a minute, Bob, don't go crazy. We were after a light little supper, I bleated. He wheeled round looking really quite shocked. "Do you wanna *learn?*" he asked, before turning back to the waiter and adding another six bottles.

The makeup artist, the most experienced crew member by quite a margin, had to work even harder than usual the next morning to cover up the shadows under my eyes. She saved many a day, not least because she had a daughter of her own and was terribly good at dandling Julia. I still hate watching myself on a screen. Most sensible people would. But I do remember how different I looked when I interviewed Bill Jekel in Monterey about his theory that *terroir* counts for nothing in

shaping wine quality. I had a broad, broad smile which had nothing to
do with how annoyed the French would be with his views, and everything to do with the fact that I knew this was the very last day of
filming.

People have often said how I look as though I am having a thoroughly wonderful time as I report from the wine regions of the world.
I'm thrilled if this is so, and there have certainly been many treats for
me and, more acceptably within the canon of film crew behavior, many
an evening when we have all a jolly good bonding time. (Working as
part of a team provides a useful and rich counterpoint to the solitary
life of a writer.) But as anyone in the business knows, there is a world
of difference between cruising round wine regions as a tourist with
your family or friends, and being in an unfamiliar place to do a specific
job to a definite timetable using very expensive equipment and technicians at the mercy of the weather and whims of participants.

I found that the bit of program-making I enjoyed most took place
back home in small, dark rooms in Soho—so convenient for L'Escargot—
the final editing and writing the commentary. So much easier than all
that checking in and out of hotels, waiting for silence and memorizing
long speeches. There's a magic in how all that footage can be transformed
by the simple transposition of two sequences, or even the substitution of a
word in commentary. The most obvious casualty of my newfound power
was a Californian acting as self-confessed ace blind taster, without notable
success.

The six half-hour films were finally ready for transmission and allo-
cated a decent midevening, midweek slot, albeit starting in the dog
days of August. To my delighted amazement *The Wine Programme* was
a great success. Admittedly, television critics didn't have much else to
write about that month, but at least what they wrote was enthusiastic.
(Mind you, arts journalists must be the bull's-eye of the target market
of a program about wine.)

We spent a weekend chez Penning-Rowsell that August of 1983
with the Bolters of Bordeaux, wine broker Bill Bolter having patiently
spent a day with us the previous September being filmed in a particularly ponderous sequence involving cars, bridges and Bordeaux traffic.
The novelist Julian Barnes, then an unknown but unbelievably heroic

character to me, was at that time yoked to his television set as television critic of the *Observer*, the Sunday newspaper of sufficiently liberal views to be allowed to flop onto the Penning-Rowsells' stone flags of a Sunday morning. I can still remember sitting in their drawing room, Sunday morning sunshine streaming into the room, my head still gently throbbing from the venerable clarets of the previous night, reading with incredulous delight Barnes's first paragraph of praise, and giggling at his second: "It's only a small grouch to note that Miss Robinson, after a mere two shows, has erased from the Guinness Book of TV Records Robert Kee's entry for the highest number of garb-changes per screen hour (set during 'Ireland—a Television History'); and that her hair keeps going up and down like a zealously practicing fireman. If there was anyone vaguely in charge of continuity in the first place, they should be tied to a chair and forced to watch 'Sin on Saturday.' "

What grabbed the attention of every television critic to notice the series at all were my big red spectacles. These were the direct result of Nick's designer friend Tom's saying portentously at around the time of our wedding that for every face there was the perfect pair of glasses. Impressionable as ever, I took this in just as I had finally despaired of my contact lenses, and just before I happened to see some big red frames in a shop window. They looked fun, and a suitable counterbalance to my large jaw even if in retrospect they looked absurdly oversized. They were extremely popular at the time; in fact, I was horrified to see, red specs became a sort of shorthand for yuppie in comedy sketches.

Before series two I had changed to the same shape in a different color, but by the late 1980s I at last saw the error of my ways and went to the smart Knightsbridge opticians run by Tony Gross, one of L'Escargot's best customers, for something slightly more discreet. "Ah yes," he said. "We've been waiting for you. First of all we had the secretaries coming in for big red glasses, and then we had their mothers. It's high time you changed." He can't have been referring to more than two or three customers in total, but I did see what he meant, and over the years my specs have consistently continued to shrink. A lorgnette next time, perhaps?

It was thrilling to be so obviously associated with a small hit on the small screen. There was the entirely novel sensation of being recognized by complete strangers. Being so very many rungs down the ladder of fame from, say, a movie star, I have experienced it just often enough to be flattering, never so often as to be an inconvenience. Oblique comments are the safest and cleverest, although I wasn't thrilled by the immigration officer at Heathrow who handed back my passport saying, "Yes, I thought you looked rather full bodied."

With that memorable exception comments from strangers are invariably complimentary. It was, typically, my father who pointed out that the people who think you're a complete pain in the neck don't actually take the trouble to seek you out and tell you so. (And it is true that once you thrust yourself or are thrust into the public eye, it is inevitable that your voice, looks, opinions or mannerisms will irritate a certain proportion of people. The trick is presumably to keep the proportion either negligible or, in the case of characters much more confident than me, so high that you become someone everyone loves to hate.)

At least one experience was a salutary counterbalance to all this head swelling. Barry and Susanna did their best to sell this rather rudimentary series on wine outside Britain too, and I was duly shipped out to the Cannes television fair for a couple of rainy late April days in 1983. The high point was our champagne party on a boat in the harbor. I don't think any potential buyers came, but we all had a very jolly time. The low point was my first sight of the exhibition hall stretching away into the far distance, each of the thousands of stands representing dozens and dozens of programs so much more exciting and/or salable than ours. In the end, *The Wine Programme* was sold to Australia, New Zealand, the odd Scandinavian market and, mysteriously, in the early 1990s to the new republics of Estonia, Latvia and Lithuania.

At one point it looked as though it might be shown in the United States, even though it was then in the grip of increasing alcophobia. There was talk of some sponsorship deal with a manufacturer of barbecue briquettes, to which end we had to alternate series of six and seven programs, the magic total of thirteen being a neat fraction of the number of weeks in a year's schedule. Despite hopefully making seven programs in our second series and six in our third, thereby maximizing our chances of an attractive run of thirteen, we never did manage to expose *The Wine Programme*, a prototype in so many ways, to American eyes.

Marathon Tastings,
and a 1787

It was at about this time that huge, communal wine tastings became fashionable. In 1983 in the space of a few months I was invited to one giant overview of the 1961 vintage of top red bordeaux and then another of the 1959, both great years and mature enough to be worth "looking at," as the wine trade euphemism has it.

I had had plenty of limbering up for these events, involving samples of more than thirty different wines. There was, for instance, the Suffolk assessment of many more than thirty 1976s, which constituted another so-called horizontal tasting, many different wines of the same vintage, as opposed to a "vertical" one of different vintages of the same wine. But the tasting that had pushed me to the limits of endurance, my wall if you like, had taken place early in 1980.

Every year Georges Duboeuf, the man who made Beaujolais internationally famous with his flowery labels and a manic dedication that involves twenty-hour working days, likes to invite his major customers to his ever-expanding headquarters at Romanèche-Thorins to taste the latest vintage and select the particular cuvées, or tank lots, they want to buy. Duboeuf is a thoroughly driven wine producer, a phenomenon only intensified by his wife's equal devotion to running the financial side of the business. A congenital frowner, he's not exactly "Hail, fellow, well met." More "Come in, what do think of this Fleurie?" He is truly a product of the age in which work was meant to be all-involving, social life its extension, and family life a mere encumbrance. As a result of all this he makes some extremely good, and a lot of perfectly good, wine.

Liz Morcom and I were invited to taste the 1979s in early February 1980. As Georges is a completeness freak we had to taste every one of his 1979s: well over a hundred four-month-old Beaujolais, from many a cuvée of simple, acid stuff from the flatlands up to the most majestic wines from the best villages, the so-called Beaujolais crus such as Morgon, Moulin-à-Vent and Brouilly. Now it is one thing to taste a hundred wines from very different grapes and places—even the standard range of top red bordeaux encompasses Merlot and two sorts of Cabernet as well as many different terrains—but it is quite another to douse your palate in more than a hundred young Gamays all produced within fifteen miles of each other. Young Gamay is notable for its acidity and a refreshingly fruity character which, after even the thirtieth let alone the hundredth sample, loses much of its charm and, especially, distinction.

We were served a feast between tasting the reds and the local whites in Duboeuf's kitsch-filled *salon de réception* (fairground organ, wine-related statuary, and a supernumerary balustrade made of double magnums), but I think it was me who suggested that only a swim after all this lot would truly refresh. Joseph Berkmann, Georges' British agent, obligingly took Liz and me in his Rolls-Royce to the indoor piscine at nearby Villeneuve where I doubt that Madame Duboeuf's swimsuit, on loan to me, had been seen before.

This marathon tasting was certainly the first time I'd been asked to taste more than forty or fifty wines at a time and it marked a milestone in my own tasting history. I think that tasters can boost their stamina by gradually increasing the number of wines they tackle at a single session until they find their own upper limit. Nowadays I often taste more than a hundred wines at a time—particularly the scores, sometimes hundreds, of very assorted wines that Britain's major retailers open once or twice a year hoping to please us columnists with as many of their lines as possible. This is much less demanding than tasting a hundred Beaujolais of the same vintage, but even so, and even though I try desperately hard not to swallow a drop of alcohol, I would not claim that I approach the last sample with as much energetic objectivity as the first. I know by comparing how much I spit during a tasting session with how much I have poured (a particularly nice experiment, as you can imagine) that however hard I try, I do take in some of the liquid, and I'm sure some of the alcohol is absorbed as vapor. Such a prolonged state of heightened analysis combined with a battle against the ravages of the enemy, alcohol; it's no wonder that tasting is such a tiring experience.

I have noticed, however, that all sorts of external factors can affect both tasting ability and how one feels afterwards, as well as the important internal factor, one's mood. You need to be willing to concentrate to taste well—drinking's easy, but tasting is a skill. I remember one blind tasting organized by Robin Young of the *Times*, a follow-up to the one in which we were all supposed to recognize our own recommendations. I can't remember this one's purpose, but I do remember that I was just about to go and choose my wedding dress, or undertake some other vital prenuptial preparation, and I just couldn't muster my tasting faculties at all.

The weather, and in particular the atmospheric pressure, has a huge effect on tasting, I have noticed. On a muggy or damp day, you feel more sluggish, and the volatile smell messages are much less ready to leave the glass and soar up your nose. On a bright, crisp day, on the other hand, everything—including smells, flavors, and the senses—seems much sharper and intense.

And then of course there are the minutiae of tasting organization. My first big horizontal tasting in 1983 was at a handsome hotel in central Scotland called Houstoun House. Its then owners Keith and Penny Knight had celebrated their son Sandy's birth in 1961 by acquiring bottles if not cases of all the important red bordeaux made in that great year. He'd turned twenty-one the previous September and, in an extraordinary act of generosity, they invited a dozen of us to join Sandy, then managing their restaurant, in a giant tasting of them. This was selfless indeed, for the parents did all the work, including feeding us the essential edible blotting paper at lunchtime, with a less essential but suitably light Mosel. Penny Knight had even given up smoking inside for the three days before the tasting so as to clear the air in their large, airy sitting room where the tasting was held.

This was not enough for Michael Broadbent, Christie's Mr. Wine.

The good thing about tasting with Michael is that he is a natural organizer of tastings. (He is now world famous for it, so you know that if
you're at the same tasting he is, you're in the right place for some very
fine wine tasted in textbook, his textbook on wine tasting, conditions.)
Most of us invited from England—Michael, Pat Grubb, his opposite
number from Sotheby's, John Avery, Clive Coates, Jane MacQuitty
and me—flew up from London that morning. Michael strode into the
tasting room with its carefully arranged little tables (one Scot and one
Sassenach apiece) and wrinkled his nose immediately. Too much
woodsmoke in the air. The Knights may have left their cigarettes unlit
but they had definitely burnt the odd log within smellable memory.
Doors and windows were hastily opened and the brisk winds off the
Firth of Forth did their bit to render the atmosphere sufficiently pristine for our delicate noses.

The thirty-one wines were served in three flights starting at noon,
2:45 and 5:30, with just the right amount of time, over an hour, to
examine the ten or eleven tasting samples poured from a single bottle.
There was a back-up bottle in case any were substandard (the first
bottle of Pichon Lalande smelled moldy and was pronounced "corked")
and surely the Knight parents treated themselves to a sip or two, for it
is easy to squeeze fifteen generous pours (or twenty-four very mean
ones) from one standard wine bottle. It was all very charmingly done.
We were asked to mark out of 20—quite a novelty in those days—and
were each given a tasting sheet with plenty of room for our comments
on Appearance, Bouquet, Taste and Overall Quality. This was the first
of many times I have been told how to allocate my marks (4, 5, 6 and 5
for these aspects respectively), all of which is fine, except that I feel
that the allotment for Appearance is almost invariably wasted. Unless
a still red wine is visibly fizzing, or a young is obviously brown and
oxidized (which will forfeit marks in every other aspect too), or the
wine has an unpleasant haze in it, which very rarely happens, then I
always end up awarding maximum points in this first category, and
wish that I had more marks left out of the total with which to signal
nuances of difference in what I smell and taste.

This was a great opportunity for me to examine this vintage I'd
heard so much about, a vintage marked like so many of the great
grape-ripening seasons in Bordeaux by drought. (The 1961 vintage

was also notable for producing a very small crop, but so for instance was the dismal 1984, so this can't have been the crucial factor.)

At twenty-two years old the wines were still exceptionally deeply colored—a sign of thick grape skins and durability in red bordeaux— and, unlike my monstrous young 1975s, most of them had so much ripe, gently perfumed fruit that one hardly noticed the tannic grip that still underpinned the most powerful of them. Some of the lesser wines, the Calon-Ségurs of the bunch, were drying out fast, but the colors and flavors noticeably deepened as we approached the third flight, the Pauillacs.

The most extraordinary thing about the 1961s is how distinctive they are, with their unusual combination of majesty, charm and bal- ance. The 1945s may be majestic, the 1953s, 1955s, 1962s and a host of wines in the 1980s may be charming, but no vintage—with the possible exception of the consistently overlooked 1959s—can, yet, rival what the 1961s can offer. I cannot imagine the 1961s tasting quite as opulent, almost decadent, in youth as the 1982s were at just the time we were at Houstoun House. But perhaps the 1990s, a vin- tage that has looked better every year in the decade succeeding it, may yet give the 1961s a run for their money.

The problem with horizontal tastings, if it can be called a problem, is that it is difficult not to be so sidetracked by the differences between individual representatives of the vintage, which is the most obvious phenomenon, that one forgets to form the most important impression of all, that of the vintage as a whole. We of course spent a lot of time after each flight debating the relative merits of the wines—well, not so much debating actually as there is precious little useful debate to be had in comparing one person's entirely unexaminable and subjective judgments with someone else's, more a repetition of points of view. Needless to say, our fervor increased as the day went on. Our host later noted a "change in atmosphere and tempo from the austere silence of the exam room during the first session to the highly charged dramatic climax of the last few wines," the three first growths of Pauillac and Pétrus, then unchallenged as the most famous Pomerol. (Little did I know that as we tasted, the buds were just coming out on Merlot vines less than a mile from Château Pétrus that would produce the most valuable case of wine I would ever buy, Le Pin 1983.)

About the Pétrus 1961 I wrote, among other things, "not quite brimstone, but not for roast lamb. Mature cheddar perhaps. Can this really be nothing but grape juice?" At Houstoun House I was most impressed by this wine, the Latour and the Margaux. Four years later, when the then distinctly embryonic Farr Vintners (now probably the world's leading trader in fine wine) organized $7,500 worth of blind comparison of even more 1961s, again in suitable flights, the most impressive wines were Pétrus and Margaux, with strong performances by Palmer, Latour à Pomerol, Gruaud-Larose and Ducru-Beaucaillou. At Edmund Penning-Rowsell's comparison of 1961 first growths, a supplementary treat to coincide with his seventieth birthday in 1983, Pétrus, Margaux and Latour had also been the favorites—a rare display of consistency.

Because it wasn't blind, the Houstoun House tasting required rather less concentration and application than Farr's, and we certainly hadn't been overworked. It had all felt like fun (to us if not to our hardworking hosts) and we were quite ready for our dinner, built round more 1961s, including the famous Hermitage La Chapelle. I can't tell you what a joy it is at the end of a hard day's tasting, to be able to sit down and enjoy wine as it is designed to be enjoyed, with food and conversation.

That Hermitage was at that stage by far the most celebrated red Rhône ever made (Marcel Guigal was yet to make his mark, his 1978 single vineyard Côte Rôties barely in bottle). It was the stuff of wine merchants' dreams—they said it tasted as good as a 1961 bordeaux— and I had been lucky enough to taste it once before. Less than a year afterwards I was to buy it for just $48 a bottle at the Dundas Arms, a pub-with-rooms in Berkshire where we spent one glorious Saturday night with my parents-in-law. The wine sells for more than $1,000 a bottle on some merchants' lists today, but the Knights' treasure trove of Jaboulet's most famous wine must have been more than one bottle, for there is nothing like a long wine tasting for making the tasters thirsty. And with breast of pheasant it tasted just like red velvet. The color was deeper almost than anything else we'd seen that day from Bordeaux and its appeal was thoroughly, hedonistically rich and sweet, yet with amazing depth of flavor, a sort of reverberation. The only other wines which approached it that day for sheer magnificence of color and flavor were the Pétrus, Latour and Palmer, the third growth Margaux that performed such a miracle in 1961.

The magnificent claret-like Hermitage had been preceded by an even more claret-like claret, Léoville-Poyferré 1961, looking almost skinny in comparison, and was followed by a grand cru red burgundy. The Musigny 1961 from Faiveley was certainly dense and succulent, but cut off fast as soon as it was swallowed (no spitting at the dinner table, thank you very much). "Nearest I've got recently to good red burgundy," I wrote rather grudgingly. Honestly, who did I think I was to be invited, after so few years in the business, to sit in judgment on these dream bottles?

But we certainly had been invited precisely to judge. Keith Knight, who had (like Michael Broadbent) been trained as an architect, turned out to be as fine a calligrapher and statistician as host. Within a few days we had each received a beautiful chart of everyone's scores for each wine, together with a summary sheet showing that the group's overall favorites were, in descending order, Pétrus, Latour, Mouton, Margaux (given a perfect mark by David Wilson of the nearby Peat Inn), Haut-Brion, and Palmer (dragged down by David Brown, Scotland's other famously wine-loving restaurateur from La Potinière). Cheval Blanc, Lafite and Grand-Puy-Lacoste followed after an interval.

After this experience I was starting to get the hang of these comparative tastings. If they were all as jolly as this, which was admittedly enlivened by the low-key confidence of so many Scots, I could handle it. Unfortunately they were not.

Over the next few years more and more tastings were organized without sensitivity for either wines or tasters. During that period it seemed as though many of the people who were spending the most on wine were determined that it should give as little pleasure as possible. Typical was the arranging of a marathon vertical tasting of *all* vintages of a certain property, even though everyone knew that mixing up the better years with the worst would make the worst taste even worse; and even among the better ones there could be only one best, with the result that all but one of these precious, painstakingly crafted wines would end up tasting like also-rans. There were times in the eighties when I would get up from a tasting full of pomp and solemnity and ache to be able to take just one bottle home, even one of the ones that was given one of the lowest scores of all by the assembled palates. Why? Because I knew that if I could only serve it in isolation, or perhaps after a wine with even fewer pretensions, with suitable food and company, it would taste delicious.

Over the years I have devised my own simple pleasure-meter for tastings of grand wines. If the majority of tasters approach the table or wherever it takes place with a smile, then I'm sure to enjoy it. If, on the other hand, most of them look gloomy and suspicious, then this is not a tasting for me. And now that I quite often lead wine tastings myself, I try to remind amateurs—I would not presume to instruct experienced professionals—that the point of wine is to give pleasure and that they should approach the wines with that in mind. I think many amateurs are wary of wine tastings, feeling almost that it is they who are on trial rather than the wines. The ideal tasting of course squeezes the most pleasure out of every wine and every taster.

Quite a number of the dreary, ascetic marathon tastings I have witnessed were organized by American wine collectors, some of them ex-collectors (in one case religion, in another an expensive divorce intervened), but then to counterbalance that I have also enjoyed some of the best meals, bottles, wine service and, especially, wines-by-the-glass in the United States.

The single most extraordinary tasting I have ever been to was in 1986, organized by one of Germany's famous band of wine collectors, the most famous of the lot, Hardy Rodenstock, a pop group promoter who has devoted much of his life and fortune to seeking out, and then drinking, some of the finest wines in the world.

I'd met Hardy and some of his Swiss and German cronies (who are almost as devoted as he to the fine wine cause) in June that year at Mouton where we tasted one of his famous, or infamous depending on which auction house you belong to, "Thomas Jefferson bottles." Hardy has never said exactly where or how he found them, but he suddenly announced that he had discovered behind some wall in Paris a cache of bottles of eighteenth-century wines that had been bought by America's third and most wine-friendly president, no less.

The collection comprised 1787s and 1784s from the eighteenth-century precursors of Lafite, Margaux, Mouton and Yquem. He knew they were for Jefferson because "Th. J." was engraved on the bottles, you see. In December 1985 Christie's sold one of these bottles, a

Lafite 1787, for what is still a world-record price, £105,000, or $168,000, to the late Malcolm Forbes. This would have worked out at about $24,000 a glass, had anyone actually drunk the wine, but Forbes chose to put the famous bottle on a suitably antique table in his Jefferson Museum, by a model of the great man. It stayed there for many months, admired as what must be presumed to be the world's greatest and certainly most valuable wine, until someone noticed that the heat generated by a nearby spotlight must have shriveled the cork, which had dropped into the wine, thereby allowing it to spoil under the full force of oxygen. Thus did the world's most expensive bottle of wine become the world's most expensive bottle of vinegar.

Our tasting of "Jefferson's Mouton" took place between the sale and demise of this famous bottle (which of course has gladdened the hearts of the millions who could not conceive of ever spending more than $10 on a bottle of wine, and even made those of us who could not imagine spending more than $150 on a bottle of wine smirk a little). Hardy had already tried one of his ancient Yquems, but this was to be the first time a bottle of red wine from his Jefferson collection would be tasted. Again, I was extraordinarily lucky to be there, the only journalist, wearing my *Sunday Times* hat, among the nineteen tasters. Hardy had flown in not just his pals but a tame sommelier, which must have put Raoul Blondin's Roman nose out of joint a little. Baron Philippe's own wine butler was already muttering about how the wine would be completely *"passé, zéro."*

The flask-shaped Jefferson bottle, our 1787 Branne Mouton, had been shipped in six weeks previously to allow it to stand upright before opening and encourage all the heavy sediment one would expect to develop after all those years in the bottle to fall to the bottom. This posed a problem for the people at Mouton because all their cellar staff were trained to put any bottle they saw standing upright on its side immediately (for the reasons that became all too apparent at the Jefferson Museum), so this historic bottle had to be carefully locked away in the darkest recesses of the then ailing Baron's personal cellar. Its oldest vintage of Mouton, by the way, was then a single bottle of 1853, the year the Rothschilds acquired the property, bought specially at Christie's a few years before, although it is certainly the finest collection of nineteenth-century bordeaux in the Médoc.

Our group consisted of many shiny-suited Germans, Baron Philippe's freckled grandson Philippe Sereys de Rothschild playing hookey from business school in Bordeaux, the highest echelon of the Mouton Cadet set, and (phew! now I knew I was right to have come) Michael Broadbent, who blew in in blazer, gray flannels and Mouton tie at the last minute and, typically, had to catch the 2:25 flight back to London for a dinner that evening. Not just Hardy's but Christie's Wine Department's fortunes depended to a certain extent on how this bottle tasted. (Subsequently there was to be much carbon dating of glass and wax seals, analysis of calligraphy and, eventually, acrimony over these extraordinary bottles, only two and one half of which have ever been offered in a public salesroom, the Yquem creating a record price for a white wine.)

Blondin led the curious cortege across the famous gravel to the cellar. We all gazed at the bottle with its thick wax turban over the top, and Michael, notebook at the ready, asked "Level? Ah, mid-shoulder. Very interesting." (If you are ever considering selling several bottles of the same wine, as Hardy presumably was, it is commercially astute to keep those with the least air in them for the salesroom.) The bottle was labeled Branne Mouton 1787, after Baron Bran (n) e who at that time owned the estate. It had consisted only of the Motte, the very slight knoll in front of the tasting room, and back then the owner was busy planting Cabernet Sauvignon vines on it in his efforts to produce a wine as highly valued as at Lafite next door.

We trooped back up into the light to watch the young sommelier put the precious bottle into a bowl and then start to chip the wax off it. That bowl, how did he know that the ancient glass was going to crack? Imagine having sufficient knowledge of antique wines in your twenties to know that you should always put a dodgy bottle in a bowl. But this could have been disastrous. We all dashed awkwardly back down the steps with many a cry of *"Schnell! Schnell!"* to retrieve the decanter Hardy had brought with him, a strange thing in the shape of a bust of George Washington with a cork sticking awkwardly out of his head, but at least the sediment-free wine was now trapped in a reasonably airtight container.

We tasted the wine in a light room overlooking the courtyard, the sommelier cradling the decanter and so cleverly managing to share out the wine between so many of us. Just a look at the depth of its treacle-brown color was enough to elicit a flurry of *"Extraordinaire!"*s from the French contingent. Michael said it looked like a 1900. Philippe raised his glass and asked permission to take it to his grandfather in bed upstairs. The pre-revolutionary bouquet was reticent at first and then built up to a great cloud of sweetness hanging over the whole room. The most extraordinary thing about how the wine tasted was its weight and intensity, almost as though it had at some stage in its life been very gently fortified (which it could have been, but none of us were going to give up a drop for the sake of cold-blooded laboratory analysis).

Far from a fragile relic, this was a wine with real life and power, the bouquet, amazingly, continuing to blossom in the glass, evoking "dunked gingernuts" for Michael, "lovely coffee" for Hardy, sheer incredulity in me. In fact the wine kept getting better and better for a full three-quarters of an hour after it was poured—quite an achievement even for a young wine. Raoul Blondin couldn't believe his senses. "I've never tasted anything like it," he kept repeating, sidling up for just one last dreg from the decanter (which most unfortunately trapped all the last drops at the end of Washington's nose). So excited was he, he poured out the deposit from the empty bottle into a giant glass and made us all taste it. "It's delicious! No bitterness. They wouldn't have done any egg white fining in those days, you see."

By the time this glass got to me, it smelled of so many expensive male unguents, I'm afraid, that I could not fully appreciate its intrinsic flavor, but there was no doubting the quality of this wine. Word came back of Baron Philippe's amazed delight (the home team really hadn't been expecting anything very much). Hardy smiled and nodded in his usual enigmatic way. "The Paris cellar was so effectively blocked up, it was almost hermetically sealed, you see." It takes a great deal for a wine to inflame Michael, but he was chattering excitedly. "I thought it would be a bit acidic, a bit decayed, but there wasn't a trace. If there was any doubt, forget it. This wine is genuine. No doubt about that."

The wine that had a little trace of both acid and decay was the *bonne bouche*, the Mouton 1858. It tasted so light, so *modern* after its predecessor. The Germans then trooped out to inspect a bottle in the back of Hardy's car, a jeroboam (six-bottle size) of Château Pétrus 1945. I must have expressed some astonishment at all this to Michael. "Oh, the Germans are doing it with knobs on nowadays. They're good people; they really know quite a lot. I spent three days in Germany with Hardy last year and it was all '28s, '29s and '59s."

I saw evidence of this full-throttle, knobs-on approach in the ornately decorated Petit Château next door, Philippine's Pauillac residence, where we repaired for lunch (the Germans loomed hugely over the spindly Louis XVI furniture). One of the Mouton Cadet team mentioned the 1865 Margaux they were planning to serve us and added nervously, "even if it's awful, we're going to drink it." Hardy smiled and let slip that at home he had every single vintage of Mouton from 1982 back to the great 1945. He proposed that we open his jeroboam of '45 Pétrus for lunch (he probably had three more in his cellar). Much loss of face among the Mouton Cadets. Grandson Philippe butted in diplomatically and argued that it would be a shame to open the Pétrus and drink it straightaway; it'll be so tannic and tough. French honor was saved but German taste buds probably felt just a little deprived.

I met this extraordinary gang of well-heeled sybarites again the following September 30 at the 1986 version of Hardy's annual tasting, this year at Château d'Yquem. This was by a very wide margin the most remarkable event of its kind, and possibly—though it's hard to tell—the highest point of Hardy's own series of vinous pinnacles, for if Hardy has a specialty in his cellar it is this, the most glorious and long-lived of all Sauternes.

In brief, we sat down at about noon on a crisp autumn day and rose from the table at one or two the following morning.

Sixty-six wines were served, with a dozen courses, by chefs shipped in specially from Germany and Bordeaux. It was a survival course for us, and a triumph of organization for Hardy.

We were driven from our hotel in Bordeaux in a bus, feeling rather foolish in our evening dress at this sober hour, and disgorged onto the lawn in front of the château, overlooked by workers in blue mending the roof. The chefs, who'd been here since 4 A.M., came out of the kitchens to greet us, their whites already reeking of good food and luxurious reductions. On our way in to the grand salon where we were to transform so much culinary artistry into so much alimentary canal stuffing we passed a notice board on which was pinned the full, stomach-churning gastronomic plan, beautifully illustrated and designed by Hardy.

At this extraordinary fest we were each issued a lavishly bound red and gold album in which to make our notes on each wine. Later on we'd be given a giant, specially blown and engraved glass as a souvenir of this occasion. During the first few courses I was seated next to Alexandre, the Comte de Lur-Saluces and our host representing Yquem. For him, although he had attended marathon tastings of Yquem in Los Angeles, Brussels and Brisbane, this was the event of a lifetime. He was supplying very much less wine than Hardy was, but even so this was the first time such an event had taken place at the Château itself. We were making serious inroads into the Château's own stocks of older wines on this single day. He noticed a Roman numeral on the front of our tasting album. "What means this seven?" he asked Hardy, who at this point was seated opposite him and the Comtesse.

"It means this is my seventh annual tasting," smiled Hardy.

The count gulped. "That's what I thought it meant," he said bravely.

"And next year will be the eighth," Hardy added, somewhat brutally at this stage, I thought.

Lur-Saluces was later to confess to me that Hardy has tasted many more vintages of Yquem than he has himself. "He probably owns more vintages too," he confided. "What makes him different is that he collects to *drink*."

This was the first time Hardy had held his annual tasting outside Germany, and he'd invited one American, fanatical tasting organizer Bipin Desai, in recognition of the transatlantic camaraderie between what was then the world's two greatest clusters of fine wine collectors, in the United States and in Germany/Switzerland. A famous Dutch wine collector had also been invited. He got very exercised about the description in the album of the host's wine as Château Yquem rather than Château d'Yquem. "It's as it is on the label," explained Hardy patiently. There were several amazed guests from Bordeaux, including my Cheval Blanc friend Jacques Hébrard, Professor Pascal Ribéreau-Gayon from the University of Bordeaux, young Philippe Sereys de Rothschild, who discussed the current vintage with Lur-Saluces (they'd just started picking at Mouton and would start in a week at Yquem) and René Lambert of wine merchants Dourthe, who is one of surprisingly few members of the Bordeaux wine trade to be truly fanatical about fine wine.

There was not a spittoon in sight, but there was plenty of still Spa water (Hardy had conducted a blind water tasting to determine which one would suit the wines best). The wines were of an order of greatness that would move any wine lover. We began with four extremely rare dry German wines (including a bizarre dry, late-picked 1976 Zeltinger Beerenauslese Trocken); four white burgundy grands crus from the likes of Domaine Ramonet; and sixteen—far too many—vintages of Ygrec, the top-heavy dry wine made at Yquem in less successful years for sweet wine-making.

All this was by way of palate whetter for the first and most important flight of Yquems: the big, almost blowsy 1976, an aggressive 1858, an 1847 that was the star of the show, so vigorously sweet, round and rich, strutting its stuff right out to the outer reaches of the palate, a slightly passé 1811 and, the rarest of all these rarities, a blue-green flask which had been engraved in white with flowers, leaves, bunches of grapes and the arms of the Sauvage family who had owned Yquem before the Lur-Saluces took over in 1787.

The Count was in ecstasies of grateful excitement. "For ze empty bottle, I kiss you," he said to Hardy. "For ze full one, I don't know what to do."

Hardy had studied the archives of Yquem and knew that the Russian Czar had bought a barrel of 1847 Yquem for 20,000 gold francs. He'd also heard that there was a cache of Czarist treasures in what was then Leningrad (who does this man consort with?), so he went to work on the hunch that some of this wine may have survived and, voilà, this single ancient bottle, glass already dated at mid-eighteenth century. A wine perhaps thirty years old when our Branne Mouton 1787 had been made. There was a mutter that this was probably the oldest wine ever tasted from the bottle. (There is an ancient but systematically refreshed barrel of a 1727 Rüdesheimer Apostelwein in the cellars of Bremen town hall in the far north of Germany.)

Michael Broadbent had already risen to his feet to remind us that these old wines have to be decanted and drunk straightaway, so we fell silent and watched the young sommelier tap gently at the wax seal.

Hardy's girlfriend hugged him. There was a squeal of delight and a clap as the cork emerged intact, only to crumble immediately but well away from the wine which, as it was carefully measured into eight glasses specially handblown and engraved by Austrian glass specialist Georg Riedel, looked from a distance like young claret with its deep reddish brown color. Each table shared one of these glasses of unctuous history, creamy-rich with a very slightly metallic edge that indicated it may just be starting to fall apart. This wine did not improve in the glass, it had to be passed around quickly, inhaled and shared like a sacrament. The 1847 served next was the better wine, but then it was probably exactly a century younger. I resolved then and there to fill my cellar with Sauternes that will taste deliciously youthful when I sip it on my deathbed.

Those special glasses were auctioned for charity by good old Michael (he works so hard) and by four-thirty, with the lovely autumn light fading, the lucky bidders were packing away their purchases in special boxes and all were anxious to stretch their legs outside. But no. The chef looked anxious, tapped a glass and reminded us we must get back to our seats for the last course of the first quarter of our meal, foie gras sauteed with freshly peeled grapes, to be washed down by the ten-year-old infant 1976 Yquem.

Belgian wine writer Jo Gryn turned to the Count. "It's a historic day, isn't it?" "More than that," said the Count (who exactly ten years later was to see the rest of his family sell their share of this great old property to Moët-Hennessy while he was traveling in the Far East).

Myself and Michael, lazy Brits, were the only ones to duck out of the cellar tour that punctuated this orgy. While the others inspected the presses and barrels being prepared for the (as it turned out, highly successful) 1986 vintage, the British contingent snoozed under a couple of trees in the afternoon sun. We were also the only ones feeble enough to ask halfway through for a spittoon. The only suitable receptacle turned out to be an ornate cache pot; German tasters have always been much less enthusiastic spitters than the British, and I suppose in retrospect it was rather rude to ask if we could spit in the dining room, but at this stage we were concerned with self-preservation. I seem to remember washing down some aspirin with Lanson 1964 during one of the other breaks.

The second session didn't begin until 6 P.M. I may have drunk far

more than I ever had done previously before sundown, but I don't
think I've ever *left* as much wine either. The French windows were still
open to the vineyards, hazy blue in the setting sunlight. A breeze was
playing on my dress, so blessedly made with Lycra. Hardy still looked
very serious, but then he had so much to organize for so many.

We'd had lobster and foie gras with grapes. With our giant bottles
of 1966 red bordeaux—including a jeroboam of robustly mature and
healthy Canon and an impériale of surprisingly well developed, classic-
tasting Calon-Ségur (trumping a rather dull jeroboam of Lafite)—we
had cèpes, the precious local fungi.

There was a sudden change of mood with the next flight of wines,
for Hardy had decided it would be fun to lay on a blind tasting at this
stage. Not just any blind tasting, of course, but eleven of the finest
red bordeaux, in magnum of course, ranging in vintage from a
1937 Latour to an 1848 Lafite! Everyone suddenly had to start paying
attention and there was much discussion of the minutiae of different
wines, for many of Hardy's guests were already familiar with these
wines. All I can tell you is that the 1921 Pétrus and, almost as delicious, the 1921 Cheval Blanc were stunning, as was the 1929 Figeac.
The 1858 Mouton (our *bonne bouche* after tasting the 1787 Branne
Mouton) and 1848 Lafite were pretty good, the 1878 Rausan-Ségla less
so, like the 1929 Haut-Brion and 1934 Margaux, while the 1928
Trotanoy and 1937 Latour were mildly disappointing. Michael identified an extremely creditable six out of these ten wines (we knew what
was being poured, but not the order). I scored a totally pathetic zero,
but quite frankly at this stage my palate had lost any edge it might
ever lay claim to. Writer Richard Olney and I were shushed like
naughty schoolchildren as we giggled over the impossibility of this
task, while Hardy was hard at work on his pocket calculator coming
up with the results of the blind tasting (someone must have developed
a special liver super-function pill for him).

A 1978 Brane-Cantenac (named after the same baron as once owned
Mouton) tasted quite lovely after all this hard work.

After a break for aspirin, a truffle flan with an ink-black sauce was
served with four more giant bottles of giant red bordeaux. The room
was very subdued as everyone chomped on their truffles, chewing over
their performances as blind tasters. Michael cheered up our table by
making comparisons between the ultra-opulent Pétrus 1979 ("of

course it's infanticide to drink it now") and Sophia Loren. "You can admire them, but you don't want to go to bed with them." The double magnum of Palmer was drying out a little we thought but Michael insisted the lively double magnum of 1947 Cantenac-Brown smelled of chocolate and schoolgirls' uniforms. (Political correctness was still in its infancy in 1986.)

Then something amazing happened. We had all, by any standard, had quite enough to eat and drink. In fact some of us were feeling thoroughly bilious and even, disloyally, starting to think fondly about our beds in the Hotel Aquitania. But three more reds were served with our artery-hardening Brillat-Savarin (this was before Michael was converted to white-wines-with-cheese zealotry) of which the third was so absolutely sensational, so utterly complete, so creamily rich yet perfectly balanced and elegant, with both power and subtlety, that it completely revived even my flagging spirits. It was a jeroboam of Mouton 1929, made just seven years after the young Baron Philippe de Rothschild had taken over the property from his aunt, on a prescient whim. For at this time wine was thoroughly unfashionable in much of cocktail-sipping Europe, and completely illegal in the whole of the United States.

This felt to me like the final burst of energy we would be granted that evening, but then I had never been to one of Hardy's events before and was reckoning without the seven sweet wines served with the two sweet courses at the end. A deep ruby, complex, quince-like Wachenheimer Goldbacher Gerümpel Trockenbeerenauslese 1937 tasted like the most reviving elixir one could imagine, so lively yet delicate. And then finally (or at least finally for those of us who resisted the temptation to try the four rare spirits Hardy had laid on with the coffee) there were three more wines from the Lur-Saluces stable with a 1949 from Yquem's sister property de Fargues as introduction: richly burnished, attractive if very slightly rustic in this company with a bitter note at the end. Then, our swansong into the rest of our lives, the last wines I would taste before returning to my more usual diet of Coonawarra Cabernet and Sainsbury's Corbières, two of the greatest vintages of Yquem, 1937 and 1921. The 1921 is conventionally the *prima inter pares,* dark brownish gold and fairly deep, already smelling spicily exotic, still hinting at something left unrevealed yet that night, just starting to dry out very, very slightly. I was completely smitten by the

1937, which was so much more youthful and vivacious, absolutely intriguing and lovely yet with riches hidden behind more than seven veils. We slipped into a new month, the harvest month of October, as we sipped the 1937. A good omen surely.

The Comte de Lur-Saluces rose to his feet, admirably steadily I thought, to hymn the praises of Hardy. He'd heard some bottles had come from Leningrad, some from England, some from Scotland, some from Caracas. Certainly he had nothing in the Yquem cellar to rival the collection of wines we'd been lucky enough to drink that night. Chaban Delmas, the mayor of Bordeaux, should award Hardy a medal. It was people like Hardy and his friends who provided the spur for people like Lur-Saluces to keep on making top-quality wine.

Eventually we heaved ourselves up from the table, too, and slowly, reluctantly, filed on to a vehicle as prosaic as the bus that had brought us that morning. Surely Hardy could have organized horse-drawn gilt coaches.

You may feel that the tasting notes above hardly do justice to the great wines they attempt to describe. The reason is simple, if ignoble. I was exhausted and took the first seat I could at the front of this bus. Glassmaker extraordinaire Georg Riedel of Austria, whom I had never met, came and sat next to me, and happily put in the return journey to Bordeaux telling me about his family firm's very special efforts to design wine glasses perfectly suited to each different style of wine, according to where it hits the tongue, lips and so on (at least that's what, from later discussions, I assume he was saying; I was not taking in much at this stage). The result was that at the other end, in my haste to reach my hotel bed and oblivion, I must have left my beautiful red tasting album with all its detailed, if increasingly untidy, notes on these miraculous wines on the bus.

I discovered this the next morning just before setting off for the airport and an early flight to London. (What could Bordeaux possibly tempt me with after Hardy's feast?) Thank goodness, and Hardy, that we had each been presented with a copy of the menu and full array of wines. I sat in the departure lounge at Mérignac feverishly trying to recall tasting notes on every wine. I still have the notebook. Against the 1953 Pichon Lalande served in marijeanne, a rare bottle size containing the equivalent of three regular bottles, all it says is "appalling to admit that I have absolutely no recollection of this wine."

I still feel unworthy of all these treasures, still sure that I could do full justice to any one of them if served in splendid isolation, still convinced that my constitution must be built differently from those of Hardy and his collecting cronies. He invited me to the two or three subsequent annual tastings, held in the mountains of the Austrian Tyrol, with a few walks in between sessions, which sounds a bit more sensible. For various reasons I was never able to go. I'd love to one of these days but I feel convinced it would never be as extraordinary as the 1986 vintage.

In the last ten years there has been much speculation about Rodenstock, his motives, his methods and, in particular, the provenance of his bottles. Michael Broadbent and I have, for instance, spent many a tube journey discussing him.

Hardy remains a mysterious figure in both his buying and selling of wine, but he is exceptionally generous and shows no sign of holding these great tastings of his for publicity or personal aggrandizement. He doesn't court the press because he knows far more about fine wine than any of us could afford to. He is a genuine, diligent, fanatical, if enigmatic, connoisseur.

Mastering Wine

By the mid 1980s life seemed very busy indeed, not with the social round of the previous decade but with more serious obligations. Nick was hard at work building on L'Escargot's early success, although he was dogged by ill health and, increasingly, by a strange and financially damaging phenomenon.

I can well remember the first time he came home in the evening complaining that two women had come in for lunch—our friend the journalist Sue Summers was one—and *drank nothing but water.* This worried him. If this became a trend, then restaurants, which at that point depended heavily for profits on their wine sales, would have to start charging more for food. The accepted wisdom then was that everyone knew how much a butcher charged for a steak but the price of different wines was a trade secret. (I would argue that nowadays in fact typical London restaurant customers probably buy far more bottles of wine for themselves than steaks—and butchers have all but disappeared anyway.)

Nick and I had many an argument about the right profit margin to add on to the wines on L'Escargot's constantly updated list. "You can't bank percentages," was my constant cry, while Nick would patiently try to explain laundry and gas bills to me. Luckily for Julia, Nick and me, the restaurant was too big to demand his physical presence day and night and most evenings he was able to eat with me—either at the restaurant or, increasingly since Julia's birth, at home. The real menace of the time were telephone calls in the middle of the night. They inevitably told us of attempted break-ins, leaks, flooded cold stores or, something shockingly condoned by British law at that stage, chefs who had been detained by the police simply because their skin was darker than was usual for a BMW driver.

Broken nights apart—and with a young baby I was used to those—I was a very obvious beneficiary of the restaurant. The staff, who were a rather exceptional lot picked mainly because of the strength of their personality rather than from the Soho catering agency pool, were unaccountably nice to me. I was able to make the crucial realization that I would never go short of a good meal. I had a fashionable place to meet my friends and colleagues in, not to mention launch my books in. And, with Nick's blessing, I also had a friendly arena in which to try out various forms of wine event. Before long L'Escargot became a popular place for daytime wine tastings, especially in the glass-roofed, barrel-vaulted room on the second floor where, high up among the Soho rooftops and fire escapes, many a wine merchant showed off his wares.

I had taken to holding the blind comparative tastings that had become a feature of the *Which? Wine Monthly* up there and my successor Jane MacQuitty carried on the tradition, often dovetailing it with proofreading her columns for the *Times* from Nick's office. "No, *garnet*-hued . . . " But L'Escargot with its four large, very distinct and separable rooms was perfect for wine events in the evenings too.

In the early years wine dinners, another relatively novel phenomenon, helped to fill the restaurant on quiet nights. We had winemakers of world renown and local luminaries such as dear old Edmund present a collection of their favorite wines. On other evenings I organized tastings that I, selfishly, was interested in myself. I remember in particular a blind comparison of Barolos that had been decanted 24, 12, 4 and 0 hours before serving to see if it really made a difference. (It didn't seem to.)

L'Escargot was an inevitable meeting place for the Zinfandel Club, for its new Australian counterpart the Coonawarra Club and for an arguably long-overdue society, Forum Vinorum, designed to celebrate Italy's best wines. (During this period it was common for even the most celebratedly open-minded wine commentators in Britain to claim that Italy produced no wine of interest, or that the trouble with Italy was that it was so complicated—these complaints coming from people quite happy to navigate their way around France's intricate language and geography.)

I was busy not only with nappies and nannies (drawn initially from my native Cumbria) and trying to find a larger house at an affordable price, but with the aftermath of the first television series, trying to outline a second, finishing my book *Masterglass*, and satisfying my many masters at *The Sunday Times*. Soon after I joined the paper, Rupert Murdoch bought Times Newspapers from the compliant old Thomson regime and a new era in British newspaper publishing began. Harry Evans was moved to the *Times* and briefly replaced by Frank Giles, the only editor I have ever had to have claimed knowledge of my subject. An editor trying to steer you in the direction of his own particular wine favorites ("How about an article on Odette Pol-Roger?") is much worse than a supportive, noninterventionist one.

In 1983 Frank Giles was replaced by a combative outsider called Andrew Neil. At my initial audience with him I suggested that a wine column in a regular slot would be a good idea. It would give Britain's swelling band of wine enthusiasts a reason to buy the paper as well as a specific place to look for information, and the lavishly designed pages of the magazine where I generally appeared were often slightly wasted on my difficult-to-illustrate articles. He would have none of it, although anyone less suitable as a roving reporter beholden to everyone from news editor to literary editor would be difficult to imagine. It was one thing to get by as an untrained journalist on *Wine & Spirit*, quite another on a publication as sophisticated as the multisection, market leader *Sunday Times*.

One of many Escargot lunches with colleagues from the paper was with James Adams, defense correspondent and Neil's right-hand man, who had been charged with cutting down the paper's notoriously wasteful expenses budget and staffing levels. Rather belatedly I had recently been sent to the mediterranean port of Sète by the news desk in the vain hope that I could sniff out a story on France's imports of Italian wine (this was a year or two after the notorious wine wars with smashed tankers and firebombs as militant French growers tried to protect themselves from the consequences of joining the Common

Market). Adams gave me a dressing down. Not because of the disappointingly mild nature of the story I filed (I just couldn't find any violence, and lacked the training to create some) but because of the shockingly modest nature of my expenses claim. It really was letting the side down to claim only for the basic hotel I stayed in and the few simple meals I ate. It would set a dangerous precedent, I was told. Alas, although I'd been hired by the paper in the notoriously slack old days, we retained freelances enjoyed none of the famous privileges such as twenty-five-hour work weeks, six weeks' annual holiday and frequent sabbaticals.

In early September 1983 Nick and I found the perfect family house up Haverstock Hill on the much-disputed border between Belsize Park and Hampstead. It had been occupied by the same family since the 1930s who had done mercifully little to its late-Victorian origins— although this meant that we would have to spend a great deal on paint, rewiring, replumbing and a new roof. After a hard summer slaving away in Soho Nick needed a break, so we flew off with Julia for a hot October week on Cyprus, discovering that in this hot climate, where temperature control was still a novelty, the cheaper (i.e., younger) the wine, the fresher and more appetizing it was. Fifteen-month-old Julia, stomping around the beach in her pale pink bathrobe, soon had a troop of older children in her thrall.

The week after we got back, as we were starting to get alarming estimates of just how much money the new house would absorb, I was telephoned out of the blue by an advertising agency. They were working on a new "fresh" ground coffee and someone had come up with the idea of using me in the advertising campaign. I suppose it's easy to imagine the parallels a hard-pressed copywriter might draw between wine tasting and coffee tasting, but it's extraordinary that, after just one six-week television series on Channel 4, with audiences of less than two million, they thought I would be recognized by enough people to warrant using me. For a fraction of an instant I considered slamming the phone down with an "Advertising? Me?," but then I realized this would have absolutely no impact on my authority as a wine writer other than possibly making me better known, and considerably more comfortably housed. The most important thing, therefore, was how the coffee tasted, so I asked the guy on the phone if I could try it before giving them my answer. "The *product*?" he asked in disbelief. "You want to taste the *product?*" There was a doubtful pause. "I suppose we've probably got some somewhere. If not we'll get the client to bike some over." (Ad agencies never believed in the Royal Mail.) So I made up this coffee, probably pretty badly since I am far from the world's most enthusiastic coffee drinker, and decided it tasted perfectly fine, before going over to meet this extraordinary team in their Knightsbridge offices.

They showed me a script with lines in it like "Jancis in helicopter over Andes," which puzzled me. Were they going to mock it up in Wales? "Oh no, we'll all go out to Colombia. Would early January suit you?" And so began one of the more surreal, and certainly most lucrative, episodes in my life—and what timing! The Goldcrest crew may have been generous but the profligacy of advertising budgets defies, or at least defied, belief. We were to double our numbers with local expertise once we got to Bogotá, but we still filled the first-class cabin on the British Caledonian flight out. Two representatives from the agency accompanied us with the sole job of transporting packs of The Product and keeping them sufficiently pristine to feature in a TV close-up. (They filled them with dummy white powder instead of the actual coffee, which *really* confused the Colombian customs officials.) Coffee terraces were scoured for the perfect coffee bush, and when the little red berries weren't in absolutely the camera-ready position, others were stuck on. I was treated to one of the grandest make-up artists in the business, who insisted we start work at five every morning—which was probably understandable but not great for someone who had just discovered she was expecting her second baby.

The best bit was the shopping for clothes beforehand. A film wardrobe specialist and I spent a happy day or two whizzing round clothes shops grander than I would ever contemplate, buying rafts of outfits for the director Bob "Clarissa" Bierman's approval. I treasure, and indeed wear, some of them to this day. A spare pair of red specs was ordered for me, just in case.

We stayed way up in the Andes not too far from coca country in Manizales, a large town with a magnificent church and a fleet of ancient yellow taxis in retirement from Manhattan. They sounded eerily reminiscent of New York as they bounced over the ruts in the street at night. As when filming *The Wine Programme*, I was introduced once more to the running jokes and factionalism involved in working as a team, even if because of my pregnant state and pivotal role I was handled with kid gloves. I think the makeup artist was rather shocked that I wanted to go and explore local restaurants with the gang instead of having an early, literally face-saving supper in my room, and it must have made her job more difficult the next morning that I didn't.

I was intrigued to see wine lists dominated by Chile, a country whose wines I had hardly tasted before (Argentine wine was not exported much before the 1990s). Communal dinner on our last night taught me a lesson. We all went out to a fish restaurant, where the makeup artist confessed she'd been dreading working with a nonprofessional like me but it really hadn't been too bad, and the cameraman started fiddling round in a large carrier bag he'd brought along. What he produced were not just some seriously fine tapes to substitute for the restaurant's muzak, and some liar dice to entertain us after dinner, but two bottles of Krug 1976 he'd bought at the airport on the way out for this very purpose. What style, and what an extraordinary place to be drinking it. I resolved to put this lesson into practice some time myself.

The coffee—and the ad agency—sank without trace (its name, Master Blend, was subsequently borrowed for a range of instant coffees), but for me it was all frightfully exciting. All this cossetting doubtless turned me into the most terrible prima donna for the second series of *The Wine Programme*.

Barry's wife, Susanna, who took over as producer of this seminal series, had a serious problem on her hands. Channel 4 was demanding a second series as soon as possible, but it's a waste of time to film Northern Hemisphere wine country between December and April (nothing but stumps in the vineyards), and my baby was expected at the end of August. Susanna therefore had a narrow window of opportunity, between April and, say, June, when the bulge got too big, to do all the filming. (Fortunately, I was not privy to the discussions about how and why pregnant women could not be shown in a television series about wine, but this was before Fetal Alcohol Syndrome had been identified, magnified and let loose on the public. I suspect the decision was taken with continuity, viewer sensibilities and television convention in mind rather than any health issue other than my likely sluggishness. In those days, television maintained the myth that pregnancy did not exist.)

Consequently, it was decided that we would go on an extended trip to northern Spain and northern Portugal in early April and then Tuscany in late April, picking up the British bits in early June (Simon Loftus, whom we filmed buying chianti at Castello di Volpaia, striding magisterially around Southwold) and even a day or so in early July in an English vineyard, using the rampant summer foliage to disguise my swollen abdomen.

I don't recall why we didn't film in late May, but I know all too well why early May was out. The next, very substantial, stage on from the Wine & Spirit Education Trust exams I'd taken in my first three years at *Wine & Spirit* was a coveted, if curious-sounding, qualification known as Master of Wine. The Institute of Masters of Wine had been founded in the 1950s as a superior (in every sense) trade educational body and held a grueling week of exams every May to sort out worthy candidates from the rest. Thirty years later there were still only about a hundred Masters of Wine, only about 10 percent of whom were women, even though scores of hopeful candidates jumped through the necessary hoops each year. It was one of those infuriating exams where reading the papers gave you no clue as to what depth of answer was required. The questions all made sense to those of us who had taken the Trust's most difficult exam, the Diploma, but clearly if the pass rate was only about 10 percent, there must be a lot more work to it than met the eye. I had been delighted, therefore, that in the late 1970s there had been no question of my going on to the "MW" treadmill since the exam was open only to those actually in the wine trade.

Then in the early 1980s those running the Institute were faced with the unpalatable truth that even Masters of Wine are not immortal. Some of the early (and not so early such as lovely Martin Bamford of Château Loudenne) MWs died. The senior MWs did their sums and worked out that the Institute, already thought dangerously elitist and introspective by outsiders, could well wither and die if limited to members of the British wine trade. The result was that in late 1983 they relaxed the admissions requirements to include people who *made their living through wine* and, as someone who'd done well in the Diploma in 1978, I started to be taken on one side by MWs for quiet little words of encouragement.

I used to think if I hadn't gone to a grammar school I wouldn't have given this gruesome possibility of hard work and public humiliation a second thought. But I did, and am thoroughly imbued with the old-fashioned need to see ticks and "VG"s in my exercise book. (The more I read biographies of women writers, however, the more I am convinced that this need to achieve has nothing to do with education and probably reflects some sort of driven escapism.) In my working life, if someone presents me with an opportunity, I assume (often wrongly, I have learnt) they've asked me because they think I can do it. I therefore feel duty-bound to have a go. I was also feeling increasingly out of touch with the reality of winemaking, what with all this playing at being a television presenter. I'd seen more makeup brushes than fermentation tanks in the past year or two and felt it would do me no harm at all to be forced to confront the many lacunae in my wine knowledge.

Another factor too, I'm sure, was that with the telly and my most recent book, *Masterglass*, I was viewed as very much a popularizer of wine. If I did by any chance succeed in becoming an MW, there'd be no question that whatever the result of my work, it was based on a high level of expertise. I even remember an article in which we wine writers were compared to various different wines. Edmund was of course a grand old bordeaux, slightly austere but magnificently worthy. Oz Clarke was, I think, a please-all Chardonnay. I was a flighty, evanescent Beaujolais, perfectly agreeable in the short term, but would I last?

I'm most of all sorry for Nick that that article was written because it probably provided the final spur for me to try the MW exams in 1984, the first year I was able, and he suffered as a result. He and virtually all my friends were adamant that what I stood to lose by failing was far more than what I might gain by passing these exams. With the television shows, the *Sunday Times* columns and books such as *The Wine Book*, *The Great Wine Book* (which had won much praise and several awards) and *Masterglass*, not to mention the *Which? Wine* experience, I had no need to prove myself. I had to admit to the sneaking suspicion that in the highly likely event that I would fail the first time (few candidates pass more than the theoretical or "practical," i.e., tasting, half first time around; they are then free to concentrate on the other half the next year), this would fuel the wine trade's widely held belief that the wine writers don't actually know all that much.

But I must have felt some confidence because I agreed to make my taking of the Master of Wine exam part of the second series of *The*

Wine Programme. Perhaps I knew it could always be edited out, but at least this way I could combine taking the exam with making the series, and having a baby—I really must have been mad. Of course we weren't allowed to film the actual exam itself, but we filmed a practice tasting session which looked identical. The most serious effect of my decision, for me and anyone who lived or worked with me, was the amount of work involved. Quickly sucked in to the camaraderie of supplicants, we MW students circulated copies of past candidates' revision notes, poring over hieroglyphs and trying to make sense of equations. It became clear that those exam questions were very deceptive indeed in their simplicity ("discuss the relative merits of the various types of vessel used for the storage and maturation of wines"). We were obviously required to absorb and memorize some relatively sophisticated science.

The MW exam is not nearly as deep as, say, a degree in oenology (winemaking), but it is very broad, requiring knowledge of all aspects of wine production, consumption and marketing as well as skills in writing and, most important of all, tasting. Most candidates fall by the wayside because they are extremely good at, say, tasting, but just can't write an essay, or perhaps have a fine brain but deficient tasting faculties. (It is particularly cruel for Northern Hemisphere hay fever sufferers that the exam takes place in May.)

In 1984 there were papers on viticulture (growing vines), vinification (making wine), handling wine (an increasingly outdated reflection of Britain's role as a bulk wine bottler), and the commercial aspects of wine (a sop to those who tartly pointed out that Masters of Wine tended to be very good at buying wine but hopeless at selling it). There was also an essay paper, my lifeboat but a fatal whirlpool for many talented tasters, and no fewer than three tasting papers during each of which we were presented with a dozen glasses of wine and asked to assess and identify them as closely as possible. The most stultifying aspect, now excised from the syllabus, was having to mug up on the code numbers of various customs documents required to move wine from one place to another.

Because the Institute began as a tiny elite cell in a particularly cozy trade, it inherited an obsession with secrecy. Papers are, quite understandably, numbered rather than named so that examiners don't know whose paper they're marking (although in the early, manual correspondence days, they must have recognized some of the handwriting). It is also an absolute principle that the identity of examiners is equally shrouded in mystery. Admirable as this is, it prolonged for years longer than necessary an almost complete and infuriating lack of communication between examiners and tutors, generally the most recent successful candidates.

It has to be the most recent MWs who coach their would-be successors because they are the most likely to understand the current standard of the exams, which have evolved organically over the years. In the 1960s, for instance, MW candidates had one two-hour lecture called "Other Wines of France" that included the Rhône, the Loire, Alsace, the whole of the south, everywhere in France, in fact, apart from the traditional wine trade staples of Bordeaux, Burgundy and Champagne. Because the range of wine regions selling their produce on the international marketplace expands every year, and because wine and vine science is more completely understood all the time, the exams are naturally more complex, if not actually more difficult, each year.

There is certainly no doubt that however much glory is reflected onto the successful MW candidate, zero glamour attaches to the life of the student. In my case there were many hours sitting in an airless lecture room wondering whether I wouldn't really be learning more communing with my own treasured files of revision notes.

My diary for early 1984 records MW course days interspersed with antenatal appointments and visits to possible nursery schools for Julia. Then suddenly on April 1, just six weeks before the exam, I flew out to Barcelona for a couple of weeks' filming. It would be fair to say that I was not wholly engaged in this second series, which showed in some of the end result. It was partly overcommitment, and partly that strange sense of either limbo, or perhaps proportion, that comes with pregnancy. Barry and Susanna must have many a time cursed the fact they'd chosen a presenter both female and fecund, for the pressure it put on their schedule.

We spent our first day filming Miguel Torres, darling of us British wine writers at the time for most publicly breaking the mold in Spain. He studied in France and, in a bold move, imported French grape varieties such as Cabernet Sauvignon, Sauvignon Blanc and Chardonnay into his native Catalonia. All females on the crew, including me, fell in love with his big eyes and coy violinist's air as I interviewed him in one of his new high-altitude vineyards, an escape from the high temperatures and accelerated growing season on the flatter land below.

We spent the second day at another winery representing the new Spain, Raimat, a vast wine estate well inland from Barcelona owned by the giant Spanish sparkling winemaker Codorníu. It had been carved out of the arid plains thanks to financial muscle, advice from Davis in California and a nearby canal. I interviewed its industrial grandee owner who produced a bottle of Chardonnay as evidence for his revolution which, in its flatness, dark color and vapid flavor, showed exactly why this was the wrong grape for the region, or at least for the techniques available to them at that time.

Our ambitious cameraman from the first series had succeeded in graduating to the movies, so a new, personable young fellow called Pascoe Macfarlane had been hired for this series. He told us over lunch at Raimat how the most recent series he'd worked on had been about health and how it had encouraged him to take up running. That evening we drove over to Olite in Navarra, an old monastic center on the pilgrims' route to Santiago de Compostela, where the director Tim Aspinall, himself a Catholic and part Spanish, wanted to film a particular doorway that would signify the close connections between wine and religion. The whole town, a network of narrow stone passageways with clerics and nuns apparently at every turn, was shrouded in a light mist and had a dreamlike quality about it. We stayed right in the center in one of those dark, baronial paradors, Spain's network of state-run hotels in ancient palaces, castles and monasteries, a late-twentieth-century way of generating income from the remnants of a more feudal past.

The following morning Susanna was presented with the most terrible event imaginable. Pascoe had gone out for an early morning run, collapsed and died. (We discovered later that his family had a history of heart problems.) Tim, who had been out early walking and planning the day ahead as he often did, was a marvel. He tracked down the priest he'd been planning to film that day and went to the nearest hospital with him and Pascoe. He navigated the most efficient path through Spanish bureaucracy, but it was left to poor Susanna, the producer, not just to break the awful news to us and, far more importantly, to Pascoe's family, but also to decide what to do next. I'm sure normally we would all have flown back to London straightaway and resumed filming only after a decent interval, but Susanna had to bear in mind her schedule and my swelling belly. In the end, another cameraman, Paul Summers, was flown out and, callous as we must have seemed, we tried to carry on.

My memory of the next few days is hazy. I just remember sitting in our bus rattling through the moonscape of northern Spain feeling entirely out of touch with reality and worried most of all about Pascoe's young assistant, who had spent so much time with him that he found his death particularly hard to grasp. He was flown home, as was I for a brief but restorative weekend with Nick and Julia, and we reconvened, firing on more than half our cylinders at last, in the Douro for one of our funnier programs, about the people and places involved in making port.

It was in Oporto's Factory House (inside at last!) that I learnt that old-school Brits make marvelous subjects for documentaries, because they are absolutely determined not to do anything so ill bred as take any notice of a roving television camera. I was allowed into the dining room for one of their famous Wednesday lunches but, being a woman, was not allowed to actually sit at the table. I had to interview Richard Delaforce, the port shippers' chairman that year, from a chair a pace behind him. Up in the silent wilds of port country, on a terrace above the Douro at the Quinta de Vargellas, Gillyane Robertson of Taylors was so delightfully indiscreet on camera that, for the first and last time, we felt honor-bound to show her her interview before broadcasting it to allow her to retract some of her most outrageous revelations.

My strongest memory of the Portuguese trip, however, was trying to balance my increasing bulk on one of the low whitewashed walls outside Taylors' winery at Pinhão with Emile Peynaud's textbook on winemaking, then unavailable in English, trying desperately to drum in the principles of various different sorts of fermentations before my MW exams. It was, incidentally, a real problem for Master of Wine students in the mid 1980s to find suitable textbooks in English. This was before Australia and the sterling, balanced, useful work of the Australian Wine Research Institute had burst upon the international scene (Australia was exporting only a fifteenth as much wine as she was ten years later) and virtually the only really detailed English textbooks on the sciences of vine growing and winemaking were American.

At this stage American enology and viticulture was dominated by

Davis, the University of California's specialist outpost near Sacramento, which operated in virtual seclusion. European traditions were regarded with skepticism at best and horror at worst. The principles adhered to by the eminent professors at Davis throughout the fifties, sixties and seventies were that nature was there to be subjugated, mastered and tamed so as to transform wine production into a commercially thoroughly efficient process. Wine's duty was to be technically sound rather than interesting to taste. Thus, for example, there was absolutely no question of using anything as unreliable as the yeasts naturally present in the atmosphere of any established vineyard or winery; specially cultured, entirely predictable yeasts were used instead.

Similarly, everything erred on the side of safety. Because risks are involved at higher temperatures, all fermentations tended to be a little too cool, resulting in somewhat clenched, neutral wines. This was just a natural expression of the era, and a reaction against bad winemaking habits learnt during Prohibition and mom-and-pop wines made by recent immigrants in their own backyards. This philosophy clearly represented just one part of the wine producing picture—and we Master of Wine students could see that textbooks from the University of Bordeaux, for example, which embraced all the modern theory with centuries of successful practice, was preferable at that time to any gospel according to Davis. This is why, until the late 1980s when there was widespread recognition in California that the Old World had something to contribute, the state may have been good at producing technically sound inexpensive wine but, with a few cosmopolitan exceptions, was yet to produce seriously fine wine in any great quantity.

Toward the end of April there was another week's filming in Tuscany, although this being 1984, the year Chianti Classico ascended to the great bureaucratic height of achieving DOCG status rather than common or garden DOC, it was miserably cold and gray for much of the time. And we discovered just how many expensive film crew hours can be spent navigating the back roads of Chianti country unless a researcher has surveyed the territory first.

The exam was now only a couple of weeks away and it was too late to make much significant progress on the theoretical side, but we candidates were determined that our palates would be in perfect shape for their three days' trial. The fifty or so of us tended to split into geographical and sentimental affiliations and take it in turns to organize blind tastings for each other, or decide on a theme and each bring a bottle or two representing it. The important thing was to taste blind and to get one's blind tasting faculties as finely honed as possible. Fellow candidates in my year included Maureen Ashley, then working at the Wine Standards Board, the wine trade's somewhat skeletal police force; Jane Hunt, who now represents the wines of South Africa as a generically promotable entity; and Liz Robertson, who had imported, among other things, Britain's first branded Argentine wine Franchette, but is now in charge of Safeway's wine department and a budget of many millions of pounds a year.

Since the beginning of the year we had gradually increased the frequency of our informal blind tastings, in the denouement trying to share as much as possible the clues we'd used in our deductions, for there is no ceiling on the number of passes awarded. It is still very much Candidates versus Examiners. By the week before the exam we were meeting to taste every day, usually early in the morning in an effort to minimize the interruption of the working day, just as a group of us had back in Diploma days. (It was then that I learnt how inimical minty toothpaste is to the taste of wine, or almost any other vaguely acid drink for that matter—certainly orange juice. So began my careful substition of homeopathic, non-minty toothpaste whenever I know I'm soon going to be tasting wine.)

By the time the exams started on the following Tuesday morning we were like athletes, groomed specially to be in top form for the day of an important race. I don't think my tasting faculties have ever been sharper—although I nurse the assumption that I could, with sufficient practice, get them back to that peak of condition. I was probably helped rather than hindered by my pregnant state. Unlike the odd candidate who has been known to carelessly let some of the tasting samples down their gullet in the desperate hope of inspiration, I had absolutely no desire to drink any of the wine I had so assiduously been analyzing. My only nagging doubt about being five months pregnant was whether I could survive each two-hour paper without needing exceptional and embarrassing dispensation to go to the lavatory.

About the papers themselves I have little memory except that I somehow managed to include a reference to heroin in my essay, and I do remember Jane Hunt turning round just before the start of the red wine paper saying "don't forget Beaujolais," which I had entirely and the first wine turned out to be one. I found it a great help, in theory anyway, to write down a long list of, theoretically, all possible options for the dozen wines I was about to taste. For the red wine paper, for example, I'd write down a list of the major grape varieties, and then the important blended wines (Médoc, Rioja, Châteauneuf-du-Pape, for example). This was part nerve-steadier and part inspiration for when the senses failed.

Once we were told we could start to tackle the mystery glasses I would carefully describe their color, and intensity, and any development of color at the rim, as well as any other visible clues such as that blackish orange that seems peculiar to mature Barolo and Barbaresco or the greenish tinge found only in old madeira, or the gamboge that in the eighties was a giveaway for an Australian white. Then a bit of calming deep breathing was needed before the most important bit, the "nosing" of each glass.

What I was hoping for, but rarely got, was inspiration from the very first gentle inhalation, what I call the intuitive sniff. There are times when you just know, without any thought process at all, that this must be Syrah, almost certainly French, probably Hermitage with that color, and the tasting process merely confirms all this. There are other times, many more of them in my case, when you sniff and get an indistinct soup, blurred in olfactory outline, a smudge of a wine. Too depressing to worry at it for the moment. Best to come back to it relative to something more obvious that you spot along the lineup, and then to work doggedly away at eliminating most of the possibilities on your long list and narrowing it down to a handful of probabilities. At that stage there will usually be at least one overriding reason why it has to be A or B, and you can even write down both these answers and why you have come to them.

The good thing about the MW exam is that most of the marks are for analysis and deduction rather than identification, so that as long as you keep your nerve and describe with absolute objectivity each of the dimensions (sweetness, acidity, tannin, alcohol, balance and persistence) together with any flavors that strike you "on the nose," as we say, you will do reasonably well. A typical tasting question is: "Wines

1 to 4 are made from the same grape. Identify their geographical origin as closely as possible and comment on their quality, making reference where approproiate to winemaking techniques." This group might include a premier cru white burgundy (barrel fermentation, low yields), a Chilean Chardonnay (oak chips, high yields), an unoaked Chablis and a California Chardonnay with a very obviously milky stirred lees character.

After this ordeal it was time to forget the exam and concentrate on *The Wine Programme* and *The Sunday Times* until July. We were on holiday in Cornwall when the results were due. George Perry-Smith who had done so much to revive Britain's culinary reputation in the 1970s was in his last years cooking like an angel at the Waterside at Helford, a jumble of whitewashed cottages overlooking a lushly wooded inlet full of lobster pots and rowing boats. We'd been given the perfect room just over the kitchen, with a little bedroom off it for Julia. We were woken each morning by the smell of freshly baked bread (far more exotic even then than the smell of reheated croissants) and our appetite for dinner was revived each night by wafts from the Waterside's many subtly complex stockpots. Perry-Smith himself would dart around the place from one bothy to another in his admirably thorough preparations for each dish. (Alt-na-harrie in the far north of Scotland is slightly similar, though its isolation brings a certain spookiness.)

We were sitting on the rocky terrace in front of the kitchen having breakfast when the postman arrived and I was given, thrillingly, a vast brown envelope. This was deeply exciting as I knew that only a small envelope would be needed to tell me I'd failed, and indeed, there it was, a short letter of congratulation and a long list of all the rules and principles to which I must swear allegiance (including, especially, an assurance that I would never sell fake wine). I can still remember how wonderful it felt to have somehow pulled this off. And how relieved Nick must have been to realize that this drain on my time and attention could now be shut once and for all. Doing the MW exam is a bit like I imagine climbing Everest: great when it's over.

An enormous amount of luck is undoubtedly involved in these even more than any other exams. I had a very fair wind behind me for most of my thirty-six wines (I think they had been particularly difficult the year before) and was asked to lecture the next year's students on tasting techniques. To my eternal chagrin I advised them they could automatically discount first growth red bordeaux as the Institute couldn't possible afford to offer it in an exam. The next year, as though to prove the treasured dysfunction between examiners and educators, candidates were given four vintages of Château Lafite.

Today the Institute is open not just to British people outside the wine trade but to anyone anywhere in the world who can write a satisfactory dissertation on one of that year's three chosen subjects. They can even write in languages other than English, provided they pay for the translation. Despite some substantial benefactions from wine producers and retailers, the Institute is still underfunded. Nowadays there are Norwegian, Swiss, American, Canadian, Australian, New Zealand, even French Masters of Wine, and the exams themselves are held, almost concurrently except for differences in time zones, in Sydney and New York as well as London (although for obvious reasons tasting cribs are not given out until the last paper has been collected from the last American candidate).

I feel grateful to have taken the tasting exams in the mid 1980s when, for example, Australian wines tasted unmistakably Australian, California wines betrayed the relatively warm climate they were then generally grown in, Spanish reds always smelled of American oak and Portuguese ones were always unbelievably tannic. Although the examiners say they try to find wines that are as representative as possible, there has been a universal move toward emulating just a handful of archetypes, notably red and white burgundy, red bordeaux and red Rhône. New vineyards have been planted in the coolest parts of warmer wine regions so that the distinctions between New and Old World wines have become blurred. Top-quality French oak, gentle handling of red grapes, barrel fermentation and lees stirring of whites are all techniques that are now used routinely throughout the world, making it more and more difficult for the geographical origins of a wine to struggle out from under all this technique to impress themselves on the blind taster. I will return to this hobbyhorse of mine.

On my first post-MW book jacket blurb, the hyperbolic pen of Chris Foulkes, then wine editor at Mitchell Beazley, described me as "the first and still the only journalist to have been accepted into the wine world's most respected fellowship." I had to insert a "British" a few years later when our friend the New Zealand wine writer Bob Campbell finally succumbed to nagging from Nick and me and flew all the way to London to sail through the exam first time round (had he waited a few years he need have flown only as far as Sydney).

Many MWs turn to writing once they have qualified and the canon of wine literature has been immeasurably enhanced by the rigor of such MW authors as Maureen Ashley, Nick Belfrage, Liz Berry, Michael Broadbent, Clive Coates, Mary Ewing-Mulligan, Rosemary George, Anthony Hanson, Remington Norman, David Peppercorn and Serena Sutcliffe. Some of the more recent MWs, on the other hand, have only the most distant relation to the wine trade; there is a lawyer at Fox Studios in Hollywood who decided he'd have a go in his spare time. Another wine lover with an Everest-climbing streak perhaps?

Distractions

The nascent Lander who had patiently accompanied me to so many Master of Wine courses, tastings and, eventually, exams was a sturdy boy, William, born like Julia later than expected, in early September 1984. I was quite busy enough with my commitments to *The Sunday Times* as well as contributions to a terribly glossy, very designer, archetypally eighties magazine called *A la carte*. I also wrote for *Cosmopolitan*, which at that stage was so keen on wine it devoted some of its popular Saturday course days to tastings conducted by me at L'Escargot. They were apparently nearly as popular as the ones called Assertiveness Training. In long overdue acknowledgment of my new status as mother, however, I took a two-year sabbatical from writing books: 1984 and 1985 are the only years in the eleven from 1979 to 1989 free of a volume written or edited by me.

Nevertheless there was one, perhaps inevitably, if not on the boil then certainly simmering. Way back in the early eighties I had been taken out to lunch by the two men running Mitchell Beazley, which was at that time the world's foremost wine book publisher. It had been founded by James Mitchell and the late John Beazley and their greatest publishing success, after *The Joy of Sex*, was *The World Atlas of Wine*. The combination of Hugh Johnson's matchless, if all too constricted, prose and cartographically irreproachable maps of the world's most famous wine regions was a winning one. The first edition appeared in 1971 and it has continued to be updated regularly. The domineering James Mitchell and his then henchman Adrian Webster (who has since branched out into his own imprint for Oz Clarke's wine books) had commissioned Hugh to write his historical *Story of Wine* but, as they put it, having sliced the wine cake geographically and historically, they were looking for someone to slice it another way, varietally, by grape variety.

They must have asked Hugh to take up this third sort of cake knife and found him less than keen, but it was a project that appealed to me enormously, however ill at ease I felt at that initial meeting. Author of just one published book at that early stage, I had been taken to the fashionable Neal Street Restaurant and sandwiched both literally and strategically between these two very determined, very cunning publishers. I have never in my life felt more like a naive, tender piece of wild game being trapped by a pair of experienced hunters with some very sophisticated equipment.

The book had been put on hold while I filmed the first two series of *The Wine Programme*, for reasons more connected with international co-editions, Mitchell Beazley's specialty, than my availability, but I finally got down to writing the first thousand words on Thursday, November 15, 1984, Beaujolais Nouveau release day, already a date of waning significance in Britain's wine calendar. The book was eventually published in autumn 1986 as *Vines, Grapes and Wines*, with the by now inevitable launch party at L'Escargot.

This wasn't a book I could rattle off in a few weeks like my first *Wine Book*. It really did break new ground. Even the word "varietal" was a new (American) one, and the concept of varietal wines was embryonic. Of course all wines are made from grapes and all grapes are some variety or another, such as, most famously, Chardonnay and Cabernet Sauvignon or, much more commonly, Trebbiano and Grenache. But until the early to mid 1980s most consumers had hardly heard of any grape names; the great majority of wines were sold either by the name of the place they came from—Mâcon and Médoc, for example—or, at the bottom end of the market, as a branded wine such as Charbonnier ("the legionnaire's liter") or Nicolas, whose cleverest blend was called Vieux Ceps ("old vines," or "old socks," as many of its devoted followers called it).

Within the European Community there were now tight controls over the use of geographical names so that any wine labeled Chablis, for example, had to come from the strictly demarcated vineyards of Chablis and be made according to the local rules. This was France's treasured appellation contrôlée, AC, system at work (aped in Italy as the DOC system and, when they joined the European Community, in Spain and Portugal as DO). Elsewhere, however, particularly in North America, the old European place-names had been thoroughly traduced. Chablis was used as a marketing tool for selling any old white wine that was drier than one sold as Sauterne (*sic*). Burgundy came to be used as its conveniently capacious red wine equivalent. Australia, New Zealand, South Africa, South America, all the emerging New World wine producers had been using Europe's treasured wine names with such abandon that they had become virtually meaningless. On the other hand, specific wine regions within these new wine producers were generally too young to have established any great reputation for themselves—certainly not one that could be used to sell a specific style of wine to the consumer. We were already some years from having established, for example, that Cabernet was *the* great variety for the Napa Valley and Coonawarra. The solution, therefore, was to rely on varietal labeling, as devised by the late Frank Schoonmaker in California way back in the 1940s. Neither producer nor consumer had a clear idea at that stage of what was to be expected of a wine from Sonoma, but once consumers became familiar with the word Chardonnay, they could be persuaded to buy it wherever it came from.

Chardonnay was the golden goose of the 1980s. This was before anyone had whispered there might be a connection between red wine drinking and good health. White wine outsold red more than two to one, and wine growers everywhere—well, everywhere outside Europe's carefully circumscribed vineyards—were kicking themselves for planting so many red grape varieties. All sorts of *vieux ceps* bearing unfashionable grapes such as Zinfandel, Mourvèdre and Shiraz were pulled out to make way for self-selling Chardonnay or, at the hands of growers in a real hurry, suffered the ignominy of having Chardonnay cuttings grafted on to their own established root system. Throughout the New World of wine and then throughout southern Europe, including southern France, there was a population explosion in Chardonnay vines. Growers in countries such as Australia and South Africa, which have particularly strict plant quarantines, formed an impatient line at the gates of official nurseries, desperate for cuttings of this fashionable variety. Some of them smuggled their own cuttings in anyway.

Following grape names rather than geographical names was so much easier for the consumer, it is hardly surprising that today Chardonnay and Cabernet are better known than Mâcon and Médoc. The danger of this new varietalism was clear even when I began to write *Vines, Grapes and Wines*. With a handful of varieties gaining universal fame, there was a real risk that more obscure, but often more suitable and interesting indigenous varieties might be abandoned. The book was in its own way a celebration of variety in its most general sense. This involved a great deal of detective work, however, for communication between different wine producing countries, and even between different regions within the same country, was much less advanced than it is today.

Few French growers of Ugni Blanc, for example, were aware that it was the very same variety as Italy's ubiquitous Trebbiano. Spanish growers had been taught to scorn their workhorse Garnacha, the same grape so treasured, as Grenache Noir, in Châteauneuf-du-Pape. It took the Australians years to fully appreciate the worth of their Shiraz, the same grape revered for centuries as Syrah in the Rhône valley and, increasingly today, all over southern France. And for many years growers in California and Australia would sell for a song the produce of the old immigrants' vines they'd been taught to call Mataro, without realizing that it was the ultra-fashionable grape called Mourvèdre in southern France. (It is still available at bargain basement prices in Spain where it is widely planted and known as Monastrell.)

Clearly I couldn't assemble my corpus of knowledge by tramping through every vineyard in the world. I had to depend largely on desk research, comparing already published works such as those of the great ampelographer Pierre Galet of Montpellier with the best available texts elsewhere. What was fascinating was to see how the range of grape varieties planted reflect the history of each wine region. Australian vineyards, for example, have a number of ancient Portuguese varieties, probably because they were taken on board when the ships bound for Australia stopped at the Portuguese island of Madeira. Chilean vineyards accurately reflect the vines planted in early nineteenth century Bordeaux which supplied them.

I included a sort of historical sketch map of major grape variety movements in the book but it is one of the few maps in the book I feel is really worthwhile. In the wake of their *World Atlas of Wine*, Mitchell Beazley had come to believe that all wine books had to have maps, and *Vines* has far too many of them, often rather confusingly keyed in my opinion, but in those days I was far too obliging and assumed even more readily than today that all my employers knew better than me.

I was delighted of course that Mitchell Beazley had sold the book to an American publisher, Knopf. The only trouble was that *Vines* came out at the same time as a long-awaited book they'd commissioned from the American wine writer, Bob Finigan, so it was always a rather poor relation in terms of publicity and sales push. Mitchell Beazley also underestimated demand for the book in Britain and ran out of stock for the crucial book-buying months of November and December. They did sell it in German, Danish and Finnish, however, and eventually cracked France, the toughest nut of all.

The French were, and still are, deeply suspicious of varietalism, or *cépages*, as they call grape varieties. They see it as an opponent of their organically evolved appellation contrôlée system. No one else in the world can produce a Chassagne-Montrachet, whereas everyone can produce a wine labeled Chardonnay, so why on earth should they bother with the latter? This is French wine hierarchy speaking. There are of course vast tracts of suitable vineyard land in France where Chardonnay can grow perfectly well and nowadays fetch a higher price than the appellation wine permitted there—the Languedoc is the most obvious example, where the appellations Minervois and Corbières are too recent to command high prices and where there is no shortage of suitable land for planting fashionable grape varieties. Amazingly, however, the French publishers Hachette decided to translate my book and boldly called it *Le Livre des Cépages*. In the end it sold extremely well there, probably more to curious professionals than to consumers who were, and are, still kept largely in the dark about the exact grapes that go into their geographically named wines.

Hachette managed a hugh publicity coup in having me appear on what was then an extraordinarily popular and extraordinarily French television program, a late-night book program, *Apostrophes,* presented by the nation's beloved Bernard Pivot. Pivot is himself a great wine lover. His brother has his own wine estate in Beaujolais. He read every book discussed on his program and I think he was genuinely tickled by the novelty of my book, and by the fact that it had been written by an Englishwoman.

The Englishwoman was not looking or feeling so hot when she appeared on the screen, however. I had got back from Australia just the day before, so was in that sort of trance that severe jet lag and extreme nervousness can induce. I'd also been to an unfamiliar Parisian hairdresser and, thanks to my confusing the French for "middle-aged" with "Middle Ages," she'd fashioned my hair into my very own wimple. Very strange.

I'd been invited on the show with four or five other wine writers, all French, all men, all older than me. The great Professor Emile Peynaud was one, the impish Michel Dovaz another. We'd been invited to bring a wine to be served blind to the others, so I'd brought back a bottle of Australia's now world-famous Penfolds Grange, the wine that matches first growth bordeaux prices. Unfortunately—another example of how I should have gone on one of *Cosmo*'s Assertiveness Training courses—they said they'd run out of decanters so my wine could not be served blind. They all knew in advance therefore that my wine not only came from outside France, it came from somewhere as far beyond the pale as Australia. This makes a huge difference if you are a Frenchman tasting a wine for the first time. Their noses were wrinkled in distaste before they even came within sniffing distance of the glass. It was dismissed outright as "a pharmacist's wine" and I was a very silly little girl for having wasted their time with it. It's difficult to mount a spirited defense of something as subjectively appreciated as a wine, even in your own language. In jet-lagged French it was impossible, but I think I won so many sympathy votes on the screen that night that it helped sales of the book enormously.

In between starting and publishing *Vines*, both my personal and professional lives were in a fair degree of turmoil. Nick's health visibly deteriorated during 1985, so that by September he had turned the same *eau-de-Nil* as the walls of L'Escargot. From all too many possibilities, we assumed it was the ulcerative colitis that had been diagnosed when he was a teenager, but when he finally had ten feet removed from his intestines his surgeon diagnosed Crohn's disease, a deeply uncomfortable chronic inflammatory bowel disorder which has continued to attack him indiscriminately ever since.

Rest is the only cure and he clearly needed a break from something as stressful as running a large restaurant. We therefore holed up for a week's convalescence and nurturing, Nick with his siestas, me with a prototype laptop, at Chewton Glen, a luxurious hotel, with particularly attentive staff, a suitably gentle walk from the Hampshire coast.

Nick hates being an invalid and I am a terrible nurse, so the pleasures of the 1980s were punctuated by considerable pain. He tends to suffer, far too often, in stoical silence, while my memories of the decade are laced with constant explanations of why we had to cancel arrangements at short notice, how Nick couldn't eat onions, and why we tended to leave parties about two hours before anyone else.

In spring 1985 the second series of *The Wine Programme* had been shown (reviewers differed as to whether it was "even more fun than the first" or "lacks the panache of the first"). Channel 4 were so keen they commissioned a Christmas special which we shot that November at the suitably atmospheric Studley Priory hotel, an Elizabethan manor house outside Oxford. With Simon Loftus, Martin Lam, Alice King, Nick Davies, Jane MacQuitty and Bill Baker who had very kindly contributed a bottle of 1961 Château Pétrus to be consumed on-screen, it was rather like having our very own house party.

I was continuing to write about wine for virtually all fiefdoms within *The Sunday Times*: for the "News" section on a survey that showed, with only a small amount of statistical juggling, that for the first time there were more wine drinkers than beer drinkers in Britain; for "Business News" that Bollinger was investing in the Australian winery Petaluma; for the "Atticus diary" a paragraph about Margaret Thatcher's request for a list of contaminated Austrian wines before setting off on holiday for Liechtenstein; for the "LOOK" pages of *The Sunday Times* the inevitable article about women in wine; and a host of longer pieces within a section now called "Leisure and Lifestyle," the latter a very eighties word.

By this stage supermarkets had become important wine retailers in Britain. In fact by the mid 1980s the Sainsbury grocery chain sold more wine than any other retailer, and the supermarkets between them were effectively introducing wine to whole new segments of the population previously intimidated by smart wine shops and unenthused by the scruffier sort. One by one the traditional importers and retailers were folding or amalgamating. On the prices of inexpensive wine, the stuff that makes up the great bulk of the British wine market, they just could not hope to compete with the buying power of a huge supermarket chain.

But various people at *The Sunday Times* encouraged me to write about things other than wine. Suzanne Lowry was a fastidious editor of the "LOOK" pages. I say this because I remember her response to one of my better ideas: "It's a good subject but we'd have to put someone who could *write* on to it." She did let me write a few articles about food, however, which in a complete fluke somehow won me the Glenfiddich Food Writer of the Year award as well as the Drink Writer award.

Toward the end of 1985 the new editor of the paper's magazine, Genevieve Cooper, commissioned me to write a series of personal pro-files. By January 1986 I was setting off for the Lake District to inter-view the reclusive Wainwright (always known as such), writer and illustrator of the cult fell-walking guides to the Lake District. It helped enormously that I'd regularly spent my teenage Sundays, thanks to the fell-walkers' bus from Carlisle, on the fells and occasionally rock faces of this beautiful part of northwest England.

And another, even more interesting journalistic possibility had been dangled by News International, the Murdoch company that owned *The Sunday Times*. Affecting to have particularly enjoyed an article I'd written guying Australian gastronomy after our trip there early in 1985, a Murdoch emissary from Australia, Mike Hoy, came to see me at home. News International was going to launch a London evening paper to rival the *Evening Standard*, he said. Would I be its restaurant reviewer, its counterpart to my friend Fay Maschler? I remember thinking at the time that he and the paper's supposed editor Charlie Wilson were strangely unmoved by the journalistic problem posed by the fact that I was mar-ried to the owner of one of London's most successful restaurants.

In fact, as we now know, this London evening paper was a complete fiction, a ruse to cover the tracks of Murdoch's most trusted employees' setting up a complete printing works for all the News International titles at Wapping, notoriously breaking the stranglehold of the print unions once and for all. The entire staff were moved there overnight early in 1986 and suffered a demoralizing few months as Fortress Wapping was picketed, often violently. Andrew Neil's charmless ebullience didn't help and finally I, like so many *Sunday Times* writers, resigned in September 1986. Not that long afterwards some hapless editor was detailed to sound me out about returning because, entirely predictably, they'd decided to institute a regular weekly wine column. I declined with thanks. Was Wapping a factor in my decision? Oh, we thought so, he said glumly.

Fay persuaded me to join her at the London *Evening Standard* where for two or three years I enjoyed the rapport a consumer writer can have with their readers if they are all relatively local. Meanwhile I was filming the third series of *The Wine Programme*, including a beautiful film of Jerez in which I tried desperately to enthuse people about real sherry, the dry tangy stuff served in wine glasses, often with food, as opposed to the syrupy stuff served by the thimbleful in British pubs. We also made a reasonably lyrical film about Burgundy, a region that lends itself well to such treatment, and included a dinner chez Lafon of Meursault when Dominique, now one of Burgundy's most admired winemakers, was still relatively new to the family domaine and was distinguished in this most traditional of regions by having actually worked in California.

By the spring of 1987, when the third series was being transmitted, I embarked on a couple of fascinating television projects unrelated to wine, one on design for BBC2—some classics thereof and an awards scheme—and a series of interviews for the commercial, and soon-to-be-defunct Thames Television. Design was the watchword of late 1980s retailing and it was fascinating for me to be catapulted into another specialist arena. I still occasionally stumble across my voice, very slightly squeakier than it is now, narrating some film about Levi's jeans, the Coke bottle or the VW Beetle, on in-flight audio systems—and apparently these "Design Classics" are regularly hauled off a shelf somewhere at BBC Television Centre to fill an embarrassing gap when some sporting event finishes unexpectedly early.

The Thames series was fascinating for a different reason—less for the content, although the author Ruth Rendell and Australian artist Sidney Nolan were particularly intriguing interviewees—and more for the way in which the programs were made. This was the last-gasp era for overmanned television crews. Thames had its own scams to rival those Murdoch had expunged from Fleet Street.

To make this simple half-hour daytime film about Ruth Rendell, for instance, we had a crew of more than twenty and a giant pantechnicon of an outside broadcast unit, virtually an editing suite within a removals van, which squeezed and scraped its way down the narrow lane leading to her cottage. One of the crew regularly turned up on location in the London taxi he ran alongside his job at Thames. And woe betide me if I unplugged my own microphone or even touched up my own makeup. That was specialist, union-protected work. Even those of us with the strongest socialist tendencies could see there was something wrong here. Meals and breaks were rigidly observed. Even if an interview was going terribly well and it was clear that only another couple of minutes were needed, if those minutes impinged on official coffee time, then it was just too bad. Some official would shout "cut" and we'd have to start the whole cumbersome process of getting everything wired up, the lighting and sound in place, and so on and so on, half an hour later after the coffee break.

Meanwhile, in the summer of 1987 there were more personal considerations: Nick spent another two weeks in the hospital under close observation. To the delight of his mother and his wife, who had been nursing this thought for some time, Nick decided that it would be sensible to sell L'Escargot and find something less strenuous to do. It was of course very sad for him (and meant his brother had to hurry up and get married so that he, like Nick and his sister, could have his wedding reception there), but in retrospect it was a pretty good time to sell.

The lasting legacy of Nick's eight-year career as a restaurateur was that he became absolutely riveted by the workings of Martin Lam's kitchen. From a base of almost total ignorance, he became completely hooked by cooking and, I'm delighted to say, is now in charge of all victualing in our household. Before long Nick was taken on as restaurant and food writer for the *Financial Times* and, after a few tetchy weeks trying to share one telephone line, we added another and today both work in relative harmony sharing a study and even a desk. Nick goes out to lunch much more than I do, and I travel much more than he does, but otherwise we are parents who work at home. Although Crohn's keeps coming back to haunt him, he now has the time to prove that he is the most perfect husband and father I could imagine.

The Wine Revolution,
and My Cellar

By the time we were married, in 1981, and I felt that at long last I might be able to establish some sort of long-term cellar, I had drunk most of my first serious purchase of fine wine, my two cases of red bordeaux 1976, admittedly an early-maturing vintage. A bottle of La Lagune 1976 somehow survived until early 1990 when it was by no means unpleasant but seemed full of lead pencils and earthiness.

During the late seventies I had begun to amass a collection of odd bottles which moved around London with me from underneath one set of basement stairs to an (extremely damp) coalhole in the late 1970s, to a draughty dining room off Oxford Street and eventually, as my somewhat diminished dowry, to a small wine rack in a passageway in the house Nick lived in when I met him.

Very fortunately for me, our setting down of roots coincided not only with acquiring a house with a cool, dark semi-subterranean space that I have converted from bicycle shed to cellar but also with the run of great eighties vintages in Bordeaux. The first vintage we bought together in any quantity, as soon as it was released *en primeur*, was the 1982. We had the full justification not only of all the brouhaha over that vintage's potential but also the convenient coincidence that this was the year our first child was born.

In those days, I felt extremely guilty about buying even one case of first growth claret. Good heavens, our dozens of Château Margaux 1982 and 1983 cost about $480, a sum I am sure we justified by assuring each other that "we could always sell it to pay for school fees." As it happens, those two vintages are being sold for $4,800 and $2,700 respectively a case at the time of writing. But this entirely notional profit is dwarfed by what has happened to the price of the Château Lafleur 1982 I bought for $215 a case in 1983 and the then practically unknown Pomerol Le Pin 1983 for $240 in December 1984. A case of Lafleur '82 is currently priced at over $8,000 and single *bottles* of Le Pin '83 are now listed at well over $1,000 each.

I know I should feel triumphant about this but in fact I feel almost physically sick. I hate the way that something I bought to give myself and my friends innocent, escapist pleasure has been transformed into a financial asset that is crying out for management. I don't want to manage my cellar. I want to drink it. I want to feel free to continue to be slightly vague about exactly how many bottles of which wine are in there. I enjoy the serendipitous nature of nosing around its wooden boxes and wine racks. I don't want the responsibility of bottles worth hundreds of dollars each. It's inhibiting. I hate this notion that one "can't afford to drink" something. And, moreover, it's not what wine is for.

I like to repeat Edmund Penning-Rowsell's mantra "You must never think of what a wine is worth when you drink it," but then he devised this in an era long before the absurd fine wine inflation rate of the nineties. And he sold enough wine at Christie's recently to under-pin an entire sale. I much preferred the state of the wine market before all these new, must-have buyers came so inflammatorily on the scene. Wine is supposed to bring pleasure, not remorse.

I have a horrible feeling that talk among those who take fine wine seriously is going to become increasingly dominated by money. I have already come across too many bores who confuse wine appreciation with financial appreciation ("I managed to get mine for only £280 a case from Bonham's in 1985"), and thoroughly disapprove of anyone who deliberately uses wine for speculation. But presumably now that wine prices are soaring skywards, there are hundreds of wine investors hoping eventually to sell their bottles for profit. And what, we wine lovers and Omar Khayyám (or at least his inventive translator Edward

Fitzgerald) may wonder, could they possibly hope to spend their money on that would bring them half as much pleasure as the wine itself?

Another puzzle is the lack of correlation between price and pleasure. Perhaps it is not so surprising that a first-rate example of a little-known wine can seem much more memorable than something more famous selling at ten times the price; part of the thrill is the excitement of discovery and the feeling of having beaten the system. What is much more extraordinary is the wild price variation at the very top end. Demand bubbles up mysteriously, apparently fueled by fashion and rumor as much as by intrinsic quality.

One of the strangest phenomena of recent times was the extent of wine buyer obsession with the red bordeaux produced in 1995. For once the Bordelais themselves did not overstate its appeal; in fact they were rather taken aback by the extent of consumer demand. The wine press didn't rave about the vintage. But still demand was furious and prices quickly spiraled, to such an extent that they matched those of mature, drinkable, proven vintages such as 1985. Fine wine traders would point this out and, especially for some of the wines in shortest supply, suggest customers might also like to buy something to *drink* as well as this punt on an infant liquid that would not be bottled for many months. But there were few takers. This may have been because their cellars were full of mature wine already, but I doubt it.

Most of the demand was coming from consumers new to fine wine buying—particularly but by no means exclusively in the Far East. They had heard from a friend of a friend that 1995 was the vintage to buy, and that was all they were interested in. I know myself from listening to the sort of hot air that fills any London trade tasting open to the pin-striped public, that Britain's City slickers were equally excited about the prospect of the 1995s—perhaps partly because this was the first incontrovertibly good vintage in Bordeaux since 1990. People who'd been hanging around wanting to start a cellar for five years at last had their chance, or could wait no longer. I couldn't help seeing parallels with the overenthusiastic reaction to the 1975s I'd witnessed twenty years earlier. But I also realize that the difference in price between the world's most expensive and cheapest wines has widened to such an extent (ironically, at a time when the gap in quality is probably narrower than it has ever been) that I shall probably never feel able to buy the seriously sought-after wines again. Farewell first growths, grands crus, Penfolds Grange, Guigal single vineyard Côte Rôties, top Italians, and the rest.

Bordeaux and burgundy fetch higher prices than practically anything else—certainly far higher than most Rhône wines and all Loires, practically all New World and southern European wines—and yet these wines certainly don't have a monopoly on pleasure. What they do have is resale value; this is the stuff that makes up the great bulk of lots for the auctioneers and the burgeoning army of fine wine traders and brokers who have been taking an increasing share of their business.

Bordeaux from one of the hundred-odd châteaux in the famous 1855 merchants' "classification" of five divisions of hot properties (thereafter known as *crus classés,* or "classed growths"), or their unclassified equivalents in Pomerol, is by far the easiest wine commodity to trade, because its status is so easy to understand. Yet a great deal of the classed growth claret made even today, with the benefit of improved, more user-friendly vinification techniques, is merely respectably classic rather than heart-stoppingly gorgeous. Like vintage port, classed growth claret is unimpeachably correct, and the lodestar that guides so many wine producers and consumers the world over, but only the very best bottles actually manage to make my heart beat faster and invade my reason (unlike some more artisanal wines, which are perhaps less polished but often more visceral).

Time after time I have opened or been served bottles of classed growth claret from respectable to very good vintages and found myself unmoved by them. They have no faults. No one could take them back and complain. But they lack the excitement, the sheer bull's-eye quality of wines such as Pichon-Lalande 1979 (with 1982 and 1983 waiting in the wings), Chasse-Spleen 1978, Gloria 1970 and many a more celebrated combination of château and vintage. I am deliberately excluding here seriously expensive proven wine classics that cost a bomb, such as Cheval Blanc 1947 and Palmer 1961.

Burgundy of both colors reaches parts of you that other wines cannot. Great burgundy is the ultimate sensualist's wine, but it is even rarer than great bordeaux, and a much, much riskier purchase. This makes one treasure bordeaux's somewhat plodding predictability, but when burgundy succeeds—which it can do for me at all price levels, even some of the most modest appellations can be a real, heady, flirtatious joy—it brings such singular pleasure that it spurs me on to keep trying. Red wine making in Burgundy has improved if anything even more notably than in Bordeaux, but the real trick is to know exactly when to open burgundy of either color, so many different evolutionary phases does it seem to go through.

For this reason, the cases of burgundy in my cellar tend to be opened quite early, and many a bottle from the longer-lived vintages is sacrificed to often literally fruitless experimentation. In my tasting diaries I can read, for example, how bottles of Nuits-Saint-Georges from the light vintage of 1982, made by Jean Grivot from vines grown by his sister-in-law Jacqueline Jayer (the great Henri's first-cousin-once-removed in typically tortuous Burgundian fashion), steadily improved throughout 1987, only to start losing their fruit the next year.

At the time the wine merchants all urged us to buy 1983 rather than 1982, because the grapes had much thicker skins and the wines were much more "substantial" (i.e., hard as old boots). The relatively widespread rot was never mentioned. I didn't buy anything grand from the 1983 vintage but did buy a case of Tollot Beaut's modest Savigny Champ-Chevrey 1983 which I kept sampling with increasing dissatisfaction and desperation throughout the late eighties. About the very last bottle, opened in March 1991 I was at last able to write: "An absolute revelation. This wine has always been a stubborn old thing with a very tannic finish until this bottle, which was divine. Round, supple with mushrooms and good fruit on the nose and palate. Nowhere left to go but at its very peak." As I write, I rather regret the cellar space taken up by 1988 burgundies, and wish I had something more approachable to supplement the still surly 1990s.

I understand those wine lovers who just refuse to play the Russian roulette that is burgundy buying, but when I survey my tasting diaries I see a pathetically obvious, relentless pursuit of The Burgundy High. Like some drug addict determined to duplicate the seminal experience at whatever cost, I track myself continuing to choose burgundy from the lists of restaurants and wine merchants in the often futile hope that *this* will be the bottle.

It was once, one winter's day in 1990, for instance, at the White Horse Inn at Chilgrove, the Sussex mecca for many British wine lovers.

We did our best to re-create my seminal Oxford bottle as closely as possible, by ordering a 1971 Chambolle-Musigny, Les Amoureuses, the most promising vintage after the original 1959. This Drouhin bottle of ruby riches was perfect: headily enveloping with its hint of spice but beautifully balanced, showing much of burgundy's delicacy too. And Drouhin's 1959 Griotte-Chambertin tasted three years before was even more sumptuous; its truffles and licorice still perfuming the leftover glasses the morning after a particularly good dinner the night before. Nowadays I should probably ignore the market and follow my own nose toward the lighter, less commercially admired years, for they have given me so much more reliable pleasure: that combination of fruit, scent and place that red burgundy is so much better at than bordeaux.

Anyone who drinks older wines in the 1990s, even ten-year-old wines, is in a very particular sense tasting history, often a quite noticeably different way of making wine than that employed today. By the late 1980s the sort of wines being made, sold and drunk in the world's most important markets such as the United States, Britain and Germany were almost unrecognizably different from the distinctly retentive liquids that had made up the bulk of my tastings in early *Drinker's Digest* days ten years before.

The most startling difference was the technical skill with which even the most basic, everyday wines were made. With very, very few exceptions they looked healthy (no sluggish hazes and fewer gray tints) and smelled *clean*. Permitted levels of sulphur dioxide had been systematically reduced so that this compound, the winemaker's antiseptic, could no longer be used to cover up careless production of, particularly, sweet wines. As a direct result, the acrid reek of anthracite was very much less common in the tasting room.

Another very visible difference in the wines on offer in the late 1980s was a direct result of varietalism. Now that inexpensive examples of wines labeled with famous French grape names were available from places like Australia, Bulgaria and northern Italy, common or garden table wine sold only on the basis of some brand or fantasy name sank very obviously to the bottom of the barrel where it had always belonged.

These new varietal wines went out of their way to broadcast their charms. Subtlety was no longer a virtue, but a strident aroma and very obvious fruit certainly were. Wine drinkers prepared to spend a little bit more were also introduced to a new, and extremely easy-to-appreciate flavor, that of oak, the wood with the greatest affinity with wine—and they loved it. The apparent sweetness, a whiff of vanilla, and extra depth that oak seems to bring to a wine, in some ways replaced the actual sweetness which made Liebfraumilch and Lambrusco so appealing to newcomers to wine in the late 1970s and early 1980s. What was extraordinary in retrospect was how many wine producers got wine and oak so hopelessly wrong, particularly in the mid to late 1980s.

The real asset of an oak barrel is physical. It allows just the right amount of interplay between oxygen, wine and the wood's own characteristics to encourage red wine to settle gradually and acquire extra smoothness and stability. If a full-bodied white wine is handled fairly roughly and actually fermented in barrels, it seems to shed its harshness, and much of its color, and emerges as delicate yet as complex as a prima ballerina. If, however, it is fermented in a tank, following the late-twentieth-century principles of fierce control of temperature and shielding the wine from any oxygen, and then transferred into a barrel, it tends to soak up every bit of color, flavor and astringence the oak has to give it.

Because barrel fermentation is quite a complicated, expensive technique (one that now provides employment for hundreds of young "cellar rats" around the world each vintage), the first obviously oaked whites we saw in the mid to late eighties were the products of this horrible halfway house, wines fermented in stainless steel and then aged in the barrel. They tended to be made by winemakers who thought if a little oaky flavor was good, then a lot of oaky flavor would be very good. Some of them were monstrous: redolent of steeped matchsticks, they almost demanded to be chewed rather than sipped. They arrived on the shelf already a deep butterscotch color. Many rapidly darkened in the bottle. And the worst of it was that these new oak barrels (the newer the barrel, the more oaky flavor it has to give) had cost the wine producer a fortune, a fortune we consumers were subsidizing, in the first flush of our love affair with this exciting new, if all-pervasive, ingredient.

The oak barrels took over from the bottling line as the most significant investment. Much was made of the exact provenance of the oak

("47 percent Allier, 40 percent Vosges and 13 percent Nevers") by producers who lived so far from these ancient French forests that coopers were able to tell them any old tosh. What they should have told them was that far more important than the exact corner of which forest the trees providing the barrels were grown is how long the wood is left outside for seasoning before being transformed into a barrel. This, it is now much more widely understood, is the key ingredient in barrel quality.

But what consistently amazed me on my travels around the dynamic New World of wine—in the late 1980s I visited Australia three times, New Zealand twice, California several times and Oregon once—was how wine producers anxious to shave a penny off costs here and another penny there seemed prepared to spend any amount of money on their barrels—in some cases even before they fully understood how to use them. This could easily double the cost of the wine.

Oak fixation was perhaps partly influenced by one of the most publicized "research programs" of Mondavi in the Napa Valley. It reviewed in minute detail the results on wine of oak provenance and, particularly, how heavy the "toast" was, how long the half-built barrels were left to char over an open fire before being formed into the right shape.

Another reason for the extraordinary fortunes to be made in the cooperage business was that fine French barrels were also the most obvious "special ingredient" in making absolutely top-quality bordeaux and burgundy. Producers in the world's newer wine regions fell over themselves to import their own stake in France's government-run oak forests. The (entirely crackpot) theory was that if you bought barrels from the guy who supplied the Domaine de la Romanée-Conti, then maybe your Chardonnay would end up tasting like their Montrachet.

Nowadays, thankfully, much of the oak hype has died down. There is a recognition that only the finest wines designed for long aging deserve the investment required for top-quality barrels. There is widespread and increasingly subtle use of cheaper alternatives to new barrels for wines designed to be drunk young. If consumers merely want an oak *flavor* in a young wine rather than the physical properties that oak barrels bring to wines designed to be aged, then it makes sense to use merely a flavoring agent such as a bag of oak chips as an infusion in the fermentation vat, or new oak staves dangled inside an inert container. And from a consumer point of view we are now seeing the predictable reaction to the oak craze: wines being marketed specifically as Unoaked, or Unwooded, as though a special cachet attached to this novel concept.

The white wine revolution of the late 1970s, driven by salesmen of refrigeration plants and resulting in superclean fruity flavors on to which oakiness was rather ineptly grafted, was followed by a revolution in red wine making. This was inspired by the fact that some of the world's most influential producers of red wine, notably in Bordeaux, gradually came to realize that long-term storage of wine was becoming a distinctly minority sport, fraught with practical difficulties in an age when so many people live in centrally heated apartments. The excessively tannic, often rather acid style that had been traditional for young red bordeaux may have inconvenienced no one in an Edwardian age when it was normal to keep such wines in a private cellar for several decades until they tasted more supple, but it certainly was at odds with the frenetic pace of late-twentieth-century life.

The result was a sea change in the style of red bordeaux, resulting in much deeper colored, more intensely flavored wines that were at the same time softer and gentler to taste young. Thanks to anti-rot sprays that took the panic out of picking dates, grapes were allowed to ripen more fully and sumptuously, so the wines became notably lower in acidity and the tannins themselves in the grape skins, stalks and pips were also riper and less harsh tasting. Once picked, the grapes began to be sorted much more rigorously than before, with special sorting tables, slow-moving belts at the cellar door between truck and fermentation vat so that rotten or unripe grapes could be physically eliminated. (This replaced the old-fashioned tip of an entire truckload.)

There was much more careful control of fermentation temperatures throughout the whole two-week fermentation process, typically heating the vat a little at the beginning to get things started and then deliberately cooling the vat after a couple of days so that no useful traces of anything would be boiled off, as can easily happen if a ferment is allowed to go its own heat-generating way. Some producers redesigned their cellars and wineries so that wholesome gravity rather than powerful pumps were responsible for moving the must and wine around (Australia's ultra-pragmatic winemakers tend to be cynical about the theory behind this).

One key element in red wine making is the extraction of color, tannin and flavor from the skins, and all quality-conscious producers have been particularly careful of the way they encourage this by mixing up the skins and liquid in the fermentation vat as gently as possible, often using only the wine that will naturally drain off the skins and deliberately excluding the much tougher liquid that is eventually squeezed off the leftover skins in the wine press. And then throughout the barrel aging and bottling process, an inert gas such as nitrogen is increasingly used to fill spaces that would otherwise be filled with air, to eliminate any possible oxidation. Bordeaux being the hub of the red wine world, subject to scrutiny furtive and otherwise from winemakers elsewhere, these techniques have been adopted as far as is financially possible for most of the world's fine red wines, and certainly by most ambitious producers of bordeaux-like wines made from Cabernet Sauvignon and Merlot grapes.

Few financial sacrifices were required by the important Bordeaux proprietors to achieve this stylistic change. After several lean decades they were awash with cash thanks to an unprecedented combination in the 1980s: a run of excellent vintages together with a worldwide market eager to buy them.

And another thing. The consumer no longer has to rely on wine information filtered through the hardly dispassionate commentary of a wine merchant; producer performance is fully and objectively monitored and available to anyone anywhere prepared to pay a subscription or, now, access the Web. The producers may have moaned about a bad review in an influential newsletter or wine magazine, but at least such publications provided—and continue to provide—an international bulletin board for what is happening in the world's vineyards and cellars. The publications helped to whip up demand, the merchants fueled it with their exhortations to buy while stocks last, and the auction houses serviced it by offering a marketplace for surplus stocks and an arena for (sometimes) making money out of fine wine buying.

Whenever I visited the Médoc in the second half of the eighties I was agog to see which château looked newest-scrubbed, and had installed the smartest new marble-floored tasting room, the grandest salon for receptions, the most avant-garde barrel cellar. The only one of these that affected the quality of the wine, and crucially, was the barrel storage area. The one essential luxury for an ambitious wine producer is to have enough suitably cool space to keep each vintage's produce for as long as that year's conditions demand before it is bottled. Even on an estate as exalted as Château Margaux, it was only in the 1980s that a suitable second-year barrel was installed, carefully humidifed and temperature-controlled under a lawn by the famous avenue leading up to the main building, so that the wine could be bottled when it was ready rather than to make way for the next year's crop. The problem of finding or building sufficiently cool cellars and warehouses is even greater further south in Europe and in most New World wine regions; Californians have taken to boring expensively into hillsides, especially but by no means exclusively for maturing sparkling wines, a much-needed attempt to replicate the *crayères,* chalky caverns, of the Champagne region.

Thanks to these manifold blessings and otherwise of the agrochemical industry, yields began to soar in Europe. Toward the end of the eighties the Bordelais became almost embarrassed by the quantity of grapes their carefully managed vineyards could be persuaded to produce, particularly if the weather cooperated during the all-important flowering of the vines. The result has been a widespread fashion among Bordeaux's top producers to cut what they judge are surplus grapes off the vines during the summer, so-called summer pruning. This doesn't sound to me much like man in perfect harmony with nature—more like man determined not to risk losing a penny by pruning hard during the winter.

Another more recent technique adopted by some Bordeaux producers who have perhaps overreacted to the modern taste for deep, dark concentrated reds is to physically concentrate the grape juice in much the same way as, say, other fruit juices are concentrated. These expensive bits of machinery are still used strictly experimentally, almost under cover of darkness, and are reported, strictly thirdhand of course, to have the usually unfortunate effect of concentrating everything. They are theoretically most useful in cool years which have failed to ripen the grapes fully, but then the acids tend to be relatively high in the first place and the effect of the concentrator is to concentrate the acidity and make it even more unpleasantly marked.

I have certainly noticed over the last few years that the most common red wine faults have changed. In the old days there were too many mean, thin, underripe wines but today the disappointments in a lineup of red wines are most likely to be deep-colored but unbalanced because the color, leeched out of the grape skins by long maceration (or possibly even concentration), is not matched by a similar intensity of appealing ripe fruit. In fact all this contact with the grape skins may well have made the wine uncomfortably high in tannins and thoroughly unpleasant to drink.

The new, softer generation of red wines, especially classed growth bordeaux, was not met with universal acclaim. Those with cellarsful of more attenuated, old-fashioned counterparts had a vested interest in wondering aloud whether these new wines would last. It is still too early to answer that question. Presumably some Hardy Rodenstock figure of the twenty-second century will be kind enough to provide an answer, but the question becomes less and less relevant with every year. No one I've ever met is seriously buying wine for their children, let alone their grandchildren. Indeed I hear many serious wine buyers explaining exactly how they intend to open the last bottle in their cellar just before they die, as André Simon is said to have done so percipiently. All that seems to be demanded of great wine today is that it has a life of between ten and twenty years, and sometimes not even that.

Red bordeaux, most of it made under the influence of new techniques, is certainly the largest single component of my relatively small cellar, which is full to bursting with about a hundred cases, both rottable cardboard and tights-snagging wood. I know that I could store my bottles in a professional wine warehouse, but I prefer to know they are all under my own roof and subject to no more bureaucracy. I'm not at all sure I want the added organization required to administer stock in different locations at different stages of maturity. I like the spontaneity of being able to get my hands (in theory anyway) on any bottle at any time. In practice, however, I know that even under my own roof bottles in dark corners are in sufficient danger of being overlooked, so I dare not trust my wine to any third parties.

In addition to the cellar I draw from a giant wine rack under the stairs deep enough to store two bottles in each of its 120 holes. This is my sort of pending tray, where I put wines not long-lived enough for the cellar, as well as a selection of more serious bottles that I know I can always put my hands on without even having to find the cellar key, brave the outdoors and trip over our younger daughter's tricycle.

The bordeaux is a fairly haphazard collection of mainly classed growths. These handsome wooden boxes of claret tend to just sit there, most still nailed down, except for the 1985s that were so delicious during their first eight or nine years that they were wolfed down with indecent haste—although some of the odd bottles left have suggested that the wines are hardening up a little for the beginning of their second decade. Wines have this annoying habit of changing character just when you think you have them fathomed.

Mind you, I see that I actually wrote the same strange tasting note, "slithery," for two bottles of Eglise-Clinet 1985 even though they were consumed almost a year apart in the early nineties. I don't think I have ever used this word before or since, but what I meant was that this Pomerol, while being lively and exciting to taste, seemed to have no *edges* whatsoever, no perceptible tannin or acidity to latch on to, just one concentrated, glossy mouthful. Just one bottle remains of the two cases I bought in 1987 for less than $200, but this wine style clearly fulfils the modern wine dream, for the case price is currently more than $2,000. (The 1962 Eglise-Clinet on the other hand, which was also in my cellar, was an archetypally old-fashioned gamey red bordeaux.)

I know all these vintages from the eighties are nowhere near that horrible turning point when they start to fade and lose their appeal, so perhaps I can eke them out for several more decades. I should, perhaps, weed out the cases of 1977 vintage port taking up room at the back of the cellar because our consumption rate is so low.

There are certain wines, however, that I seem to drink almost as soon as I buy them. This is true of the odd case of particularly successful Pinot Noir from Martinborough in New Zealand. I've enjoyed the truly Burgundian variability of Martinborough Vineyards' Pinots over a span of vintages, and have added the most recent vintages of Ata Rangi's exuberant Pinot Noir to my cellar. Quality has soared at this winery since I tasted some initial offerings, a soft 1986 and rot-plagued 1987 at Oregon's International Pinot Noir Celebration in 1988. Truly successful New World Pinots tend to run out of their cardboard cases and on to the dinner table, perhaps because I know how much pleasure they can give—and how unlikely they are to make my fortune as investments. The same argument is true in spades of fine Alsace from the likes of Faller, Trimbach, and Schoffitt. Trimbach's Riesling Clos Sainte-Hune is the classic example of slow-maturing Alsace, with so many admirers of its unimpeachably steely purity that its price has been steadily rising out of the "simple pleasure" category. Plumper Rieslings, superior Pinot Blancs, sleeker Pinot Gris and the most savory Gewürztraminers are some of the wines that disappear fastest from my wine racks. These full-bodied, scented whites seem just so *useful,* either as aperitifs, or with all sorts of food—even quite sturdy "red wine" sort of food, although too many of them for my taste nowadays taste sweeter than I'm expecting, which cuts down on their versatility.

Top-quality German wine is one of my cellar's specialties, representing a minority but, I assure you, very refined taste. Those of us who *know* that a bottle of mature Mosel Riesling is just as fine an aperitif as any champagne are not numerous, but we all understand each other, our J. J. Prüms, our von Schuberts, our Ernie Loosens and our Reinhold Haardts well. We also know that these wines demand time. One of the most sublime was a seventeen-year-old, a J. J. Prüm Wehlener Sonnenuhr Auslese 1971 opened on New Year's Eve 1988 that was a little gold but still had the hint of green that can betray Mosel origins to the eye alone. It was still tingling with life and youth (Prüm's wines almost fizz in their very early years) but it definitely had a mature bouquet rather than a youthful aroma, of toasted minerals rather than fruit, perhaps some blackcurrant leaves, even a little spice. It was so delicate it almost danced, yet underneath was a great undertow of extract. You could tell just how much would be left in the petri dish should you be foolish enough to waste a drop on the scientific experiment of evaporation. There was perceptible sweetness, but the great welter of lively acidity kept this from being A Sweet Wine. Of the telltale sign of aging, drying out of fruit, there was not a solitary sign. The finest 1959 German wines demonstrate the same attribute even today. The one tasting I bitterly regret missing, because of a stomach bug, was a revelation of the greatest treasures in the Bremen Ratskeller in 1996.

The slow evolution of my cellar is entirely due to my enthusiasm for Mosel Riesling coinciding with one for top-quality red bordeaux, for these two sorts of wine mature at more or less the same, extremely stately pace. I wish I had more bottles of Mosel 1983s left. I should padlock my 1989s, and am slightly embarrassed by my inability to keep the powerful wines made by the stars of the Pfalz such as Müller-Catoir and Rainer Lingfelder unopened in my wine rack for more than a few weeks. These have much more substance than their spindly cousins from the Mosel in the north, and combine the weight of a white burgundy with far more racy acidity and food-friendly structure.

I am amazed that German wine hardly features on the lists of the world's fine wine traders, when it can provide all sorts of thrills completely unobtainable elsewhere. Of all the world's fine wine styles, delicate, racy, long-lived, aristocratic Mosel Riesling is the only one that will probably never be copied elsewhere. It's not surprising that California and Australia, for example, cannot match the Mosel's natural conditions, but it does surprise me that there is so little commercial incentive for them to try. Is it the low alcohol, the slight sweetness, or the curiously petrol-like aromas that puts so many wine drinkers off Riesling?

If the wines of Germany are currently underappreciated by us Brits, Italian wines always have been. For some reason, with the exception of a few really knowledgeable and enthusiastic specialists, we have allowed almost all the best bottles to go to the better-heeled customers of Germany, Switzerland and the United States. Every time I go to Italy I feel as though I have just received the most beneficial transfusion of my life. Not just the wine but the food is also of a different order, a different taste profile to the British or French norm, as is of course the thrilling experience of being so visibly surrounded by so much history. When I get back to London from elsewhere, I'm usually aching for the antidote (something brazen and New Worldish after a Bordeaux trip, or still and red after a few days in Champagne) but Italy is different. Everything about Italy, for worse as well as better, gets under my skin. I come back and feel aesthetically challenged that the oldest building I can see from our house is only two hundred years old. The objects in my house and wardrobe seem pedestrian; even my Nordic coloring seems vapid and lacking in Latin charisma and glamour. My normal diet seems somehow less vibrant, and the wines I drink with my meals are built quite differently from the average good Italian red with its dashing twist of acidity and bitterness on the back of the palate.

I feel less discontent about the lack of Spanish and Portuguese wines in my cellar. Winemaking skills in Iberia seem to improve with each vintage, as does the range of flavors and styles available to wine lovers abroad. My Iberian affairs seem short-lived and fashion-driven. After Rioja prices soared in response to our enthusiasm in the late 1970s, I flirted with Torres's Catalan bottlings, which always seemed, Mondavi-like, to be on the way somewhere rather than having arrived there. I drank many a fine red, such as Camarate and Periquita, from vineyards near Lisbon before discovering that port grapes could also produce fiery table wine in the Douro valley. And this was merely a reflection of what was going on upriver. For years I had treated Spain's famous Vega Sicilia as a one-off, but ex-blacksmith Alejandro Fernandez put Pesquera on the map—even turning up at the Groucho Club in Soho once to show off his wares, despite speaking not a word of English. In the middle to late eighties, he opened the floodgates for dozens of wanna-be bodegas in Spain's fashionable Ribera del Duero (i.e., Douro) region northwest of Madrid. Although I'm ready to be seduced by whatever comes along from Spain's extremely active winemakers, I am currently most excited by the slightly austere but definitely noble whites of Galicia in the far northwest.

All over Spain things have changed so rapidly over the last few years that I am loath to buy more than a bottle or two at a time. This is true of practically every one of the scores of new wine provenances that have been emerging over the past decade. Skills tend to improve so dramatically with each vintage that younger wines are routinely better than older ones.

We have on the other hand consistently bought small quantities of the top-quality reds that have been made in California for twenty years now, however difficult that has been when the dollar has been particularly strong. (It was useful that 1984, the year our son Will was born, was so much better a year for California Cabernet than for red bordeaux.) These American interlopers tend to languish there, Monte Bello making friends with Mouton, Dominus sitting on top of Cos, but California Chardonnays as sumptuous and fine as Kistler's tend to vanish from my racks within all too short a time of delivery. They're perfect for serving to visitors from mainland Europe.

The other day I managed to find in the depths of the pending tray the last bottle of a case of 1988 Kistler Dutton Ranch Chardonnay that was by no means put to shame by the Ramonet Bâtard-Montrachet from the same vintage served blind alongside. (For many years after the fateful Paris tasting of 1976, the French promulgated the idea that it was a solecism to compare wines from different countries. The head of Champagne de Venoge, for example, unusually worldly as author of the French style bible *BCBG*, received an official reprimand for condoning comparative tastings of champagne and other sparkling wines. I think it perfectly justifiable if the wines are strongly related to each other yet not immediately recognizable for what they are.) Chalone's Pinots from the 1970s and whites from the 1980s served us well, including a toasty seven-year-old "Pinot Blanc" drunk in 1991.

We are yet to make any significant investments in cellaring modern Australian wine, a few magnums of particularly concentrated South Australian Shiraz apart, because so many of them seem ready to drink the moment they're put on sale. Several cases of Australian relics shipped all the way from Sydney in the mid 1980s gave enormous pleasure, however, not least when served to skeptical wine drinkers never previously exposed to the delights of mature Clare Riesling or Hunter Semillon and Shiraz (still cheekily called "Hermitage" on these labels).

Perhaps the single most striking development in the history of recent wine production has been the speed with which Australia has imposed itself on the world's wine map, especially considering how relatively little wine this vast landmass produces. By the late 1980s it seemed to people like me as though my friends had given up European wine for good. Every dinner party in the land, it seemed, was lubricated by bottles and bottles of deep golden Australian Chardonnay. Steadily, as Australians planted more and better grapes in more and more suitable vineyard areas, the percentage of Britain's total wine intake supplied by this ex-colony rose, as France's steadily declined and Germany's plummeted. It has taken longer for Australia to make any real headway in a market as enormous and labyrinthine as the United States but the magnificent existence of Penfolds Grange certainly unlocked a few prejudiced palates (if not those of my French television co-tasters), not to mention purses. As a result, increasing numbers of Australian wine exporters nowadays begin their overseas travels by crossing the Pacific rather than the Indian Ocean.

A key element in Australia's reverse colonization, of the wine world, has been the country's impeccably pragmatic approach to wine science, more au courant, more fluid, less fustily dogmatic than the old Davis regime in California—and oiled by the much closer links possible with a wine industry only a fraction of the size of its California counterpart. Carefully trained Australian winemakers and vine growers emerge from the colleges at a lick each year, ready for the specific challenges of the late-twentieth-century wine business, and with a keep grasp of how to make technically perfect wines. This may be true of California's graduates in enology and viticulture nowadays, but there are strong cultural differences. Australians are not troubled by introspection or self-doubt. They are downright cocky in fact. The wine industry is so relatively tight-knit in Australia that more or less everyone agrees on a common winemaking policy. There is none of the identity crisis that dogged California's wine producers in the last 1980s resulting in a switchback of wine styles, most notably in whites, from oaky to hollow and finally back to some admirably well balanced wines in the 1990s.

Furthermore, young, educated Australians take long-distance travel (known there simply as "O.E.," or overseas experience) for granted. Anxious for specifically vinous experience, and based in a country which needs them most during the Southern Hemisphere's vintage in February and March, these highly trained Australians are free to roam the varied wine regions of the Northern Hemisphere during its vintage months of September and October.

Australia has provided the impetus and technical expertise for the trend toward big, fruit-driven (as opposed to France's more austere, terroir-driven bottlings), user-friendly, open wines, particularly in the bottom and middle price ranges. The casualties in this late eighties obsession with full-flavored, oaky white wines and big, fruity reds were many of the wines of northern Europe. German wines of course, but also many of the wines of the Loire Valley, for instance, are so marked by their high natural acidity, light color, relatively low alcohol level and lack of oak flavor that they fail to meet the criteria of a thoroughly modern wine. Apart from in their native country, and most particularly their native region, such wines as Beaujolais, Bourgueil,

Chinon, Vouvray and of course something as defiantly unmodernized, and probably unmodernizable, as sherry fell from favor—even though they had all been particularly popular in the 1970s.

What I want most from a wine for drinking (as opposed to one for tasting) is that it is appetizing and goes well with food. This means that if it is high in alcohol or oak influence, these characteristics must be perfectly balanced by a concentration of everything else. I want each mouthful to encourage the next, not punch me between the eyeballs or nostrils. The last thing I need is something that tastes hot or syrupy or molten with its charge of excess alcohol. Alas, because wine reputations are increasingly made on the basis of comparative tastings nowadays, there is ever more encouragement to make wines that stand out in a blind lineup, that titillate in the short term rather than beguile over the long term (or at least over a meal). This poses a real problem for both wine competition organizers and, perhaps more importantly, those of us who want to be delighted rather than overwhelmed.

Although flamboyant French wines and reticent California wines exist (in increasing numbers), in very general terms it is the Old World that produces wines which demand concentration rather than admiration, wines whose charms may not be immediately obvious on the first sniff, or even during their first year in bottle, while that great swath of land colonized by the vine up to four hundred years ago that we patronizingly refer to as the New World is largely responsible for the most upfront, obvious and often obviously impressive wines. They are usually easy to appreciate from the moment they're put on sale, although don't necessarily get much better afterwards.

Increasingly, the great debate in wine production, retailing and consumption has been boiled down to Old World versus New World, with France most usually representing the old guard, and California or Australia the New. Sometimes it seems that practically every wine tasting is some sort of Old versus New confrontation. By late 1987 this had already evolved into the fancy California versus Australia taste-off I organized for Condé Nast *Traveler* magazine. I somehow managed to persuade Alexis Lichine, Michael Broadbent, Ezio Rivella (Italian), Jo Gryn (Belgian), Patrick de Ladoucette (French) and Hubrecht Duijker (Dutch) to assemble in London for a blind comparison of some of the best of each of these New World pretenders. (Australia in general and Penfolds in particular were the "winners.") De Ladoucette's misplaced verdict at the end of the tasting was: "The French should definitely not be frightened of *these.*"

By the early 1990s they definitely were. For years the French underestimated the challenge to their wine supremacy, interpreting the fact that they produce indubitably the best wines in the world as proof that all their wines were superior. This arrogance has been infuriating, perhaps particularly for those of us who worship the best of France's wine culture. (It has merely confirmed the prejudices of those determined to champion the excitement and freedoms evinced by the New World.) In the long term I think competition from outside, especially from cheeky upstarts, will prove to be the very best thing of all for both the traditional wine regions and for consumers everywhere.

A Stake in
the Motherland

————

While tensions grew between the Old and New Worlds of wine, I was quite unwittingly moving myself toward precisely the arena in which this battle was most obviously to be fought.

In 1987, when the third and final series of *The Wine Programme* was shown, I wrote a little book of short essays on specific food and wine matches called *Jancis Robinson's Food and Wine Adventures*, intending it to be preparation for a long, definitive tome on the subject. John Lawrence provided some stunning illustrations, reminiscent of some of my mother's work as an illustrator before she married; the publishers provided counterbalance with some quite extraordinarily inventive page layouts. When the time came to write a synopsis of the serious longer work, I realized that I'd said everything I felt was sayable on the subject.

Appreciating food and wine combinations is an even more subjective and variable business than appreciating wine in isolation. I have found that it is perfectly possible to drink pretty much anything while eating pretty much anything else. No thunderbolt from on high comes down to strike those daring enough to essay a bottle of Pauillac with a fillet of sole (a combination most Bordelais would insist on). Even supposed enemies of fermented grape juice such as vinegary dressings, chocolate, eggs and chilies can be persuaded to mop up mouthfuls of certain wines. I think that for every dish there probably is one perfect wine, but that for most of us, life is too short to work out what it is. The one milieu in which customers have a right to be directed to a perfect food and wine combination is a seriously expensive restaurant with a relatively static menu. Menus in three-star restaurants in France are typically quite short and change only with the seasons, so their sommeliers really should be able to guide patrons to ideal unions between the solid and the liquid.

My next book reflected another, very different subject about which I felt passionately, alcohol. Some people thought I was completely mad to even consider this inflammatory subject, but I still can't understand why. In any case, I sensed a sort of sea change in consumers' attitudes to alcoholic drink—perhaps signaled by those uncooperatively aqueous lunchers at L'Escargot—and felt that as a regular drinker, I was probably not wildly atypical in wanting to know just how much harm or good my regular intake of alcohol was doing me.

At this stage American antialcohol sentiment was boiling up vociferously, and an increasing amount of editorial space was being given over to the British counterparts of these neo-Prohibitionists, as they were called. I found it hard to believe that alcohol was quite as evil as some organizations were suggesting, but I wanted an excuse to study and disseminate the medical as well as social facts. I felt that more and more social drinkers were being bombarded by tendentious propaganda about alcohol and that they deserved an objective assessment of the issues. (A temperance campaigner might have accused me of being far from objective because of my work, but once the book had come out I had the strange experience of being treated as a fellow-thinker by people on both sides of this fierce and emotive debate.)

I researched and wrote this book before the recent emergence of so much evidence of a link between wine drinking and low rates of heart disease. But I had already come to the most reassuring conclusion that, with the exception of certain people genetically predisposed to being physically wrecked by alcohol (a minority which surely didn't include those with a hard-drinking ninety-year-old granny), social drinking really wasn't nearly as dangerous as so many newspapers and television programs were then suggesting it was (most of them written by journalists who daily flouted their own recommendations). Wine enthusiasts who bothered to read my somewhat chaotically organized book were cheered by it.

But I ran into serious trouble when wily Charlie Wilson, then editing the *Times*, decided to serialize it. Try as I might, I could not persuade the paper to give me any hint of what they proposed to publish and was horrified when the extracts appeared, not only illustrated with terrifying *Struwwelpeter*-like cartoons of what supposedly happens to you if you drink too much, but with key phrases or even words excised so that only the negative side of the argument was reprinted. I suppose Wilson thought that it made a better "story" to feature a wine writer pointing out the evils of alcohol than to faithfully reproduce my more balanced view. But because far more of my older colleagues in and around the wine world read the *Times* than would ever consider spending £9.95 ($16) on a book about an active ingredient they enjoyed greatly but rarely acknowledged, they got a seriously distorted impression of the book's overall message. At a Master of Wine committee meeting which coincided with the most lurid of extracts I was virtually threatened with expulsion. And for months afterwards I was cold-shouldered by traditionalists at tastings (the congregational form favored by the wine trade). I even remember one veteran taster hissing "How *could* you?" as he passed me on his way back from a spittoon.

Contemporaries, however, didn't seem to sense the same treachery, and the next generation down is now completely, and surely beneficially, sensitized to alcohol in a way that their parents are not. This doesn't mean of course that young people today enjoy an untroubled relationship with alcohol (part of being young for many of us is to misuse pretty much everything we can lay our hands on), but I think young people are much less likely to commit the occasionally fatal mistake of pretending they are not affected by alcohol. Perhaps the most remarkable social miracle I have witnessed in Britain is the change not just in attitude but in behavior relative to drinking and driving among people born after about 1960.

Most notably, while my tract on alcohol may have been by far my most meager seller, it has consistently been the most borrowed of my books from public libraries. Perhaps this indicates that people are in fact very interested in the subject, but would feel embarrassed to demonstrate that they were by anything more obvious than including it in a stack of several volumes borrowed.

Publishers sometimes ask me to update this book, but it is the 1989 vintage of the J Robinson oeuvre that consumers most often want updated. Chris Foulkes, then overall wine editor at Mitchell Beazley, persuaded me to write a book about how wines age, eventually called *Vintage Timecharts*. This was an archetypally Mitchell Beazley book, dominated by graphics rather than words, in this case arresting graphs charting the maturation of different paradigmatic wines, typically a spread of the last ten consecutive vintages on a horizontal time axis and a vertical one for quality (ranging upwards on a determinedly unscored axis toward "Perfection"). All this geometry, and the fact that the period under scrutiny began with the 1978 vintage, particularly fine in many key areas, made the job particularly suitable for a wine-loving mathematician. I was even more obedient and reactive then than I am now, so I simply set about providing the most useful book I could within these parameters, although of course it means that the book ideally needs to be updated frequently.

The book's existence and acceptance opened my eyes to how little information the wine trade at that stage was giving its customers on possibly the most important aspect of wine consumption of all: when to open the bottle. Even as recently as the late eighties, the general belief among wine consumers was that wine was something that improved with age, and that this applied equally to all sorts of wine. Indeed, my most frequent letter from readers of my columns went something like this: "I have three bottles of Blue Nun Liebfraumilch left over from our wedding reception thirty years ago. When do you think we should drink them? What sort of value to you think they have nowadays, should we decide to sell them?" The answer of course is that practically any basic wine of either color that sells in any quantity (and the quantities of Blue Nun sold in the sixties and seventies were vast) starts its rapid deterioration just a few months after being shuttled off the bottling line. If letters like these are rarer, and if British wine consumers at least are more aware of the modern reality that most wine is an ephemeral commodity, then credit must go to our supermarkets which several years ago took a deep breath and began to spell out the brutal modern truth on the back labels of their own bottlings: "best consumed within six months of purchase" and the like. Wines, even the most basic wines, made in the first half of the century when the mellowing second, "malolactic" fermentation and its accompanying acceleration effect on aging was hardly known, did last longer, but they were by no means more fun to drink.

The only wines worth cellaring, or in the jargon "laying down" (ho, ho), nowadays are those we'd all class as a special treat, priced well above the surprisingly low average price for the wine trade as a whole. Even they vary enormously in their likely lifespans, according to the type of wine, how it's made, how it's stored, the character of each vintage and even the size of the bottle.

In the old days the traditional wine trade, who were the ones most likely to be selling wines worth aging, had learnt what they knew about the life cycles of various different wines from personal experience and wisdom passed on by their mentors. They failed to realize that so many of their customers had no access to this sort of arcane, privileged knowledge. Things are much better today, as at the bottom end of the market. Most of those selling or keeping fine wine tend to give a possible drinking period for each wine—another example of the wine trade slowly catching up with the needs of those who keep it afloat.

One delightful side effect of writing the *Timecharts* book was that I had an extremely good excuse to conduct all sorts of fascinating vertical tastings of inspirational wines. I took the precaution of choosing only particularly good quality examples of the various types of wine that are most suitable candidates for aging, and as far as possible, traveled to taste the wines with their producers in situ.

In September 1988 I made a fateful journey to Burgundy to taste the last ten vintages of the various wines I'd chosen as Burgundian paradigms. I thought superior Beaujolais of the longest-living type deserved a place (and some attention), so I went via Duboeuf and tasted, among other vintages, his last bottle of the 1976 Morgon from Jean Descombes that I had served at my thirtieth birthday party so many lives before.

At a rather more elevated level, grand cru white burgundy had to have a place, *bien sûr,* and so it was that during this visit I met the famous Vincent Leflaive, head of the family lucky enough to own some of the finest vineyard holdings for white burgundy. In the late 1980s it seemed as though I drank very little white burgundy *other* than those made at Domaine Leflaive, especially their super-charming 1982s (a vintage not unlike the 1992s) and even the odd distinguished bottle of mature 1977.

Vincent Leflaive was effectively the squire of the southern Burgundian village of Puligny-Montrachet, a handsome roué who had the reputation of suffering fools with extremely bad grace. I had made the appointment with Vincent's much more approachable nephew Olivier Leflaive, then in the process of setting up his own small *negociant* house, Burgundy's response to this quality-driven age for wine, a welcome challenge to the more blasé, well-entrenched big merchants. When I finally worked out where the office was, up some steps above the unusually large but anonymous courtyard, I found the two Leflaives sitting on one side of an enormous empty desk. I was expected to sit on the other and submit my application for their attention. I felt as though I were applying for a visa to a particularly xenophobic country.

"Are you married?" asked Vincent who, incidentally, was one of the very few wine producers keen to know exactly which other wines were to be included in the book. We tasted Chevalier-Montrachet in the spotless Leflaive cellar in a historical progression back from some elegant 1987 drawn straight from one of the remarkably few casks needed to house all the Chevalier that their four acres produce to their last bottle of vigorous, fumey 1978. This was Vincent's favorite, but Olivier favored the 1986 and a star, though as yet an unformed star, the 1983, which reached an alcohol level of 13.8 percent purely on the basis of the natural grape sugar (in Burgundy it is normal to rely partly on adding beet sugar to the fermentation vat to provide a few extra degrees of alcohol, a process known as chaptalization after Chaptal, the agriculture minister who dreamt it up two hundred years ago). In 1988 this wine was merely massive and impressive, though too young to suggest any particular flavors. We all paid lip service to the notion that it was a shame even to taste it at this stage (I couldn't go along with this entirely) and that it would only start to reveal itself in five or so years' time.

In January 1997 I had a chance to check my own prediction of Domaine Leflaive Chevalier-Montrachet 1983's maturity when it was served, in generous quantity, at the extremely large dinner table of wine collectors Michel and Diane Klat. By then it had lost none of its immense weight and persistence, but had acquired the delicious patina of, shall we say, early middle age. The color had deepened and it had that uniquely savory interplay of nuts and minerals that great mature white burgundy can deliver. Anne-Claude, Vincent's beloved daughter

who has run the estate since Vincent's death, must be proud of this
wine—if she gets much of a chance to taste it. Few family-owned
French wine domains have the habit of deliberately keeping back any
quantity of their produce to see how they age, and this can be particularly true of outfits owned by many different family members, some of
whom are interested in the estate purely for the income it brings them
rather than anything more cerebral or hedonistic.

Family tensions were just starting to rend asunder another famous
Burgundian domain I visited that September, the world-famous
Domaine de la Romanée-Conti in Vosne Romanée. I braved this
particular lion's den to put my palate diligently through a vertical tasting of La Tâche, a wine that even then was selling, partly
because of its rarity value, for hundreds of pounds a bottle. The
Provence-based American writer Richard Olney, whom I had last seen
in a hotel lift in Bordeaux just after the Rodenstock Yquem tasting,
when we'd exchanged lifted eyebrows, had turned his monograph-
writing attentions by then from Yquem to DRC, so he also took part
in this unusually luxurious tasting.

The co-managers of the Domaine, respectively representing the two
families which jointly own it and enjoy its fabulous income, were the
scholarly Aubert de Villaine and the glamorous, highly strung
Madame "Lalou" Bize-Leroy. For the sake of form, they would receive
visitors to "the Domaine" together, but passion and angst were already
in the air in late 1988. Lalou, for example, broke rank with Aubert
during our tasting, denouncing the Domaine's 1983s. Presumably
sensing she would soon be ousted from the Domaine, she was already
laying plans to set up her own rival establishment in the same village,
buying up some of the area's finest vineyards, in some cases even plots
contiguous to the Domaine's own vines. (This was to give her a marvelous excuse to demonstrate to visitors the contrast between vine
health in the two holdings.)

Lalou already ran the highly successful négociant business Leroy that
she and her sister, with whom she quarreled, inherited from their father,
whose enviable stocks of mature and maturing wine are still housed in
eerily quiet stone warehousing in the village of Auxey-Duresses. But
Lalou was sharp enough to see that négociant wines, blends of wines
made by others and bought in to be bottled by the merchant, had
increasingly limited appeal. Today the consumer wants to know as much

as possible about the provenance of their wines, and the reputation of négociants in general had been tarnished by the mediocre bottlings available from the least conscientious of them. (I thought of this eight years later when making a television program about British super-markets' newfound obsession with the traceability of the food they sell.)

I had cunningly timed my visit so that I could accept my invitation to Lalou's annual wine tasting and dinner at her sumptuous farm-house at Auvenay in the hills above Saint-Romain. I had heard about this annual event but this was the first time I had witnessed it. As I approached Auvenay by the back roads through wild farmland, the sun was setting behind immensely tall, ancient beech trees. It all seemed very *Grand Meaulnes.* I turned in to the driveway to see virtually *tout le monde gastronomique* standing rather awkwardly on the gravel in front of the house, sipping a glass of Bourgogne Blanc d'Auvenay. Lalou, in shocking pink satin shift, was dashing about welcoming the likes of Georges Duboeuf, Paul Bocuse, the impish French wine writer Michel Bettane, his Belgian counterpart Jo Gryn, Andreas Keller of Germany, wine collector Bipin Desai who had come from Los Angeles, a rather late Michael and Daphne Broadbent, and James Suckling, a young American whom Marvin Shanken had cleverly put in place as Euro-pean bureau chief of his increasingly influential and glamorous *Wine Spectator.*

Although we were invited for "18.00 *précise,*" it was not before seven when the light started to fade that we were eventually invited inside to marvel at the giant displays of heavily perfumed lilies and equally distracting heavily truffled food on the buffet tables in her inter-connecting salons. We were eventually served a supper of Lalou's own foie gras, with a slight shortage of bread, and lobster risotto with a marked shortage of rice. But before then we had to work. We were carefully allotted seats (mine was next to Bettane, a formidable taster) and given little tasting books made up of a series of top sheets with carbon copies underneath for our "answers" to the blind tasting mara-thon she had so carefully organized.

It soon became clear that the supper was designed to provide some recompense for the ritual humiliation that was the main point of the evening. A series of wines along the lines of Chambertin 1949 were served which we were to do our best to identify, and at the end Lalou collected all our top copies so she could mark them and award a prize to the top taster. It must have been useful to have documentary evidence of the frailties of some of the world's best-known wine experts, but Lalou made the most of the buildup. I particularly remember her looking with extra keenness over Michel Bettane's shoulder. "Oh, you think it's *that*, do you?" she would observe with a triumphant smile. After a range of infant 1985s she toured the room giving us a little impromptu speech about how she didn't have the time to read what the *mauvaises langues* said about her—especially not the little bird who claimed her wines were expensive. Now that she is concentrating her not inconsiderable winemaking talents on Domaine Leroy, heavily bankrolled by a Japanese company whose name she has difficulty spelling, she no longer hosts this annual event. I'm so glad I managed to witness two of them.

On that fateful visit to Burgundy I also tasted chez Jadot, and was most impressed by the négociant's career winemaker Jacques Lardière. André Gagey, the head of the firm, coincided my visit with a major vertical tasting of wines from the firm's own Clos des Ursules vineyard on the outskirts of Beaune. Because this involved extracting bottles back to the previous century from the firm's unusually well stocked cellar, he had invited wine writers from Japan, America, Switzerland, Holland, and Belgium, including James Suckling, Clive Coates, Jo Gryn and Frank Prial of the *New York Times*.

The most significant effect of this visit to France's loveliest wine region had nothing, directly, to do with wine. For my few days in Burgundy I decided to stay at the Auberge du Moulin in Bouilland, a tranquil village at the head of a lyrically pastoral, narrow green valley that cuts through the famous Côte d'Or just north of Beaune. I knew the Michelin-starred restaurant of old, but its owners had recently carved rooms out of a medieval barn across the road (in true French provincial manner, installing gold taps and down-lit fake masterpieces). I would sit at a table in my room in one of its eaves, listening to the cows munching on the hillside beside me, trying to plot the likely aging curves of the wines I had tasted that day. In the golden light of the early evening, however, I would wander around the village, marveling at how much more truly rural the French countryside was than its British counterpart. Here, little old ladies would tootle to their neighbors with a couple of eggs, freshly laid presumably by the syncopated, confidently vocal hens that strutted around the village.

Tomatoes had been carefully left to ripen on windowsills on what passed for a main road. No Neighborhood Watch notices here; the whole village was in a state of perpetual vigilance on behalf of every member of the community. And also, of course, the bucolic setting of this Burgundian backwater and its luminous gray-mauve stone buildings were just so hauntingly beautiful.

I came back to London enthused by these rustic charms, an allure both aesthetic and gastronomic, and the knowledge that at that time a pound sterling could buy you so many French francs that property in the French countryside seemed virtually to be given away. (Because of this there was an influx that amounted almost to a flood of Brits buying in France in the late eighties, many of them spurred on by the allure of drinking cheap, virtually untaxed wine. Some of them even dropped out to realize the dream of making it.) Nick, bless him, put up only the shortest of token resistances so that by the beginning of 1989 we decided we would definitely try to find a little slice of French countryside to call our own, with a view to enjoying it as much as possible during school holidays.

Although it was Burgundy that had initially inspired me, I was fearful of choosing to spend my holidays in such an engrossing wine region. I would feel that I could never relax; every moment I could theoretically be nosing round some cellar or vineyard enlarging my wine knowledge. The same was true of all the classic wine regions, unfortunately, for most them are very beautiful. But there was a visually memorable part of France that I had visited on my travels that seemed to be so torpid in terms of the direness of the wines it produced that it would surely allow me as much holiday languor as I felt like: the western Languedoc.

I remembered in particular the countryside around the Château de Gourgazaud in the ragged Minervois hills, a handsome property to which the head of Chantovent, Roger Piquet, had chosen to retire when only in his early fifties. I'd gone back there to film for *The Wine Programme* and to try (desperately) to dig up some material for my Shock! Horror! article on the wine war for *The Sunday Times*. The area had already demonstrated its tug on my affections. What I liked about it was the uninterrupted sweep of vines, brilliantly but warmly lit in golden evening light, between the dramatic crags of the foothills of the Cévennes to the north and the wildness of the Corbières mountains to the south. Each little huddled stone-and-stucco village seemed to harbor at least one mysterious and uninhabited old château, locked with its overgrown garden behind a high stone wall or dilapidated railings. And through this delightfully rustic passage between mediterranean and Atlantic cultures flowed the seventeenth-century miracle of the Canal du Midi, linking the two oceans, virtually unchanged in 330 years, but for the age of the double ribbon of plane trees which marked it out in the landscape and provided shade for those who traveled on it.

A few canal cruisers apart, this was French mediterranean countryside without the foreigners (except us) and high prices of Provence, but with a wild gypsy streak thanks to Spain's proximity just over the Pyrenees and generations of Spanish influx. Garcia and Sanchez are much more common names in the local telephone books than Blanc and Dupont. But what am I saying? You wouldn't like it, really you wouldn't. There aren't the thyme, pine and lavender smells of Provence, and there's absolutely nothing to do. Definitely not worth even inspecting, I'd say.

We, on the other hand, decided we'd fly out to the south of France at Easter 1989 and try to find a house to buy. Roger kindly put out some feelers in advance, telling the locals how much we had to spend. By a strange coincidence, absolutely every property we looked at, from half of a medieval castle to semi-ruined shepherd's hut, cost exactly that! We decided we liked the medieval castle and even made an offer for it. But the Belgian representing the family that owned it, who lived in another château nearby, decided to raise the price by 50 percent—which fortunately opened our eyes to just how much work there was to be done on it.

After two or three frustrating days in the Languedoc we set off for the other area we had in mind, Gascony, and in particular for the family-run, one-star hotel in Plaisance. This was several years before we abandoned car ownership in London, so Julia and Will were still able at that stage to sit in a car for longer than half an hour without complaint. We had a lovely journey southwest across the hilltops, marveling at the snowy Pyrenees. By day we would sniff around empty properties quite musty with damp, and in the evenings we would stuff ourselves with goose and duck in every form imaginable, all washed down with lovely tangy proud white Jurançon, backboned red Madiran and the good value bottles that local dynamo André Dubosq was wheedling out of the local Plaimont cooperatives. But we had to admit that we had left our hearts in the Languedoc. Gascony was just too damp and green for us, too reminiscent of home in fact.

We were meant to fly back from Toulouse on the Monday afternoon but on Sunday morning, Nick's birthday, we couldn't resist haring back to the Languedoc just to see whether we couldn't find a suitable property. By then we'd realized it was the arid mediterranean terrain we loved, and we'd worked out what we wanted in estate agent's jargon: a *maison de maître* (or what an English wine merchant friend with a seventeenth-century house in Provence once described dismissively as "a nineteenth-century box"). It had to have a garden, it should not be overlooked, and it should ideally be just on the edge of a village.

By some miracle, the last of three houses we saw that Monday, in a rainstorm, just half an hour before we had to set off for the airport, fulfilled all criteria and Nick and I flew down again on my birthday later that month from a weekend in Paris to sign all the documents chez the local notary.

We went to Vinexpo in June, the big biennial international wine show in Bordeaux (a preferred alternative to participation in Britain's National Drinkwise Day back home). The grand dinners of the vinously great and good at Châteaux Latour and Cheval Blanc we viewed as mere warm-up acts for our trip down south to buy furniture for our new house. (This despite the fact that the Saint-Émilionnais used the Cheval Blanc dinner to decimate their stocks of great vintages, and the Latour dinner starred Cristal 1981, Haut-Brion 1961, Latour 1959 in magnum and, for Nick, the thrill of sitting next to ex–Beirut hostage Jean-Paul Koffmann and hearing his tales of how he kept his sanity in captivity by reciting the 1855 classification to himself.)

During that first year of ownership we were like demented lovers, flying to the south of France whenever we had a few free days. Our longest stay by far was, and continues to be, the long summer holidays in July and August when we could fully indulge the passion shared by so many inhabitants of these cold gray islands of ours, eating out of doors. We have amazed our fellow French villagers, who tend to eat all year round in shuttered gloom, by having lunch in our overcoats in the

garden on New Year's Day. The Penning-Rowsells are so keen on outdoor eating that they have been known to take lunch outside in what
they call their loggia on the sunnier days of an English winter overlooking a garden covered in snow. Snow is unimaginable in a
Languedoc summer. We move our table between breakfast, lunch and
dinner to catch the dappled shadows thrown by the Judas trees, and go
to elaborate lengths to construct shade for the food, providing those
clear plastic vacuum cylinders to keep the bottles cool.

Our first Languedoc summer, one of concentrated wallpaper-
stripping and painting, was 1989, the first of two particularly hot, dry
summers in France, whose fruits I hope to enjoy in many a bottle over
the next few decades. We fair-skinned northerners sweltered, and
loved the sweltering. And our wine-drinking habits changed considerably as a result.

Despite being the part of France with arguably the longest history
of wine production (the Narbonne region was famous for wine in even
Roman times), in the 1980s the Languedoc was still regarded by the
French as an embarrassing appendage to their glorious image as wine
producers. Most of the wine made down there came from carelessly
farmed, overburdened, inferior vines that had been planted on the
plains to provide oceans of cheap plonk for industrial workers in the
north who regarded thin red wine as a more reliable alternative to
water and drank it in great quantity.

As this habit, and more particularly its practitioners, died out,
France had an increasingly inconvenient wine surplus on its hands. One
of the most obvious benefits of European Common Market membership was Brussels' ability to buy up this surplus (and distill it into
a surplus of industrial alcohol), and to institute schemes to bribe
vignerons in the less good areas to pull up their vines for good. It was
already clear to the relatively few Languedociens who were serious
about wine that the impoverished soils of the higher ground favored by
the Romans could produce really quite fine wine. Gourgazaud's wines
were getting more impressive with each vintage, and two years previously I had tasted an extremely ambitious red 1984 Minervois made by
Daniel Domergue (one of the Languedoc's most passionate winemaker-
historians whom I now know well), imported into Britain by, of all
people, Corney & Barrow, the ultra-traditional City of London wine
merchant.

The problem with the Languedoc's image was that such wines were hugely outnumbered by the vapid produce of the thousands of acres of flat, baked, fertile plain that were far from ideal for wine quality. A typical Languedoc vigneron in the late 1980s was simply a farmer in charge of a small area of vines, often in several disparate parcels inherited from various forebears. He would do his best to deliver as great a weight of grapes as possible to his village cooperative winery each September. Almost all the vines grew as low, unwired bushes in summer (black stumps in winter) and needed minimal treatments other than copious sprays of turquoise copper sulphate powder whenever it rained and rot threatened. Our first two hot, dry summers were not popular with such vine growers because drought produces small, thick-skinned grapes. I remember the uninhibited joy of a large group of vignerons we had lunch with one Sunday in July 1990 when the heavens opened and we were all trapped inside after our barbecue. Every drop of rain represented a bit more cash to spend over the following year.

Back in the late 1980s there were a few individual wine estates such as Gourgazaud where the owner actually made the wine, but they were relatively rare and certainly of strictly local interest. I felt no compunction to go and find out more about them during my first long summer in the Languedoc with the family. Nick and I, by now partners in one of Britain's new army of independent television producers, badly needed some R&R after the nervous exhaustion brought on by persuading the intensely private food writer Elizabeth David to allow us to make a film about her.

Unlike Burgundy, where even the most modest Bourgogne Rouge and Blanc sells for quite a robust price, the Languedoc allowed me to luxuriate in extremely keenly priced wines, of all hues and styles. Even in 1989 we could choose from the local, surprisingly fine sparkling Blanquette de Limoux as an aperitif; a wide range of well-made dry whites and rosés for really hot weather; more reds, of the same sort of ultra-digestible, not-too-alcoholic dimensions as red bordeaux, than one can dream of, either from appellations such as Minervois, Corbières and Coteaux du Languedoc or some of the newer, often varietal Vins de Pays; and a host of sweet and often strong wines such as golden Muscats and port-like wines from Banyuls and Maury.

The previous owner of our house, a retired gentleman from Lorraine, was a wine enthusiast. He had not only made wine himself from the produce of the vines in the garden (of which he courteously left us a bottle) but had also carved out part of the garage as his cellar. I could see, however, that without special insulation, this dark shed could never be relied upon to store very fine wine in the long term. I suspect he found the local wines rather coarse to his refined northern palate. He certainly kept a much wider collection of different bottles than, I would guess, anyone else in the village in this, France's most quantitatively important wine region.

Wine was taken entirely for granted by our new neighbors, to such an extent that few of them did anything more adventurous than turn up at the local co-op every now and then with a giant plastic jerrycan, to be filled either with their entitlement as *"adhérents,"* or contributing vine growers, to the co-op or as customers who were no more demanding. The local *vin ordinaire* was really pretty ordinaire—and the commercial bottlings available in the village grocery shop both ordinaire and heavily industrialized. Instead I took pleasure in seeking out the best bottles from the best local domains.

I had no desire to move part of my "serious" wine cellar out to the south of France. The process would have been tedious beyond belief for purely practical reasons anyway, because of France's manifold bureaucratic disincentives to actually importing wine into the land of the vine. Nor did I feel I wanted to turn our rural hideaway, designed to provide a rustic antidote to London life, into a fine wine showcase. Somehow, part of being on holiday was consuming the best of the local wine, which can be very good, but rarely demands the attention and protocols that more expensive bottles do. We could choose from Corbières a mile to the south or Minervois even less to the north. Since then I have ventured further afield, but I have yet to buy anything made closer to home. Our village squats on the flatland in between and the soil is too alluvial to produce anything above the then extremely dreary Languedoc norm.

But change was already afoot in the Languedoc. The first inkling I had came before we even moved into our house, during our post-Vinexpo stay at a local hotel (where we heard an anguished cry from an American wine importer in intense negotiation over breakfast by the pool with a local wine bottler: "Just give me Chardonnay, any Chardonnay!"). We saw an ad in the local paper, the *Midi Libre*, from a local girl looking for holiday work and thought she might prove useful while we were busy stripping off those of our house's fourteen feverish wallpapers we could bear least. We went to meet Nathalie's family and were surprised when her stepfather told us he too had a wine connection; he was currently buying some vineyard land for an Australian, an Australian called Monsieur Eric.

This was an extraordinary revelation. A representative of the New World, planning to invade the Old? For the past decade we had seen, time after time, venerable French wine producers take a slightly embarrassed stake in California, Oregon, Chile, Australia, South Africa and New Zealand. But with the exception of Len Evans's abortive strike in Bordeaux many years previously, this was the first time I had heard of reverse investment. I was intrigued, especially as at that time the Languedoc was regarded with such scorn by the wine establishment, not least the French themselves. I set about asking my contacts in Australia who this mysterious Monsieur Eric was and was eventually given the Montpellier fax number of an English-language wine newsletter called the *Frog-Line*, run by this person, who turned out to be called James Herrick.

James Herrick was not at all pleased by my fax enquiries. Which is not surprising since he and his Australian partners, who had made a mint selling Australian wines in the United States, were planning to invade Languedoc by stealth. They had identified it as one of the few regions of France where land was inexpensive and the climate reliable, and were in the process of acquiring three of the extremely rare extensive holdings of contiguous vineyard land that existed in the region. If their vendors heard they had grand plans, the price would immediately rocket (as our Belgian with the château had demonstrated). The return fax, addressed to Hercule Poirot, virtually told me to button my lips.

During the autumn the Herrick deals were put in place and we were finally to meet this mysterious personage, in neutral territory over lunch in Carcassonne one very cold day in January 1990 with his glamorous Californian wife and baby so tiny that James still had his Alfa Romeo. Since that time they have had twins, moved twice to larger houses in our area, and he has established a new wine brand, James Herrick Chardonnay, that has enjoyed enormous success in Britain, by applying a bit of marketing and Australian viticultural and winemaking techniques to these three large vineyards around Narbonne—and provided me with acres of good copy, not to mention a fine scene for a television series.

But this was not an isolated invasion. Very soon afterwards, the giant Australian company Hardy's caught takeover fever and added a dilapidated winery, La Baume near Béziers, to their European holdings which for a time included the Ricasoli estate, then a financial drain in Chianti country. More recently the Australian wine giant, Penfolds, has been combing the region and finally decided to embark on a joint venture with Val d'Orbieu, the biggest cooperative group down there. And these Australians have been joined by a host of other foreign investors, as well as all manner of producers from the smarter French wine regions to the north. My old friend Georges Duboeuf, true to form, was already there, but in the nineties he has been followed by scores of others who now use the Languedoc as their production base for their diffusion labels.

The cliché most often applied to the transformed Languedoc is "France's New World," a reference to the fact that so much of the available land produces France's Vins de Pays, a special category devised by the French for wines they see as not up to scratch for full-blown Appellation Contrôlée status. Non-French consumers and many producers are not so derisive about these "country wines." Wine buyers who were introduced to wine through New World varietals found a Chardonnay or Merlot Vin de Pays d'Oc belonged to the same family and could be appreciated without any grasp of French geography at all. For wine producers in France, Vins de Pays have the great advantage of being burdened by far fewer constraints. Vins de Pays can be made from a wider range of grape varieties (dry table wines made from the ubiquitous Muscat, once used solely for dessert wines, were exported to the U.K. from 1989, for example) with fewer constraints on production techniques (including yields) than Appellation Contrôlée wines. And while the quality of the Vins de Pays has been escalating, the French, even those based six hundred miles north in Paris, have increasingly cited the Languedoc, with Roussillon, its neighboring Catalan region to the south, as providing the best-value AC wines in France too.

Every time I go there I learn of some new, quality-driven wine domain in Corbières, Minervois, Fitou, Pic-Saint-Loup, Saint-Chinian,

Faugères or some other Coteaux du Languedoc or Costières de Nîmes that has either been established or revived. Meanwhile, some of the biggest wine producers in the United States, the Gallos, Mondavis, Kendall Jacksons, Château Ste. Michelles and Sutter Homes of this world, have been scouting round the Languedoc to fill the gaps in their inventory left by short crops back home and the ravages of phylloxera in California. As I write, a significant proportion of all the cheaper bottles sold nationally in the United States are filled with wine from Languedoc, or Chile—however covertly this fact is acknowledged on the label.

I am flummoxed, and secretly delighted. I go to the Languedoc for a bit of peace and quiet and all of a sudden I find myself at the hub of the wine world. But the joy of our house is that, although one side faces the village, the other faces the sunshine, the Corbières mountains and a walled garden, which allows me quite literally to turn my back on such toil as is associated with my chosen subject and to concentrate on some of the simplest of its pleasures: wines made with passion and dedication but only the slenderest of means and pretensions.

Discovering
France's Stomach

***

One of the many pleasures of having a base in the south of France was that it meant we were freer to explore the French countryside. This was the theory anyway. In practice, it was just too hot in summer to travel far in our old banger, and there was the small matter of two, soon to be three, children. Rose was born in March of 1991, a less-than-inspiring vintage, like Will's, so she has had to make do with liquid puns such as Quinta de la Rosa port. I see that my note on the Roederer Brut Premier we sipped at a nearby hotel before going to the hospital to have her induced was an entirely unironical "very young but well made and rounded out."

By the time she was three weeks old she was in the Languedoc for Easter, graciously receiving tributes from our French friends and neighbors and the Hardys, who had worked at L'Escargot in the early days and now wanted to absorb some French village life. The combination of them and an adoring grandmother in situ to look after Julia and Will, together with temperate Easter weather, gave Nick, me and the still highly portable Rose the chance to travel a bit further afield than we could on a day trip in summer. So it was that we got to explore our own reactions to the extraordinary cathedral of Albi, as well as to the exceptionally varied wines of Gaillac. The appellation's most famous, most vocal and most philosophical producer, Robert Plageoles, was only slightly put off his stride by being interviewed by a reporter *mit* baby. I don't think I actually fed her in his office, but she was certainly making a fair old racket as we bid our farewells. If nothing else, the visit made me realize what an extraordinary region this high country is, still smarting centuries later from having its wines taxed so punitively by the protectionist merchants of Bordeaux (a long way) downriver. Like the middle stretch of the Loire, the vines planted on the rolling green hills of Gaillac (which have attracted more than their fair share of expatriate British would-be vignerons) make wines of all colors, degrees of sweetness and fizziness. Plageoles even makes a flor sherry-like *vin de voile.*

By this stage both Nick and I were writing for the *Financial Times,* on restaurants and wine respectively—a nauseatingly cozy arrangement. Because this unusually intellectually rigorous newspaper is as widely read outside Britain as in it, we did not have to confine our articles to London's newest brasseries or what was on sale in British supermarkets. This meant that even our trip to Albi and nearby Cordes could be fashioned into an article for each of us.

I used the next year's Easter excursion from the Languedoc, to taste great white burgundy in Roanne, as the basis for a column in another, more specialist publication I was now writing for, the American *Wine Spectator* for which, quite coincidentally, I had reported from London back in the late 1970s and early 1980s.

A rather ragged two-color newspaper had since been transformed into a magazine and polished by the man who was later, in a stroke of publishing genius which must also have revived the entire economy of the Dominican Republic, to launch *Cigar Aficionado.* Marvin Shanken had invited me to speak at the 1989 version of his annual hoopla The Wine Experience, which alternates each October between San Francisco and New York. I had never seen anything like it: the monumental Monsieur Louis Latour himself standing at a booth for two nights running pouring out his Corton-Charlemagne for the 4,000 ticket holders; Rémi Krug pouring Grande Cuvée on the other side of the Marriott Marquis ballroom; André and Laura's daughter Corinne Mentzelopoulos and Paul Pontallier conducting a tasting of first growth Château Margaux back to that wonderful 1953 for the first thousand applicants who are allowed to sit down to the day-long events.

I had to address these folk, an audience Len Evans has since described as the toughest in the world, on I know not what. I certainly didn't have the advantage of any liquid props, and it was in some bum spot like nine-thirty on the Sunday morning, with Marvin unnervingly prowling around the auditorium the entire time I spoke. The upshot, however, was that he hired me to write a column, a reversal of our arrangement on *Wine & Spirit* a decade earlier.

A weekend that we spent near Roanne with the Robelin family in April 1992 taught us a great deal about French life. It is shockingly easy, we had found, to spend months and months in France, without really discovering anything very much about the French, other than that the shopkeepers are exceptionally polite, that this is remarkable in view of the French obsession to the point of brutality with food quality, and that the French have a marvelously logical way of numbering postcodes and license plates. (Until very recently, when our mayor must have had a surplus of road signs to dispense, our French address was a single line: the name of the village and its number.)

We had met the Robelins because they were regulars at a wine weekend I had hosted for years at Gleneagles in Scotland, a sort of golfing palace with its own railway station built to amuse young things in the 1920s. They usually came as an eight- to twelve-strong party of family and friends all the way from France to the Highlands of Scotland because, they said, there was nothing like this concentrated opportunity to taste good wine back home. (This is true as far as I can make out. Wine as a leisure interest is a very new concept in France. Until recently a tasting of something as ubiquitous and unremarkable as wine would have been regarded as rather akin to a tasting of potatoes—a strange way of passing time.) The Robelins based themselves between Paris and the family's country home in a little village outside Roanne, a small country town thought of as being in the environs of Lyons, but in fact is over a crucial ridge of hills that puts it in the upper reaches of the Loire Valley rather than on France's other great river, the Rhône. For the greedy, Roanne means Troisgros, the world-famous restaurant built by the family of the same name, serious *amateurs de vin* themselves, from a modest station hotel.

We were invited chez Robelin *père et mère* for a weekend of gourman-

dize, built around an unprecedented vertical tasting of Meursault-
Perrières, traditionally the longest-living, densest Meursault of all.
But these had the distinction of having been made by the village's
most respected vigneron, Jean-François Coche-Dury.

The tasting took place on the Saturday afternoon in the well-lit,
extraordinarily well preserved, anything-but-flash art nouveau salon of
their friends the Thinards, fellow Gleneagles graduates. The bottles
came from the Thinards' well-kept, gravel-floored cellar in the bowels
of their townhouse. The Thinards and the Robelins had been wise
enough to establish an early rapport with this sought-after producer of
white burgundy, so they received a decent allocation of bottles each
year. I had admired the purity of Coche-Dury's winemaking style for
years, picking out his offerings from some of England's better wine
lists. In fact we had once shared a bottle of his straight Meursault
1986, drinking beautifully at three years old, with Elizabeth David,
who abhorred champagne but adored fine dry white wine.

What made our French tasting all the more remarkable was the
presence of Monsieur et Madame Coche-Dury themselves, who had
never undertaken such an exercise before. He is one of Burgundy's
most reticent individuals. "I don't travel much because there's no one
to take over the work when I do," he explained. The sturdy Madame
Coche-Dury, Mademoiselle Dury in her youth, is also yoked to this
small, functional but internationally admired family enterprise. Long
and solemn of face, somewhat lugubrious in manner and well over six
feet (which posed problems for the Dury family and their duty as
bride's parents to provide the bedroom furniture for the newlyweds),
Jean-François Coche is widely compared to a monk, being obviously
dedicated to the nuances of each plot of land and each individual cask
of wine—not that there are that many of them in his cellar, for he
regularly sells off a third of his produce on long-term contracts to the
Beaune merchants.

We tasted—with beautifully arranged glasses, water, tasting sheets
and spittoons, the essentials of wine tasting—every vintage of Perrières
back from 1989 to his second vintage of 1976 (apart from the 1980
which the Thinards hadn't bought) and found not a weakling among
them, which is something of a record for white burgundy. Even the
heavily chaptalized, and therefore fast-maturing, 1984 was truffley and
meaty (although the first bottle had been tainted by a substandard cork).

The enormous 1983 was saved from the shortcomings of that notorious vintage by being picked before the rot arrived. "Others made sauternes that year, not burgundy," said Coche-Dury. According to him the exotically unctuous 1986 would probably turn out to be the best of the lot, but wouldn't be ready for many a year, while the gloriously rich and savory 1978 (described as having *"le goût anglais"*) had, he assured us, been that glorious for years and showed no sign of deteriorating one jot. He told us how the late Jean Troisgros, who had hoped the 1978 would see him into ripe old age, would come to his cellar and unfailingly identify every glass lined up for him, both vintage and vineyard. "His brother Pierre is almost as good," he said. "He got the over-toasted oak on the 1981."

Now here at last was a man who understood oak. Coche-Dury told of how he bought from three coopers for his white wines and one for his red, always selecting the wood himself before the long seasoning, and bemoaned the fact that Burgundy had only about a dozen small coopers left. "The big ones don't really supervise the toasting, you know. You have to stand over them to make sure." He never used more than 50 percent of brand-new oak barrels even for his Perrières, and often less than 10 percent for less concentrated wines and vintages. He reuses his barrels and sells them eventually to Vieux Télégraphe in Châteauneuf-du-Pape. Very different from Santa Rita, one of Chile's largest bodegas, for example, which was boasting at about the same time that it had bought 7,000 new oak barrels in a single year. Listening to Coche-Dury suggested that there was only one way of making great wine: intimate knowledge and diligent application. Very heartening.

But just as remarkable as the wine lessons I was learning was this French crowd's attitude to solid matter. The wine tasting was no arid, hushed tones affair. (To silence French tasters you have to put them in white coats and call them *oenologues*.) We punctuated the tasting with great fat slabs of toast buckling under the strain of even fatter slabs of Troisgros pâté de foie gras, and then toward the end of the tasting, steaming wedges of feather-light quiche lorraine. Pierre Troisgros, who had seemed to hover unseen over the proceedings, turned up in the flesh with his son and clone Michel toward six o'clock, so we could start discussing dinner while they whipped through the remains of the Perrières. The Troisgros clan aren't the demigods portrayed in some of the more reverential gastro-mags; they are simply talented locals servicing a strongly felt need, that extends through a very much deeper cross-section of society than in any other country.

Barely an hour after we'd got up from the tasting table, after inspecting the Troisgros cellar, wine shop, jam shop, and all the accoutrements any self-respecting three-star chef is expected to sport nowadays, we reconvened in a private room at this renowned restaurant.

We heaved ourselves up from that table at one o'clock in the morning, having devoured yet more foie gras, seven more courses (including half a lobster each—I'm sorry I seem to mention only foie gras and lobster in my table notes; it's probably because I eat them so rarely) and an increasingly baleful sidetable-full of emptied 1985 burgundy bottles. (One bottle of red bordeaux was essayed, but rejected pronto. It rarely works to jump across the Massif Central in a single sitting.)

Funnily enough, we slept quite well in our gleaming sleigh-beds chez Robelin—better than the Coche-Durys over whose accommodation there had been some terrible mix-up, we learnt the next morning. We just had time for a short wander round the backstreets of the village, peering into the fiery depths of the wood oven of the local baker hard at work for the villagers' Sunday lunch tables, between our croissants and what was billed by the Robelins as brunch. This meal out of doors in the watery spring sunshine turned out to be just as big a feast as the previous night's dinner, with wheels of crusty bread, giant platters of the local charcuterie, hunks of juicy Charolais beef, the soft, smoky lentils of Puy (another local specialty) and no fewer than three cheeseboards.

To drink we had to sample all of the produce of one of the Robelin sons' own vineyard, Mas de l'Escattes, near Nîmes, before tackling some great Rhône wines from Condrieu, Guigal, Beaucastel, Vieux Télégraphe, Rayas and Fonsalette. These reds were quite sturdy enough to withstand being tasted in the breezy open air. Two 1979s still sang on my palate as we sped home down the autoroute: Guigal's Côte Rôtie from his Mouline holding, and Coche-Dury's own powerful, lively Meursault Rougets.

I really do think the French are built differently from us and that, try as we might, we are wasting our time trying to reconstruct the so-called French paradox in our own cultures. The great lesson the French

can teach us is to relax about eating and drinking. To view it as a pleasure worth investing with effort, but not awe. I can't believe how
many solemn, tense, dumb-struck faces I see at wine tastings and the
tables of smart restaurants—as though the experience of eating and
drinking is a test of the consumer rather than the consumed. The
enthusiastic chatter at chez Robelin contrasted most agreeably with a
marathon tasting of Saint-Juliens in New York exactly three weeks
later: every vintage; it seemed like every château; at a great lick and
without food. It did not feel like fun, and I didn't realize at the time
that we were merely being used as drains by a collector who had fallen
out of love with collecting.

We thought of the magical weekend in Roanne two years later in
Berkeley, California. We took some very old (by which I mean pre-wine
existence) friends to Chez Panisse, the restaurant that changed a nation's
eating habits. Nick spotted Coche-Dury's Corton-Charlemagne 1991
on the list, for a relatively modest price, considering this is his only
grand cru of which he made fewer than 100 cases that year. It was one of
those magical bottles, unanticipated, serendipitously consumed, foot-
stampingly impressive and, I hope, remembered as long by our Berkeley
friends as by us.

Nick and I drank a toast to the still-perceptible presence of the late
Elizabeth David. Two years earlier Alice Waters had torn herself away
from Chez Panisse to speak, along with Hugh Johnson and her great
friend and host in California Gerald Asher, at ED's memorial service at
St. Martin-in-the-Fields in London. The night of her funeral near the
family home in Sussex, when Gerald had come to dinner, we'd served
him exclusively Australian wines of which the most attractive was,
extremely appropriately, Cape Mentelle's Margaret River version of
California's great Zinfandel grape. It was thanks to Gerald that Elizabeth had fallen in love with California and its wines.

Our most regular excursion from our base in the Languedoc is one
we can if necessary do in a day, south to the next-door region, Roussillon. Now, admittedly, Roussillon is part of Catalonia, and therefore
shares at least as much with northeast Spain as it does with Languedoc
(despite wine literature's fondness for the portmanteau expression
Languedoc-Roussillon), but it is notable how much more regional
variation there is on mainland Europe than in England, for example.
Admittedly our architecture and accents change from one end of the

country to the other, but I don't feel there is much cultural variation. Unlike Roussillon, which feels, looks, sounds and tastes like another country from the Languedoc. Everywhere there are the yellow-and-red-striped banners of a proud Catalan heritage. There is a heat and intensity that is somehow lacking just to north, and the soft valley bottoms leading to the baked, vine-covered coastal plain are lined with fruit trees famous for yielding France's first of everything each season.

The narrow stone passageways of seaside Collioure have their charm, especially out of season, and the steep terraces of Banyuls vines are as dramatic as anything in Côte Rôtie or the Mosel, but our favorite destination is the small town of Céret, famous for its cherries in spring and for its Picasso Museum all year round.

The double allure for us in midsummer is the refreshing sound of water running from the Pyrenees down the sides of its plane tree–shaded streets, and Les Feuillants, a Michelin-starred restaurant with an extremely well-informed female sommelier. Thanks to Marie-Louise Banyols, I have been able to follow the very variable fortunes of Roussillon wines over the last eight years, and found such marvels as Fernand Vaquer's defiantly aged white Vin de Table and ambitious modern reds from the likes of Domaine de l'Hortus and Canet Valette much sooner than I would have done otherwise. Marie-Louise is a far more useful guide than anything published in Paris; in fact, many of the world's most perspicacious wine merchants such as Kermit Lynch, also of Berkeley, and Richards Walford of England have systematically used her and her like in other restaurants to track down some of the best wines on their lists.

At the same time that I was falling in love with France, I had embarked on another, almost as long-lasting, act of folly. Dear Caradoc, my literary agent, had come up with the idea, over lunch with someone from Oxford University Press, of an addition to its range of venerable, durable, definitive but discursive reference works, *The Oxford Companion to Wine*. And who better to edit it than one of his oldest clients? I had already turned down an invitation to edit an encyclopedia; it sounded just too dull for the hundreds of thousands of words entailed. But I could see the attraction of working on something with as much attitude as an *Oxford Companion*, a series of alphabetically listed articles of widely varying lengths on everything the editor considers important. Besides, I was such an admirer of the prototype on *English Literature* that I felt flattered on my own account to be considered as editor, and flattered on wine's behalf that the formal university committee that had to approve any new title with Oxford in its name saw it as a subject worthy of a *Companion*.

Although I could see the attraction of editing a *Companion*, and at the end of 1988 had signed a contract to deliver it within five years (celebrated rather cautiously at a North Oxford restaurant with a bottle of Kuentz Bas 1986 Pinot Blanc), I had no idea what I was letting myself in for. Fortunately for Nick and the children, nor had they. The million-word, thousand-double-column-page *Companion*, hereinafter called The Work, was to take over our lives, certainly for the early years of this decade.

In 1989, the first of my five years under contract to OUP, I was busy finishing *Timecharts*, buying the French house and making the Elizabeth David profile for Channel 4. According to the detailed tasting diaries I kept until Bollinger changed the design of their desk diary and the demands of The Work made it physically impossible, I see we treated the crew to Dom Pérignon 1982 at the end of this shoot. Times were different then. When during the next year our Eden Productions—named after the valley I was born in and the company's conjugal structure—filmed a Channel 4 series of documentaries on food- and drink-related subjects, we drank things like Henri Jayer's Nuits-Saint-Georges. Admittedly only 1984, and admittedly in a restaurant in the far north of Scotland so quite keenly priced, but wines like this have simply zoomed out of film crew reach in the last couple of years. They were always out of reach of BBC crews.

All I did on The Work in the first eighteen months was draw up lots of lists, write lots of letters to potential contributors, come to grips with the art of cross-referencing, learn how to use a strange, supernumerary tic of punctuation known as the Oxford comma, and suffer an increasing number of panic attacks in the middle of the night. The trouble with anyone who has ever been a journalist is that we tend to view deadlines as dates *on* rather than *by* which things should be accomplished (a bit like the way many of us view train departure times as indications of when we should arrive at the station). Even I could see, however, that it would be dangerous to delay the start of this huge enterprise until the last minute. It was clearly important to get the key contributors in place.

As soon as we got back from the Languedoc in September 1990 we had a succession of potential contributors to dinner. Hanneke Wirtjes was the first, and may have been won over by roast grouse and a particularly entrancing bottle of 1959 Latricières-Chambertin from Averys via wine finder Bill Baker of Reid Wines. ("Perhaps a hint of Rhône," I wrote, "but gloriously rich stuff that lasted well in the glass. Lovely, powerful, quite sweet and subtle.") Hanneke, an earnest, intensely intelligent, wide-ranging and wine-loving Oxford academic, who looked about twenty-two but referred wearily to her duties at Wadham teaching "the young," had been recommended by Pam Coote, my editor at OUP. She was to make a huge difference to The Work, not only by contributing a wide range of witty, well-informed, often highly original historical articles, but by filling in a few gaps at the last minute.

Oxford connections helped greatly with finding the right historical specialist to tackle each subject, and corresponding with them was one of the more intriguing joys of the project. A few were already highly technically literate, but most sent in contributions which had to be sent off to be keyed on to disk, enabling all sorts of possibilities for error, particularly with Ancient Greek, accents and numerical references.

The next contributor lured to our dinner table was high tech incarnate, Richard Smart, the cosmopolitan Australian viticulturist who had already agreed to be viticultural editor. He really entered into the spirit of the project and we were to hold each other's hands via disk and fax continuously over the next three and a half years. It was a serious problem finding the right scientific contributors because many potential candidates wrote in languages other than English, and we had neither the time nor the money for translation of such enormous chunks of the work. Richard and his enological counterpart Professor A. D. Webb, in retirement from Davis in California, each contributed a good 10 percent of the finished book in all.

But, although by then I had most of the major contributors in place, and I was to write about 40 percent of the tome myself, all sorts of minor contributors were still needed, whose caliber would do much to determine the overall quality of The Work. I had already identified the

long essay on "wine in English literature" as being a key article, one
that should provide fun for even half-literate readers but that would
have to be written by someone dauntingly well read. I tried once
feebly, and I knew fruitlessly, to persuade Julian Barnes to tackle it,
and then pinned my hopes on the much more senior connoisseur novelist Sybille Bedford. We took her out to dinner at Hilaire, again in
September 1990, again with burgundy (Corton 1982, Bonneau de Mar-
tray, very pure if neither substantial nor intense) but she passed on the
buck to Richard Olney. He got me quite excited by saying he and his
brother would produce the goods, but then ran out of time or inclina-
tion. Eventually, good old Bill Baker was recruited to fill the gap and
did it with real substance.

Our Channel 4 documentary series was aired in 1991, and in 1992
we jumped ship to the BBC and made a series of ten-minute profiles of
some of the British wine trade's more colorful characters (including
Bill Baker) called *Vintners' Tales*. But these were minor distractions
relative to the enormity of my commitment to OUP. I felt as though
I were literally in retreat. At least this, and my dramatically reduced
income, was in tune with the recessionary mood of the times. The *Companion* felt like a ball and chain.

Certainly the Toshiba laptop containing The Work to date went
everywhere with me, including to the Languedoc where I spent most
of two long summers in the cool, north-facing study rather than in the
garden or by the pool. Since I had recently given birth in a more literal
way, it was no bad thing that I was hardly free to travel for Rose's first
three years, but after a decade of producing a book every twelve
months, I felt terribly gray and inadequate. Between the autumns of
1989 and 1994 it appeared to anyone who might take the slightest bit
of notice that all I wrote were my columns in the *Financial Times* and
the *Wine Spectator*, when in fact I had never worked so hard in my life.

I remember feeling in a perpetual state of tension. I would walk
one of the children to school and then hare back home, conscious of
the writing or editing task I had set myself that day. My minimum
goal was to advance The Work by 2,000 words a day (not counting ad-
min, or correspondence about contributions already commissioned or
edited). How anxiously I examined the mail, and how relieved I was
when a nice meaty chunk of material arrived from one of the more reliable contributors. The worst days were when there was nothing to edit

into the straitjacket of *Companion* style and I actually had to create something off my own bat.

Because The Work was so enormous (and there were illustrations to organize too), I felt as though I would never even reach halfway. Nick could not have been more supportive, and put in long hours as a single parent just to bail me out. My diaries for 1992 and 1993 are painfully sparse. But then there was relatively little to put in them. During 1993, for example, I had precisely six weekday lunches away from my laptop: one of the first *FT* Lunches for a Fiver, Nick's brilliant scheme for filling empty restaurants with satisfied customers at a quiet time of year; helping judge the Oxbridge wine tasting competition (which that year nearly deteriorated into a brawl); lunch at the *FT* celebrating E.P.-R.'s eightieth birthday; lunch with Will and one of his friends at the local Chinese in his half-term holiday; a truly magnificent tasting of old Australian wines organized by Len Evans at the Capital Hotel; and the launch at Claridge's of a new Oxford dictionary (precious time away from my own Work that I bitterly resented—how can these publishers expect me to meet their deadline?).

I wonder whether I looked as gray as I felt. During the day it was just life at the keyboard, shuffling papers and filling filing cabinets. I couldn't imagine how Margaret Drabble, for instance, had managed to produce her equally long *Oxford Companion to English Literature* without a word processor and fax. I suppose she wasn't having to collate contributions from all over the world, which was one of the more extraordinary elements of my Work—especially during the summer months when we'd wake up to find that reams of paper from, say, New South Wales or Santiago de Chile had been sent to our little French village during the night. One very tricky moment came about a year from the deadline, November 1993, when I realized that my laptop, not surprisingly for a machine bought in 1989, wasn't big enough to store the entire *Companion*. That did force me to transfer everything on to floppy disks (which I had done too desultorily up to then) but I felt very unsettled for the morning during which all the material to date was transferred on to a more capacious model.

As I rounded the corner into autumn 1993 I switched into top gear. It was far too late to back out, and I had a major commitment looming on the horizon for 1994. I couldn't possibly ask for an extension of the deadline for my own reasons, and anyway the Oxford team were far too hard-working, enthusiastic and revved up to disappoint. As we entered November, even evening and weekend engagements disappeared from the diary, to be replaced by understandable references to "N out." N was not only out but filming a cooking contest on the night before I was due to deliver my million-word baby. I think I got to bed at three, having finally transferred everything to a surprisingly small number of plastic disks.

After all those years of effort, I was determined to deliver The Work in person, but sat on the Thames Turbo in a state of catatonic exhaustion, not least because before boarding the train at Paddington I had dropped in on the hospital next door to visit James Rogers, the wonderfully open-minded wine merchant, less than a week before even he finally gave up his fight to live. Birth, death, exhaustion. Like my laptop, I was suffering from overload. None of my diary entries for the end of November 1993 make any sense to me whatsoever.

Some Very Special
Bottles

James Rogers's death, followed less than eighteen months later by that of Britain's California wine pioneer Geoffrey Roberts, helped to crystallize some of my thoughts about wine. We are all, presumably, powerfully affected by the loss of the first of our contemporaries. But there are other considerations when wine enthusiasts die. I remember having dinner about four months before he died with Geoffrey and Sally Clarke at her famous restaurant in London (heavily influenced, incidentally, by Alice Waters and therefore by Elizabeth David). Geoffrey was a generous host. He had already treated us, twice, to the particularly succulent 1962 vintage of Yquem, and regularly dredged up fine relics of California's, especially Chalone's, past. (One evening at his Chelsea flat overlooking the Thames he behaved less than impeccably though by serving us *blind* two halves of the same magnum in different decanters, and letting us pontificate for hours about the possible identity of the second one.)

On the evening of our dinner at Clarke's he had brought along a bottle of Leflaive's 1984 Bâtard-Montrachet, the first from a dozen he'd bought, I think. It turned out to be corked, which was absolutely infuriating because we could all tell that underneath that intolerable mustiness lurked a magnificent white burgundy. Geoffrey promised to share another with us, but of course he never had the chance. I often think of those eleven untried bottles of Bâtard when trying to decide what to open in my own cellar. We can never be sure what we're saving our wine *for.*

I had learnt another wine lesson at exactly the same corner table in Clarke's earlier in 1993. Same personnel plus Gerald Asher. By coincidence both Geoffrey and we had brought a bottle of Mouton to drink over dinner. Our contribution was relatively modest, a bottle of 1987, the most successful Médoc made in this unsuccessful vintage. It was already, even at six years old, relatively mature, beautifully constructed and a fine, if hardly block-busting drink with our chump chop of Devon lamb and Mrs. Kirkham's Lancashire cheese.

Geoffrey had been much more generous and brought, thoughtfully decanted, a bottle of the salesroom darling, a Parker 100-pointer, Mouton 1982, an exotic but tannic monster of a wine that will be slugging it out with Latour '82 in a hundred years' time over which is the longer lasting. So intense was it that at first sniff I wondered whether it could be Guigal's Landonne. It was clearly going to be stunning but was curiously dense and expressionless at that stage. We all agreed that we much preferred to drink the sleek little 1987, currently on sale for one-tenth the price of the 1982. Like Abe's sardines, subtitle of Simon Loftus's exceptionally elegant *Anatomy of the Wine Trade,* there's wines for drinkin' and wines for tradin'.

Practically the minute Big Ben had chimed in 1992 as the New Year, and the traditional first decade of repose for red bordeaux was over, impatient wine lovers were planning their comparative tastings of the highly touted 1982s. The first I went to was on January 22, a look at the best 1982 Pauillacs organized by the London wine merchant La Vigneronne a.k.a. Master of Wine Liz Berry.

Edmund's first-growth-only session for '82s took place that July, and a giant charity gala dinner the following February at the Savoy was preceded by another comparison of the 1982 first growths.

At this stage most of the wines were still incredibly opulent (some are closing into their shells and hardening a little now), with amazing depth of color and flavor, and so much exuberant fruit that you had to work quite hard to detect the ballast of tannins and acids underneath. At La Vigneronne where we tasted blind, these tastings being designed specifically for serious wine lovers, Grand Puy Lacoste surprised us all by its sheer concentration and earned almost as many marks as the magnificent Latour. Mouton was third, then the two Pichons with Lafite some way behind. Chez Edmund I rather feebly marked every wine somewhere between 19 and 20 out of 20, with top marks to Mouton, Latour, Cheval Blanc and, for good measure, Ausone. Margaux, a quite delicious wine, consistently more expressive of the vintage than the appellation, dropped 0.25 for its very slightly perceptible acidity.

Before the charity dinner at the Savoy, in less than ideal tasting circumstances (the charity's patron, Fergie, was dotting about in green satin), my order of preference was Latour, Mouton, Haut-Brion, Lafite, Margaux and a strangely inexpressive bottle of Cheval Blanc. The Pichon Lalande 1982 served with dinner was also curiously formless, and much less attractive than the Léoville Barton 1985. Many great wines go through a dumb phase in adolescence and the trick is to know when these are likely to be. Here's one good use for the Internet—more worthwhile than a recent discussion in CompuServe's clearly understimulated Wine Forum on "Is Jancis Robinson sexy?" (*I* dunno.)

Sometimes just too much good wine comes at people like me too fast. If an evening is designed around nothing but the best, then one tends to spend it trying to work out which wine is the least dazzling rather than luxuriating in the quality. Sotheby's wine department once organized the most amazing dinner to which they'd persuaded each of the first growths to show off their very finest vintage. So about 150 of us solemnly sat down to a Roux brothers dinner with a run of Haut-Brion 1961, Margaux 1953, Latour 1952, Mouton 1949 and Lafite 1945, in either magnum or jeroboam. One can imagine how many conversations between the various proprietors and managers were involved before this tour de force of organization, largesse and showbiz was achieved. The most important consideration will have been that no direct competition between wines was involved. It may be churlish to point this out, but in the end this leaping from mountaintop to mountaintop can be less satisfactory, and certainly less flattering to the wines, than a steady uphill climb in quality from beginning to end of the meal.

Another much more educational succession of superlative magnums was served one evening in 1993 at Les Saveurs restaurant in Mayfair by the young turks at Farr Vintners (who will be known as "de boys" so long as they draw breath, so congenitally upstart is their highly successful pitch in the fine wine business). Steve Browett, in true iconoclastic form, had wanted to put on a tasting that would compare all of the first growths. About two seconds after he'd voiced this proposal in Bordeaux he was told firmly that the proprietors would never ever agree to it. They may all meet every now and then to discuss the market, but they are fiercely, truly, proprietorially competitive as far as the wines themselves are concerned. He then set to work on Château Latour who agreed to provide wines from the château's own cellars, wines in as pristine a state as possible, for a big tasting. The commercial director of Latour sounded out his opposite number at Mouton who, much to everyone's amazement, also agreed. So there we were, sitting down to compare the two most consistent first growths during the last half-century, over a span of great vintages which took us back, ever more hazily, to the great 1945s. This was Bordeaux, however, so the precise vintages representing the current regimes of each property were chosen with great care, to put the best gloss possible on the rival reputations.

We were allowed to see hand-to-hand fighting for supremacy over the 1982, however (which neither party could bear to omit), as well as the more historic 1970, 1955, 1949 and 1945 vintages. And what a fight! All of these wines constitute some of the grandest monuments in any conceivable landscape of wine tasting. The Latours were magnificently consistent, brooding hulks in youth with such concentration of elements knotting together in there that they would start to emerge after a couple of decades in bottle with the most intellectually intriguing array of flavors in the "masculine" spectrum of leather and earth. The Moutons on the other hand tended to be immediately exotic and opulent, often tasting like essence of cassis in youth (we still have a bottle of dark purple sweet blackcurrant liqueur, made by the maître de chai at Mouton, in our drinks cabinet). They were more likely to take on scents reminiscent of an oriental bazaar or, in Len Evans's memorable phrase, old ladies' handbags—at their most alluring, of course.

There was a particular poignancy about this tasting. Until three weeks beforehand Latour had been the one first growth in British hands, and we all felt some of the glory reflected by its sterling performance. The Pearson family, who also owned the *Financial Times*, had taken a majority stake in it in 1963, topped up by a smaller one owned by Harveys of Bristol. They'd since been taken over by Allied Breweries, subsequently Allied Lyons, on to which Pearson had off-loaded its stake in the late 1980s (just after I joined the *FT*, in fact, thereby saving me any possible worries over conflict of interest). Allied put David Orr, who had arranged such a banner launch for my *Timecharts* book in New York, in charge and his debut vintage 1990 was an absolutely sensational Latour. Just when he was getting into his stride, turning out an admirable 1991, Allied, now much more interested in Ballantine's whisky and Courvoisier cognac, sold Latour to the French businessman François Pinault. He sent a bemused female executive, whose first official duty relative to Latour this was. Baroness Philippine de Rothschild was there herself—and not even late on this occasion, I seem to remember.

It was easy to pick the stars from the younger vintages: Latour '90, Mouton '86, both '82s, my beloved Latour '70, indeed Latour right through the 1960s, but by the time we got to the 1955s, every single wine was sensational, literally, the sweet and scented Mouton '53 contrasting with the dry and minerally Latour '52, a particularly jewel-like Latour '49 (a bottle this time, not a magnum) contrasting with the notes of coffee and torrefaction on the Mouton '49, while the 1945s were extraordinary.

The first bottle of Latour '45 was slightly oxidized, a bit flat and musty, and even the second bottle was dusty, blurred stuff that furred the tongue rather than excited the senses. But all the tasters invited there knew better than to consign Latour '45 to their vinegar plants; these were just two examples of a wine that is known on other occasions to be great. Mouton '45 is a legend that I have been lucky enough to taste three or four times and each time I find its relationship to fermented grape juice more and more difficult to fathom. At Les Saveurs it smelled unnervingly of peppermint toffees, with a hint of that cough medicinal eucalyptus that is the giveaway scent of Heitz's Martha's Vineyard Napa Valley Cabernet. (This is not a comparison I would care to make to Philippine, for she would doubtless be insulted; and would certainly point out that Martha's Vineyard didn't exist in 1945, when the Napa Valley was a sleepy enclave of post-Prohibition prune farmers.) Nick, Julian Barnes and I reeled into a taxi afterwards and sat bog-eyed and speechless all the way to north London.

The first time I'd had the chance to compare these two magnificent examples from a magnificent vintage was the most unfortunately timed tasting I have ever been involved in. Edmund decided that it would be a waste to let 1990 pass celebrated only by his usual first growth tasting of 1980s, a fairly dismal vintage. The year provided the perfect excuse to celebrate the '45s' forty-fifth birthday. And so he invited the usual crew to the usual place for an even more indulgent dinner than usual at the end of June 1990.

I had discovered the day before that I was expecting Rose and felt absolutely exhausted. As soon as we reached the Penning-Rowsells I had to go and lie down, and for the next few weeks was heavily under the influence of that bovine haze that is so common in early pregnancy. The worst thing was that most unusually, as we sat down to this bevy of '45s, the last thing I felt like was a glass of wine—and yet this was such early days in the hatching process that I felt I couldn't broadcast my enfeebled state. I see from my notes that I somehow managed to complete the course, and actually my handwriting is noticeably neater than usual, which is presumably because I didn't drink very much.

That night I thought the Lafite was the most impressively complex, if most evolved of the wines and, like the Penning-Rowsells and the Broadbents, was nearly as taken by Haut-Brion, which was extraordinarily rich, supple and velvety—not as typically tobacco and warm brick as Haut-Brion usually is. The Latour seemed to have the greatest future ahead of it, with a very dry finish but much more powerful lusciousness on the palate than either of the Saveurs bottles did. The Mouton on the other hand, which Edmund had bought for £1 ($1.60) in 1949, tasted exactly like the Saveurs magnum would. My tasting notes even referred to Martha's Vineyard and cough medicine.

Edmund served his remaining bottles of Latour '45, bought for eighteen shillings ($2.50) each in 1950, at his eightieth birthday party at the Travellers' Club in March 1993. It was clear this was a Winston Churchill of a wine, admirable, venerable, but the bottle I was served from seemed a little too dry and dusty that night. The wine that made way for it was another red bordeaux classic, an absolutely glorious example of Palmer 1961, kindly donated by Peter Sichel, the co-owner of Palmer who seems to have an infinite cache of this famous wine—or perhaps the Sichels are just particularly generous.

I first drank (as opposed to tasted) it, in much the same circumstances as I experienced my first windblown hints of Cheval Blanc 1947, out of doors under the hot Suffolk sun. This magical wine celebrated the fortieth birthday of Simon Loftus, then mere wine buyer for Adnams of Southwold, at a small birthday lunch in his garden. It was served in quantity on a much more formal occasion, the dinner in 1987 in Vintners' Hall given to Edmund as retiring chairman of the Wine Society, the historic co-operative mail-order business that is such a defining organization of the British professional classes. It had been decanted at five o'clock, which turned out to be a bit too soon even for an event as uncomfortably early as dinner in one of the City of London's livery halls, where M'lords, ladies and gentlemen tend to be called in to eat at seven-thirty on the dot and the staff are so anxious not to miss the last buses home they virtually throw the cheese plates at the tables. On this evening it was easy to see what made Palmer '61 so famous, but this epitome of both opulence and elegance was already fading by the time it was served.

Edmund himself superimposed a brilliant example on my palate memory a year later, a bottle of Palmer '61 straight from his cellar that was big, meaty, gamey, almost Saint-Emilion-like in its plush fruit. It was utterly complete. Everything in perfect balance, intensity without brashness. This must be the wine that inspires Peter Sichel on his one-man crusade against modern bordeaux's propensity to bust as many blocks as possible. Although when Sichel brought yet more bottles of this wine to a dinner for two hundred organized by Colchester wine merchants Lay & Wheeler, I must admit that my tasting notes contain the phrase "Gina Lollobrigida."

(I once read an account by one of Britain's very few professional funny columnists, Miles Kington, of how his brewer father had dispatched him to Bordeaux to work a vintage and catch the wine bug, which he singularly failed to do, even though the year was 1961 and the property at which he worked was Château Palmer. *Incroyable, ça.*)

It's strange that sweetness, usually described as richness in red wines as it sounds more flatteringly substantial, is such a desirable attribute in mature red wines, when so many wine drinkers see sweetness as a drawback in whites. Conversely, one of the things I admire most about great white burgundy, as opposed to the more obvious charms of many other Chardonnay-based wines, is its dry, savory character. Perhaps it's because red wines have so many other elements, chewy tannins in particular, to counterbalance obvious ripeness, and in great white burgundy one is similarly looking for the texture of extract and oak aging, as well as a good level of acidity, to stop a white wine made from very ripe grapes from being cloyingly too much of a good thing.

I will always associate both Palmer and the Travellers' Club with Edmund. He is of a generation that believes current restaurant prices are iniquitous and therefore does his entertaining in London at this fusty gentleman's club in Pall Mall. (As ever he combines nonconformism with strict adherence to certain protocols.) It is his habit to invite his *Financial Times* editor of the time to the Travellers for lunch once a year. He carefully chooses a bottle of claret suitable for the occasion from his Cotswold cellar and brings it up to London, preferring to pay the Travellers' nominal corkage charge rather than choose a relatively callow wine from the club's own list.

Not long ago the then editor of the *Weekend FT*, Max Wilkinson, one of Edmund's newspaper colleagues least interested in wine, arrived at the Travellers to find Edmund on the steps in a state of great agitation. "There's been the most terrible mistake," he said. "I thought I'd brought up a bottle of Palmer '81 for our lunch. It's been opened but it turns out I brought one of my last bottles of '61 by mistake." If only they'd rung me, I would have been there in a flash, and would have appreciated it ten times more than Max—or probably even Edmund in the circumstances. There's probably a rule against women lunchers, come to think of it.

The way life works, there are not only particular people with whom you end up sharing a disproportionate number of great bottles, but particular places where this happens a lot too. I don't think of myself as a regular at Michel Roux's restaurant, The Waterside at Bray, but it is associated with almost as much fine wine flowing down my gullet as gray Thames-water flows past the restaurant's windows. Hugh Johnson, Michael Broadbent and I shared the most fantastic bottle of Palmer '61 only the other day at our annual "wine summit" with our British Airways colleagues. This was yet another bottle yielded up by the Sichel family cellars, consumed with almost obscene expressions of pleasure. Can there be enough for *any*one else to have tasted it?

Len Evans organized a great dinner at The Waterside not long ago that was almost certainly more notable for the rest of us than for him since he organizes great dinners wherever he is. It was high summer so we sat outside in a little summer house popping Krug corks at a great rate (another Evans commonplace). Len had persuaded Sam Chisholm, an old friend from Australia, to come out to Bray, but he wouldn't be tempted to stay for dinner; he was probably planning to gobble up a few companies for his boss Rupert Murdoch instead. The rest of us swooned over yet another of those magnificent 1959 red burgundies from Averys (I bet that's where my Chambolle-Musigny came from) which Len had bought from John Avery on his recent travels round England, and a very special bottle of Bollinger 1945 brought out from his London cellar by David Levin of the Capital Hotel. It was one of those miraculous champagnes that has aged in the bottle the way you want all white burgundy to, getting denser and deeper flavored, yet losing none of its refreshing acidity. This one, not a special late-disgorged example, even had quite a sparkle, despite having been parted from its life-giving dead yeast cells almost half a century previously.

It was at The Waterside, too, that we were invited to dinner back in 1989 to meet a friend of some friends, an English businessman who was just starting up a wine business in California. Would I taste the first vintage of his Chardonnay? I did not hold out particularly high hopes. California was and is full of rich dropouts pursuing a dream of having a winery. But this 1987 Chardonnay had an unusual depth of flavor. The welcoming ripe gloss so common in California also had a nicely appetizing lick of acid that, instead of sticking out as the acid that winemakers use to compensate for warm climates often does, was beautifully integrated. This was promising stuff and put Bernard Morey's slightly flabby 1985 Chassagne-Montrachet Les Embrazées in the shade. The businessman's name was Peter Michael and his wines nowadays command enviable prices on the best wine lists in Manhattan.

I also have great wine memories of every visit to Gidleigh Park, Paul and Kay Henderson's hideaway near Dartmoor in Devon. As one would expect of a founder member of the Zinfandel Club, he has a first-rate collection of California wine, including some increasingly rare better bottlings of the early 1970s. But the great joy here is his benevolent attitude to wine pricing. The more you spend, the more you save—well, not quite, but his pricing certainly rewards those prepared to choose the finer bottles, which is admirable but distressingly unusual. Whatever is the point of eating some of the best food in the country if you feel you're being penalized by a percentage markup for drinking wine of a suitable standard to go with it?

Like Hugh Johnson and Michael Broadbent and our friend wine merchant Bill Baker, I have conducted a few "wine weekends" at Gidleigh. These are quite different from their Gleneagles precursors and are basically an opportunity for Paul to monitor the progress of his cellar. We share a deep love of Riesling in general and Trimbach's single vineyard Clos Sainte-Hune in particular, so that was the excuse for one great weekend. The sensational quality of Italy's 1985 reds was another. I still regret not ordering a bottle of the most sensational wine of all, Sassicaia 1985, that we saw on the list of Leith's in London several years later at "only" £70 ($110). Needless to say, by the time I got back there, not a bottle was left.

But if there are some places you can reliably expect to find good wine, there are others where unremarkable wines taste absolutely sublime, precisely because they are so unexpected, or so unlike what you have been drinking, or because of the circumstances and company. I have very fond memories of Mondavi's Fumé Blanc, for instance, even though I would not classify a relatively oaky wine made from Sauvignon Blanc grapes among my favorites today. But in the early days of courtship it seemed terribly smart and satisfying, and will always remind me of our wine-buying trip to the West Coast in 1981.

Another bottle that I realized even as I was drinking it would not taste particularly special back home but tasted like surreally stimulating nectar under the stars of a southern sky viewed through a palm tree in Tahiti, contained nonvintage Charles Heidsieck champagne. Today I am a great fan of this revitalized brand, but this particular wine, given to us for no apparent reason by an Air New Zealand hostess just before landing at Papeete, had been made before the palace coup in the champagne cellars there. Nevertheless, I doubt whether any other champagne will ever taste as good—although I am constantly amazed by how distinctive and delicious every single vintage of Dom Pérignon is, and how well Pol Roger's top bottlings last. Not just 1959 but a 1921 and 1914 have all been sensational.

Another wine, consumed later on that same 1988 trip to the south Pacific in New Zealand, seemed quite incredibly wonderful, simply because it was so different in build from everything that had passed our lips since we'd landed. Auckland wine and food writer Vic Williams asked us to dinner and generously opened up a stream of top domestic and fine imported bottles. The Krug was gorgeous. Te Mata Elston Chardonnay 1984 convinced me in a way that not many bottles have since that New Zealand is capable of making Chardonnays that improve with keeping. Château Batailley 1989 was textbook classed growth claret, i.e., not mind-blowing. But Guigal's 1983 regular bottling of Côte Rôtie bowled us all over with its exoticism, its apparently mind-blowing concentration of ripe fruit—its explosive lusciousness being quite enough to distract from the clearly impressive tannin level. It was difficult in these circumstances, in an isolated corner of the globe where hardly a Syrah vine was known and most reds struggled to ripen, resulting in pale reds smelling of green leaves and grass, to imagine that red wine came any better than this. This was despite the fact that intellectually I knew very well that were I to be presented with a glass of one of Guigal's fabulously priced single-vineyard Côte Rôties, or even his regular bottling from the 1978 or 1985 vintages, I would have been far more impressed.

Over the years in the Languedoc we have observed how exciting a sudden taste of something entirely unfamiliar to the region, such as a fresh fino sherry or a particularly grand red bordeaux, can be. We made this last discovery during our second summer down there when the wine writer Alex Bespaloff came to stay, laden with bottles, straight after a few days' researching first growths in Pauillac. I still can't imagine making first growths part of the daily round in the Languedoc—or anywhere—but I have made one outsider a regular feature of Languedoc life. So perfectly refreshing did one example of a well-made Mosel Riesling seem to be in the heat of the summer, its delicacy contrasting with the weight of most Languedoc whites, that I now have consignments of Ernie Loosen's wines sent down from Germany to the south of France directly—a feat that is accomplished with almost miraculous ease to someone usually fenced off from the rest of Europe by sea and, much more of a barrier, complex excise duty requirements.

You may think on the basis of what you have read so far that all the wines I taste and drink are superlative. This is very far from the truth, and I would hate to drink nothing but grand wine. Because of my work I have met the odd very successful businessman or highly paid artist of some sort who really can afford to drink first growths every day. But I don't envy them one little bit. For me part of the thrill of conventionally great wine is that it is a special treat. And much of the thrill of wine in general is discovering bottles that cost a fraction of the universally acclaimed greats but which give every bit as much pleasure.

A Languedoc favorite is the Simone Descamps cuvée of the local Château de Lastours, an extraordinary property that doubles, or rather sextuples, as a home for the mentally handicapped, a four-by-four test track, an art gallery, a restaurant and an oasis of ecologically sound practice in France. This bottling of earthy, spicy incredibly intense old Languedoc vine varieties (including the bane of much of the region, Carignan) is named after a particularly faithful secretary at the bank which owns the property as part of its good works program. A favorite trick played by the man in charge, who trained both as a psychologist and an enologist, is to show visitors Lastours reds blind alongside first growth Château Haut-Brion and to ask them to pick out the Lastours. They are invariably floored. I certainly was and so, I read in France's leading wine magazine the other day, was a group of Parisian wine writers recently. Lastours' top reds, which sell for only about £5 ($8) to £7 ($11) even now in Britain, are decidedly underpriced, but then so are all but a handful of the best wines of the Languedoc.

In exceptional vintages the Loire can also produce gently under-priced, and certainly undercelebrated reds. The soft, scented, vigorous Anjou-Villages 1990 Nick and I enjoyed on a brief trip to Brittany in 1993 have lingered more vividly on my palate memory, for instance, than many more conventionally fine reds. At first I was rather ungracious about this long weekend, proposed by Nick in connection with a restaurant in Cancale on the north coast. After all, everyone knows Brittany is not a wine region, I did not intend to write about the local cider, and anyway my *Companion* deadline was only six months away and this eating trip would eat up one whole precious weekday. Needless to say, it was wonderful—literally full of wonder, at Mont-Saint-Michel, at the concentration of shellfish activity along the luminous shore, at chef Roellinger's ability to integrate the spices he sought out each winter in the Caribbean, continuing a long trade link with Saint-Mâlo. We enjoyed ourselves so much we left two drawersful of clothes in our hotel, and I can still remember how well the crispness of Lebreton's 1990 red went with my morels sautéed with potatoes and baby scallops, just as its roundness flattered the lamb raised on the salt marshes of Saint-Michel.

But France by no means has the monopoly on bottles that cost only half as much as their quality would indicate. The quality of the better and best wines from Australia, Spain, South Africa and South America has been zooming up, at a rate that should terrify the French. Bargains from Italy and California are less common, but on the other hand they have already established a loyal following for their much more expensive offerings. The single most exciting development in the wine world I have observed these last twenty-odd years is the fact that good and sometimes great wines come now not just from one European country but from nearly a score of countries in five continents.

Contrary to the impression given in these pages, I do taste—though do not drink—an awful lot of very *dull* wine and, just occasionally, once every few years, some extremely bad wine. It says something about the overall improvement in winemaking standards, though, that the last seriously horrible wine I remember tasting was four years ago.

We had first met food writer Sophie Grigson when we filmed her mother, the great food writer Jane Grigson, reminiscing about how terrified of Elizabeth David she was. A few months later she came for roast duck and red burgundy (yet again) and we subsequently invited her to the press preview of our Channel 4 series of food and drink documentaries. She sat next to me watching our first film, *Mad About Fish*, about a friend of ours who then commuted, in a very smelly van full of French fish, between London and Boulogne-sur-Mer. A year later Sophie and the fish-commuter were wed, and when they finally managed to organize a honeymoon, in Ecuador, they brought us back a souvenir bottle of local wine, a 1991 Scheurebe from Domaine de la Marquise (*sic*). Many good things come out of Ecuador. Sophie's husband could tell me a great deal about the country's fish, I'm sure. I've admired many a jumper and woolly hat and gloves made in Ecuador. But this wine tasted as though it had been used as a marinade for both fish and some woolly socks. The smell reminded me of some of the first wines I every came across—thoroughly nasty and a powerful disincentive to try wine ever again. It was a truly exceptional bottle, and kind of William and Sophie to add to my experience and education.

Some wines smell rather disgusting simply because of storage or because they are too old. Some wine-loving captains of industry invited me to one of their wine dinners not long ago and one of them brought the most beautiful, barnacle-encrusted flask, shining black, blue and bronze in the muted light of the executive pied-à-terre in which this dinner was held. It had been dredged up from the wreck of an ancient Dutch merchant vessel and dated in the 1730s. We were each poured a little glassful with great ceremony. It was a most arresting dark brown. Unfortunately it also *smelled* a most arresting dark brown. And, even worse, tasted of essence of seawater. Difficult to write a flattering tasting note on that one.

This wine was clearly not designed to be aged for many years in bottle, and until relatively recently that has been true of the wines of almost every place in the world, with the exceptions of Bordeaux, port country in the Douro valley, and some of the best German and Loire white wines. Fortified or very sweet wines in general last much the best.

A potent dark tawny syrup, for instance, made from grapes ripened and then dried on the Greek volcanic island of Santoríni in 1895, was still very much alive and kicking when I tasted it at 101 years old. Sherries may not generally improve in bottle but the dark rich styles take a great deal of time to deteriorate (unlike finos and manzanillas which fade fast once drawn from under their life-preserving film of special flor yeast). A nut-brown old oloroso sherry bottled in 1951 that had been bought at auction for about £4 ($6.50) by a friend of our host, was absolutely stunning when sipped at the end of a meal in the early 1990s, all raisins and that strange "rancio" (almost rancid) character that wines and spirits aged for years and years in wood take on. We seriously underestimate the nobility and versatility of sherry.

It can be quite difficult for the modern wine fanatic to get his hands on really old wine. The world's fine wine traders and auctioneers like to keep tabs on every cache of classic mature port and bordeaux, and collections of older bottles of other wine types scarcely exist. Some Burgundian producers such as Madame Bize-Leroy and Maison Jadot have serious collections of older vintages, but there is little continuity in most other regions. Older champagne can be delicious, but it is not a wine designed for aging. There was a great flurry of interest in the late 1970s when someone persuaded the Touchais family of Anjou to unhand their stock of fine old Loire whites—and if ever anyone gives you a sweet but tart deep golden wine that smells pleasantly of damp straw and honey, it's a fair bet that it will be one of a collection of more than a thousand bottles of 1928 Anjou Rablay bottled by Prunier's fish restaurant in Paris that were auctioned by Christie's in 1982. Old Monsieur Prunier had bought this great wine in quantity but was hijacked by the economic slump and the fashion for dry wines.

Most wine regions outside France, the Douro valley, Jerez and Madeira simply don't have the historical continuity to make keeping ancient bottles a very sensible practice. Even Italy's two greatest regions, Piedmont and Tuscany, have suffered, or rather benefited from, enormous upheaval within current lifetimes. A historic tasting of Tuscan wines in early 1996 merely demonstrated how much better things are today than earlier this century. Another, most unusual, historic vertical tasting of rioja later in the year managed to field two bottles of 1871— but the Marqués de Riscal bodega is a Spanish exception. The Marqués, a Spanish diplomat who learned a thing or two about wine when stationed in Bordeaux, virtually created Rioja when phylloxera struck Bordeaux. Most wine regions, even European ones, just don't have long histories to show off to us. The notion of providing international consumers with bottles from all over the world to keep in their cellars is a relatively new one.

I have been lucky enough to taste one or two sensational old wines from regions we think of, with varying degrees of accuracy, as new to wine production. André Tchelistcheff, grandfather of the modern California wine industry and the wisest wine man I ever met, brought two extraordinary bottles of old California red to dinner once. A 1916 "Calwa" Hillcrest Cabernet was over the top and could have been used to dress our salad, but the Inglenook 1943 Cabernet Sauvignon was quite extraordinary. All of us around the table—Hugh and Judy Johnson, Helen Thomson of wine merchants O. W. Loeb, James Rogers, Sally Clarke and ourselves—were terribly privileged to have our palates exposed to such a historic bottle, in whose making Tchelistcheff had been instrumental. Like another historic bottle of Napa Valley Cabernet consumed at that table, a 1937 from Beringer, this was no copy of

Bordeaux, but a definitively California wine with lots of mouth-filling depth and spice which showed that, like great Médoc, this particular combination of grape and place could provide liquids that not only lasted but continued to grow when trapped for years inside a bottle. In fact I can think of nowhere in the world that is so obviously suited to producing Cabernet-based wines designed for the long term than the Napa Valley—and Bordeaux's prime sites in the Médoc and Pessac-Léognan, of course.

The greatest old Australian reds to have come my way, largely thanks to Len Evans but also thanks to a dinner that a generous Melbourne collector organized for us in 1988, have been based not on Cabernet Sauvignon but on Syrah (Shiraz), or rather Hermitage as it was called in Australia until the Australians encountered French local pride, and the appellation contrôlée system. Their massively warm, mineral-scented style is a million miles from the intellectual austerity of a fine Cabernet. I often picture how wines strike the senses, the nose in particular. Among whites, Chardonnay approaches the taster in a cloud, while more aromatic varieties like Riesling and, especially, Sauvignon Blanc attack like a rapier. Similarly, Cabernet's impact is more rapier-like, but the impact of these old Australians is definitively smudgy, blurred with sensual pleasure, a cloud of desert dust.

Penfolds' jewel is their Bin 60A 1962, a wine that was even greater than the Penfolds Grange Hermitage 1955 served just before it at Len Evans's memorable Australian retrospective in London in 1993 (inspired by his irritation at so many British wine writers' dismissing Australian wines as sprinters rather than long-distance runners). This is a wine to astound anyone wedded to the concept that all great wine must of necessity express one particular spot on the globe, for it is a blend of grapes grown more than two hundred miles apart, in Barossa and Coonawarra. The scent hung heavily throughout the hotel suite where we tasted.

Just as gorgeous was a bottle from Len's own cellar of the famous Lindemans Bin 1590 1959 (despite yet another pedestrian name), the greatest wine the Hunter Valley has ever produced. Very, very rich, this mainly Syrah wine may also have contained Pinot Noir, however unsuited to the sweltering Hunter, and had managed in its time to win top prizes in classes for both "claret" and "burgundy" styles in Australian wine shows.

I haven't tasted great old bottles from any other New World

country, but the 1959 vintage has certainly provided more than its fair share of thrills in the northern hemisphere too. Two of the most unusual treats to have come my way have been sparkling wines from Huet of Vouvray in the Loire Valley: one a pink fizz cleverly tracked down by Danny Meyer for his Union Square Cafe in New York (where I always find something new) and the other a miraculous golden 1959 Huet Mousseux provided by the owner of London's RSJ restaurant, a Loire wine fanatic, when we went to dinner there one summer's night in 1992. We'd just been to a party given by an *FT* colleague who, most uncharacteristically for this determinedly understated paper, had chosen to serve champagne cocktails. The extraordinary thing about the ancient sparkling Huet was that it had all the sweetness and strength of a champagne cocktail, but in this case it was the product of superbly ripe, flavor-packed grapes rather than added brandy and sugar.

Another great 1959 is Château Latour, an archetypally classic wine that most obligingly followed me around during the late 1980s and early 1990s so that I could monitor its stately progress. It tasted like still-youthful essence at the château when I went there to write a story about how they selected the final blend for the 1987 vintage. (The then director, for Pearson, Alan Hare, was to accuse me of being responsible for Latour's less-than-stunning 1987, by distracting them.) I identified a magnum served blind early in 1991 as very good, very young bordeaux. (It was followed by another 1959 Vouvray, a sweet still version from Marc Brédif that was so good it managed to stand up to Sally Clarke's chocolate truffles.) A bottle served at another dinner party three months later had been decanted too early to bedazzle, but a bottle brought to our dinner table in February 1992 was sensational— *much* more evolved than the magnum had been twelve months before but absolutely magnificent. Very, very concentrated and majestic in the deepness of each layer of flavor. Krug 1959, the creamy wine we were served when we visited the Krugs the year we were married, was the best of an extraordinary collection of Krug champagnes from vintages ending in 9, although an amazingly youthful, compact 1929 gave it a run for its money.

These are some of the best of the liquids squeezed from grapes grown by previous generations that my nose and palate have been introduced to. By no means are all old wines great wines, and there is nothing so sad as a wine you know is well past its prime. I know of one or two wine collections which are predicated on age and have several times been invited to share so many bottles so obviously past their drink by date that I have felt both ill and morose. The conditions of storage are obviously important, but so are the expectations. Wine professionals who come across venerable wines regularly are reasonably sanguine about the disappointing bottles, but I feel a great weight of responsibility if a friend—a real, nonwiney person—invites me to share with them one very special bottle, possibly the most special bottle they will ever taste in their lives. Will the bottle perform as it should? Will I?

Two writer friends live nearby and were already married in 1970 when I met them. They eat and drink well but wouldn't dream of buying something as stratospherically priced as Château d'Yquem for their own consumption. However, when they moved into a new flat in Hampstead in the early 1970s and found that the previous owner had left behind a bottle of Yquem 1945, they knew better than to throw it out. Nor were they unromantic or poor enough to decide to sell it. Instead they said they'd keep it for a special occasion, the birth of their first child perhaps. They waited, with great fortitude, more than twenty years, which did the wine no harm, except that the sweet, sticky wine, kept so carefully on its side, started leaking through the cork. Alex had apparently asked my advice on this problem, but must have asked me too late in an evening for me to appreciate its gravity and I had blithely told him to keep on storing it horizontally when I should probably have advised him to recork it, or at the very least stand it up. By the sunny Sunday evening in July 1994 when about eight of us gathered to celebrate the conclusion of their agonizingly protracted adoption process, the bottle was only about four-fifths full. The cork was alive with weevils or some other form of wildlife and disintegrated as it was extracted. No food technologist would dream of consuming the liquid beneath it. No wine lover would dream of doing anything else.

As it turned out, Yquem is such a robust wine that it seemed completely untroubled by all the air and fungi it had been exposed to. Some of the others there were no great fans of sweet wine and may well have found it too creamy and syrupy, but I was absolutely knocked out by its richness and concentration. Its trick was that it managed to combine a honey texture with being very much a wine. In fact it was quite intoxicating to sip at this golden relic of the end of the war, while watching the sun set over Hampstead Heath and nibbling the pâté de foie gras I'd brought back specially from Bordeaux (where else?) earlier that week. An ultra-rich experience on all fronts, which we found so agreeable we even broached the 1960 Rabaud Promis, a backup bottle I had guiltily taken along just in case the Yquem had been ruined. This particular event managed to combine all the necessary ingredients for tasting a special bottle: low expectations, some suitably delicious food, no outrageous expenditure, great company, a good excuse, and resultant happiness.

The Ball and Chain
Cast Off

The pattern of my working life changed unrecognizably the minute I delivered the *Companion*—or at least the minute I'd finished answering the seventeen pages of queries from OUP's admirably well educated copyeditors. Instead of spending four years hunched over a word processor, unmade-up, in leggings and a T-shirt, I was to be set loose on the wine world, far too much of the time in full makeup, with freshly done hair and clothes subsidized by an official BBC budget.

Eden Productions was about to embark on its most ambitious project by far, a $1.6 million, ten-part series filmed all over the wine world which depended for financial underpinning not only on the usual tie-in BBC book, but on a terrifying large slice of what Nick had made from selling L'Escargot. This was therefore a very different undertaking from my rent-a-presenter role on *The Wine Programme*. We were risking a considerable amount of our own money as well as acting as producers. In my case, I had the strange sensation of being both puppet and puppet-master. Knowing that we were responsible for every foot of film, for example, made me keener than ever to get my lines right.

However bold and dynamic this undertaking sounds, it was, yet again, entirely reactive. Most television projects are born over lunch but this one nearly died over a lunch at Clarke's in 1990 with Alan Yentob, then controller of BBC2. The purpose of this lunch was to discuss our forthcoming series of ten-minute vignettes, *Vintners' Tales*, but over a particularly succulent bottle of Au Bon Climat Chardonnay Reserve 1987, Yentob asked me rather wistfully whether there wasn't a more substantial series I'd like to start planning, too. At that stage I felt Hugh Johnson's historical, but thoroughly international, TV series *Vintage: A History of Wine* had rather queered the pitch for anything big and grand—and besides I knew I had the *Companion* to finish—so I demurred.

It was therefore more than a year later, in August 1991, that Jancis Robinson's *Wine Course* was born—again as a result of an external stimulus. One hot summer's day in the Languedoc I was called out of the blue by someone from BBC Wales, suggesting a wine series built around grape varieties. This was a brilliant device which allowed us within a single program to visit more than one region—and therefore vary the scenery, architecture and climate. It also reflected my passionate interest in grape varieties and my conviction that coming to grips with the most important grapes provides the easiest route to learning about wine. Thanks to personnel changes, the labyrinthine structure of the BBC and the usual tortuous business of funding international television productions, it was to be two and a half years before we actually started work on the *Wine Course*, which was fine by me.

The conflict between the New and Old Worlds of wine was coming nicely to a head at just the right time for our series, and this inevitably became the subsidiary theme of many of our programs. But before we could embark on our round-the-world, twelve-month filming schedule, trying to catch as much as possible of the 1994 vintage in the Northern Hemisphere and the 1995 vintage in the Southern, there were offices to be found and a team to be hired.

We chose the partner of a friend of ours as producer/director. Until now David Darlow had been known to us only as someone unfailingly able to produce a receipt to match any given combination of date and location for anyone at work on an expenses claim. He turned out to be an equally reliable producer of television programs about wine, and took on as second director a softer man, Tony Bulley, for us to take comfort in when he got too hard. Our miles of precious film were the responsibility of respected cameraman Ernie Vincze, who came complete with tales of

working with Merchant/Ivory and also making anthropology films
sleeping with barely civilized tribes in the Amazon jungle. We assured
him the *Wine Course* would be tame stuff in comparison to either of these
experiences, but after my first research trip for the series, to Australia, I
wasn't so sure.

The first of the sixty-odd flights involved in making the *Wine Course*
set me down for a research trip at six o'clock one morning in early
March 1994 in the clean, warm, eucalypt-scented air of Adelaide airport. Adelaide is such an insignificant city for everyone apart from
those of us interested in wine or the arts that the international ter-
minal car park routinely is closed one hour after each flight arrival.
This first day of my trip was dedicated to getting used to the killer
nine-hour time difference, so I was in no hurry. I decided to take the
transit bus into town, and found its driver to be one of those defining
Australians, who usually turn out to have emigrated from England
only five years before. "Where you going?" he asked me. "The Hyatt
Regency? Oooooh! La di dah. They're so stuck up there, even the staff
say [he put on what I assumed was supposed to be a posh Australian
accent] none of *our* customers use a transit bus. I say to them, do you
wipe yer arse after you've been to the toilet? 'Cos I do." Yes, this was
Australia.

A large German backpacker climbed on to our bus and offered my
new friend his smallest note, a hundred dollars, for his $4 fare into the
city. "That is one bad start to your visit to Adelaide, mate," said the
driver, shaking his head. "I know it's not your fault. It's that sheila
who does the currency exchange. Thick as a brick toilet, that girl."

I asked whether Glenelg, Adelaide's seaside suburb, was far from
the airport. "Oh, no, lady, I could piss it," he assured me, adding with
a touch of pride, "Excuse me, but we Australians don't mince words."

Curiously, he did when giving us a commentary on the city's Victoria Square with its predictable population of dispossessed Aborig-
ines. "Be careful," he warned us, "the Abos do their bathroom business
out in the open." Soon after this circumlocution he dropped me off at
the bus stop opposite my hotel, insisting on carrying my bags across
North Terrace's six busy lanes of traffic. The Australians are nothing if
not pragmatic, blunt, and *very* non European.

There could be no greater contrast with the determinedly relaxed,
not to say phlegmatic, approach of the Australians we filmed (they'd

be *mortified* if any guest ever caught them doing anything as formal as laying a table) than the hospitality we encountered in Germany, one of our earliest filming locations. Tension is inevitable the first time a film crew goes out together at the start of a long project that will involve many arduous journeys, difficult conditions, changed minds, unpredictable weather and a presenter—especially if the cameraman and director have never worked together before, for theirs is a crucial, intimate but recondite relationship.

Our very first week of filming, in May 1994, had been our introduction to the brutal (i.e., no lunch) directing style of David Darlow. There had been nervousness as well as bubbles in the air as we filmed in, or rather several hundred yards beneath, the champagne town of Épernay. As David flew back to London, rolls of precious exposed film packed into his hand baggage, the rest of us crossed the border into Germany for this second week's filming, which was to be Tony Bulley's first experience of working with cameraman Ernie Vincze.

It would have been difficult enough without the helicopter. Tony is a keen rambler and map reader and had spent much of his research week making calculations about bird's-eye views. He had found a terrace outside a ruined castle on the top of a hill overlooking the Mosel and, quite rightly, thought that it would make an arresting opening sequence to have Ernie film me talking to the camera from this terrace, before pulling away into the sky, wheeling round the tower and over the winding river and its steep-sided banks. David was all for it. This was just the start of his and Tony's joint plot to turn our wine series into transport programs. Hot-air balloons, ancient aircraft, trains, a floating gin palace, a kayak, horses, mules, motor bikes, jet skis, a First World War ambulance, all sorts of automobiles, including open-topped sports cars with cameras on the side and long-distance trucks, were all pressed into action on our behalf, so frustrated were David and Tony by wine's essentially immobile state. (They were to go on to make series about plane crashes and war respectively. Surely they missed wine then.) Helicopters are particularly difficult, though, because they are expensive to hire and notoriously dangerous. Both Tony and Ernie had recently lost friends in helicopter accidents and they sat up talking long into the night the day before the helicopter shoot, trying to prepare themselves for the feat ahead.

I wasn't worried until the frail craft approached and hovered above my terrace. There seemed to be a pair of little legs dangling from a completely open side. Those legs belonged to an extremely expensive cameraman on which our series depended. And so early in the enterprise too! Apparently cameramen are belted in with some special sort of harness but I learnt this only later. I thought the whole thing was crazy, and it seemed particularly strange to be talking intimately about my great love of Riesling to a thundering chopper a hundred yards away. In the end the shots looked great—they would have looked even better if the sun had happened to shine on the day we'd booked but it was a nerve-racking experience for us all, involving distance, physical danger and walkie-talkies (which the French, I was to learn, call *talkies-walkies*). We were all so exhausted by the emotional and physical rigors of filming in Germany that we were far from suitable candidates for the formality of German hospitality.

Even something promised as "a very casual supper" chez Ernie Loosen, the wild boy of Bernkastel, turned out to involve a dazzling white tablecloth, giant black plates and a phalanx of giant, ping-able crystal glasses at each place setting. There had been some misunderstanding about exactly how many of our six-strong team were coming, and every time the doorbell rang, Ernie tried desperately not to look surprised, while his wife, Eva, ran up and down stairs to the kitchen to unpack more boxes so that she could, as discreetly as possible, lay another place fit for a lifestyle magazine. We glugged our way through vintage after vintage, including tasting some fine California Pinot from Williams Selyem (whom we were to film three months later), but we continued to sit, stiff-backed, round the white tablecloth.

The white tablecloth seems to rule German social life. And upright chairs. You can spend a week on the Mosel in some of the most prosperous vintners' homes without setting eyes on a sofa or a chair more comfortable than a particularly generously upholstered dining chair. You sit up. You do not lounge. Even Ernie Loosen's parlor consisted of two large tables, covered with tablecloths, surrounded by their satellite dining chairs.

A couple of days later when Dr. Manfred Prüm invited me and our indefatigably cheerful researcher Robin Eastwood for dinner, I knew better than to suggest that anyone else come along. Breathlessly enthusiastic Manfred and his blond pigtailed wife, Amei Prüm, are the current custodians of the Middle Mosel's most admired and envied wine estate. The J. J. Prüm holdings flank the calm, green river from the village of Wehlen. From a grand terrace in front of the handsome nineteenth-century stone house you can look across the river at the steep, slate, sun-seeking slope of the famous Sonnenuhr vineyard, the sundial at one time being of real practical use to the vineyard workers. One look at the house tells you that this is not a place where people drop in.

Robin and I had been so looking forward to plundering Dr. Prüm's famous cellar but we had to drive all the way back from filming in the Rheingau to get there. Thanks to Just One More Shot syndrome and a particularly stately beer truck, we reached Schloss Prüm a whole hour late. So for an hour the Prüms had sat in their salon overlooking the river with our fellow guest, wine writer Stuart Pigott, in upright chairs round a beautifully ironed white tablecloth, five slender-stemmed wine glasses and an expectant silver wine coaster. For an hour they had talked, and looked at the sparkling, beckoning, empty wine glasses.

When we eventually arrived chez Prüm, Manfred was charmingly sympathetic. "Did you have a very, er, *stressy* day?" he asked in his smiling, breathy way. He guided us through the late-Victorian, tiled and be-antlered hall to the salon, made formal introductions (Stuart giving us an understandably dirty look) and then asked, as though struck by an entirely novel notion, "Now what would you like to drink before dinner?"

Robin, who was driving and is committed to the purest of diets, was probably tempted to ask for chamomile tea, but showed German restraint instead. Of course this man, who makes some of the longest-living white wines in the world and has bottles in his cellar going back to the last century, including unctuous Beerenauslese by the dozen, knew exactly which bottle that coaster had so patiently been waiting for. The German custom is, rather like that of the Burgundians, or the English at tea, to work one's way through bread and butter toward the cake. In this case to begin with a dryish Kabinett and process with stately logic via slightly sweeter Spätlese and Auslese to the highly charged, honeyed drama of a Beerenauslese and, on very, very special occasions indeed, a richer than rich ultra-ripe Trockenbeerenauslese.

I understand the logic of progressing up the ladder of quality (and quality in the coolish vineyards of Germany equals ripeness) when choosing a serving order of wines, but you need to be very sure that the wines en route aren't so tempting, and your guests so enthusiastic, that the nuances of the final and most valuable bottle are not lost on them. Many's the time I have reread my tasting notes at home after a particularly indulgent wine dinner the night before to find that I have written in impeccable detail about the first, rather ordinary young cru bourgeois, but my account of the thirty-year-old first growth served with the cheese is little more than a scrawl saying "Mmmmm."

So, with Dr. Prüm, a firm believer in approaching the summit from the foothills, we began with a Wehlener Sonnenuhr Kabinett from the meanest of recent vintages, 1977. The carefully considered point of this bottle was to demonstrate that he can conjure elegant, sinewy refreshment from ingredients that generally produced the skinniest, most meager of wines. Polite chat accompanied this bottle—Dr. Prüm is a great believer in not progressing to the next one until every drop has been drunk—so it was not until we were in the green-brocaded dining room being served with salmon and potato pancakes that the Wehlener Sonnenuhr Spätlese 1981 was poured. It was a youthful thirteen-year-old, a straining thoroughbred with more muscle than the Kabinett thanks to being made from riper, literally "late harvested," grapes. Manfred was literally teasing our palates on the way to the truly great bottle of the evening, an antique rarity made from even riper grapes, an Auslese from the five-star year of 1949. This sublime essence of Mosel tingle, still heady with peaches and apricot fruit but with a steely undertow of minerals, was served, not with something sweet, or on its own as a "conversation wine" (and it has to be said that Manfred hardly distinguishes between these two words), but with venison from the Hunsrück hills just a few miles away. It was a sensational combination, and shows just how the extract in top-quality Mosels makes up for their lack of alcohol, often being more than a third less alcoholic than most other wines. After this, the extraordinarily rich, pear-scented 1976 Beerenauslese seemed not nearly ready, but gorgeously, dancingly, elegantly revitalizing. Amei, with her lovely thick plait over one shoulder and her crinkly-eyed smile, doubtfully offered us sorbet at this point but, quite rightly, we were expected to demur and admit that no dessert could possibly improve the sensation of this wonderfully complex liquid. Robin and I made our contented way back to the hotel, agreeing that the boys really wouldn't have enjoyed it one bit.

Most of the characters we filmed for the *Wine Course* were people I had met before. Filming gave me an excuse to put a face to such famous names as Aldo Conterno in Barolo and Alejandro Fernandez of Pesquera in Ribera del Duero. But there was one character whom I had never set eyes on, nor read a word about, but I just knew that if I could possibly persuade her in front of a television camera, she would be a star.

It seemed extremely unlikely. I had been trying to meet Madame Descaves for fourteen years. When I first saw the delightfully appropriate name of Maison Jean Descaves on the side of a little white van delivering to Château Margaux, the doyenne of the Bordeaux wine trade was a mere seventy-eight years old. The first growth's private cellar had many a gap when the Mentzelopoulos family bought the property in 1977 and, as has been their custom, they sought help from the most impeccable source, in this case, Bordeaux's most admired, yet most discreet, wine merchant of the old school. It is typical of the Descaves style of business that Madame Descaves was able to sell old vintages of Château Margaux to its owner.

There are certain people who lead a respectable life for so many years that their first names are worn away. Those who once played with them in the schoolyard are long since dead. Their friends in early adulthood have also perished. They survive to be addressed only by those who call them Mr. This, Colonel That or Lady The Other. Madame Descaves is one of these miraculous beings, who gives us all hope of a fulfilling and prosperous tenth decade.

She lives quietly, as is normal for a ninety-four-year-old. But, since the death of her wine merchant husband in the early 1970s, she always has done. She hates to be thought to be courting publicity. She lives alone (*seule* and *métier,* a French word that covers the middle ground between a job and a craft, being her two most used words) in a giant house over three warehouses in the Cours du Médoc in the Chartrons area by Bordeaux's once-busy docks.

Ever since I first heard of her, I felt she would make a great subject for a profile but she had never agreed to meet me. Whenever I wrote I would receive a scrupulously courteous handwritten letter explaining that she was particularly busy at that time, or had been ill, or some other excuse. The more I heard about her, the more intriguing she became. A British wine merchant told of calling her to inquire about buying a large quantity of a certain wine. They discussed the price. Madame Descaves won. "May I have an option on the wine, then, Madame?" he asked. "Of course," she replied. "And when will the option expire?" he asked. "When I put the phone down," she said firmly.

As we were preparing the *Wine Course*, I rang her from London but she protested she'd had a fall on the stone staircase that connects her apartment to her work and that she was therefore *trop villaine* (too ugly). When Robin went researching in Bordeaux before we arrived, I gave her all Madame Descaves's details, but the closest she got was to be allowed to hand a bouquet of flowers through the tall double doors on the Cours du Médoc.

I was resigned to never being granted an audience with Bordeaux's *"monument historique,"* but toward the end of our filming trip to Bordeaux, the day before I was due to fly back to London a little ahead of the rest of the film crew, I thought it would be worth calling her one last time and asking whether she'd see me on my last morning. To my amazement, she agreed. I still don't know why. The night before, we filmed a dinner at Château Margaux with some German merchants who knew her through their fine wine business. They warned me that she would either dispatch me after three minutes, or I would reel out of her extraordinary office-cum-salon full of champagne, whatever the time of day.

At 10:05 the next morning I was being asked to choose between Ruinart or Laurent Perrier, and I was bewitched by this extraordinary being who can claim to have seventy-four years' experience of the city's lifeblood, the wine trade. Almost deliriously, I opened the bottle (Laurent Perrier, though it was a difficult choice) and poured the creamy morning mouthwash into two *coupes de champagne.* Such shallow, tawny, engraved saucers are deeply—shallowly?—unfashionable in wine circles today, but are as much part of Madame Descaves's entourage as the antique, free-standing globe and the fax machine incongruously perched on an ornate escritoire in her baroquely decorated office.

Madame Descaves worked with her husband, Jean Descaves, from her marriage at twenty until his death. There is no question of her tottering in for an hour's light paper-shuffling each day while this exceptional négociant business is run by someone younger. She lives above the warehouses holding her unrivaled stock of 37,000 cases of "Grands Vins de Bordeaux Authentiques," as she describes them on her price list. When you ring Maison Jean Descaves, it is her exceptionally gruff, manly voice which is most likely to answer the phone. As she boasts on her ancient letterhead, headed haughtily "Sans Engagement," she has three lines, and is quite capable of carrying on a conversation on two of them, with a visitor in her office, while keeping another customer on the boil in another room.

"So what do you want? I haven't time to read you my tariff. Twelve magnums of *what?*" she snorts into a heavy telephone receiver. "So, a double magnum of Pape Clément." Typically, the heavy, old-fashioned receiver is put down on her desk in mid-negotiation (well might she be called a négociant) while she bends over the precious tariff, muttering prices the while. "I have the 1982 at 725 francs. Or you can have the 1981 at 575 francs. Cash or a check, either's fine." She looks pained when she has to explain to this customer how to find the Cours du Médoc.

"I'm one of the top buyers of *grand vin*. The châteaux know I can pay. I've never needed banks. The others are jealous because I get the first tranche. But I don't like publicity, I live quietly. I don't go out. Not even when Baron Philippe de Rothschild invited me personally to dine. My recipe for living happily is to live hidden." She smiled proudly at me. Much of her conversation was about the problem which most preoccupies her. Who will take over the business after her?

None of the Descaves family is remotely interested. Seven people work for her, and the succession is a constant topic of Bordeaux's "aristocracy of the cork." She had for long been grooming a man in his sixties, whom she referred to as *"jeune homme,"* but to her chagrin claret proved a less efficacious preservative for him than for her. She told me she was always being courted by companies who wanted to buy the firm. "It'll have to happen one day," she said, hoisting her breasts beneath the patterned silk. "I'd prefer French to Japanese." She described how her fall had left her lying one night on the dark, stone stairs on her back, splitting open her head so badly that she needed three transfusions. She had been found by her gentleman lodger on the second floor. "I would have died during the night otherwise."

But this summer of 1994 she looked absolutely indomitable, like a handsome seventy-year-old with curves and a full head of chestnut hair, moving purposefully about her domain, commuting between the little fridge full of champagne and Sauternes and the outer office where Ingrid, or *"ma petite,"* tried to keep up with the paperwork generated by Madame Descaves's unconventional telephone sales technique.

By the time I'd spent five minutes with her, sitting nervously in front of her desk, listening to a steady stream of Piaf-like French addressed in turn to me, to telephone callers and to a woman who had somehow won access to Madame Descaves's lair on a female solidarity ticket (she wanted to buy one very special bottle for her husband's birthday), I was in love. She may have been a complete pain for the first fifty years of her life, but now she was a national treasure, completely unselfconscious, master of her beloved *métier*. Meeting her made me all the more frustrated that she had never to my knowledge been captured on film. So just before leaving, because I knew the film crew were in Bordeaux for a little longer even if I had to leave within a couple of hours, I threw the dice one more time. To my complete amazement she grunted assent, if not explicitly to the idea of being filmed then at least to the idea of the film crew's arriving in her offices that afternoon. I knew this meant rearranging their schedule completely at short notice, something we tried very hard not to do, but I also knew it would be worth it. After our farewell, when she drew me to her and asked me to kiss her, I made a series of excited, champagne-drenched calls and hoped David Darlow would find her as captivating as I had. He did, of course.

The researcher that afternoon was a charm school graduate with perfect French and was well able to conduct such interviewing as was necessary from behind the camera. But then Madame Descaves didn't really need any prodding; her self and her conduct behind her desk was all that was needed to make one of our most riveting film sequences.

In the spring of 1997 she was still going strong. She had sold a small holding in the company to an impeccable rival merchant to ensure continuity after her death and shrewdly responded to price rises in Bordeaux by buying from Farr Vintners in London $400,000 worth of the wines on which her life has been based.

Even though we filmed sporadically for a week or two at a time rather than continuously, we managed to work almost exclusively with the same tight-knit crew: one of the two directors; Ernie Vincze the cameraman; and two somewhat frustrated beer and whisky drinkers— Jonathan Earp, his hard-working assistant, and sound recordist Simon Clark. Like most film technicians, they'd been everywhere, done everything and were cool, calm and hard to impress. Because the wine world is so full of colorful characters, they were often intrigued by individuals, but only one of our subjects really agitated them, Francis Ford Coppola, because he was a very grand one of their own. We were all thrilled when the film director agreed to be filmed at his Napa Valley wine estate. It added texture to the cast list and the broader perspective of someone able to view the wine industry from both inside and out.

One late afternoon in August 1994 we turned west off Highway 29 and drove up a long, increasingly dusty track to a large, atmospheric white house pressed right up against the hills on the western edge of the valley floor. This was the old Inglenook homestead, built more than a hundred years ago by the Finnish merchant-turned-wine pioneer Gustave Niebaum, and bought by Coppola in 1975, very much as a family home, with the proceeds from *The Godfather*.

It was only when we were setting up all the equipment on the wide veranda before the interview that I realized how nervous everyone was. They were about to perform in front of a major player at their own game. We used some of our precious stock of real, old-fashioned film because, as director Tony Bulley said indignantly, leaving long spaces between the last three words, "I'm not going to use videotape on Francis Ford Coppola." What would he make of them? Would he by any chance be so impressed that he'd make one of them an offer on a major motion picture then and there? I may be fantasizing here but I think they were too. They had never been so jumpy.

And there was a further twist which, as usual, concerned social arrangements for the evening. John Skupny, the *"gérant"* of Coppola's wine venture Niebaum-Coppola, had invited me *plus one other* to stay on for dinner which, I was told, the great man would cook himself. This was quite a responsibility. Protocol suggested that the one other should be Tony, but then on the other hand he was always saying he felt he ought to stay with the lads, and Robin the researcher would have enjoyed it so much too . . .

In the end it was Tony and I who rather guiltily bid farewell to our colleagues as they drove off down the long, dusty drive to experience yet another spit-roast chicken sandwich at the Rutherford Grill.

The interview had been fine. Someone had thoughtfully set out a pretty vase of roses and baby tomato shoots and a bottle of Coppola's best wine on the low table between the white wicker chairs. Ninety minutes after we arrived, thirty minutes after nerves had been tightened to maximum torque, Coppola padded on to the deck in a pink Hawaiian shirt and obligingly expounded on the evils of alcohol warning labels and the almost tangibly special quality of Napa Valley life, influenced, he felt, by the still present karma of its original Indian population. Yes, the interview was fine—no one made any terrible mistakes, no one was invited to jump ship to a more glamorous production—but the evening was wonderful.

First of all, Tony and I did what winery visitors do everywhere, tour the winery. Except that the winery at Niebaum-Coppola was no late-twentieth-century architect's showcase or owner's ego trip. It was the original barn built by Niebaum himself. Amazingly, it had cupolas on the roof long before it had a Coppola as proprietor, as well as marvelously dilapidated lacy fretwork round its Victorian eaves. It was built as the prototype winery before Niebaum's giant stone "chateau" was ready to do service as the Inglenook winery, and had subsequently been used as stables and a carriage house. But nowadays half of it was back in use as a folksy winery, while the other half housed a production base for Coppola's serious business interests.

Inside this extraordinary dual-product factory the film production suite and script unit were separated from the winery by a single glass door. Skupny claimed to observe great symbiosis whenever troupes of film actors arrived. At first they would press their noses against the glass gazing curiously at the barrels. Then they would get seriously involved, tasting and giving their views. The winemaker and vineyard manager on the other hand could easily find themselves carting props around the property. Another barn is stuffed with souvenirs of Coppola's film career, including many a tribal weapon from Southeast Asia to remind him of the *Apocalypse Now* episode in his varied and colorful career.

For someone who has achieved so much, including international fame and Oscars, Coppola was remarkably normal and unHollywood.

Mount Saint John, now glowing above us in the golden Napa twilight, was clearly a good trade for Beverly Hills.

In the old wooden winery we earnestly tasted barrel samples of the sturdy, rather uncompromising '93s. Coppola wandered off, probably disgusted at my spitting. ("It looks so awful I've never done it," he explained with a slightly pained expression, but then he has the sort of bulk that allows that attitude.) His perceptive Irish American wife, Eleanor, who's responsible for the day-to-day running of the estate, showed us the attic of the barn which had been fully insulated, lined with an Art Deco carpet and equipped with a comfortable viewing studio and a stack of editing machines that had Tony crying with envy.

We tore ourselves away from this dream playhouse and reluctantly allowed ourselves to be led back to the homestead, past a plastic Little Tikes playhouse in the garden, the swimming pool, aromatic gum trees and the splayed, gnarled old oak in front of the house.

In Coppola's gravel-floored cellar in the basement our job was to find a 1958 Inglenook Cask Selection Cabernet while trying some of his tiny production of white wines, a rather neutral Chardonnay and a second vintage Viognier.

Finally we climbed back up to the steamy kitchen to tell Chef Coppola, by now hovering over a cauldron of hot water, that we were ready and yes, he could put our pasta in now. Coppola as pasta cook is clearly a persona he is very comfortable with. A sizable entourage of friends, family and colleagues was assembled round the massive table in the wood-paneled dining room that looks as though it hasn't changed a chip since Niebaum's day. Coppola is very Italian and very, very keen on family life. "You should have some children," he told his consultant enologist Tony Soter sternly, adding as an aside for my benefit, "the only trouble with a family is that you don't see them often enough." A large portrait of his son Gio hung over the main fireplace. He was killed in a waterskiing accident several years before. The vineyard block straight in front of the house is named after him.

With the famous rigatoni and tomato sauce came the house red, and more evidence of the importance of the family. Coppola's Edizione Pennino Zinfandel's evocative label is modeled on the labels on the rolls of sheet music sold by his maternal grandfather, Francesco

Pennino, when he first arrived in the United States. He had shown us his collection of these yellowed rolls of paper with great pride. Two diamonds, one depicting Francesco's native Bay of Naples where he'd initially left his wife and two children to seek his fortune in New York, the other the Statue of Liberty, are joined by a slim band, which in the early twentieth century did not represent communication by telephone or fax, but sweetly painful letters.

Coppola's mother, once Signorina Italia Pennino, lived in one corner of the big white house and sat at the other end of the table from the two Tonys, me and our host. She still looked remarkably sprightly and was to bid us all good-night with real showmanship before taking off up the stairs. (She was born over the family's Empire Theatre in Brooklyn; Signor Pennino became increasingly successful in the music and film business, although he expressedly forbade any of his six children from going to Hollywood.)

This Zinfandel was just my style of wine, hearty, gutsy, made as though in an Italian family cellar with real gusto. The sort of wine that makes you feel healthy as you gulp it. And the poignant family story probably added to the appeal. It was followed by a 1979 Rubicon, only the second vintage of the new Niebaum-Coppola estate's signature wine. This grand red Cabernet blend which had been made with help from André Tchelistcheff now fetches fancy prices at charity auctions. I could imagine these two thoughtful men getting on extremely well, once they got over the repressive effect of their mutual admiration. It was kind of Coppola to show us this early vintage, not as well structured as the more recent 1987 we had tasted for the camera, but it was very kind indeed to open the 1958 Inglenook, made on the same land, and a fascinating example of bottled history. This marvel of life, fruit and subtlety was served with lamb chops, rosemary and sweetly juicy green beans straight from the garden, lavishly and justifiably eulogized by FFC. Then came lots and lots of cheese (none of this American for-maggiophobia in this household) and biscotti for Coppola's homemade grappa with its as yet unapproved label.

Coppola was in an expansive mood. He wanted, he said, more room to expand his film activities, but he also wanted to complete his dream of putting Niebaum's great Inglenook property back together again. Frustrated by owning only part of what was clearly once a great estate (as witness our bottle of '58), he now wanted the old stone Inglenook château that was so tantalizingly close and now almost abandoned anyway, and the remaining sixty-five acres of vineyard. I was urged to persuade Grand Met, to whom the remaining piece of the jigsaw now belonged, to sell to him, thereby reuniting the 120-year-old property. Perhaps this was why I'd been invited to dinner. Perhaps it was why we'd been treated to the '58. If so, it was based on the serious misapprehension that I was capable of influencing the people who ran this giant, London-based multinational corporation, but his intention was obviously a noble one, and he is so intuitively attuned to what is important about wine, that I promised to do what I could.

Skupny proposed a toast with his grappa to the estate's officially getting organic certification that very day—even though it has always been run thus in this hot, dry spot where an excess of the famous Rutherford dust, subject of many a wine lover's curiosity, is far more likely a hazard than the sort of vine pests and diseases that need lots of chemical treatments.

We all had a lovely time. We discussed wine a bit, film a lot, families a great deal. Coppola took me over to a side table to show me a photograph of three women, his wife flanked by their beautiful daughter (now, contrary to family tradition, based in Hollywood) and her Irish mother. "Just look what an infusion of Italian genes does to their looks!" he exclaimed, pointing proudly at the youngest of the three generations.

Tony and I walked the mile or so back to our hotel as the fogs crept up the valley from San Francisco Bay, buzzing with stories and observations about who had said what to whom and how. "I can't believe I've just had an argument with Francis Ford Coppola," said Tony happily, "with me telling *him* that film's so much better than videotape."

When I got home I dutifully wrote to Grand Met's chief executive George Bull, about whom I had written an article way back in *Wine & Spirit* days, to put Coppola's case. I never got a reply but Coppola, in a surely quite unrelated coup, got what he wanted three months later just when, thanks to *Bram Stoker's Dracula*, he could afford it. He would probably not want the mantle, but with his current holdings he could now claim to be a count himself, Il Conte di Napa.

Traveling the wine world to make television programs undoubtedly has its perks, but, as Coppola knows so well, it has the huge and sometimes painful disadvantage of family separation. This was unavoidable during term time, but we decided to make the most of the fact that this American filming trip was timed for the 1994 summer holidays. Nick and I arranged a house swap with a family in the People's Republic of Berkeley just north of San Francisco so that we could spend nearly three weeks there with old friends and our children before the crew arrived.

That had been the plan, but in the end, flattered to be recruited all the way across the Atlantic, I was sidetracked into devoting a weekend of our Berkeley stay to yet another television enterprise, this time for the American specialist cable network, TV Food Network. The idea of *Grape Expectations (sic)* was to provide a sort of wine version of the popular movie-rating show by Siskel and Ebert. In each half hour wines in three different price segments would be tasted and rated either a Buy or a Pass by a pair of wine pundits. TVFN decided they definitely wanted one of them to be a woman and claimed, unlikely as this sounds, that they couldn't find anyone suitable in the United States.

En route to the West Coast I'd spent a couple of preparatory days dodging the heat in New York, where the network is based, learning about business breakfasts (that some customers are so obsessive about what they regard is the best table they will get the maître d' to ask a lone woman to move in a near-empty restaurant) and dashing from Saks to Donna Karan with a wardrobe advisor choosing my outfits. I still regret not realizing that I would be allowed to keep them. If I had, I'd have concentrated much harder. There were so few dates that both I and my co-host Frank Prial could manage that the whole caboodle had to be flown over to California where we were.

The mind-boggling plan was to tape thirteen shows, six and a half hours of television, in a studio south of San Francisco in less than two days. It was no wonder that my *Wine Course* colleagues were so sniffy about TVFN's hectic timetable, making scornful scissor movements as though at either end of a length of blithely unedited videotape. On the BBC series, we were devoting eighteen months and miles and miles of precious film to our ten thirty-minute programs.

Certainly no one could have accused the TVFN team of neurotic overplanning. The details of my work permit were sorted out about half an hour before I left our temporary Berkeley home for the studio.

The scores of wines we needed as fodder had been rapidly assembled in the studio from San Francisco wine stores only one or at most two days before taping. And it was not until 7:30 on the Saturday night, after our long first day's taping, that, realizing we needed a bottle of top-quality champagne for one of Sunday's segments, we made a local liquor and video store's owner's day by buying his only bottle of Dom Pérignon. Production values were not the highest of priorities, and I can't remember ever being asked to do anything twice—a marked contrast with perfectionist documentary work.

The great attraction of this show for me, however, was that so many bottles of seriously fine wine had to be opened, thanks to the director's wise insistence that at least one "dream wine" should be reviewed in each program. The bit I liked best was when our wine-loving English director Tony Hendra, Frank and I got to drink such leftovers as Château d'Yquem 1970, Domaine de la Romanée-Conti Grands Échezeaux 1991, Château Latour 1981 and Pavillon Blanc de Château Margaux 1990 with our $20 fish supper in Palo Alto on the Saturday night.

The actual taping was pretty tiring—especially for Frank, who did no spitting. Since we had to taste about two dozen wines each day, I rather wimpishly asked if I could spit instead of swallow after tasting. Tony Hendra, late of *Spy* magazine, was so tickled by this that he made my silver spit bucket a central feature of the set. He was to regret it.

During the second day, my palate was exposed to Château Pétrus 1988 (worth hundreds of dollars), the Dom Pérignon 1985, Dow 1966 port, Mouton 1966, Pichon Lalande 1983, Chapoutier's fabled Hermitage 1990 Sizeranne—oh, and Gallo's new estate Cabernet Sauvignon (a Pass at $50, I thought). Some of these had washed down our Chinese take-out lunch and by the end of the day, despite doing my best to spit, I felt quite giddy with the succession of contrasts to which I'd been so rapidly exposed.

The giddiness turned to disbelief when, at the end of this exhausting weekend in studio darkness, I was ushered, clutching my unexpected new wardrobe and blinking in the stark West Coast sunlight, into a ten-seater limo for the journey home. I'm sure it was the result of a misunderstanding on the part of an overzealous studio manager, and perhaps the average American child is familiar with these absurdly overgrown vehicles, but I could hardly wait to show our children its black leather casting couch, its cut-glass decanters and the video screen that provided its focal point. In the determinedly whole-meal university town of Berkeley stretch limos are probably regarded with deep suspicion, I realized with a smile. Too bad. I settled back to enjoy the view through the smoked windows, San Francisco's building-block skyline shimmering across the choppy blue water at me as we crossed the Bay, champagne glasses clanking every time we hit a bump on the San Mateo Bridge. I was so looking forward to bathing three-year-old Rose, and wondering how to thank Nick enough for being a mother as well as a father for a weekend.

The taping timetable sounds hectic, and it was tiring, but what actually held us up considerably was the executive producer's insistence on using a standard issue TV hostess to serve our wines and, painfully, pronounce their names. By the time we came to make a second series, in New York this time (no wardrobe), she had been dispensed with and we finished fourteen shows in less than a day and a half. I still insisted on spitting but Tony knew better than to make a feature of it. When the Midwest stations saw the first series they insisted that women don't spit, especially not in the homes of strangers, and demanded a major and expensive re-edit.

The only trouble was that while Siskel and Ebert can easily be enlivened by showing film clips, the one diversion in *Grape Expectations* in addition to listening to us pontificating was the dramatic moment at which we held each glass up against a carefully placed white background. Not exactly high drama. I am more surprised to meet people who claim they really loved the show than that we did not run to a third series.

After this long and varied American trip there was just enough time for two weeks in the Languedoc and to settle the children back into school before we were all off again, chasing the grape harvest round eastern France in the particularly rainy September of 1994.

We hated filming in the rain. It's wet, it's depressing, it's difficult, and nothing looks as beautiful as it does with stronger light. But thanks to the structure of our programs comparing and contrasting New and

Old Worlds, this unfortunate weather at least accentuated the climatic differences, and added contrast to the images. I got to wear Henry Jayer's galoshes (very smart brown ones), we got some great shots of Lafon's muddy pickers being hosed down, and my umbrella became a bit of a TV star in its own right.

As the autumn wore on, we went to film later and later harvests in increasingly cool wine regions, in Ribera del Duero, Austria and Piedmont—all on the same culturally confusing trip which was nearly truncated by an officious Alitalia employee at Vienna airport. (How on earth could we be expected to check in and clear with customs our forty pieces of luggage in *less* than an hour, for heaven's sake?)

I drove myself from Madrid airport to the village of Pesquera, on deserted motorways that coasted straight up and down quite major mountainsides. I marveled at this spectacular landscape of wide valleys with their stands of larches, overlooked by crumbles of rock that look so crude they almost ought to be draped or sandpapered to make them acceptable. Wherever there was a settlement, there was all too obvious evidence of zero regard for planning. Man had done his best to ruin this landscape but competely failed. The gimcrack constructions looked so temporary compared to what Nature accomplished.

By the time I got to Duero plateau, I realized that we didn't actually need to go all the way to South America to see old-fashioned peasant life. Here it was in the ultra-dramatic Spanish landscape: horses still being used as principal means of transport and for tilling the soil. When we filmed Alejandro Fernandez of Pesquera it was a national holiday and the village seemed to be full of little girls in beautifully pressed dresses and gleaming white shoes. I watched an old man walking home to lunch with a large demijohn of wine in his wheelbarrow.

Northern Spain looked so much more primitive than northern Italy, where the equivalent sight was of toddlers in designer strollers being wheeled past the fancy leather shops of Alba, their eyes and the shop doors open till past midnight.

We ate superbly in Piedmont, better than anywhere else on our filming schedule. Every simple little village café turned out to want to serve us dish after stylish dish until we had to tell them to stop. We did make things easier by arriving slapbang in the middle of the truffle season. We filmed a man and his truffle hound. He explained how the

dogs had to be pale so they could be seen at night, truffling time, when
the woods were as busy as *"autostrade,"* as he put it ruefully.

The plan was that Piedmont's most famous winemaker, Angelo
Gaja, and I should be filmed eating truffles together (Oh all right,
then, I said) one rainy Sunday afternoon. The first restaurant he suggested was the old Fascist headquarters in Treiso, all square pillars just
like Angelo's jaw. At four o'clock this giant hall of a restaurant was
still heaving, children running everywhere, grandmothers, hands in
laps, looking at them contentedly. We climbed back in our cars and
drive toward the next village, Neive.

Angelo suddenly clapped his hand to his head. Why didn't he think
of this place? It's perfect, he said, there's a little wine shop across the
road from the restaurant, a particularly smart place full of Germans.
The wine shop was also full of German tourists spending a fortune on
wine and truffles, weighed out on tiny scales. Angelo's friends the
owners rustled up a little table and two large plates of risotto for us in
a corner of the wine shop. He turned his back on the throng and began
to grate great wodges of white truffle—about $300 worth, I worked
out—on to my risotto. His answer to my protests about the costs (this
was on a BBC budget, after all) was a wide grin and a "Be 'appy, my
dear!"

By now it was November, so it had to be Australia—to get the last
of the famous wine shows, at Hobart, the miniature capital of Tasmania. But first we had several days' filming in New Zealand, sched-
uled to star in our Sauvignon Blanc program thanks to its reputation
for this grape, Cloudy Bay, et al.

David Darlow flew out ahead of the rest of us to set everything
up. He was able to greet us in nauseatingly good health after we
experienced the most stomach-churning flight ever—in a four-
seater plane with windspeed one mile an hour less than the legal
maximum—across the notorious Tasman Straits from Wellington
after a tortuous thirty-five-hour journey from London. (It was even
worse for the smokers among us, who were thwarted on every flight
and at every stopover en route. One of them, our recently engaged production manager, seriously doubted on the last, storm-buffeted leg
that she would live to experience her carefully planned wedding.)

The next morning this sadist we'd hired lured us out on to a flashy speedboat in the Marlborough Sounds, and we were hard at work before we knew it. It was particularly good fun when the propeller got trapped in the Sounds' salmon nets and we were left floating helplessly away from the camera and crew who were now stranded in the middle of the Sounds on the floating salmon farm.

We flew on from New Zealand to Hobart, Melbourne and Adelaide where I experienced the strangest sensation, being in Australia and *not* feeling jet-lagged. I had never spent long enough on Australian time before. I didn't meet my favorite airport bus driver again, but we did all pinch ourselves at the miracle of enjoying warm sunshine, and eating out of doors, in November.

Back home for the rigors of a British winter, there was the small matter of writing the 300-page book designed to accompany the series, but then modern word processors give off so much useful heat, they seem almost designed to keep deadline-driven authors warm.

By the beginning of March much of the initial editing had been done, this parsimonious northerner squirming as more than 90 percent of everything we shot was rejected, the documentary norm. We knew, or at least we thought we knew, exactly where everything was going to go and what we wanted out of our very last location, exotic Chile, then in the throes of the 1995 harvest, in March in the Southern Hemisphere. I had stopped here briefly a year previously, trying to find suitable candidates for our camera, but I had hardly even sniffed the extraordinary other-worldliness of southern South America. As a European, you really do feel very, very distant here. And thanks to differences in time zones and relatively poor communications, you can be incommunicado for large chunks of time, especially if you take to the countryside as we did.

There was a definite end-of-term feeling in the air, marred only by the fact that Simon the Sound had been lured away to the Himalayas, so it wasn't quite the long-serving, core crew who had shared so much toil and trouble. Tony was the director on this last segment, David having flown back out to Australia to pick up harvest shots with an Australian crew. A young British wine writer who'd been living in Santiago for some time, Richard Neill, acted as our organizer and researcher and introduced us to some of the country's contradictions. I never thought I would see someone parking a horse and cart in the parking lot of a giant Blockbuster video store, but that unexceptional sight paints a fair picture of the state of the Chilean economy when we visited. The rich were getting much richer and the poor were beginning to experience at least some of what the late twentieth century had to offer.

Thanks to the magical quality of the light in Chile, a mixture of sparkle and shimmer, we got some wonderful footage, and some particularly evocative music. We'd talked to some fascinating characters (mainly non-Chileans, to Richard's chagrin) and one day filmed some particularly beautiful scenery on a journey that took us so far up into the Andes that we reached a checkpoint for the Argentine border. Tony had been amazed when researching this godforsaken area the week before to find his passport greeted by a border guard who smirked, "Ah, Nick Leeson, I presume?"

It was good to end this long, stressful odyssey on a high note, and we certainly made sure that we celebrated the last night. Remembering how wonderful that Krug had seemed on our last night in Colombia eleven years previously, I had also brought two bottles of champagne out from Heathrow as a surprise and we drank them together in the subtropical garden of our Santiago hotel before going out for our final dinner. But far from seeming like nectar, the champagne seemed oddly displaced and inappropriate. We went through the motions, but the fact is that we had all been turned off wine by the dreadful quality and condition of the wine served in Chile itself. The Chileans equated age with quality. If a wine was brownish and sherry-like, then it must be good. They were deeply suspicious of fresh fruit flavors. So the bottles on offer even at hotels as smart as the Santiago Hyatt where the Oddbins buyers were holed up and limos lined the approaches, were hardly worth ordering.

We had all turned our attentions instead to a particularly stimulating local alternative, pisco sours. Pisco is Chile's national spirit, an aromatic, colorless grape-based distillate that tastes absolutely delicious provided it is blended with the juice of Chile's particularly limey lemons, and drunk in Chile. On this last night we made for the Bellavista district of Santiago, had a long, thoroughly Chilean meal (lots of corn and beans) and took to the bustling streets where the regular street theater includes jugglers, amateur dramatics and transsexual dancers by the score. We strolled and gawped and finally settled on a pavement bar at a judiciously placed crossroads.

Toward midnight Jonathan, the one crew member who had been on every single one of my filming days (Ernie had had to fly back from Bordeaux to go to Cambridge to see his son graduate, for instance), turned to me and said kindly, "You look sad, Jancis." So began the most terrible deluge from my eyes which can, I suppose, only be called tears. I sniffed and sniffled, mopped and moped, with so little sign of relief that the only Chilean member of our party firmly found a taxi to take me back to the hotel. I sobbed my way into my room, into bed and finally to sleep, and then when I woke the next morning, I sobbed some more. I just couldn't stop. I was desperate for a voice of sanity to plug those tear ducts so I rang home in London, but Nick and the children had gone out. My mother, in Cumbria, must have been very surprised indeed to hear me all the way from Chile when I was flying back within a couple of hours. By the time I got on the plane I was just sniffing rather than sobbing, and at Heathrow I was fine, quite robust enough to carry the wicker laundry basket I'd bought from its maker, by a country roadside, proudly out of the baggage hall. I think it must have been the particularly potent combination of pisco, homesickness and the relief of cumulative tension. Worrying about everything and everybody and feeling so damn responsible must have been more of a burden than I realized. At last, it seemed as though we'd finally made it.

Half Centuries

Is it the approach of a new millennium that is making us all so anniversary-conscious? Or is it that I have been a parasite on the wine business for so long that more and more people are asking me to share their significantly celebratory bottles with them? I don't know.

What I do know is that December 14, 1995, was one of the more extraordinary days of my life. Sir Christopher Mallaby and his French wife were as keen on fine wine as you might expect of Her Britannic Majesty's then ambassador to France. (His brother Anthony is responsible for Bollinger's fortunes in Britain.) At the beginning of that year he'd been reminded by Hugh Johnson and Peter Sichel that 1995 was the fiftieth anniversary of the great 1945 vintage, a crop that produced such fine wine all over Europe it has come to be regarded as Nature's celebration of the peace that had just broken out. Wouldn't it be a fine idea, they suggested, to organize a dinner at your magnificent embassy in Paris at which some of the best 1945s are drunk with important representatives of the most significant nations involved in that peace, and us of course, and a few mates?

I was absolutely thrilled to find myself counted a mate, not least because my diplomat cousin Michael Arthur, an Oxford contemporary and another great-grandchild of James Forfar Dott the cooper, was

Head of Chancery in Paris at that stage and stationed in the embassy's handsome gatehouse where I could so conveniently stay the night. There were just two problems with this dream date. One was that it coincided with the BBC Governors' Christmas Lunch. This may seem to have little to do with the story but, if you are an independent television producer and depend for much of your income on how you are viewed by the nation's most important broadcaster, your instinct is not to refuse invitations from the BBC, especially ones as significant as this.

The 1945 dinner was due to start at 8:00 in the middle of Paris, so in normal circumstances, even with the hour one loses flying to France from London, it would have been a fairly leisurely journey from the lunch to the dinner table. But this was December 1995 and Paris was in the grip of the most crippling industrial unrest it had seen for years. Public transport systems had ground to a halt. The newspapers were full of stories of people walking five hours to work, sleeping in offices, and twenty-mile tailbacks on the *péripherique* (ringroad). It was impossible therefore to know how long it would take me to get from the airport to the embassy, always assuming my four o'clock flight wasn't affected by strike action.

I therefore carefully chose an outfit that would do for both engagements and arrived at BBC Television Centre deliberately early, straight from Will's end-of-term assembly, because I knew I would have to leave so early. To my horror I found that at this Governors' annual get-together, routinely leavened with notable characters from BBC programs of the year, I'd been put in the place of honor, on the right of the chairman of governors Marmaduke Hussey. I was amused, not least by his uninhibited conversational style, but also embarrassed about leaving a gap on the top table so early. On the other hand, it was not difficult to choose between staying for BBC Christmas pudding and maximizing my chances of tasting Pol Roger 1945, the aperitif planned in Paris. So I dashed off with unseemingly haste in search of a taxi, still trying to work out which vintage of Roilette Fleurie had been served with the turkey.

The flight was mercifully unscathed by militant air traffic controllers and touched down at snowy Charles de Gaulle just after six o'clock French time. I sped off toward the city in a taxi feeling pretty optimistic. We did very well for the first half of the journey, but after about twenty minutes the traffic slowed virtually to a standstill. I seemed to sit under a big Grundig sign for hours. Lorry drivers got out of their cabs to swap horror stories. We crawled toward the apartment blocks on the edge of the city. Instinctively, I pulled out my plan of Paris and tried to work out whether I could escape to some outlying metro station, before remembering that of course there was no metro, just as there were no trains and no buses. This cab, on a four-lane highway into town, was my only hope. I imagined arriving at the heavy gates of the embassy at midnight, asking if I could please be allowed to sip what was left in the bottom of the bottles.

Slowly, agonizingly slowly, the four-lane highway gave way to three-lane boulevards. High-rise apartment blocks gave way to the six-story tenements which constitute central Paris. It was 7:30 and I was inching into town, but still two or three miles from my destination, I worked out after peering through the darkness at the street signs and my little street plan. I paid the frightening number of francs on the meter and set off south as directly as I could, teetering on and off narrow pavements listening to the horns and low rumble of idling engines. At one point I was accosted by a woman in that state of near hysteria which can be relieved only by telling one's tale. She'd found herself like me, stuck in a taxi, but in such tightly packed traffic that she couldn't open the door to get out. She also babbled a story of how the traffic in some areas was crammed so tight, bumper to bumper, that to cross some streets pedestrians were having to clamber over car bonnets.

Walking was so preferable to being imprisoned in a car in these circumstances that I felt quite liberated, and triumphant when I found myself at the embassy gates by 8:20—almost early by French standards. Michael had already crossed the courtyard to the ambassador's residence, so I just threw my overnight bag in my room in the gatehouse and hurried across the courtyard toward the grand entrance that for so many of us will be forever associated with Mrs. Thatcher's downfall five years before. It was on these steps that we saw her reaction to the news that a crucial vote back in London showed she'd lost the support of her party. It was here, we knew, and she didn't, that all that lay ahead for her was speechifying and memoir-writing. As I crossed the gravel I couldn't resist trying a brisk little running dip with my handbag, just the way she used to. What a good mood I was in. I'd made it!

And there they were, still sipping the warm-up champagne, not the deeply savory Pol Roger 1945 but "just" a magnum of Pol Roger's 1979 vintage of its top blend, Cuvée Sir Winston Churchill, an appropriate enough name in the circumstances.

It was possible to work out more or less what we were going to drink by looking round at the company: Christian Pol-Roger of course, cousins Eric and Philippine de Rothschild (Philippine being stuck for two hours in her limo), Peter Sichel co-instigator, of course (so Palmer), urbane Anthony Barton who'd brought his Château Langoa-Barton, Alistair Robertson of Taylor's port (what a lovely thing to look forward to), most significantly for this celebration of peace Egon Müller from the Saar in Germany, and Jean de Castarède from armagnac country.

Hugh Johnson and Michael Broadbent, without whom no serious wine party is complete, were there and, like everyone else, had a story to tell of pilgrimage in difficult circumstances. The one guest who had no excuse to be late, the glamorous Pamela Harriman from the American embassy next door, duly made an entrance and I had the unnerving experience of apparently being invisible even when introduced to this famous man-eater. The French prime minister, Alain Juppé, and the German ambassador had been invited to add diplomatic gravitas, but were engaged in weightier matters, not least the social unrest in France and the signing of the Bosnian peace accord with Clinton and Chirac that was also taking place that night in Paris.

I felt quite ridiculously privileged as we moved through to the Borghese salon that is now the embassy's dining room. What had I done to deserve an invitation to this absurdly grand and wonderfully sybaritic event? I felt sure that thanks were due yet again to Hugh. A grand cru Chablis from Simonnet-Febvre and Chapoutier's Chante Alouette were served with the first course salad and it was the fifty-year-old Chablis that was the nervy, steely revelation. How dare people use the name of this obviously noble wine on any old medium-dry white rubbish? A fellow crusader against this travesty, and my TV co-star, the *New York Times*'s Frank Prial, arrived, delayed as all of us by the strike, during this first course. He had come only from the other side of Paris but had done the decent thing when faced with a particularly challenging social dilemma. In view of the strikes, the embassy Rolls had been sent for Frank, but it, inevitably, became enmired in the traffic by the Louvre, some distance away. Frank managed to restrain himself from ungraciously leaping out of it to finish the journey, far more effectively, on foot. I'm not sure I would have done.

With our sautéed foie gras (it had to come) was a Schloss Johannis-berg Auslese and the last two bottles of the wine Egon Müller himself made from a blend of everything he could produce in that extraor-dinary year from his family's Scharzhofberg vineyard in the Saar. He told movingly of how he'd returned from the Russian front to find the weeds higher than the vines, which had been so neglected that yields were minuscule. Perhaps that's why the soaring descant of this dryish, still-youthful 1945 was so thrilling, although the lively richness of the coppery Auslese suited the sweetness of the dish better.

Aubert de Villaine had sent a Grands Échezeaux from the cellars of the Domaine de la Romanée-Conti to provide the perfect light, game-scented bridge from whites to reds. The array of 1945 bordeaux was prodigious: Langoa and Palmer followed by the three Pauillac first growths, Hugh as a director of Latour having persuaded its new owner, François Pinault, to do the decent thing. Both of the third growths acquitted themselves well in this company. I would have felt terribly nervous if I had been Anthony Barton or Peter Sichel, although I sup-pose they must have used the occasion as an excuse to open another bottle beforehand. Peter Sichel had brought with him some extracts from the diaries of the famous Bordeaux merchant family Lawton. A typical entry read: "Very bad frost this morning. Hitler dead."

If anything the three Pauillac greats had become even more polar-ized, the Lafite all dancing and ethereal and reaching the heights that only Lafite at its best can ("just like Eric: bashful, elegant, puckish," I wrote); the Latour a big solid Winston of a wine, powerful and gentle-manly; the Mouton, with eucalyptus and cassis again obvious on the nose, so sweet and alcoholic it was almost porty. About the Mouton I wrote "E-N-O-R-M-E . . . to think was only a second growth when this was made!" The Doisy-Daëne was a very respectable accompani-ment to our almond tart but was trounced by the '45 Taylor's. Alistair Robertson of Taylor's was sitting next to me, and told me how he'd been evacuated from Portugal to the north of England during the war, and how many in the port trade doubted that 1945 would be a great vintage. "But it just closed up for years and years and then emerged tasting like this." This was my sort of port, burnished with many a layer of experience and a round, jewel-like whole, rather than a callow mixture of alcohol and sugar. With great restraint, I declined the brandy and coffee, and was amazed, when I finally floated back over the courtyard to my gatehouse billet (no Thatcher imitations this time), to find Madame Christian Pol-Roger, who'd presumably had a sandwich supper, sitting patiently in her husband's car, leather driving gloves ready on the wheel, waiting to drive him home. There's another test I would fail.

One of the completely unexpected side effects of my work is the social entrée now provided by it. When I first thought about wine in the early 1970s, the subject seemed so veiled in frivolity that I hardly dared confess in public I was interested in it. But over the last ten years or so, wine (and food) has become so respectable a leisure interest with the same sort of cultural associations as opera or fine art, that people I might merely have admired from afar, had wine not brought us together, have become good friends.

The most obvious of these is the novelist Julian Barnes, whose work I have always admired, and not just his flattering television reviews. He not only writes beautifully but manages to communicate on the printed page better than most writers of contemporary fiction that he also thinks and feels.

We first met in the mid eighties over a couple of dinners organized by, and then with, the writer Paul Levy, designed as selective vertical tastings of properties as relatively modest as Châteaux Poujeaux and Haut-Bailly. The first time we went to dinner with him and his wife, literary agent Pat Kavanagh, there was another theme, the southern Rhône, which has become Julian's most enduring wine passion. Star of the show, also enjoyed by that other literary wine lover Auberon Waugh, was a wine that would be served at Julian's forty-fifth birthday dinner—Les Cèdres, the 1962 vintage of Jaboulet's top Châteauneuf-du-Pape. It is typical of his generosity that he gave Nick and me a bottle left over from this dinner in January 1991 to enjoy at home.

I don't know anyone who has taken up wine quite so devotedly as he has over the last ten years. A substantial part of his house is now given over to housing a wine collection that is far grander than ours. He spends far longer than I do checking sale catalogues and comparing merchants' lists, plotting dinners and tracking down special bottles. Another major brake on his literary output (or perhaps addition to it—I haven't read them) are his regular transatlantic faxes to and from a fellow wine lover, the American novelist Jay McInerney. I sense there is as much one-upmanship in these as male bonding, but good old wine is clearly providing these two men of letters with enormous pleasure.

We first met Jay in the summer of 1988 over a dinner of 1974s— California Cabernets, of which Sterling Reserve was the best, plus a slightly less impressive La Mission-Haut-Brion. Since then he makes regular detours to London, mainly, it seems to me, to the Barnes cellar and table. The author of *Bright Lights, Big City* has even taken up wine writing, for heaven's sake, in the American *House & Garden*. But if Jay has taken the obvious route to learning more about wine, Julian shows all the symptoms of true devotion, not to say fanaticism.

A typical dinner chez Barnes begins with some very special champagne, zips through a bottle of top-quality Alsace and then gets down to the serious business of what feels like about two bottles of very grand red per person, before moving on to a sweet wine and, very possibly, port.

This generous host and considerate guest inflicts mental as well as physical pain. He loves nothing more than to bring, say, a magnificent vintage of red to your table decanted into a Sauternes bottle and then listen to you, with a poker face, mire yourself deeper and deeper into a completely irrelevant quicksand as you try to guess what it is. The first time he did this, quite soon after our dinner of California '74s with Jay, I told him firmly that the Latour '71 he'd brought was a California Cabernet. "You're not just saying that because of what you think I have in my cellar?" he asked gently. No, no, I assured him, before letting him tell us, still completely straight-faced, what grand bottle of bordeaux he'd spent all that money on.

There was also the memorable Barnes dinner at which Bron Waugh dismissed a bottle of Guigal's La Mouline 1976 as Moroccan port. The only time I can remember showing any flair when tasting Barnes wines blind, and that was pretty oblique, was at dinner there in 1993 when I said a red reminded me of the sort of old-fashioned burgundy favored by Bron. It turned out to be a bottle of Cheval Blanc 1970 which had come from the bat-infested cellar beneath the Waughs' house in Somerset.

But Julian excelled even himself as host of his fiftieth birthday celebrations. On the Sunday night after the actual day in January 1996, he gave us, Jay, the food writer Simon Hopkinson and Stephen Fry not just one but two of the greatest wine thrills I've ever had. Even better, the wines weren't served blind. A magnum of Dom P 1975 was just a warm-up—"meaty, lively, more huts than the '71 we'd had at New Year" is what I wrote about it the next morning. I think I meant guts. Laville-Haut Brion 1966, a great dry white bordeaux thoughtfully chosen with Simon and me in mind, smelled oily and heavy. Its tang and full-bodied character made it a perfect match for the fennel and shallots roasted in olive oil, but it would not have been much fun to drink on its own.

After this heady start came the two amazing magnums, of Pétrus no less, really cleverly chosen vintages that only a true connoisseur knows enough to value—1967 followed by 1964, both great years for Pomerol but not necessarily for the Médoc, which so unfairly makes a year's reputation. The 1964 took ages to open out, even once it had been poured into our glasses. It still looked very deep and crimson, much less evolved than the 1967, and sat brooding while we allowed the 1967 to wash over us. This younger wine was at the peak of its power, all flesh and opulence and sheer perfumed pleasure. There were only seven of us but this showed all the virtues of having a whole magnum to wallow in. Just as the '67 was starting to get a little bit furry and indistinct at the end of the palate, the 1964 marched magnificently center stage, much tauter and more structured than the 1967, quite a different style of wine, more Médoc in a way, but with a much longer life ahead of it. This was Pétrus at its concentrated best, even if we weren't.

But there was more to come: the coppery depths of Climens '47 that were wonderfully sweet, enlivened with a nice kick of citrus and acid, and—as if we deserved or needed it—a decanter of Cockburn '12 (1912, that is) which seemed to be drying out at the end but was an extraordinary treat, a souvenir of a world in which Sarajevo was yet to assume historical significance. There were real as well as gustatory fireworks halfway through this meal, which exercised the Barneses' North London neighbors considerably, especially when a particularly loud rocket set off a car alarm.

Julian decided to celebrate his birthday *again* with the same team, a sort of end-of-the-birthday-year, as he put it, although it was well into February 1997. The star magnum this time was Cheval Blanc 1955, served refreshingly cool so that we lost nothing and could enjoy every new facet as it opened up. This was so beautifully complete, so *nourishing*, that the lamb served with it was almost superfluous. It was not that this forty-two-year-old wine was monumentally enormous, intense or alcoholic; more that it was so perfectly, sweetly harmonious you just wanted to stick your nose in a bowl of it. We'd had a bottle of the same vintage eighteen months previously at our nearest smart restaurant in the Languedoc to celebrate someone else's fortieth birthday. It had been delicious then, but this magnum seemed to have been tightened up three notches. The bottle of Calvet-bottled 1952 Cheval Blanc served with it, also blind, seemed so much tauter it was almost impossible to believe the two wines could have come from the same property. This was a magnificent wine, for intellectuals rather than hedonists, and I fear our intellects are usually overcome by our senses by the end of the first (me) or second (everyone else) bottle chez Barnes. (A 1953 Cheval Blanc served at an anniversary dinner at The White Horse at Chilgrove two years previously had also been sensational.)

Nick and I thought we were doing rather well to stay the course until the Sauternes was served—after a very respectable bottle of Chateau Montelena Cabernet 1976 we'd brought. The Yquem was from the great 1947 vintage which Julian has clearly adopted as preferable to his own 1946. It was deep, dark and instead of enormously obvious sweetness had massive weight and substance, enlivened by vague hints of orange peel. This combination of wine and vintage is very, very special indeed. Although not quite as plump and sweet as the 1945 Yquem I'd enjoyed *pace* weevils, it was the sort of wine, not to say purchase, that only a very dedicated, very generous host would share.

This is a man obsessed. He let slip that he'd taken delivery of the magnificent magnum of Cheval Blanc 1955 only that morning. He'd ordered it from a merchant in the depths of the country the previous week and it had been delivered by mistake to a similar address also, dangerously, housing a wine cellar and a wine lover. Simon Hopkinson tried to formulate politely a question that several of us were fuzzily grappling with. How come you went out and bought yet more, even more expensive wine for tonight when you've already got three cellarsful downstairs? But both he and Julian failed to find the right words, and I'm sure the arrival of the port (coincident with that of our cab) did nothing to help find an answer to the essential attraction of wine to one who has so willingly succumbed to it.

On Writing
About Wine

I have never lost my taste for a small scoop, and was pleased during my last few months on *The Sunday Times* in 1986 to introduce the British public to a new phenomenon in the world of wine, an American ex-lawyer called Robert M. Parker Jr. He had started up a newsletter called the *Wine Advocate* in 1978, just a year after the dear old *Drinker's Digest* was born, and had built it into such an authoritative publication that he was already accused of single-palatedly steering the American wine market. His unique selling proposition was that, as well as providing copious notes he gave wines points out of 100. So inimical was this notion to traditional British wine lovers that when in 1985 Hugh Johnson was sent proofs of Parker's first book, on Bordeaux, he thought they were printer's marks, but by then American retailers were already complaining: "If Parker scores a wine less than 85 you can't sell it; more than 90 you can't buy it."

I flew to Bordeaux in mid March to meet him and see him in action assessing the newborn 1985s. Make that *one* 1985. Château Margaux was the only property relaxed enough to allow a third party to witness such a pivotal encounter as the annual one between their infant wine and Parker's palate. We met the Sunday night before his major two-week assault on the '85s. He'd brought with him his new part-time assistant, clinical psychologist Jay Miller, to show him the full rigors of his schedule. Then as now Parker was typically tasting a hundred young wines a day, a punishing assault on the olfactory and nervous system. In Bordeaux it involved an early start from the unglamorous Novotel, five châteaux before lunch, and many more after.

From the start I was particularly intrigued by his self-confidence. Since my early days on the *Digest*, when I felt I was so inexperienced I needed someone like Anthony Hanson at my tasting elbow, so to speak, I too had come to the conclusion that the most useful assessments of a range of wines come from a single palate rather than a tasting panel. The more scores and opinions are taken on board, the more likely that someone will not like an exceptionally distinctive wine, dragging it into the apparently innocuous middle ground of communal assessment. Tasting panels can all too easily have this sort of smudging effect so that everything they recommend will please everyone, but the really interesting wines get overlooked. This makes them perfect for deciding on, say, wines for airlines, but they can shortchange wine-loving consumers. Individual wine consumers are better off, my argument goes, following an individual wine critic's preferences and prejudices and getting to know how they relate to their own—in the same way that we filter what we're told by, say, individual theater or film critics. For, make no mistake about it, wine judging is every bit as subjective as the judging of any art form.

It is because I am constantly aware of this, and because I am all too conscious of my own fallibility, that I make my wine recommendations somewhat hesitantly—much less confidently than Parker, for instance—knowing how human preferences, sensitivities and even individual bottles can vary. (Funnily enough, however, when years later both of us were invited to join a famous French tasting group to evaluate a great range of red bordeaux, it was me and not him who turned out to have the dubious honor of tasting closest to the group norm.)

And another thing. What makes writing about wine so rewarding to me is the chance to describe where and how wines are made and, particularly, the people who make them. For me wine is so much more than a liquid in a glass; the liquid is merely our link to what is so often a fascinating story, a spot on the globe, a point in time, a fashion in wine-making, an argument between neighboring farmers, rivalry between old schoolmates, perhaps proud new owners who want to make their mark at any cost.

Parker, on the other hand, appears to be completely untroubled by self-doubt and barely interested in the human and geographical context that makes a wine. His working life is to report on his reaction to a succession of glasses. He goes to Bordeaux every spring because the hyper-protective Bordelais wouldn't dream of letting samples of their infant wines cross the Atlantic, and he travels the Rhône every year because that is effectively the only way to keep up with developments there, but one has the impression that he would really much rather stay at home in Maryland and, say, have anonymous glasses pushed through a hatch for evaluation. Whereas I would call myself a wine writer, he has always styled himself a wine critic.

So, I was intrigued to find out, what gave Parker such oracular confidence? He seemed to have no qualms about going out on a limb to castigate some individual winery (sometimes with disastrous consequences for its owners) or tell his readers that, without any shadow of a doubt, wine X, which he tasted at only five months old before it had been properly blended or aged in cask, let alone bottled, would be the best wine of the vintage? On the basis of reading his work I was expecting to meet someone talented, hard-working but arrogant.

I was wrong. It was not arrogance that fueled him. We met over an indifferent dinner at a Bordeaux restaurant suffused with Sunday night torpor. According to the article I subsequently wrote in *The Sunday Times* we drank a cru Beaujolais, a Moulin-à-Vent, which seems an extremely perverse choice, not to say exotic wine for a restaurant in western France. Parker was great fun to have dinner with. We had lots to gossip about, after all. I could see at a glance that he had the ideal wine taster's constitution, really useful critical mass, one might say. A young head on a statesman's body. Fast-talking (so fast he makes no audible distinction between the words "winery" and "wine writer"), relatively serious, sensitive to criticism, very cynical about Americans, if anything overreverential toward the French (his beloved wife's being a French teacher played a major part in his conversion to wine) and a thoroughly good dinner companion.

What I should have already worked out about Parker's take on wine is that it is inspired less by arrogance than by anger. Very much a child of the Ralph Nader generation, he sees himself as an outsider, and a lone champion of the wine consumer. As he started to get interested in wine, he told me that night, he became increasingly convinced that the American public were getting a raw deal. Too many American wine writers, he felt, were simply writing what publicists were telling them to. They depended on free trips, free meals and free bottles, for none of them was able to make a decent living out of wine writing. One or two of them were even doubling as wine publicists themselves. No one was actually *criticizing* wines. What really fired him up in the early days of the *Wine Advocate* were his occasional sorties to the jungle called Manhattan to make some of the more important wine writers aware of his new publication. He gave one of the best known a fancy lunch with something even fancier to drink, only to find that the next time they met, the wine writer failed to recognize him. As has been evident throughout the history of the written word, there is no more effective spur than a chip on the shoulder.

The next morning we met at Margaux, in the château's smart new tasting room with a fresh white linen tablecloth, a copy of Parker's Bordeaux book placed just so on it, along with six sets of six gleaming tasting glasses. There was Parker (in college suit and loden overcoat); Jay Miller; Parker's minder, Archie Johnston of the négociants Nathaniel Johnston (he has a network of fixers throughout France); Paul Pontallier, who had been in charge of winemaking at Château Margaux for just three years; the estate manager, Philippe Barré, and me. This was an important moment for the fortunes of Château Margaux 1985. How Parker reacted to these first samples from as yet unblended different lots would determine how the wine would be seen in the market and how it should be priced. This was impressive, considering the man had published his first words on wine less than eight years previously. I was also touched by his determination to speak French throughout, no matter how great an effort this entailed.

Pontallier wanted to talk him through the four Cabernet and two Merlot samples first, but Parker couldn't resist getting that famous nose straight into the glasses. They'd heard he liked to taste in silence, or at least silence punctuated by some extraordinarily noisy intakes of air during the process. So there were only the most awed of mutterings from the house team. Some chance visitors were hurried out of earshot.

Parker liked the big, bold sample number six best. Pontallier was brave enough to venture that perhaps sample five was more typically

Margaux. By judicious pouring and mixing between samples, Parker made up a glass of what for him would be the ideal blend and everyone tasted it reverentially. He was given the 1984, 1983 and 1982 to taste too, the youngest with many an apology. We all drooled over the last two—which continue to be stars in their own starry galaxies. Parker remarked that the type of tannins were very different in the two vintages. Pontallier ventured, very politely, smiling, taking his courage in both hands, that the analyses suggested that they were identical. We tasted the fabulously priced white Pavillon Blanc, Laura Mentzelopoulos's pride and joy, as a rinser and then, wham, Parker's little red notebook was slammed shut, slipped into the pocket and we all realized that the audience was now officially at an end. The entourage was about to move on to my friend Michel Delon at Château Léoville-Las-Cases, but I was barred, left forlornly waving farewell in the courtyard.

Parker's great gift, apart from a strong constitution and unshakable confidence as a taster (and in any group the most confident taster becomes the arbiter of taste) is his ability to synthesize, to draw conclusions from what his senses tell him and compare those impressions with relevant others. Following the same track, I ventured to extrapolate from our small tasting of Margaux '85. Pontallier was quite right that that fifth sample had the elegance, the lift, the perfume for which Margaux was always famous. The sixth sample of 1985, Parker's favorite, was much more like The Sort of Wine Parker Likes (and indeed Parker himself): big, a model of concentration, slightly chunky, set for the long haul.

I have the greatest respect for Paul Pontallier and am making a more general point than one merely about Château Margaux 1985, but the trend in Bordeaux over the last ten years has been without any shadow of a doubt to make more and more wines in the Parker mold, rather than to be absolutely true to their geographical origins. Because of the tradition that classed growth châteaux choose every spring exactly which lots of wine go into the main blend (the rest may be bottled as a "second wine" such as Les Forts de Latour or Pavillon Rouge de Château Margaux or simply sold off in bulk) and because all sorts of factors such as picking dates, fermentation temperatures and exact details of oak aging can be manipulated, there is ample opportunity for château owners to dictate to a certain extent the style of wine they make.

In the Médoc, with its huge estates, we are not talking about bottling the hand that Nature inescapably deals every year. So as a region it has been ideally adapted to Parkerization, not least because it depends so crucially on the international marketplace. Since the early 1980s when Parker really rose to prominence—notably with his forecast of the greatness of the 1982 vintage—communal differences, those say between Saint-Julien and Margaux, have become increasingly blurred, even if overall quality of winemaking has risen. With skill has come uniformity, and I'm sure Parker is proud only of his part in encouraging the former.

Already from that brief encounter I could see just how diligent and thorough a taster Parker was, and is. And when in April 1987 I was sent by the American magazine Condé Nast *Traveler* (Harry Evans editing me again) to write a profile of Parker in situ at his modest home in pretty woods outside Baltimore I was further impressed by the fact that as well as being such a hard-working taster, he is perfectly aware of what wine is for: to convive with, to wallow in, sitting round a table in good company with good food.

He's called Dowell, or Dow by his nearest and dearest, after his middle name McDowell. His wife, Pat, is the vivacious one and must have opened many a door for him in the early years when the only certain argument for starting the newsletter was its tax advantages for wine buying or, as he puts it, "when I labored in obscurity." When I'm at home writing I think of Parker, or rather his mother-in-law, every time I go to the lavatory. This is simply because this is where I keep the giant conch that Pat Parker's mother gave me from those she and her husband used to collect on their sailing days in the Caribbean.

Now, does this compromise my relationship with Parker? Given that he occasionally reviews my wine books and vice versa, are we perhaps too close to give our readers objective advice? He gave me a delicious dinner during my Maryland visit: Comtes de Champagne 1976, Pétrus 1971, a stunning bottle of Latour 1966, La Mission Haut-Brion 1964, British bottled Chasse-Spleen 1949 and a half of Yquem 1980.

Six months later we had him to dinner at our house, exposing him to some Australian treasures I thought might not have come his way: Bollinger RD Tradition 1976, Dom Pérignon 1976, Leo Buring Rhine Riesling Watervale 1973 DWC 15, Lindemans Hunter River Burgundy 1970 Bin 4000, the miraculously good Châteauneuf-du-Pape

Chante Perdrix 1961, Taylor 1948 and Thévenet's botrytized Mâcon-Clessé 1983. (The Bollinger was disappointingly surly. A week later I was rung by the champagne house's U.K. importer who had heard via the owner of Bollinger, via someone whom Parker had just met in New York, that this bottle had not found favor with Le Grand Palais du Monde. What exactly did Parker say? I was asked. How displeased did I think he was? The upshot was that another bottle of this extremely expensive wine was dispatched from Bollinger to Maryland in order to expunge the poor tasting note.)

There is a noticeable contrast between the American and British points of view on the relationship between wine writers and those they write about. The official Parker line, now embraced by the great majority of American wine writers, is that wine critics should remain as distant as possible from those who make and sell wine for fear of having their judgments clouded by personal feelings, their palates contaminated by emotion.

This is more difficult than it sounds. How are we to learn about wine without spending time with those who produce and sell it? And wine people are congenitally generous hosts. For them the most natural way to introduce someone to their wines is to do so with food. This can occasionally bring the wine writer into dangerous contact with not only a wine producer and his table but also his—not usually her—family. Perhaps our critical faculties might be swayed by exposure to a pretty wife, wise parent or particularly cute child?

In practice, as Parker knows as well as anyone else, it is impossible to operate as a wine writer without some sort of contact with those one writes about. And in practice it is perfectly possible to operate as a human being when in their company and still be a dispassionate adjudicator when the moment comes to report on their wares. Just as Parker depends on certain wine people to facilitate his punishing tasting schedule, and all American wine writers of my acquaintance owe many a meal to the world's wine trade, so do we Brits. In fact I feel more guilty about my *lack* of collusion than the reverse. I suspect many wine producers and merchants are puzzled that I seem so friendly in the flesh, yet so inscrutable in print. I am ashamed by my own callousness verging on hypocrisy, my ability to set personal feelings on one side when communing with my word processor.

As is clear, I am troubled by my relationship with the wine trade. It contains many extremely sympathetic people. Having met them I find it next to impossible not to interact with them and I now count several dozen of them as friends. Some of them make or sell extremely good wine. Some of them make or sell good wine, some of them good-value wine and some of them earn their living dealing in wine I would never dream of recommending. Ernst Gorge, the little Czech so beloved by Liz Morcom and I, could not have been more charming, nor more generous a host, dispensing first growths at his lunch table throughout his latter years in the wine trade. I may have arranged an eightieth birthday dinner for him, yet I don't think I ever wrote a word about the wines he was so good at selling. Nor did he ever reproach me for it. The first Christmas I worked at *Wine & Spirit*, out of the blue one of the old school of London wine importers sent me a case of their bottlings. If they hadn't, I would never have known quite how bad their wine was. So much for buying praise.

Nowadays, dozens of unsolicited bottles arrive on my doorstep most weeks, as they do chez every wine writer I know wherever they are in the world. (On my London doorstep I regularly sign couriers' delivery lists that have them circling London on a continuous wine correspondent loop, from Atkin of the *Observer* to Simon of *The Sunday Times*.) Some of these bulky packages are routine mail-outs from the supermarkets and major retail chains to all national wine correspondents. Very, very few of them come direct from great wine producers. Most of them come from obscure and often indifferent wine producers, not infrequently with bills for excise duty and storage attached. I feel duty-bound to taste practically everything that arrives (with the exception of the odd bottle of, say, Lite White Lambrusco that I cannot possibly imagine would be of interest to readers of the *Financial Times*), but find that only about one bottle in every fifty is sufficiently interesting to make me want to drink any more of it than the routine tasting sample. The beneficiaries of my policy that life is too short to drink less than delicious wine are friends with less finicky palates who can be bothered to collect restoppered bottles and the odd casual charity event. Chez Parker I was shown the sylvan slope down which his assistant regularly empties the slops. The grass really is greener there.

The real difference between American and British wine writers is that so many Brits have or have had a commercial involvement in the wine trade. Generally speaking, the less mature the wine market, the closer the connections between those who comment on wine and those who sell it, because it is so much more difficult to make a living as a wine writer. I met a central African wine importer once who told me how blissful it was to be the only person for thousands of miles who knew the first thing about wine. His customers hung on his every word and recommendation. In South Africa, New Zealand and especially Australia there is still considerable crossover between wine writers, producers and consultants. Britain can hardly be said to be an immature wine market—we've been trading in it for centuries—which is partly why Americans find it so difficult to understand how so many British writers have been recruited directly from wine importers. Don't they see how vulnerable this makes them to criticism?

Our most celebrated pundit and one of the few to make a seriously good living out of writing about wine, Hugh Johnson, is quite open about his directorship of Château Latour, his involvement with the mail-order Sunday Times Wine Club outfit, his investment with Bordeaux producer Peter Vinding-Diers in the Royal Tokay Wine Company in Hungary and, of course, his range of glassware and wine paraphernalia shop in one of the most expensive quartiers in London. Like most of the traditional wine trade, he just can't see what all the fuss is about. British wine merchants are decent chaps and wouldn't dream of favoring their own produce, runs the argument. And certainly there could not be a more decent chap than H. Johnson. Along with Harry Waugh, he is the archetypal gentle man in wine, however much the sales figures of his books might suggest sharp commercial acumen. He has been unaccountably generous to me.

Every now and then a younger wine writer is dispatched to the Johnsons' beautiful house, garden and arboretum in one of the prettiest corners of Essex to snap at the great man's heels. The idea is that they will come back with a story of just how clay-like his feet are, having confronted him with his wicked conflicts of interest. Time and again, however, they return confounded by his natural warmth and bonhomous nature. He may make money from his forays into wine retailing and production, but Hugh convinces that they are fueled by his boyish enthusiasm rather than avarice. The idea of setting sail on a reconstructed schooner or ancient trade route with a group of Sunday Times Wine Club members fills him with excitement. Whenever I see him, he has just got back from a trip to somewhere with the most amazing three-hundred-year-old parawana oaks, or sensational scenery, or extraordinarily pure Rieslings or whatever. He is above all an enthu-siast—as is evident in his approach to writing about wine, which a new generation of wine writers at one stage may have found too blindly uncritical, especially of France. But then in Britain at least there has been a simplistic polarization of wine thought into the "if it's French it must be superior" Johnson and Broadbent school, and the more vociferous "if it's French it must be rubbish" school of New World protagonists.

I see Messrs. Johnson and Broadbent even more often than I used to now that I have joined them and the once heavily insured Master of Wine Colin Anderson as wine consultants to British Airways. I was filming in New Zealand when in late 1994 Nick sent me a copy of a fax inviting me to join this distinguished tasting panel. I remember it particularly because only the day before all of us concession card-carrying television crew members had been cursing ourselves for for-getting to claim the air miles on two days' car hire in Tasmania. I felt honored. Here was a noncompromising wine consultancy (the only even vaguely commercial connection I have) which seemed to signal that I had finally joined the grown-ups. Now, I felt, my work in wine seemed to be flatteringly recognized by an external but powerful body (no one in the U.K. buys more champagne, for example). When I was back in Britain and went for my initial meeting with the BA man in charge, known quaintly as Head of Culinary Concepts, I gushed some-thing about how honored I felt to be included in such august com-pany. "Well, we thought we needed a woman," was the deflating explanation.

If Hugh has an Achilles' heel, it is the vituperation he reserves for the business of awarding points out of 100 to wine, pointing a not so dis-creet finger at Parker. In the mid to late 1980s there was a public transatlantic polarization of views on scoring wine, with most British wine professionals—and Hugh Johnson most publicly—pouring scorn on this crude marking system which offers the illusion of precision where none is possible. The line is that it might seem useful to wine consumers as unsophisticated as Americans perhaps, but it is superfluous to those who genuinely understand the variation of different bottles and palates. British wine consumers, on the other hand, have proved rather more enthusiastic about the notion of drinking by numbers. Those who earn their living in wine may be able to afford the time to commune closely with the nuances of hundreds of different wines, but many of those with even quite large amounts to spend on their cellars find the scores an easy, time-saving device.

I find all of this deeply depressing. Of all nations Britain has managed to establish a reputation for connoisseurship, partly because of the English language and its widely published wine writers, partly because, thanks to the auction houses, London is as much a trading hub for fine wine as it is of less liquid financial commodities. I would be unhappy to see the British wine-buying public transformed into a satellite of zombies buying what someone else tells them to. My somewhat vain aim has always been to enlighten and enthuse my readers and viewers as much as possible, so that they can make as informed a choice as possible, based on their own tastes. But more and more I reach the conclusion that however hard I try to instil confidence in wine consumers, the great majority of them just want to be told what to buy.

A certain proportion, those with a real passion for wine and a substantial budget for indulging it, become Parker postgraduates. The course initially involves slavish comparison of their own impressions with those of the great man, resulting in confusion and lack of self-esteem when they fail to tally exactly. But eventually most students graduate to the realization that this is inevitable and reach a new confidence in their own taste.

I keep wondering whether Britain could have produced a Parker. The British traits of self-deprecation and irony would sit uneasily with the Parkeresque pitch of omniscience. The closest we get is our Clive Coates, whose newsletter *The Vine* provides many a useful tasting note on young French wines, especially burgundies, but he is more equivocal in his judgments than Parker and, another typical result of Anglo-American comparison, works less hard.

The American approach depends on being exhaustively, and presumably exhaustedly, thorough and requires a high tolerance of fact-checkers. British journalists tend to argue that their natural brilliance of thought and felicity of expression supersedes any requirement to be so ploddingly diligent (and every one of them who has ever written for an American magazine has at least one fact-checker story). We are less earnest but probably lazier. A certain laziness is now apparent in British wine columns, which are all too often just like shopping lists, with little thematic connection between the "bargains" recommended. To judge from what is published in the national newspapers, the British wine-buying public is famously mean, and interested almost exclusively in wines selling at the cheapest end of the price spectrum, which surely can't be right. Nevertheless, it is not just British wine columns but wine books that are increasingly dominated by mere lists of recommended bottles, which suggests that fewer and fewer people share my romantic fascination with the context in which any given wine is produced. Perhaps the modern wine consumer, typically short of time, really does want nothing more than a quick sensory hit?

One man who manages to straddle the Atlantic in terms of approach, being both erudite and readable, is Gerald Asher, the Englishman who went to work in the American wine trade and now writes regularly for *Gourmet* magazine. Most of the elegant prose in his long articles is devoted not to wine itself but to the stories behind them, which is wise because words are such impoverished little things with which to describe taste. Most of the perceptions that go together to form our impressions of taste are deeply buried in our nervous system. We can't extract them and compare them with anyone else's, or any objective scale such as, for example, the musical scale that is so useful for communicating about music or the spectrum that validates our language for color. The closest we can come to describing flavors (which we actually perceive as aromas, whether we're tasting food or drink) is to find flavor similes. "Smells like raspberries with a hint of burnt toast," for example. But even setting aside just how useful these similes are (and I cannot imagine someone feeling they just have to have a certain wine because it smells of raspberries and burnt toast), we know how approximate and inadequate these flavor similes are.

There are thousands of compounds in the smell of any really good wine and it is their cumulative effect that is so ineffably captivating, together with their interaction, their persistence, their variation with time and with whatever we happen to be eating or thinking. Wine professionals in any case tend to use a common but terribly imprecise tasting vocabulary. "Spicy," for example, is the word widely used to describe the most common and powerful characteristics in the smell of wine made from Gewürztraminer grapes. The word has come to be used not because Gewürztraminer smells at all like any particular spice, but because *gewürz* is German for spiced (and is used as a prefix for this particularly aromatic strain of the Traminer grape). This is just one particularly obvious example of unhelpful wine jargon.

Besides these flavor elements wines have dimensions, usually easier to measure, such as alcoholic strength, total acidity, residual sweetness, and levels of tannins. In general, these dimensions really are useful to potential buyers of the wine. It's important to pass on the style or build of the wine because that is its single most important characteristic. Some people just don't like even a hint of sugar in their wines, others have an aversion to aggressively astringent wines, others feel physically irritated by high acidity. For all these reasons, I try to spell out wines' dimensions, but I fight shy of the long list of flavor similes. I can enjoy skillful personifications of wines of the "quavering little old lady with a wicked sense of humor" school but am extremely wary of them myself, for obvious reasons.

So, the lives of us wine writers are not completely without problems. Like practitioners of any craft, we have our little spats between craftsmen, our differences of technique and creed. Because of this, and because we have annexed such unusual territory for our work, it is extraordinary how easy it is to forget how lucky we are to be able to devote so much of our lives to a subject everyone else so rightly associates with pleasure. All wine writers, critics, commentators—however they style themselves—should be reminded to pinch themselves at the start of every working day.

Vin Fin

———

The wine world today is almost unrecognizably different from the one I first surveyed in the early 1970s. The number of countries with a stake in wine production has increased even since 1993 when I assembled *The Oxford Companion to Wine*. For the second edition I will have to add entries on Korea, Thailand and Vietnam, and possibly several others. Today the world's wine drinkers—and consumers of wine books and television programs, as Nick and I have delightedly discovered—are scattered all over the globe.

As recently as the late 1980s we European wine writers complacently regurgitated the accepted view on the Chinese, for example, that they would never take to wine because of some culturally deep-seated preference for brandy and rice-based liquors. Since the mid 1990s, however, the international fine wine market has been turned on its head and heated to boiling point by a new generation of enthusiastic Asian wine lovers, some of whom are drinking a sizable proportion of the world's finest wines in Taiwan's new generation of wine bars. This has been reflected in my own life by recent, eye-opening trips to Thailand and Vietnam, places I would never in a million years have thought wine would take me.

Wine lovers today are much more varied socially too—a thoroughly refreshing phenomenon—but this doesn't mean they have less respect for wine than their more patrician antecedents. I suspect they may even be more genuinely discriminating, buying more on the basis of inherent quality than on names and reputations alone. I hope they are a bit more confident as wine buyers than those who used simply to leave wine selection to their own, single wine merchant.

Wine has certainly acquired resounding respectability during my tenure, as both a leisure interest and raison d'être. The idea that as a wine writer I might be awarded an honorary doctorate by an eminent university would never have occurred to me when I started, but doesn't seem so absurd in 1997. When wine takes hold of a person, it tends to sink its claws in pretty deep. One of our researchers for the *Wine Course* abandoned her twenty-year career in television for the wine trade after her stint in Burgundy and the Rhône. I smile when I think that exactly twenty-five years after I automatically discarded the idea of a postgraduate career in wine, my oldest god-daughter, Hester Mc-Intyre, left Oxford with her first in history and went immediately into the wine trade (with zero encouragement from me, it pains me to admit). I frown, on the other hand, when I think that the dream of being a vigneron has become so universal that we woke up one morning in the Languedoc to find that the old *cave* next to our house had been bought by a Home Counties accountant who had dropped out with his wife and family to live out that dream. Now I see Lay & Wheeler are importing their first vintage, a liquid we'd been passed over the fence to assess straight from the barrel. *That* wasn't in the holiday plan.

Perhaps we should have invested in one of the many vineyards we were offered as soon as we bought the French house (many of them now patches of bare land, thanks to government bribes for pulling up France's surplus vines). And perhaps we should have bought the lovely old stone building next door when we were offered it by the elderly brothers who once made their wine there, but *(a)* I was scared off by their claim that only dynamite would remove the ancient concrete tanks and *(b)* I have no desire whatsoever to make wine myself. I know my failings all too well and am acutely conscious that not only am I not at all practical, but I lack the necessary equanimity to be a farmer. I would hate to be at the mercy of the elements.

For me one of the excitements of the newly expanded world of wine production to which I am looking forward most keenly will be the gradual discovery of which grape variety is most suitable for which new and newish wine region. It has already started, what with Napa and Coonawarra Cabernet, for example, but I hope to enjoy the fruits of many more proven combinations. I recently tasted evidence—at last, after all these years—that Welschriesling really *is* probably the best grape in the Ljutomer region of Slovenia. I finally managed to taste a pure, unadulterated example of this wine, so besmirched in my memory by all those heavily sweetened and sulphured brown bottles labeled Lutomer Riesling, just last year at the London Wine Trade Fair. The manager of the local co-op beamed proudly at me as I tasted his tingling essence of Slovenian mountain stream. This was a significant moment in my wine odyssey, vanquishing forever memories of a liquid that did almost everything it could to put me and hundreds of other Britons off wine in any form. The presence of this proudly nationalistic Slovenian contingent at the Fair, rather than being subsumed into the vast communist exporting body that had organized our 1977 trip, provided one of those rare confluences of wine with politics. Occasionally wine and politics do bump into each other.

The most important event in my twenty-odd years has been wine's role in the international rehabilitation of South Africa. When I went to the Nederburg auction in 1977, all but two of the many nonwhites there were serving rather than being served. On my second visit to South Africa, in March 1996, there were signs of a very gradual normalization of the country's social fabric. The wine industry had its token high-profile black wine promoter (an immigrant from New York) and there was talk of winemaking scholarships specifically for the black and Cape colored population. I cannot imagine that in my involvement with wine there will ever be a repeat of the extraordinarily universal hope and heartfelt optimism about the human condition generated by images of the release of Nelson Mandela and the country's first multiracial elections in 1994. Of all the wine regions I have visited around the world (which by now must include the majority), the Cape of Good Hope is by quite a stretch physically the most beautiful and socially the most heartrending.

There are still wine regions I would love to visit and scores I am impatient to revisit. My fantasy is that by the time Rose has left school, Nick and I will gently tour the world's vineyards, cellars and finest restaurants, in semi-retirement, at long last getting the balance between reception and transmission of information right.

As the bottles, books and years have rolled by and I have become older and supposed by others to be wiser, I have found responsibility and respectability an increasing strain. Last year someone even called me a doyenne, for heaven's sake. I would rather not make statesman-like judgments on wines and wine regions and would much prefer to rave unguardedly about their attributes or dash off an intuitive, flamboyant attack on their shortcomings. But I feel, perhaps wrongly, that such a thing would be inappropriate in the *Financial Times* or from the editor of *The Oxford Companion to Wine*. Nor does it help to have inherited, from my parents, a terribly inconvenient desire to please. I now know what Ron Hall, once my *Sunday Times* master, meant when he said that columnists write all their best work before their fifth decade. Maturity is a fine thing in a wine, but I for one value it much, much less in a wine writer.

Index